JUSTICE AND GLOBAL POLITICS

19

Edited by

Ellen Frankel Paul, Fred D. Miller, Jr., and Jeffrey Paul

CAMBRIDGE
UNIVERSITY PRESS

PUBLISHED BY THE PRESS SYNDICATE OF THE UNIVERSITY OF CAMBRIDGE
The Pitt Building, Trumpington Street, Cambridge, United Kingdom

CAMBRIDGE UNIVERSITY PRESS
The Edinburgh Building, Cambridge CB2 2RU, UK
40 West 20th Street, New York, NY 10011-4211, USA
477 Williamstown Road, Port Melbourne, VIC 3207, Australia
Ruiz de Alarcón 13, 28014 Madrid, Spain
Dock House, The Waterfront, Cape Town 8001, South Africa

http://www.cambridge.org

First published 2006

Printed in the United States of America

Typeface Palacio 10/12 pt.

A catalog record for this book is available from the British Library

Library of Congress Cataloging-in-Publication Data
Justice and Global Politics / edited by Ellen Frankel Paul,
Fred D. Miller, Jr., and Jeffrey Paul.   p.   cm.
Includes bibliographical references and index.
ISBN 0-521-67440-9
1. Justice.   2. Distributive justice.   3. World politics.
4. Intervention (International law).   5. Internationalism.
I. Paul, Ellen Frankel.   II. Miller, Fred Dycus, 1944   III. Paul, Jeffrey.   IV. Title.
JC578.J875   2006
320'.01'1–dc22   2005054298

The essays in this book have also been published,
without introduction and index, in the semiannual journal
Social Philosophy & Policy, Volume 23, Number 1,
which is available by subscription.

CONTENTS

1006284563

INTRODUCTION

Since the end of the Cold War, there has been increasing interest in the global dimensions of a host of public policy issues—issues involving war and peace, terrorism, international law, regulation of commerce, environmental protection, and disparities of wealth, income, and access to medical care. Especially pressing is the question of whether it is possible to formulate principles of justice that are valid not merely within a single society but across national borders.

The idea that justice applies between nation-states may be traced back to Aristotle (384–322 B.C.), who criticized the rulers of Sparta and other regimes for trying to gain despotic power over their neighbors. "[T]o a reflecting mind," Aristotle said, "it must appear very strange that a statesman should be always considering how he can rule and tyrannize over others, whether they are willing or not." Aristotle argued that such people are fundamentally inconsistent: "[T]hey are not ashamed of practicing towards others what they deny is just or advantageous in their own case; they seek just rule for themselves, but where other persons are concerned they care nothing about just things."[1] Aristotle's insight that even the practice of war must be subject to principles of justice helped to inspire the theory of "just war" that was developed during the Middle Ages. In the early sixteenth century, two Aristotelian philosophers in Spain, Francisco de Vitoria and Bartolomé de Las Casas, wrote scathing critiques of the widespread violations of the human rights of native American Indians by the Spanish conquistadors. In the Netherlands during the same period, Hugo Grotius published two works that are widely viewed as watersheds for modern international legal theory: *De Jure Belli ac Pacis (The Law of War and Peace)* and *Mare Liberum (Freedom of the Seas)*. During the twentieth century, principles of international justice were applied famously in the Nuremberg trials of Nazi war criminals. In recent years, however, the traditional theory of just war has been sorely tested by the rise of international terrorism.

While questions of war and peace remain central to contemporary discussions of global politics, there has also been increasing interest in issues of distributive justice. What do people in one country owe, if anything, to people in other countries? Aside from duties of charity, do the citizens of wealthy nations have duties of justice to impoverished people living elsewhere? According to some theorists, notably John Rawls, strong principles of distributive justice stop at the border, on the grounds that one people should not have to bear the costs of decisions made by

---

[1] Aristotle, *Politics* VII.2.1324b1–36.

another people.[2] According to other theorists, such as Allen Buchanan, "justice is a morally obligatory goal of international law."[3] If there are principles of global distributive justice, what are they and how should they be enforced?

The essays in this volume—written by prominent philosophers, political scientists, economists, and legal theorists—address these questions and explore related topics. Several essays examine issues related to international aid and the global redistribution of wealth and resources. Some deal with just war theory, tracing its history and considering how it should be applied to judge the legitimacy of military interventions undertaken for humanitarian ends. Other essays address the influence of culture on global interdependence, or the effect of international law on individual liberty. Still others look at the impact of imperialism on the international order, or at the concept of global citizenship.

The collection opens with four essays that deal with distributive justice. In "The Mirage of Global Justice," Chandran Kukathas argues that the political pursuit of global justice is not a worthy goal, and that our aims in establishing international legal and political institutions should be more modest. He begins by sketching two broad positions on the pursuit of social justice: the Rawlsian view that justice cannot be achieved globally but should be pursued within individual nation-states, and the cosmopolitan view that there are standards of justice that can and should be applied globally. Kukathas rejects the cosmopolitan view, contending that the pursuit of justice in the international order is dangerous to the extent that it requires the establishment of powerful supranational agencies, or lends legitimacy to frequent exercises of political, economic, and military power by strong states or coalitions. His view also differs from the Rawlsian one, however, in that it rejects the pursuit of social justice within nation-states as well. Modern societies are marked by a diversity of opinions on what justice requires, and institutions designed to redistribute wealth or resources are likely to be manipulated by political elites in pursuit of their own interests. Kukathas concludes that the primary concern in the establishment and design of all legal and political institutions should be not to secure justice but to limit power: it is a mistake to think that a distinction can be drawn between power created to do good and power created to do evil, or that we are capable of devising institutions that can honor the distinction.

While Kukathas rejects Rawls's theory of justice, Samuel Freeman defends it in his contribution to this volume, "The Law of Peoples, Social Cooperation, Human Rights, and Distributive Justice." Cosmopolitan critics of Rawls argue that the account of human rights and distributive

---

[2] John Rawls, *The Law of Peoples* (Cambridge, MA: Harvard University Press, 1999), 116–18.
[3] Allen Buchanan, *Justice, Legitimacy, and Self-Determination: Moral Foundations for International Law* (Oxford: Oxford University Press, 2004), 86.

justice in his book *The Law of Peoples* is incompatible with his argument for liberal justice. Liberal societies, on Rawls's view, guarantee their citizens a strong set of basic liberties and arrange their social institutions according to the difference principle, which states that the benefits and burdens of society should be distributed in a manner that works to the greatest advantage of those who are least well off. According to Rawls's Law of Peoples, however, nonliberal societies may nevertheless be considered "decent" if they meet their citizens' basic needs and guarantee them a narrow set of human rights (which may not include some rights that liberal societies take for granted, such as rights to political participation, freedom of expression, or freedom of association). Critics insist that Rawls should extend his account of liberal rights and distributive justice to apply to the world at large. In response, Freeman notes that the Law of Peoples should be viewed not as a scheme of global justice, but as a set of principles of foreign policy for liberal peoples. Rawls grounds his principles of justice in social cooperation, and human rights are among the necessary conditions for social cooperation. So long as decent societies respect basic human rights, a common good, and the Law of Peoples, it is not the role of liberal societies to impose their own views of liberty and rights upon well-ordered decent societies. Moreover, Freeman argues, the difference principle is not primarily a principle for allocating wealth or alleviating poverty. It is intended to govern the design of institutions of property and other social institutions necessary to economic production, exchange, and consumption, and it presupposes political cooperation. The principle requires a legislative body to apply it, and a legal system to which it can be applied, yet there is no feasible global state or global legal system that could serve in these roles. Critics who would apply the difference principle globally are misguided, Freeman suggests, since the principle embodies a conception of democratic reciprocity that is only appropriate to cooperation among free and equal citizens who are socially productive and politically autonomous.

In "International Aid: When Giving Becomes a Vice," Neera K. Badhwar takes a different approach to the issue of distributive justice, focusing not on the design of institutions but on the obligations of individuals. She offers a critique of the views of Peter Singer and Peter Unger, who argue that moral decency requires giving away all one's "surplus" wealth for the relief or prevention of "absolute poverty," because not doing so is analogous to refusing to save a drowning child in order to avoid making one's clothes muddy. Badhwar argues that this analogy is flawed and, moreover, that there are four independent moral objections to the Singer-Unger thesis. She maintains (1) that the thesis is monomaniacal in ignoring the variety of morally worthy ideals and in elevating self-sacrificial aid to the global poor into the sole ideal; (2) that the thesis is misanthropic in its indifference to the happiness of moral agents who are called upon to sacrifice their interests; (3) that it is incompatible with integrity; and

(4) that it would have disastrous effects for the poor if it were generally adopted. Genuine beneficence, Badhwar contends, aims at creating or restoring the conditions that enable its beneficiaries to become self-sufficient creators themselves—creators of wealth and of meaningful and enjoyable lives. Small-scale beneficence is necessary for moral goodness, but large-scale beneficence is optional, so long as its absence is not due to a lack of regard for those in need. On Badhwar's view, the uncharitable person violates a neo-Lockean proviso which states that we should acquire or keep for ourselves and those we love as much, but only as much, as we can use or invest meaningfully or enjoyably, now or in the long run. Thus, someone who invests all his resources in creating something of worth leads a morally worthy life even if he reserves nothing for large-scale charity. Both our capacity for beneficence and our capacity for creation are important aspects of our humanity. Ultimately, Badhwar concludes, the Singer-Unger thesis promotes not genuine beneficence but the profligate giving away of wealth to prolong lives, while failing to appreciate what makes life worth living.

Like Badhwar, Iris Marion Young examines the obligations individuals have toward disadvantaged people in other parts of the world. In "Responsibility and Global Justice: A Social Connection Model," Young considers the responsibilities that moral agents may have in relation to structural social processes that have unjust consequences. As an illustration of one such process, she discusses the production, distribution, and marketing of clothing—a system of economic relationships that extends widely across regions of the world. When such processes lead to injustice toward workers in undeveloped countries, how should individual agents and institutions conceive of their responsibilities in relation to that injustice? To answer this question, Young proposes a model of responsibility based on social connection. This social connection model states that all agents who contribute by their actions to the structural processes that produce injustice have responsibilities to work to remedy these injustices. Young distinguishes this model from a more standard "liability" model of responsibility and specifies several key features of the social connection model: The social connection model does not isolate perpetrators of injustice; rather, it conceives of injustice as the result of the actions of many agents who participate in global systems. The model scrutinizes the widely accepted norms and practices that form the background conditions of injustice. It is more forward-looking than backward-looking, concerned with remedying injustice rather than assigning blame. Finally, it conceives of responsibility as essentially shared, and as capable of being discharged only through collective action. Young concludes her essay with a discussion of a set of considerations that agents should take into account when thinking about their own responsibilities in relation to structural injustice.

The next two essays in this collection deal with issues relating to international law and international order. Paul B. Stephan's essay, "Process Values, International Law, and Justice," focuses on the formulation of international law and the efficacy of various checks that might prevent the making of arbitrary laws that are harmful to individual liberty. It might appear, Stephan notes, that the principle of state consent provides a sufficient check on international lawmaking. If a state (and by extension, its subjects) can be bound by a rule of international law only after that state manifests its consent to the rule, then the adoption of the rule should meet basic criteria of procedural justice. States will simply refuse to consent to unjust rules. Stephan argues, however, that this reasoning is mistaken. International lawyers argue for the existence of norms that should apply regardless of state consent. The concept of state consent is subject to interpretation, and opportunistic decision makers have some freedom to construe consent in ways that circumvent conventional checking processes. Moreover, political and economic coercion can reduce state consent to a meaningless formality. If state consent turns out to be insufficient to constrain international lawmaking, what other checks might exist to protect liberty? Stephan addresses this question and explores the problems that arise when lawmaking authority is delegated to international institutions, with specific reference to the International Criminal Court established in 1998. He concludes that the threat to liberty posed by international institutions does not justify blanket opposition to international lawmaking, but that those who are interested in making and enforcing international rules need to take this threat seriously and provide another layer of justification for their efforts.

In "What's Wrong with Imperialism?" Christopher W. Morris considers the role of empires in maintaining international order. He acknowledges that imperialism is thought to be wrong by virtually everyone today, and with good reason, since empires have historically been associated with conquest, plunder, exploitation, and the domination of subjugated peoples. Nevertheless, he believes that these may not be essential features of imperialism, and argues that empires may not be harder to justify or legitimate than nation-states. Imperialism's negative reputation seems to be due to a methodologically suspect comparison of malevolent empires to benevolent states. Yet Morris suggests that it is possible to conceive of an empire whose governing institutions are relatively just and responsive to the interests of its subjects. Such an empire could do all or nearly all of the things that legitimate governments do: it could protect its subjects from foreign invaders and prevent internal conflicts, establish a legal system and civil service institutions, and provide roads, irrigation systems, and other public goods. Using this hypothetical empire as an illustration, Morris goes on to ask whether such an empire could be considered legitimate, in the way that many states are considered legitimate. He concludes that empires may be able to achieve a weak form of legitimacy, if their institutions are just and efficient, and if they make their subject peoples better off. The legitimacy of empires would be of limited duration, however: once their subject populations become capable of self-government, imperial rule would need to come to an end. If this view of imperialism is correct, Morris suggests, empires may be better suited to securing global order today than alternative kinds of international institutions.

The next three essays ask whether and under what conditions military intervention is justifiable. In "The Just War Idea: The State of the Question," James Turner Johnson examines the traditional theory of just war and its implications for the justification of the use of military force. In its classical form, just war theory holds that the use of armed force, to be legitimate, must be undertaken by a sovereign power charged with the protection of the common good, with the intention, ultimately, of establishing peace. Johnson outlines the early development and substantive content of the just war tradition and sketches its subsequent development in the modern period. He identifies three benchmarks in the revitalization of just war thinking in the United States over the last four decades: the writings of Paul Ramsey in the 1960s, the work of Michael Walzer in the late 1970s, and the U.S. Catholic bishops' 1983 pastoral letter, *The Challenge of Peace*. The contemporary discourse on just war, Johnson observes, differs from the traditional theory. Contemporary theorists endorse a strong presumption against the use of force and propose a number of additional requirements for its justification, including the strictures that the use of force must be a last resort, that it must have a strong probability of success, and that it must be proportional to the wrong it is intended to address. Johnson offers a critique of these features of the contemporary discourse, testing them against the context, purpose, and content of the classical just war idea. He argues that the historical substance of just war tradition needs to be respected in contemporary just war discourse, in order to discipline that discourse and to engage contemporary moral reflection with the values embodied in the just war tradition.

The justification of the use of armed force for humanitarian purposes is the subject of Clifford Orwin's "Humanitarian Military Intervention: Wars for the End of History?" Orwin begins by sketching the history of armed intervention in the post–World War II/Cold War era, noting that during this time, the use of force was most often justified as a necessary means of repelling aggression or assuring collective security. Only with the end of the Cold War did military intervention for humanitarian reasons come into its own. What were the factors that led to this shift in the motives for going to war? Orwin seeks to answer this question, examining the arguments used to support intervention against sovereign governments that threaten the lives and liberty of their own people or the people of neighboring countries. In the course of his essay, Orwin discusses a number of recent cases of intervention, from the first Gulf War that expelled the Iraqi military from Kuwait, to the UN intervention in Bosnia, to the U.S.-led intervention in Iraq. He seeks to determine whether there is a responsibility to intervene against governments that brutalize their own citizens—a "responsibility to protect" the security of people in countries other than one's own. The existence of such a responsibility would raise a number of difficult questions: What is the scope of this responsibility? Upon whom does it fall? How is it likely to be carried out in practice? Orwin contends that while a "responsibility to protect" may have a strong rhetorical appeal, it is unlikely to be consistently put into practice. The chief flaw of humanitarianism as a basis for intervention is that compassion for distant strangers is a weak motive for going to war. It is unlikely, Orwin suggests, that full-scale military interventions against tyrannical governments will be the wave of the future; it is far more likely that humanitarian crises will remain largely unaddressed, or that they will be addressed with half-measures that may lessen their impact without ultimately resolving them.

Michael Blake's essay, "Collateral Benefit," approaches the issue of humanitarian military intervention from the perspective of nongovernmental organizations (NGOs) that are concerned with the protection of human rights. Blake rests his discussion on a distinction he draws between first-order political agents, who are responsible for making decisions about the use of governmental power (e.g., the use of military force), and second-order political agents, whose responsibility lies in responding to and evaluating those decisions. As second-order political agents, human rights NGOs are in a position to pass judgment on governmental decisions that have an impact on human rights, and Blake's aim is to consider what ethical principles should guide the judgments of these NGOs. We might suppose that military interventions are only permissible when they are undertaken with the proper intention: when they are motivated by humanitarian concerns rather than reasons of self-interest or political gain. Blake argues, however, that NGOs may be permitted to ignore the motivations of governmental agents and support even substantially unjust military interventions, when such interventions would have substantial "collateral" benefits for the defense and preservation of basic human rights. While critics of this approach might claim that it would undermine the moral authority of NGOs, Blake maintains that the overriding purpose of human rights advocacy groups should be to effect change in people's lives, to bring about genuine improvements in the protections afforded to human rights. NGOs need to be careful not to squander their moral capital, but they should not be afraid to spend it when their support for a particular military intervention could bring about significant humanitarian benefits.

The next three essays examine cultural diversity and globalization. In "The Uneven Results of Institutional Changes in Central and Eastern Europe: The Role of Culture," Svetozar Pejovich sets out to analyze the process of transition from socialism to capitalism as it has occurred in various Central and Eastern European countries. He wonders why some formerly Communist countries have fared better than others in the transition to capitalism. He suggests that countries with stronger cultural ties to the West have made greater progress in this transition, as measured by a number of factors such as the level of government regulation of the economy, the stability of property rights, and the freedom of entry into markets for goods, services, and capital. Countries without historical ties to Western traditions of economic freedom and the rule of law, Pejovich argues, face higher transaction costs as they attempt to refashion their economies along free-market lines. If this view is correct, problems associated with this economic transition are primarily cultural rather than technical, and their solution will involve identifying and embracing the elements of Western culture that are supportive of capitalism. Pejovich discusses a number of these elements, including respect for individual rights and admiration for entrepreneurship, and he contrasts these with the traditions of egalitarianism and collectivism that tend to prevail in Central and Eastern Europe. He concludes that the promotion of economic liberty and strong legal protections for property could provide incentives for risk-takers to develop businesses and engage in innovative activities that would reenergize the transition to capitalism in this region of the world.

The theme of cultural differences and how they influence our conceptions of justice is taken up by James M. Buchanan in his essay, "Equality, Hierarchy, and Global Justice." Buchanan focuses on the relationships among citizens in Western liberal societies and observes that they can be characterized in terms of either equality or hierarchy. Citizens can conceive of one another as natural equals, worthy of respect and capable of cooperation and reciprocity, or they can conceive of one another as occupying positions in a natural hierarchy, filling predetermined roles, and thus relating to one another as either superiors or inferiors. The cultures of liberal societies differ and are characterized by various mixtures of these two attitudes, though one or the other is likely to be dominant within each society. After setting out this distinction between equality and hierarchy, Buchanan discusses some of the implications these contrasting attitudes have for the development of social policy. Western legal institutions, for example, are based on the presupposition of equality among citizens, while the transfer programs that characterize the modern welfare state are hierarchical, since they draw distinctions between those who are potential recipients and those who are not. The policies of different liberal societies regarding the permissibility of the death penalty provide another example. Buchanan contends that differing attitudes toward capital punishment in the United States and Western Europe might be explained by the different emphases these societies place on equality and hierarchy. Finally, turning to the realm of international relations, Buchanan argues that the tension between equality and hierarchy will need to be resolved if principles of justice are to be extended across national boundaries. In the end, he maintains, institutions based on the assumption of natural equality provide a firmer foundation for securing justice in a world of globalization and economic interdependence.

The debate over globalization and its cultural impact is the focus of Irving Louis Horowitz's essay, "Feuding with the Past, Fearing the Future: Globalization as Cultural Metaphor for the Struggle between Nation-State and World-Economy." Critics of globalization view it as a form of imperialism, as a means for developed nations and large multinational corporations to extend their power. Globalization's defenders hail it as a force for modernization and economic development through innovation, mutual cooperation, and healthy competition. Horowitz critiques both of these positions, but emphasizes the positive effects of globalization. Large-scale economic cooperation across national borders has revolutionized production processes and has led to the development of common standards in virtually every area of technology. Developments in the automotive industry and in global communications represent the more obvious examples of this trend toward standardization, but Horowitz notes that standardization impacts everything from electrical grids to the licensing of physicians and other health care professionals. Opposition to globalization often takes the form of hostility to the perceived growth of American power and influence, yet Horowitz observes that the result of globalization is a relative reduction of American power, as other nations gain power through economic development. At the same time, the visible signs of American cultural influence are everywhere, in the form of American television, music, films, and fashions. Resistance to globalization will continue, Horowitz suggests, as nation states seek to preserve their power in the face of a global economy and a global culture. Nevertheless, the level of resistance will be limited, since national governments derive their power (and their tax revenues) from the prosperity that globalization tends to bring.

The collection's final essay examines the theory of civic republicanism in our era of ever-increasing global integration. In "Toward Global Republican Citizenship?" Waldemar Hanasz begins by setting out the basic elements of the republican tradition: the idea that the good life can only be lived within a commonwealth or *res publica;* that the functioning of the commonwealth and the stability of its institutions is made possible only by the civic virtue of its citizens; and that citizens must be formed into a strong community by means of civic education. Some contemporary theorists, drawing on the classical republican tradition, claim that the republican concept of citizenship can be adapted to meet the challenges of globalization. Hanasz argues, however, that republican citizenship is unsuited to the task of organizing the cosmopolitan societies of the twenty-first century. Republican citizenship demands a level of public service and devotion to the commonwealth that can only be motivated by patriotism and a strong sense of national identity, and such motives are at odds with the cosmopolitan values of a global society. Moreover, Hanasz notes, there is a serious tension between republican and cosmopolitan views of rights and liberties. Modern political theory regards individual rights as universal, as transcending ethnic and religious identities—an understanding that is reflected in international agreements and institutions. Civic republicans, in contrast, view rights as a legal concept: rights are granted to citizens by the commonwealth and are always subject to limitation in the service of the commonwealth's interests. Hanasz draws similar contrasts between republican and cosmopolitan notions of civic duty, civic participation, and community. He concludes that civic republicanism, despite its proud tradition, is inadequate as a theory of global citizenship for the contemporary world.

In a period characterized by economic interdependence and by heightened tensions among diverse nations and cultures, questions of justice assume a paramount importance. The thirteen essays in this volume, written from a variety of perspectives, offer valuable contributions to current debates over the nature of justice and its implications for the development of international law and international institutions.

ACKNOWLEDGMENTS

The editors wish to acknowledge several individuals at the Social Philosophy and Policy Center, Bowling Green State University, who provided invaluable assistance in the preparation of this volume. They include Program Manager Nicolás Maloberti, Mary Dilsaver, and Terrie Weaver.

The editors also extend special thanks to Assistant Managing Editor Tamara Sharp, for her patient attention to detail, and to Managing Editor Harry Dolan, for providing editorial assistance above and beyond the call of duty.

CONTRIBUTORS

Chandran Kukathas is Neal A. Maxwell Professor of Political Theory, Public Policy, and Public Service in the Department of Political Science at the University of Utah. He is the author of *The Liberal Archipelago* (2003) and coeditor (with Gerald F. Gaus) of *The Sage Handbook of Political Theory* (2004). He has also coedited (with John Kilcullen) Pierre Bayle's *Philosophical Commentary* (2005).

Samuel Freeman is Steven F. Goldstone Term Professor of Philosophy and Law at the University of Pennsylvania. He has published articles on a variety of subjects in moral and political philosophy, including contractarianism, deliberative democracy, liberalism and libertarianism, deontology and utilitarianism, property and distributive justice, constitutional interpretation, and the role of judicial review in a democracy. He is the editor of John Rawls's *Collected Papers* (1999) and of *The Cambridge Companion to Rawls* (2002). Currently, he is editing Rawls's *Lectures in the History of Political Philosophy* and completing a book on Rawls.

Neera K. Badhwar is Associate Professor of Philosophy at the University of Oklahoma. Her articles on various topics in ethics have appeared in *American Philosophical Quarterly, Ethics, Noûs, Social Philosophy and Policy,* and other journals. She is the editor of *Friendship: A Philosophical Reader* (1993), and has held fellowships at the University Center for Human Values at Princeton University, the Social Philosophy and Policy Center at Bowling Green State University, and Dalhousie University. In the fall of 1999, she was NEH Distinguished Visiting Professor at SUNY Potsdam, and, in 2002, she was a Visiting Scholar at Liberty Fund.

Iris Marion Young is Professor of Political Science at the University of Chicago, where she teaches courses on theories of justice, democratic theory, feminist theory, and postcolonial political theory. Her books include *On Female Body Experience* (2005), *Inclusion and Democracy* (2000), *Intersecting Voices: Dilemmas of Gender, Political Philosophy, and Public Policy* (1997), and *Justice and the Politics of Difference* (1990). Her writings have been widely reprinted and translated into eight languages. She is currently working on a book about individual responsibility and structural injustice.

Paul B. Stephan is Lewis F. Powell, Jr. Professor of Law and the Hunton and Williams Research Professor at the University of Virginia. An expert on international business, international law, and Soviet and post-Soviet legal systems, he has advised governments and international organizations, organized conferences, edited books, and lectured to professionals, university groups, and international scholarly colloquia on a variety of issues raised by the globalization of the world economy and the transition away from Soviet-style socialism. He has been a guest professor or visiting lecturer at the University of Vienna, Lausanne University, Melbourne University, Sydney University, the University of Pantheon-Sorbonne in Paris, and the Institut d'Études Politiques de Paris. He has written extensively on international law, corruption, and the history of the Cold War, and his casebook on international business is used at law schools both in the United States and abroad.

Christopher W. Morris is Professor of Philosophy at the University of Maryland, College Park, and a faculty member of the Committee on Politics, Philosophy, and Public Policy. He is the author of *An Essay on the Modern State* (1998) and the editor of *Practical Rationality and Preference: Essays for David Gauthier* (with Arthur Ripstein, 2001), and *Violence, Terrorism, and Justice* (with R. G. Frey, 1991).

James Turner Johnson is Professor of Religion and Associate Member of the Graduate Department of Political Science at Rutgers University, where he has been on the faculty since 1969. Since receiving his Ph.D. from Princeton in 1968, his research and teaching have focused principally on the historical development and application of moral traditions related to war, peace, and the practice of statecraft. He has received Rockefeller, Guggenheim, and National Endowment for the Humanities fellowships. He is the author of seven books, coauthor of one, and editor or coeditor of five others. He is also coeditor of the *Journal of Military Ethics*, and a trustee, editorial board member, and former general editor of the *Journal of Religious Ethics*.

Clifford Orwin is Professor of Political Science, Fellow of St. Michael's College, and Director of the Program in Political Philosophy and International Affairs at the University of Toronto. He was born and raised in Chicago and studied at Harvard University and Cornell University. He is the author of *The Humanity of Thucydides* (second edition, 1997) and of numerous articles on ancient, modern, and current political thought. He is presently completing a book on the role of compassion in modern political life and thought.

Michael Blake is Assistant Professor of Public Policy and Philosophy at the John F. Kennedy School of Government, Harvard University. His research focuses on international ethics and the moral foundations of multicultural politics. He has published work on international distributive justice, international criminal adjudication, and immigration, and is currently writing a book on multicultural politics.

Svetozar Pejovich is Professor Emeritus of Economics at Texas A&M University and Senior Research Fellow at the International Centre for Economic Research in Turin, Italy. He received his LL.B. from the University of Belgrade in 1955 and his Ph.D. in economics from Georgetown University in 1963, and has taught at St. Mary's College in Minnesota, Ohio University, and the University of Dallas. He is the author of seven books, including *Economic Analysis of Institutions and Systems* (second edition, 1998). He has also edited eight books and published numerous articles in professional journals.

James M. Buchanan is Advisory General Director of the Center for Study of Public Choice at George Mason University. He retired in 1999 as Distinguished Professor Emeritus of Economics and Philosophy from Virginia Polytechnic and State University. He received his B.A. from Middle Tennessee State College in 1940, his M.S. from the University of Tennessee in 1941, and his Ph.D. from the University of Chicago in 1948. In 1986, he received the Alfred Nobel Memorial Prize in Economic Sciences. His major works include *The Collected Works of James M. Buchanan* (twenty volumes, 1999–2002, 2004), *Better Than Plowing: And Other Personal Essays* (1992), *The Economics and the Ethics of Constitutional Order* (1991), *The Reason of Rules* (with Geoffrey Brennan, 1985), *The Power to Tax* (with Geoffrey Brennan, 1980), *Freedom in Constitutional Contract* (1978), *Liberty, Market, and State* (1975), *The Limits of Liberty* (1975), and *The Calculus of Consent* (with Gordon Tullock, 1962).

Irving Louis Horowitz is Hannah Arendt University Professor Emeritus of Sociology and Political Science at Rutgers University, where he has been since 1969. He also serves as chairman of the board of Transaction-Aldine Publishers. He taught previously at Washington University in St. Louis, and has served as visiting professor at Stanford University, the University of Wisconsin, Queen's University in Canada, and the University of California. He has been a Fulbright Lecturer in Argentina, Israel, and India. Among his recent works are *Tributes: An Informal History of Social Science in the Twentieth Century* (2003), *Taking Lives: Genocide and State Power* (fifth edition, 2001), *Behemoth: The History and Theory of Political Sociology* (2000), and *Three Worlds of Development: The Theory and Practice of International Stratification* (1973).

Waldemar Hanasz is Associate Director of the Philosophy, Politics, and Economics Program at the University of Pennsylvania, where he teaches decision and game theory, the history of economic theory, and theories of rationality. Previously, he taught at Rockford College and Clemson University. His main areas of interest are political philosophy and the history of political and economic thought, and he has published articles in these areas. He is also assistant editor of *The Philosopher's Index*.

THE MIRAGE OF GLOBAL JUSTICE*

By Chandran Kukathas

I. Introduction

Theories of global justice address two main issues. First, what would a just distribution of benefits and burdens across the world look like? Second, what sorts of institutions would be required to secure such a just distribution? Many other related questions inevitably arise when these problems are addressed. Perhaps the most notable is how to establish such institutions given the diversity of sovereign nations and the fact of global inequalities of wealth and power. For many, these questions are urgent because we live in a world in which millions live in desperate poverty. They are salient not only because many people enjoy great wealth but also because the disparity in riches may itself be the product of unjust global institutions. On this view, it might be said, justice is the first virtue of global institutions. Institutions, no matter how efficient and well-arranged, must be reformed or abolished if they are unjust.

For some theories, however, the issue of global justice has a wider scope. The protection of human rights generally, it is argued, is a matter of justice. Just institutions would ensure not only that the distribution of benefits and burdens was morally justifiable but also that people were secure against the predations of despots and warlords. The security of people's individual liberties and political rights is also a matter of justice. To establish global justice requires institutions that secure human rights broadly understood.

The thesis of this essay is that the political pursuit of global justice is not a worthy goal, and that our aims in establishing international legal and political institutions should be more modest. Its primary argument is that the pursuit of justice in the international order is dangerous to the extent that it requires the establishment of powerful supranational agencies, or legitimizes greater and more frequent exercises of political, economic, and military power by strong states or coalitions. The primary concern in the establishment and design of all legal and political institutions should be not to secure justice but to limit power. It is a mistake to think that a distinction can be drawn between power created to do good and power

* For helpful comments on earlier drafts of this essay, I would like to thank Jerry Gaus, David Miller, Dan Greenwood, Peggy Battin, Leslie Francis, Erika George, Cindy Stark, and Deen Chatterjee, as well as my fellow contributors to this volume. For especially detailed and helpful editorial comments and advice, I would like to thank Ellen Paul.

1

created to do evil, or that we are capable of devising institutions that can honor the distinction.

The essay is organized in the following way. In Section II, I articulate a conception of global order in which justice has a limited part. In Section III, I advance the main reasons why our concern for justice should be limited. In Section IV, I consider some important objections to this viewpoint, particularly those advanced by such contemporary political philosophers as Allen Buchanan and Thomas Pogge, who contend that justice should be a central concern of global economic and legal institutions. In Section V, I offer replies to these criticisms, and in Section VI, I offer some general conclusions.

II. Justice and Global Order

There are two primary positions taken in contemporary political theory on global justice. The first asserts that justice, and in particular, social justice, is something that cannot be attained globally but can be pursued successfully only by the nation-state. The most influential statement of this view is offered by John Rawls in *The Law of Peoples,*[1] though there have been other notable defenders of this position who have presented independent or complementary reasons for it. David Miller, for example, has presented a case for limiting the scope of distributive justice; and Michael Walzer has argued that justice cannot be a global ideal but only a local one, tied as it must be to local understandings.[2] The second position on global justice repudiates the first, insisting that there are standards of justice that should properly be regarded as globally significant. Principles of justice that hold within the nation-state should also hold, *mutatis mutandis,* across or among states. To put the matter in another way, if individuals have basic rights in virtue of their humanity, then these are rights they hold as against the whole world; and responsibility for upholding them falls upon the world as a whole rather than upon the nations in which they happen to reside. Such views have been defended most recently by philosophers such as Allen Buchanan and Thomas Pogge, though others, such as Henry Shue and Peter Singer, have been arguing for some time that considerations of justice should inform the foreign policies of wealthy nations to a much greater degree than such considerations do at present.[3]

[1] John Rawls, *The Law of Peoples* (Cambridge, MA: Harvard University Press, 1999).

[2] See David Miller, "Justice and Global Inequality," in A. Hurrell and N. Woods, eds., *Inequality, Globalization, and World Politics* (Oxford: Oxford University Press, 1999), 187–210; David Miller, "National Self-Determination and Global Justice," in Miller, *Citizenship and National Identity* (Cambridge, MA: Polity Press, 2000); and Michael Walzer, *Spheres of Justice* (Oxford: Blackwell, 1983).

[3] See Allen Buchanan, *Justice, Legitimacy, and Self-Determination: Moral Foundations for International Law* (Oxford: Oxford University Press, 2004); Thomas Pogge, *World Poverty and Human Rights* (Malden, MA: Polity Press, 2002); Henry Shue, *Basic Rights* (Princeton, NJ:

A particularly sharp statement of this second position is put forward by Darrel Moellendorf in criticism of Rawls, and in defense of cosmopolitan justice. Rawls, he observes, conceives of the international order as one in which toleration is extended even to regimes that are "unreasonable, intolerant, [and] oppressive" by the standards of Rawls's own doctrine as developed in his *Political Liberalism*.[4] But to be tolerant of such regimes, Moellendorf suggests, is to be tolerant of unjust actions or oppressive cultural practices when there are no good reasons for being so. "In fact, just as institutionalizing an arrangement that permitted individuals to be unjust could be seen as being complicit in the injustice, so institutionalizing principles of international conduct that licensed oppression could be seen as being complicit in the oppression."[5] On this view, if there are good reasons to pursue or uphold justice within the nation-state, those reasons also support upholding justice across the globe.

My thesis in this essay is that justice should not be pursued globally. The position defended here differs from those of Rawls, Walzer, and Miller, however, because it also rejects the idea that justice is something that should be pursued within the nation-state. It acknowledges that the advocates of global or cosmopolitan justice have a point in demanding consistency from those who argue for justice at home but are prepared to tolerate injustice abroad. But it also acknowledges the force of the arguments of those who are skeptical about global justice, and who consider the pursuit of justice on that scale implausible.

Justice, it should be noted, may be understood in many different ways. At its broadest, justice could be said to be the subject of any general account of how people should live. On this view, Plato's *Republic* gives us an account of justice no less than does Marx's theory of communism— even if Marx regards "justice" as a bourgeois virtue that has no place in post-capitalist society. A narrower view of justice sees it as concerning the proper distribution of benefits and burdens in society. Justice is a characteristic of the rules or the institutions that determine the entitlements people have, individually or as groups, to parts of the material world, and to the services of others. A theory of justice would offer an account of what people are entitled to under the rules of justice, and also what measures may be taken by an appropriately constituted authority to ensure that justice is upheld. A narrower view still regards justice as a matter of the application of rules rather than a matter of the rightness or "fairness" of the rules. Justice, in this sense, may be served if the law is consistently applied, even if the law is systematically unfair.

Princeton University Press, 1980); Peter Singer, "Famine, Affluence, and Morality," *Philosophy and Public Affairs* 1, no. 3 (1972): 229–43; and Peter Singer, *One World: The Ethics of Globalization* (New Haven, CT: Yale University Press, 2002).

[4] John Rawls, *Political Liberalism*, paperback edition (New York: Columbia University Press, 1996).

[5] Darrel Moellendorf, *Cosmopolitan Justice* (Boulder, CO: Westview Press, 2002), 28.

My concern in this essay is with justice in the second of these three senses. That is to say, my concern is with social or distributive justice. Theories of distributive justice are numerous, ranging from the Nozickian view that a just distribution is any distribution that is the outcome of just acquisition and just transfer of resources,[6] to socialist views that regard all resources as collectively owned and properly allocated according to need, to views associated with particular religious or cultural traditions. Islamic conceptions of distributive justice, for example, allow for private property, but impose particular constraints on its use. Different views of distributive justice may also be shaped by particular views about the status of persons, what constitutes a violation of persons or their property, and what forms of punishment are justified. Ideas about what justice requires are at least as numerous as the different communities that are to be found in a diverse society (such as the United States), though the differences among some of them are more trivial than the differences among others. Christians have much in common in their thinking about justice; yet while some think that distributive justice requires ensuring that all women have access to medical services to terminate unwanted pregnancies, others think that justice can require no such thing, since abortion is morally wrong.

On this understanding of justice, it is something that would be difficult to pursue in a society marked by a diversity of opinions and a variety of communities, since there would be many views about what justice demands. Any commitment to accommodating a diversity of ways of life would make it difficult to advocate a single standard of social or distributive justice. I suggest that it is neither possible nor desirable to pursue justice in this sense within a single nation-state. Consequently, we should not pursue social or distributive justice at the global level.

To put the issue schematically, there are four possible positions available on the question of whether justice (or social justice) should be pursued at home and abroad. (See Figure 1.) Position A suggests that social justice should be pursued at home and abroad; B that it should be pursued at home but not abroad; C that it should be pursued abroad but not at home; and D that it should be pursued neither at home nor abroad. Position C is perhaps the view least likely to find a representative, though it is not unusual for some political leaders to argue for global (re)distributive justice, while insisting on the importance of national sovereignty, and their own immunity from international criticism. This position has been expressed in a number of international declarations, such as the 1993 Bangkok Declaration.[7]

---

[6] See Robert Nozick, *Anarchy, State, and Utopia* (New York: Basic Books, 1974), chap. 7.

[7] See the Bangkok Declaration of the ministers and representatives of Asian states, meeting at Bangkok from March 29 to April 2, 1993, pursuant to General Assembly resolution 46/116 of December 17, 1991, in preparation for the World Conference on Human Rights. While "welcoming" the attention paid to human rights in the international community, the declaration's evident concern was to downplay the relevance of human rights by asserting —

In this essay, I defend position D against A, B, and C. (F. A. Hayek has also defended position D, insisting that social justice cannot be pursued at home or abroad since the very idea is incoherent.)[8]

	Social justice abroad	No social justice abroad
Social justice at home	A: Pogge, Moellendorf	B: Rawls, Walzer, Miller
No social justice at home	C: Bangkok Declaration	D: Hayek, Kukathas

FIGURE 1. Four positions on the pursuit of social justice.

In my view, then, the international global order should, like domestic or national societies, properly be conceived as a network of independent jurisdictions bound not by any shared (or imposed) understanding of justice but simply by a commitment to mutual toleration. The most important imperative in the international order is to avoid war. International institutions, including international organizations (such as the United Nations) and international regimes (such as that established by the 1951 Refugee Convention) may be useful if they help to keep the peace, and if they define mutually acceptable conventions by which problems common to global society might be peacefully addressed.

This view might appear to be a defense of a Westphalian model of international order, one that is dominated by sovereign states recognized as the subjects of international law. The Peace of Westphalia, which in 1648 brought an end to the Eighty Years' War between Spain and the Netherlands, and to the German phase of the Thirty Years' War, greatly weakened the power of the Holy Roman Empire. It confirmed the 1555

---

and reasserting—the "principles of respect for national sovereignty, territorial integrity and non-interference in the internal affairs of States." This concern is especially apparent in the declaration's wish to "discourage any attempt to use human rights as conditionality for extending development assistance," to emphasize the importance of "the non-use of human rights as an instrument of political pressure," and to reiterate "that all countries . . . have the right to determine their political systems, control and freely utilize their resources, and freely pursue their economic, social and cultural development." Human rights, it seems, are very important—important enough to justify the spending of increasing sums of money to promote "awareness of human rights," but not important enough to justify others' invoking them to scrutinize or criticize the workings of states. See http://law.hku.hk/lawgovtsociety/Bangkok%20Declaration.htm (accessed May 2001).

[8] F. A. Hayek, *Law, Legislation, and Liberty,* vol. 2, *The Mirage of Social Justice* (London: Routledge, 1976).

Peace of Augsburg, which had granted Lutherans religious toleration in
the Holy Roman Empire, and it extended toleration to the Calvinists. In
recognizing the territorial sovereignty of member states, it is often asserted,
the Peace of Westphalia also established the principle *cuius regio eius
religio*: that the religion of the head of state would be the religion of the
people within that domain. This is not quite accurate, since the articles of
peace required states to tolerate religious minorities. The authority of the
Holy Roman Empire was dramatically reduced, however, and the sovereign power of some three hundred princes was increased. The modern
world order could be said to operate on the Westphalian model in as
much as it is a world of states, since European colonialism—and, more
particularly, decolonization—brought states into being right across the
globe. By the provisions of the Peace of Westphalia, princes eventually
became absolute sovereigns in their own dominions, immune to the interventions of the Holy Roman Emperor. In the modern world, independence and immunity against foreign intervention are central aspects of
state sovereignty.[9]

At least to a limited extent, it is the Westphalian model that is com-
mended in this essay. The virtue of the Westphalian ideal is that it divides
power, recognizing as it does the diversity of claims of political authority,
and that it appreciates the importance of avoiding war. Its weakness is that
it strengthens the hand of the state, allowing it to act with immunity within
its borders—even when its behavior is imprudent, unjust, or, at the extreme,
barbaric. But if it is undesirable that there be any authority with power that
can be so abused, it is even less desirable that such power be extended in
scope to cover more and more domains—to create empires or a world government. Better to have many petty tyrants than a few great ones.

There are, of course, other reasons to be skeptical about the Westphalian
model. In the 350 years and more since the Treaty of Westphalia was
signed, not just Europe but the world has seen countless wars in which
millions have died. Moreover, particularly in the twentieth century, the
numbers killed in war have been dwarfed by the hundreds of millions
killed by their own governments.[10] The state is a difficult institution to
defend even with mild enthusiasm. Nonetheless, the Westphalian model
may have something to commend it if only because some of the alternatives being advocated are so unattractive. One alternative is to establish
a more powerful force able to deal with the problem of bad states. A

[9] Strictly speaking, the doctrine that states as sovereign powers had the right to rule by
their own structures of authority, without intervention from other states, was not established by the Peace of Westphalia but developed later in the legal theory of the Swiss jurist
Emerich Vattel. "Westphalian sovereignty" is a widely used term, but it is probably a
misnomer. See Stephen Krasner, *Sovereignty: Organized Hypocrisy* (Princeton, NJ: Princeton
University Press, 1999). It is worth noting, as Krasner emphasizes, that states enjoy sovereignty to varying degrees.
[10] See Rudolph Rummel, *Death by Government: Genocide and Mass Murder in the Twentieth
Century* (New Brunswick, NJ: Transaction Publishers, 1994).

second alternative is to develop international institutions that will authorize systematic intervention in the affairs of bad states by other states or coalitions of states—so that good states will reform bad ones. The Westphalian model is preferable to either of these.[11] Further decentralization may be preferable to a world of sovereign states; but a world of independent states is still better than a world of states subordinated to a greater power—whether the global Leviathan is a single body or an assembly of states.

This view does not assume that states must be regarded as economically self-sufficient units, or as culturally and politically undifferentiated entities, capable of relating to one another only as bargainers pursuing their own advantage. In freer political systems, cities and provinces, as well as other forms of association, will also be internationally significant political actors. Agreements will be reached between many different forms of associations besides states. States themselves may relinquish aspects of their sovereignty when they sign treaties or enter into conventions that bind them and limit what they may do even within their own borders. Signing the Kyoto Agreement on global warming (and then ratifying it) would limit a state's freedom to make laws that violated the agreement's provisions on acceptable greenhouse gas emissions. Being party to the 1951 convention on the treatment of refugees restricts a state's ability to turn people away from its borders if they come seeking asylum, for signing the agreement meant signing away elements of state sovereignty. A world of sovereign states need not be a world in which all political relations exist only between undifferentiated polities unaffected by international ties or international obligations.[12]

Despite these ties, however, ours is not a world united by shared moral convictions or a common idea of justice. The virtue of the Westphalian model of a world of sovereign states that emerged in the seventeenth and eighteenth centuries was that it was able to secure peace in the face of religious disagreement. The virtue of this model in the twenty-first century is that it might preserve peace in the face of ethical diversity. One way of describing this model of global order is as an archipelago of interdependent jurisdictions not subject to any common power, existing under norms of mutual toleration. Justice has no significant part to play in accounting for such an order.[13]

---

[11] The virtue of the Peace of Westphalia was not that it established the authority of the state but that it weakened the forces of religious imperialism by lessening the influence of the Holy Roman Empire and the House of Hapsburg. It meant that religious questions could no longer be decided by a majority of the imperial estates and that future disputes would be decided by compromise among religious authorities.

[12] There is, however, the danger that the state will exercise its power to make treaties that end up binding provincial and local governments while also removing some responsibilities from their jurisdictions.

[13] I have offered a more elaborate account of such an order in *The Liberal Archipelago: A Theory of Diversity and Freedom* (Oxford: Oxford University Press, 2003).

III. Reasons for the Limited Role of Justice

The primary reason for limiting the role of justice in international affairs is that understandings of justice are diverse and contentious. A secondary reason is that the pursuit of justice threatens to do little more than enhance the influence of the dominant states, and of the elites that guide them, while taking us further away from self-rule. We should consider these reasons more closely.

To begin with the primary reason, though justice is a value or an ideal that is universally recognized, it is also one whose content is widely disputed. It is disputed in several different and important ways. First, there is widespread disagreement about what are the fundamental requirements of justice. This disagreement is clearly in evidence among philosophers and scholars, who have disputed the merits of liberal, socialist, libertarian, utilitarian, Marxian, and other principles of distributive justice. However, even among people more generally, there are disagreements: for one thing, the various political parties in most Western democracies favor different standards of social justice, and appeal to different concerns or attitudes found in their electorates. Moreover, while the political parties may try to win office by appealing to the median voter, the fact remains that there are also voters at the extremes. It is also worth noting that often there is a significant gap between the attitudes of party elites and the masses within the party on a host of issues—including justice.

Second, there is disagreement about issues of justice because there is disagreement about questions of value.[14] Some people may value a resource because they regard it as having spiritual significance, while others may look at the same resource and see it as a potential source of material wealth. Thus, for example, some Aboriginal peoples have been reluctant to exploit the mineral wealth on lands they hold sacred, while their fellow citizens have argued that not exploiting these resources deprives others of the income that might be generated for everyone. Similarly, the issue of whether to permit oil exploration in wilderness areas brings out the conflict between those who attach greater value to the preservation of natural beauty or endangered ecosystems and those who see the need for energy as more pressing. Even those who agree on principles of justice in distribution may disagree on what should be distributed and how it should be valued.

There is a further complication here. Often it is difficult to say just what is the value of the resources a particular society or community may have, since questions of value can only be settled against the range of background conditions that give things worth. Oil was not an asset but a lia-

---

[14] Here I have drawn on David Miller's analysis in "Justice and Global Inequality," 193–96.

bility when discovered in the days before there was any demand for petroleum. Today, uranium would be of little value to a society unable to exploit it, and soil suitable for cultivating vines would not be prized in a society of teetotalers. Even if value could be established here, however, there is also the problem of determining how different values are to be traded off. Some communities may prefer to trade off higher incomes from uranium sales for untouched wilderness and rural enterprise. Some communities may prefer to trade off future income by consuming their resources more rapidly now—opting for development rather than conservation. Some communities will simply have more children than others, and this will affect the distribution of resources. This can have a bearing on justice to the extent that these choices affect the overall distribution of resources not only within but also among different communities. Clearly, however, different communities will favor different conceptions of justice, since not every conception of justice will support the values of every community.

Third, a problem arises because different communities or societies have different understandings of property. This means not only that there are different understandings of what ownership means—what rights and duties come with possession of different kinds of things owned—but also that there are different understandings of how ownership may be transferred and to whom. Laws of inheritance vary from society to society, sometimes considerably.

Fourth, there may be disagreements about justice to the extent that there are more general ethical disagreements among people. For example, to the extent that people disagree about the morality of abortion or assisted suicide, they may also disagree about whether to subsidize pregnancy termination and related forms of medical care or to subsidize adoption—or whether to subsidize anything at all. But there are also other matters on which people disagree that have a bearing on justice. Different religions, communities, and societies have varying attitudes on the definition of childhood and the responsibilities of children and parents. They differ on what they recognize as marriage and what they consider the proper grounds for divorce. At the extreme, there are differences among people as to what constitutes harm to or violation of persons. Most people would consider female genital mutilation an unjustifiable violation of a child's body, but some communities consider it not just acceptable but a duty of responsible parents in their societies.

In the face of this great diversity of views about justice, and about morality more generally, how can justice be pursued across a variety of communities with different views about what justice demands? This is a problem not just for international society but also for domestic societies, particularly if a society is large and internally diverse. Countries such as India, China, Russia, Brazil, Indonesia, and the United States contain numerous communities with different languages, religions, customs, and ethical traditions. Under such circumstances, the most a society can reasonably pursue is the establishment of a framework or set of norms that might accommodate ethical disagreement, allowing different traditions to coexist.

An alternative view, however, is that even in the face of diversity and ethical disagreement, it is nonetheless important to pursue justice, at least to ensure that some standards of universal significance prevail. This is vital in the international realm no less than in domestic societies. This requires establishing international institutions, governed by universal ethical standards, aimed at promoting justice and ensuring that the actions of states and communities alike are governed by standards of justice. It means rejecting "moral minimalism" in favor of developing institutions governed by robust ethical standards that apply across international borders.[15] But this view has to be rejected if ethical diversity is to be taken seriously.

This brings us to the secondary reason for limiting the role of justice in international affairs. If there are substantial differences over questions of justice, then trying to establish institutions whose purpose is to serve justice can produce either of two outcomes. First, it can lead to the creation of institutions of justice on which there is general agreement, but only because the understanding of "justice" is diluted or broadened to secure agreement among the different parties. Or, second, it can lead to the dominant powers establishing their own preferred understandings of justice, and running the institutions created according to their own ethical convictions—not to mention their interests. Most likely, we will see some combination of these two outcomes, which means that we will see some kind of rule by elites in the name of something they agree to call "justice."

The establishment in 1998 of the International Criminal Court (ICC) provides an illustration of the problematic role of elites in the establishment of institutions of international justice. The impetus to create the court came from the failed attempts to prosecute General Augusto Pinochet in Britain and in Spain for crimes, including torture, illegal detention, causing the disappearance of persons, and murder, alleged to have been committed while he was president of Chile. The ICC, it was hoped, would help resolve the problem of determining the legal jurisdiction in which such charges could be brought against persons accused of war crimes or crimes against humanity. After several years of preparation and five weeks of negotiation in Rome, the ICC was established on July 17, 1998, but not before the provisions of the statute governing its operation, and the definitions of crime that it would work with, were suitably modified to placate the convictions and interests of various parties.[16] Thus, for example, the definition of crimes against humanity brought protests for references to gender persecution (from some Islamic states) and to enforced sterilization (from China). Syria and a number of Arab states insisted that

[15] "Moral minimalism" is a term used by Allen Buchanan in *Justice, Legitimacy, and Self-Determination*, 38ff.

[16] Rome Statute of the International Criminal Court. The document may be found at http://www.icc-cpi.int/officialjournal/legalinstruments.html.

the list of crimes compiled to illustrate the prohibition on attacks on civilian populations would be acceptable provided it only applied in cases of inter-state conflict. Israel objected to Article 8 (section viii), which included in the definition of a war crime "the transfer directly or indirectly by an Occupying Power of parts of its own civilian population into the territory it occupies,"[17] arguing that this provision was aimed at its policies on Jewish settlements on the West Bank.

The United States also had serious objections to the Rome Statute, worrying that the war crimes provisions could be used by its enemies to prosecute its soldiers serving abroad. Along with many other states, it expressed a concern over granting any proposed court the sole power to determine what constituted an act of aggression, particularly since this would contravene the authority of the United Nations Security Council. Since the United States is a permanent member of the Security Council, with a right of veto over its resolutions, the U.S. took a much less favorable view of such an outcome than did India, which would like to be but is not a permanent member. In the end, however, the final statute incorporated provisions ensuring the sovereign rights of states, and enabling the court to operate only at the invitation of states or of the Security Council—though even then, a number of states, including the United States, Russia, China, and all the states of the Middle East except Jordan, declined to become members of the ICC.[18]

In the end, an institution established to deal with criminal justice was shaped as much by the interests of important powers as by any concern for justice. The more general point this leads to is that international political institutions, like many domestic ones, are shaped by the interests and attitudes of elites. Unlike many local political institutions, however, the elites in question are a long way removed from the people who are ultimately governed by them.

To extend responsibility for justice to international institutions is to detract from self-government. This point was recognized in 1863 by Lord Acton in his analysis of the implications of the development of the nation-state itself and its usurpation of the powers of local jurisdictions. True republicanism, he argued, "is the principle of self-government in the whole and in all the parts." In an extensive country, he continued, self-government could only prevail in a confederacy, "so that a large republic not founded on the federal principle must result in the government of a single city, like Rome and Paris." A great democracy, he concluded, "must either sacrifice self-government to unity, or preserve it by federalism."[19]

---

[17] Ibid., 12.
[18] For a helpful analysis, see Spyros Economides, "The International Criminal Court," in Karen E. Smith and Margot Light, eds., *Ethics and Foreign Policy* (Cambridge: Cambridge University Press, 2001), 112–28.
[19] Lord Acton, "Nationality," in *Selected Writings of Lord Acton: Volume I: Essays in the History of Liberty*, ed. Rufus Fears (Indianapolis: Liberty Fund, 1986), 409–33, at 414–15.

To try to establish a single standard of social justice even within a single country is a dubious undertaking. If a standard is agreed to by different communities, with different ethical traditions, that standard will be a weak one that reflects the compromises made to secure agreement rather than anything resembling justice. If the standard of justice is imposed by the more powerful, however, self-government will be sacrificed—without there being any assurance that the standards imposed have anything to do with justice rather than the interests of the dominant powers. This point holds even more strongly for international institutions. Powerful nations or coalitions will always find it advantageous to use the language of justice to defend the arrangements they establish. But this does not mean that justice is what they will pursue or defend.

We should be wary, then, of proposals to take action or devise institutions to secure international or global justice. The chances are that such proposals will simply serve the interests of elites, and will not secure justice even to the extent that we agree on what justice amounts to. More worryingly, however, appeals to justice, particularly when institutionalized, may simply serve as a cover or pretext for intervention in the affairs of people unwilling to accept ethical standards other than their own. At worst, such appeals may serve as pretexts for war. To the extent that it is important that we consider establishing international institutions to address matters of global concern, our priority should be not working out what justice requires and how it might be pursued but how to ensure that the power of global institutions, or the power that might be exerted through them, is kept limited. In the international domain, no less than in the domestic realm, the main political problem is how to keep power in check, not how to devise mechanisms to do good.

What this position implies is that in the international realm we should be concerned not to establish institutions that facilitate intervention in the affairs of other societies but to secure norms of toleration. A further implication of this outlook must also be recognized. If toleration is to take priority over justice, this means that injustice will have to be tolerated. This may be difficult if the perceived injustice is great. Nonetheless, toleration means nonintervention even in cases of injustice. For this reason, many hold either that toleration must be redefined so that justice establishes its limits, or that toleration must be subordinated to justice— perhaps to the extent that toleration simply becomes irrelevant as a substantial moral consideration.[20] The position defended here is that toleration takes precedence over justice.

It is important, however, to make clear what is not an implication of my view. The argument advanced here is not the one offered by Rawls in *The*

---

[20] John Rawls advances the first view in *A Theory of Justice* (Cambridge, MA: Harvard University Press, 1999); Deborah Fitzmaurice advances the second in "Autonomy as a Good: Liberalism, Autonomy, and Toleration," *Journal of Political Philosophy* 1, no. 1 (1993): 1–16.

Law of Peoples, which seeks to make a case not merely for nonintervention but also for respecting nonliberal peoples and states if they come up to certain minimal standards of morality.[21] I am not suggesting that we should think about the world as constituted by "peoples," or that we need to address the issue of whether or not certain societies deserve our respect. Nor, however, am I suggesting that states or state sovereignty are worthy of respect for other reasons such as those advanced by Martha Nussbaum in her critique of Rawls. For Nussbaum, "we ought to respect the state" since the state is "morally important because it is an expression of human choice and autonomy," because it "expresses the desire of human beings to live under laws they give to themselves."[22] My position makes no such assumption about the nature of the state; indeed, it is entirely skeptical about the state's moral credentials.[23]

It is also important to note that my view denies the significance of a distinction sometimes drawn between "not tolerating" and "intervening." The philosopher Kok-Chor Tan, for example, argues that a global theory of justice based on comprehensive[24] liberal ideas "does not face the tension between tolerating nonliberal societies and protecting individual liberty—it simply does not tolerate nonliberal societies."[25] But not tolerating, Tan insists, does not mean intervening. Indeed, there is a very strong presumption against intervening, especially with military force, even on behalf of oppressed peoples. Liberal states, he thinks, may take a whole range of other actions short of armed intervention, including public criticism and condemnation of nonliberal states. Comprehensive liberals "can deploy state (i.e., publicly shared) resources to question and even criticize some nonliberal group practices without actually criminalizing or enacting legislation against them."[26] Much the same kind of view is advanced by Nussbaum, who makes a distinction between the justification and the implementation of moral standards. We may think that the standards of a nation are defective, but this does not mean that it would

---

[21] John Rawls, *The Law of Peoples, with "The Idea of Public Reason Revisited"* (Cambridge, MA: Harvard University Press, 1999).

[22] Martha Nussbaum, "Women and Theories of Global Justice: The Need for New Paradigms," in Deen K. Chatterjee, ed., *The Ethics of Assistance: Morality and the Distant Needy* (Cambridge: Cambridge University Press, 2004), 147–76, at 167.

[23] To be candid, it seems to me that the idea that the state is (ever) an expression of human autonomy is a piece of wild romantic fiction. Its hold on the intellectual imagination is surely testimony to the brilliance and ingenuity of some of the outstanding philosophers of the past several centuries.

[24] "Comprehensive liberal" ideas contrast with "political liberal" ones. Comprehensive liberals take liberalism to be a doctrine that adheres to or upholds certain views about what values are central to leading a valuable human life—values such as individuality and autonomy. Political liberals think that comprehensive liberalism runs the risk of simply becoming another sectarian doctrine rather than adhering to the liberal ideal of finding neutral ground for the accommodation of different ideals of what makes for a good life.

[25] Kok-Chor Tan, *Toleration, Diversity, and Global Justice* (University Park: Pennsylvania State University Press, 2000), 82.

[26] Ibid., 60.

be right "to intervene, either militarily or through economic and political sanctions, simply in order to implement better human rights protections"—in most cases, "diplomatic pressures and persuasion seem more fitting than any sort of coercion."[27]

The problem with relying on this distinction (between "not tolerating" and "intervening") to diminish the likelihood of being drawn down the path of intervention is that it does not recognize the significance of the presumption against intervention in the affairs of people in other states or communities. The reason for rejecting justice in favor of toleration is precisely that this stance makes clear that nonintervention is the default position. It is intervention, particularly if it is to involve coercion or violence, that requires justification. Tan and Nussbaum, in different ways, want to assert the primacy of justice or substantive standards of morality; but in insisting that such standards may only be enforced in very rare cases, they, in effect, concede the priority of the principle of nonintervention or toleration over justice. In the case of Tan's claim that criticism without intervention or enforcement is not toleration, the use of the word "toleration" seems odd to the extent that it makes even criticism an act of intolerance. It surely makes more sense to say that we are intolerant not when we reject or criticize another's views but when we try to impose our own through the exercise of force rather than through persuasive reasoning.[28]

IV. ARGUMENTS FOR GLOBAL JUSTICE

The main targets of this essay's criticism, then, are those who defend global justice as an ideal that should inform the establishment of international institutions, and would form the basis for collective action to enforce standards of morality across the world. The literature advancing the case for global justice is substantial. Rather than try to address it as a whole, the remainder of this essay will focus on arguments developed by two philosophers, Allen Buchanan and Thomas Pogge. Both reject the view advanced by Rawls and others that justice should be pursued only within the confines of the nation-state: Buchanan emphasizes the importance of protecting human rights as an imperative of the natural duty of justice, and Pogge emphasizes the importance of reforming the global basic structure to end world poverty. I will consider these arguments in turn, beginning with Buchanan's.

According to Buchanan, justice must be the primary moral goal of international law. He rejects the idea that peace should be the main goal

---

[27] Nussbaum, "Women and Theories of Global Justice," 165–66.
[28] See Glen Newey, *Virtue, Reason, and Toleration: The Place of Toleration in Ethical and Political Philosophy* (Edinburgh: Edinburgh University Press, 1999), esp. 18–35; see also Andrew J. Cohen, "What Toleration Is," *Ethics* 115, no. 1 (2004): 68–95.

of the international system, and that the ideals of peace and justice are in conflict. He writes:

> [I]t is wrong to assume that justice and peace are somehow *essentially* in conflict. On the contrary, justice largely subsumes peace. Justice requires the prohibition of wars of aggression (understood as morally unjustifiable attacks as opposed to justified wars of self-defense or of humanitarian intervention) because wars of aggression inherently violate human rights. To that extent the pursuit of justice is the pursuit of peace.[29]

He adds that "protecting some of the most important human rights *is* securing peace."[30]

This view, Buchanan insists, is not as extreme as might be thought. It does not deny that justice may sometimes conflict with peace—though, for the most part, this will be the case in the period of transition from very unjust to more just conditions.[31] Furthermore, he concedes that the principle "Let there be justice, though the world perish" is not defensible. A commitment to justice cannot require allowing considerations of justice to trump all other moral considerations in every instance, for not all injustices are equally serious. The protection of basic human rights should be the primary goal of the international system, but this is entirely compatible with the fact that justice is not all that matters.[32] Nonetheless, "the protection of basic human rights is the core of justice, and the *raison d'être* for political power."[33]

There are two arguments that Buchanan offers for the conclusion that justice is a morally obligatory goal of international law. The first is that there is a global basic structure of institutions through which people across the globe relate and that this basic structure can be assessed for its justice. If justice is, as Rawls asserted, the first virtue of social institutions, then "justice is a morally imperative institutional goal," in the global as well as in the domestic sphere.[34] Here Buchanan endorses Thomas Pogge's contention that the global basic structure is a human creation, and that to accept it uncritically would be to support massive injustices.[35] The second argument is that there is a "Natural Duty of Justice" that requires everyone to contribute to ensuring that all persons have access to just institutions, and that this implies that "justice is a morally obligatory goal of

---

[29] Buchanan, *Justice, Legitimacy, and Self-Determination,* 79 (emphasis in original).
[30] Ibid (emphasis in original).
[31] Ibid.
[32] Ibid., 80–81.
[33] Ibid., 259.
[34] Ibid., 84–85.
[35] Ibid., 85. Pogge first developed this view in Thomas Pogge, *Realizing Rawls* (Ithaca, NY: Cornell University Press, 1989), though he has developed the arguments more forcefully in his later writings.

international law." [36] This duty flows from a "Moral Equality Principle"; and equal consideration of persons requires that we help to ensure that they have access to institutions that protect their basic rights.[37] We have a duty not simply not to harm but to help, even at substantial cost to ourselves.

With this outlook comes a particular view of the state and its ethical basis. Buchanan rejects what he calls the "discretionary association" view, according to which the state is nothing more than a discretionary association for the mutual advantage of its citizens—designed to further *their* interests.[38] On this view, "the state is not even in part an instrument for moral progress."[39] This view is, in the end, entirely incompatible with the Natural Duty of Justice.[40]

The view Buchanan defends is one he describes as "moderate cosmopolitanism." It recognizes that we have moral obligations beyond our own borders, but without going to the extreme of suggesting that all our particular obligations are simply derived from our obligations to humanity more broadly.[41] Equally, he insists, it is not a view that, in rejecting the discretionary association conception, suggests that governments may simply use the resources of the state to pursue global justice as they choose. Indeed, the state is, at least in part, "a resource for global, not just local, progress toward justice."[42] But its officials must be properly authorized, ideally by democratic processes, to carry out their fiduciary obligations.[43] What is very clearly rejected, however, is the idea that the national interest is the supreme value that should guide the conduct of foreign policy.[44] This would be entirely inconsistent with a view that gives an important place to human rights.

Central to Buchanan's argument is the claim that there are basic human rights, and that there is "an expanding global culture of human rights that exhibits a broad consensus on the idea that justice requires respect for the inherent dignity of all persons."[45] In this regard, he rejects the contention that there is widespread moral disagreement, and the idea that no global moral consensus can emerge. The evidence, in his view, points the other way. Thus, he rejects arguments, such as those offered by political philosopher Michael Walzer, that the world is marked by "deep distributive pluralism"; or that societies ought to be able to develop their own prin-

---

[36] Buchanan, *Justice, Legitimacy, and Self-Determination,* 86.
[37] Ibid., 88.
[38] Ibid., 98–99.
[39] Ibid., 100.
[40] Ibid., 103.
[41] Ibid.
[42] Ibid., 104.
[43] Ibid., 104–5. Buchanan recognizes that a theory of democratic authorization is needed to make the argument complete, though it is not his immediate concern to fill in this particular gap.
[44] Ibid., 106–16.
[45] Ibid., 42.

ciples of justice.[46] Buchanan also rejects as a reason for minimizing the role of distributive justice in the development of international law the idea that the international system lacks the institutional capacity to determine the requirements for, and to enforce, distributive justice. Our aim, he thinks, should be to develop that capacity.[47]

Buchanan argues not only for theoretical innovation but also for practical reform of the international legal order. Two aspects of his argument merit special mention. First, he makes clear that it is necessary to develop "a more permissive law regarding humanitarian intervention," for "liberalizing the international law of humanitarian intervention is likely to be a necessary condition for achieving" other reforms.[48] Second, Buchanan rejects the idea of relying on the development of customary law,[49] or working through established authorities like the United Nations, to establish appropriate conventions, arguing that a serious commitment to the international rule of law may require deliberate effort, by a coalition of like-minded (and right-minded) countries, to establish new rules of international law—illegally, if necessary. He makes this plain when he writes:

> [C]onsider again the proposal for a treaty-based, rule-governed intervention regime whose members would be restricted to the most democratic, human-rights respecting states. To the extent that it authorizes humanitarian interventions in the absence of Security Council authorization, such a regime would violate existing international law. But it would embody, rather than repudiate, a commitment to the rule of law in the normatively rich sense.[50]

In fact, Buchanan insists that being "willing to act illegally to make a very unjust system more just need not be inconsistent with a commitment to justice through law; it may indeed be required by it."[51]

Buchanan's concern is to present a case for the creation or reform of basic international institutions in order to bring about a more just world. Such reforms would bring about justice by protecting or enforcing individual rights. Despite some significant philosophical differences between their approaches, Buchanan's concerns are shared by Thomas Pogge, who also calls for reform of the basic structure of international society, but whose writings on global justice have focused on the problem of world poverty and human rights rather than on international law.[52]

---

[46] Ibid., 201–2.
[47] Ibid., 202–3.
[48] Ibid., 445–46.
[49] Ibid., 446–49.
[50] Ibid., 462.
[51] Ibid.
[52] See esp. Thomas Pogge, *World Poverty and Human Rights* (Malden, MA: Polity Press, 2002).

For Pogge, the interdependence of persons in a world order makes it essential that we look at justice in global rather than local terms. Institutional interconnections across the planet, he argues, "render obsolete the idea that countries can peacefully agree to disagree about justice, each committing itself to a conception of justice appropriate to its history, culture, population size and density, natural environment, geopolitical context, and stage of development."[53] In the modern world, people's lives are profoundly affected by global rules of governance, trade, and diplomacy; and about such institutions we cannot agree to disagree, since they can only be structured one way—not differently in each country. If they are to be justified to all persons in all parts of the world, "then we must aspire to a *single, universal* criterion of justice which all persons and peoples can accept as the basis for moral judgments about the global order."[54] This acceptance is vitally important, for it matters that a society's institutional order be endorsed by those to whom the order applies. This is why "we should try to formulate the universal criterion of justice so that it can gain universal acceptance."[55]

Despite his emphasis on universalism, Pogge is aware of its shortcomings and has some sympathy for the contextualist ethics defended by philosopher David Miller.[56] Pogge's most serious criticisms of contextualism, however, are reserved for John Rawls, whom he charges with offering a theory that fails to justify applying quite different fundamental principles to national and international institutional schemes. For example, Pogge argues, Rawls rejects the difference principle[57] as a requirement of global justice on the ground that it is unacceptable for one people to bear the costs of decisions made by another—decisions on national birth-rates, for instance—but Rawls does not explain "why this ground should not analogously disqualify the difference principle for national societies as well," since one province or township may have to bear the costs of decisions made by another.[58] To the extent that Rawls argues that his theory, and the difference principle in particular, can only apply to a closed society or a self-contained system, Pogge also points out, it is hard to see why it should not apply to the world if it can apply to the United States, which is neither closed nor self-contained. If the objection is that principles of justice must be acceptable to the people who live under

---

[53] Ibid., 33.

[54] Ibid. (emphasis in original).

[55] Ibid., 34.

[56] Ibid., 102–4.

[57] Rawls advances the "difference principle" as a part of the second of his two principles of justice. Broadly, it asserts that in a just society, institutions of justice would permit inequalities only provided that social arrangements were such that the welfare of the least-advantaged or worst-off group in society was higher than it could be under any other arrangements. Rawls's most recent discussion of the difference principle is in John Rawls, *Justice as Fairness: A Restatement* (Cambridge, MA: Harvard University Press, 2001).

[58] Pogge, *World Poverty*, 105. Rawls's claim is in *The Law of Peoples*, 116–18.

them, as they are not in other parts of the world, Pogge replies that the same holds true for the United States, where the difference principle is not one that commands agreement[59]—even, one might add, among liberal political philosophers. If there are reasons why the standards of justice that apply domestically cannot be applied internationally, Pogge argues, Rawls has not supplied them.

For Pogge, there are compelling reasons why justice is an issue that has to be addressed globally. First, it is clear that many people live lives of desperate poverty and enormous suffering, even as others, particularly in the countries of the developed West, enjoy great affluence. Second, an important cause of this suffering—and affluence—is the system of global institutions that protects the wealth of some while prolonging the poverty of others. Third, to the extent that global institutions are capable of being reformed but have not been improved, those who benefit from those institutions must bear responsibility for the condition of those who suffer under them. In the world today, Pogge maintains, the affluent benefit from a system that sustains radical inequality such that they enjoy significant advantages in the use of a single natural resource base—the earth—from whose benefits the worst-off are excluded without compensation. This system itself emerged out of a historical process that was pervaded by massive, grievous wrongs.[60]

As a first step toward justice, Pogge proposes the establishment of a Global Resources Dividend (GRD)—a fund created by payments made by all states, to be used to eradicate poverty—"to ensure that all human beings can meet their own basic needs with dignity."[61] With the help of "economists and international lawyers," Pogge suggests, it may be possible to design a scheme that disburses funds to the poor—if necessary, directly rather than through their governments—and provides governments with incentives to rule better.[62] "A good government brings enhanced prosperity through GRD support and thereby generates more popular support which in turn makes it safer from coup attempts."[63] Such a scheme would not only make available funds owed to the world's poor, but also encourage the governments of developing countries to pursue much-needed reforms. "Combined with suitable disbursement rules, the GRD can stimulate a peaceful international competition in effective poverty eradication."[64]

Like Buchanan, Pogge defends what amounts to a moderate cosmopolitanism. What both philosophers share is a conviction that justice is a

---

[59] Pogge, World Poverty, 106.

[60] Ibid., 201–3. In this account, I have contracted Pogge's more elaborate, careful, and sophisticated argument, but without, I hope, misrepresenting it or failing to capture its spirit.

[61] Ibid., 197.

[62] Ibid., 206.

[63] Ibid., 207.

[64] Ibid.

global issue, though both want to give particularism some due. Both thus make what they regard as moderate proposals for reforming global institutions. Neither thinks that a proper respect for human dignity or moral principle warrants anything less.

V. Against Global Justice

There can be no doubt that we live in a world in which many people suffer poverty and oppression, or that where one is born has a greater bearing on one's prospects in life than, say, one's talents or character. A modern variant of the ancient Chinese curse might well run, "May you live in an interesting country." There is surely a case for helping the destitute, opening our borders to those looking to make a better life, and welcoming those who are trying to escape oppressive regimes. This does not mean, however, that there is a case for seeking the mirage of global justice, and the problems with the theories advanced by Buchanan and Pogge help to bring this out. Both set out to show that universal justice is desirable, and that it may be better secured across the world by the reform or creation of institutions authorized and empowered to do so. Yet the outcome of their philosophical effort is, in effect, a justification of rule by elites, guided by (and unchecked by anything other than) a commitment to a view of justice. We should be skeptical of these efforts, for they promise only elite rule, not justice.

One important reason for this is that political institutions cannot secure justice, particularly when they cover large areas of territory and a great number and diversity of people. The most they can secure is peace as people agree to abide by common laws and the rule of common authorities. There are two reasons why justice is not a likely outcome. First, given the nature of politics, the institutions or rules that are adopted will reflect not the demands of justice but the balance of power. Second, the likelihood of agreement on justice diminishes with the increasing size of the polity: any agreement reached will be a compromise, assented to in the end in order to bring negotiation to a close. To say this is not to take refuge in skepticism about justice. One might remain convinced that one view of justice is true and still recognize that political institutions are incapable of securing it, or that securing it is no part of their purpose.

Allen Buchanan takes a different view in arguing that justice subsumes peace, and that the best way to secure peace is to secure justice by protecting human rights. But this seems straightforwardly implausible. If two parties to a dispute disagree about justice but one is successful in having his view of justice prevail, there is no reason to think that this will produce peace between them. If peace is produced because one is able to persuade the other that his view of justice really is correct, it is agreement that produces peace, not the justice of the agreed-upon view. Peace would be the outcome even if the agreed-upon view of justice was wrong. If agreement were the outcome simply of the stronger party's being able to enforce his view of justice, the resulting peace would hardly be the product of justice, simply of power.

Consider as an illustration what is perhaps the most intractable of all problems in contemporary international politics: the dispute over Palestine. It would be simplifying matters considerably even to assert that there were only two sides to this conflict. We can say, however, that there are a number of issues in play: the legitimacy of the very existence of Israel; the proper boundaries of the Israeli state (whether they should be defined by the 1947 U.N. determination, or the war at the founding of the state, or the 1967 war, or the view of the present Israeli state, or some other set of considerations altogether); the right of return, if any, of Palestinian refugees; the status of Jewish settlers and their settlements on the West Bank; and the rights of Palestinians or Arabs living or working in Israel. It is safe to say that there is agreement neither among Israelis nor among Palestinians about what justice demands, let alone agreement between the government of Israel and the various groups, including the Palestinian Authority, who claim to speak on behalf of all Palestinians. To suggest that the path to peace in this land is to establish justice by protecting human rights seems utterly implausible given the unlikelihood that those who lose by the establishment of what is alleged to be justice will simply accept the outcome with good grace—even if the judgment were offered by Solomon himself. Buchanan suggests that justice requires the prohibition of wars of aggression "understood as morally unjustified attacks as opposed to justified wars of self-defense or of humanitarian intervention."[65] Yet each of the warring parties in the Holy Land believes others to be the aggressors and sees itself as acting in self-defense. If we must wait for this disagreement over justice to be settled before there can be peace, we will be waiting for a long time. If there is any plausible route to peace, it must surely involve most parties' recognizing and accepting that they will not obtain justice in the sense of receiving the full measure of what they regard as their due, but being willing to take less than justice in the interests of peace. This would surely be easier to take than being forced to accept that what one receives is all that one is justly entitled to.[66]

Buchanan, however, suggests that "progress towards justice is especially likely to require illegal acts if the system's imperfections include serious barriers to expeditious, legally permissible reform," and recommends the creation of a "rule-governed intervention regime," its membership restricted to the "most democratic, human rights–respecting states," to authorize intervention in regimes that violate human rights.[67] For him, current norms of nonintervention are too robust and are an

---

[65] Buchanan, *Justice, Legitimacy, and Self-Determination*, 79.

[66] As H. L. Mencken once observed, albeit with a slightly different point in mind, "injustice anyone can take, what really stings is justice."

[67] Buchanan, *Justice, Legitimacy, and Self-Determination*, 462.

obstacle to the establishment of justice. But it is difficult to know what to make of this call for human rights–respecting states to take matters into their own hands in the name of justice.[68] To the extent that his point is simply that illegal acts are sometimes morally justified, it is hard to disagree. It is also fair to say that those acting illegally may well be truly committed to the rule of law, in the way that, say, Martin Luther King or Gandhi were in their acts of civil disobedience.[69] But what would this mean, say, for international society confronted by the knowledge of these past acts of civil disobedience and their suppression by the American and British governments? The norm in international law is that other states not intervene in such cases, even when accusations of human rights violations are very serious. Buchanan's proposal is that a coalition of right-thinking nations should not simply intervene in such cases, but should get together, rewrite international law, authorize themselves to act, and then claim to be acting lawfully—understanding law "in the normatively rich way."[70]

This is a troubling view, but it is important to understand what lies behind it. Buchanan's concern is that existing international norms (and in particular, the structure of the United Nations) make it difficult to pursue justice or morality. Human rights abuses go unaddressed. Reform, he thinks, is necessary to make it more possible for human rights to be protected. What is troubling about this view is that it assumes or asserts that a world in which such constraints on intervention are removed or weakened will be a better world, presumably because the just are freer to act. Yet it would also leave the unjust freer to act. If the recommendation is that right-thinking states should combine when necessary, restructure patterns of international authority by establishing treaties, and then authorize themselves to act in the name of justice, this looks like a general invitation to all states to so act. No state thinks it is not right-thinking, and most even claim to recognize human rights—and indeed are signatories to the major human rights agreements, including the Universal Declaration of Human Rights (1948).[71]

---

[68] Buchanan does try to make clear that his proposal is *"not* for a single state, or even a collection of states, to intervene lawlessly. Instead, the idea is to create a new system of rules—new principles, processes, and institutions—that embody the normatively rich conception of the rule of law." Ibid., 462.

[69] Buchanan uses these examples; see ibid., 464.

[70] Buchanan's defense of lawbreaking is very different from that suggested by Robert Goodin, who argues that there may be cases in which it is justified as the only means of reforming international customary law. See Robert Goodin, "Toward an International Rule of Law: Distinguishing International Law-Breakers from Would-Be Law-Makers," *International Journal of Ethics* 9 (2005).

[71] Other important human rights declarations include the International Covenant on Economic, Social, and Cultural Rights; the International Covenant on Civil and Political Rights; and the Convention on the Elimination of All Forms of Discrimination against Women. For a fuller list, see the U.N. Office of the High Commissioner for Human Rights: http://www.unhchr.ch/html/intlinst.htm (accessed January 2005).

Buchanan's theory, in the end, requires that we accept either one of two views, the first one implausible and the second unattractive. The first view is that there is a level of consensus in the international order that would make it possible for global institutions to be restructured by concerted action of the kind he recommends. In fact, however, there is no such consensus—or at least, not yet. Now, Buchanan is aware of this argument, but he questions the claim that there is no consensus and suggests that the implication of denying the existence of consensus is a denial of the legitimacy of the international system as a whole.[72] The Universal Declaration of Human Rights, he points out, "as well as other central human rights conventions, explicitly endorses the idea that the inherent dignity of free and equal individuals entitles them to be treated in certain ways—and this sounds very much like a widely shared, core conception of justice."[73] This, he thinks, throws into question the whole "moral minimalist" perspective. Yet the most such agreements reveal is the existence of elite consensus, and a limited consensus at that. The reasons why some countries might sign on to important declarations may have less to do with acceptance (by the elites of those states) of the expressed moral principles than with the political advantages of joining. Even after declarations have been endorsed, however, there is no reason to think that the elites, or populations, of different countries interpret them in the same way. When the U.N. Human Rights Committee protested that Iran's Islamic Penal Code, which required the amputation of four fingers of the right hand for a first conviction for theft, and flogging for consuming alcohol, violated article 7 of the International Covenant on Civil and Political Rights (ICCPR), the Iranian government insisted that it was upholding not violating the covenant. Article 7 prohibits "cruel, inhuman or degrading treatment or punishment," but Iran, as a signatory to the ICCPR, insisted that it took the strictures of article 7 very seriously, while interpreting it in a way consistent with its own social norms.[74] If there is an international moral consensus, it is weaker than Buchanan suggests. He is quite right to say that we should not assume that a consensus will never emerge; but until it does, we should operate on the assumption that it does not yet exist.

The second view is that a minority of states should pursue the task of engaging in the restructuring of global institutions. The objection to this is not simply that any such effort would fail without the major powers, such as the United States and the European Union, going along with it, though Buchanan thinks there is much to be said for trying to engage in such restructuring without the United States, which is "widely regarded—

---

[72] Buchanan, *Justice, Legitimacy, and Self-Determination,* 308–10; see also 38–45.

[73] Ibid., 309.

[74] See Kristen Hessler, "Resolving Interpretive Conflicts in International Human Rights Law," *Journal of Political Philosophy* 13, no. 1 (2005).

and not without reason—as an international scoff-law."[75] The problem is that the claim is that international law, and more specifically, a "liberal-democratic intervention regime,"[76] should be created by a self-selected elite. This elite, led, in Buchanan's ideal scenario, by the European Union, would admit only those countries with "decent" human rights records and those that meet the minimum criteria for democracy. It would establish an alternative international organization that would have "a stronger claim to legitimacy than a state-majoritarian UN entity such as the General Assembly"; after all, "[i]f the goal is to protect human rights, then who would be better qualified than a coalition of states that have the best records for doing so?"[77] Yet even if the self-selected members of this regime should be satisfied that they are the best standard-bearers for human rights, why would, or should, anyone else accept this assertion, or accord this group any moral or legal standing simply because it claims to have the best human rights record?

It is difficult to see how Buchanan's proposal here amounts to much more than a recommendation that like-minded states who believe in human rights should set out to collude and enforce, whenever possible, their own conception of justice. If this is so, it does not look like an improvement on the norm that Buchanan is looking to undermine: international customary law. The disadvantage of customary law is that it changes slowly and is not a tool that may readily be used to right serious wrongs. It depends on the development of consensus, mostly among states, and does nothing to enhance the capacity of international agencies to intervene in the affairs of tyrannical regimes. Its advantage, however, is precisely that it does make intervention, and the resort to arms, more difficult.

More generally, whatever the weaknesses of the Westphalian system, it does have some important virtues. In a world of unequal power, a norm of nonintervention, even if upheld by a convention recognizing states as sovereign powers, checks the capacity of stronger states to enforce their wills. For weaker states, sovereignty is an important asset, particularly if it can be deployed with effect against stronger states whose assertions of the common purposes of states in international society can easily be self-serving and to the detriment of lesser polities. As the theorist of international relations Hedley Bull noted, "If a right of intervention is proclaimed for the purpose of enforcing standards of conduct, and yet no consensus exists in the international community governing its use, then the door is open to interventions by particular states using such a right as a pretext."[78]

---

[75] Buchanan, *Justice, Legitimacy, and Self-Determination*, 452.
[76] Ibid.
[77] Ibid.
[78] Hedley Bull, "The Grotian Conception of International Society," in Herbert Butterfield and Martin Wight, eds., *Diplomatic Investigations: Essays on the Theory of International Politics* (London: Allen and Unwin, 1966), 51–73, at 71.

In the end, the world is more diverse than Buchanan's theory is prepared to admit. We live in an international society that is pluralist rather than solidarist.[79] Until there is in fact greater moral agreement, any attempt to restructure the international order in accordance with principles of justice risks sanctioning the enforcement of international norms that serve the interests of powerful states, without doing much to serve the interests of weaker states or their members. In any case, we should be wary of setting up institutions of international justice intended to protect the weak, because more powerful agents are often better able to exploit the resources these institutions provide. This is not a decisive consideration; but it is an important, cautionary one, nonetheless.

This consideration calls into question the claims Buchanan makes on behalf of the Natural Duty of Justice. The Natural Duty of Justice is "the limited moral obligation to contribute to ensuring that all persons have access to just institutions."[80] Showing proper concern and respect for all persons, in Buchanan's view, requires doing what is necessary, within the limits of what can reasonably be expected of anyone, to ensure that those persons have access to the institutions needed to protect individual rights. Thus, "conscientiously acting on the Natural Duty of Justice means supporting institutional efforts to secure justice for all."[81] In part, the problem with this is that the very idea that the Natural Duty of Justice requires acting to ensure that others have access to institutions is not as plausible as Buchanan suggests. Here he draws on Kant's idea that there is a duty to leave the state of nature to enter a juridical condition.[82] But all that really follows from our having a duty of justice is that we must fulfill our obligations to act justly.[83] If some people wish to establish institutions to govern themselves in order better to secure justice, there is no duty for us to take part. But even if there were a duty to support institutional efforts to secure justice for all, that would give us no reason to think that we should support *any* institutional efforts that are undertaken. Indeed, one might be well advised to take a skeptical attitude toward most claims made in defense of developing institutions—particularly when the claims are that such institutions will serve justice, rather than the interests of those creating them.

These considerations also tell against Pogge's arguments in defense of establishing an international regime to secure global economic justice. There is no question that large numbers of people live in poverty. Even on

[79] On the use of these terms, see Edward Keene, *Beyond the Anarchical Society: Grotius, Colonialism, and Order in World Politics* (Cambridge: Cambridge University Press, 2002), 35–38.

[80] Buchanan, *Justice, Legitimacy, and Self-Determination*, 86.

[81] Ibid., 93.

[82] See Immanuel Kant, *The Metaphysical Elements of Justice*, trans. John Ladd (Indianapolis: Bobbs-Merrill, 1976).

[83] This is true even if one recognizes that there are positive rights that have to be upheld, and that one's duties go beyond merely forbearing from violating negative rights.

very modest assumptions about what constitutes poverty (say, an income of less than US $1.50 a day), nearly a sixth of humanity is poor. The moral imperative to address this problem is a strong one. Yet this does not mean that our obligation is to restructure the international system. There are a number of steps that can surely be taken unilaterally by individuals and governments with complete justification. First, it may be incumbent on those who are well off to act unilaterally to contribute more to relief of the poor and destitute. Since relief is often better supplied by collective action, it may be morally better to act through international agencies, such as Community Aid Abroad or Oxfam, to do so.[84] Second, the governments of various states can act unilaterally to reform their own economic policies, opening their borders to trade, ceasing to subsidize domestic industries, admitting greater numbers of refugees and immigrants, particularly from the ranks of the poor, and ceasing to finance regimes that are corrupt, inefficient, or oppressive—indeed, ceasing to finance other governments altogether. Free trade does not, at least in principle, require a World Trade Organization, or formal international agreements.[85] Third, international federations such as the European Union can themselves act unilaterally to eliminate practices, including their agricultural policies, that harm the world's poor.

Now it might be argued that these recommendations are not enough: first, because private unilateral action is not going to do very much good, and second, because it is simply politically naive to think that states will take unilateral action to open their borders to foreign goods and people. In the first instance, it is probably true that private charity will not be sufficient to make a substantial impact on global poverty. Other changes are necessary. Yet, second, if there is no possibility of states and international federations taking unilateral action to cease their harmful trade and immigration policies, there is surely little reason to think that more ambitious reforms of global economic structures are possible. What hope is there of a Global Resources Dividend in a world of butter mountains, wine lakes, and billion-dollar subsidies to grow rice in deserts, or sugar in the wilderness?

Pogge is looking for solutions that involve reform on a global scale, using mechanisms that will do justice by making possible large transfers of funds from rich to poor societies. In his view, justice requires such transfers to reduce the inequality that exists between the rich and the poor. The question is, who is to establish what justice demands, and how are we to ensure that justice is properly served? Pogge's answer is that

---

[84] For a discussion of the limits of such duties, however, see Neera Badhwar, "International Aid: When Giving Becomes a Vice," elsewhere in this volume. (For Oxfam, see http://www.oxfam.org.uk.)

[85] Even if it is useful to have the World Trade Organization to pressure other nations to lower their own trade barriers, there is no reason for wealthy nations acting within the WTO structure not to be more open than the terms of the WTO require.

these questions will be settled by states, or elites within them, who will enlist experts—economists and lawyers—to devise suitable schemes to raise and distribute funds. Whatever practical problems this may involve, two difficulties stand out. First, the GRD sets out to solve a problem of global distribution by creating yet another political institution. Yet given that the existing political institutions have struggled to address the problem of taking care of the world's poor, what reason is there to think that creating another layer of intervention will help in any way? Past experience suggests that all the problems that beset other institutions, from the nation-state itself to the agencies of the United Nations, would simply reappear. In particular, if a fund were created making available for redistribution tens of billions of dollars, it is hard to see how there could not be another scramble for a slice of the largesse, with the spoils going to those who know best how to manipulate the system. Even if the outcome of this was a greater share of the world's wealth going to the poor, it is not clear that this would be desirable if it means that poor nations put their energies not into learning how to develop and manage their productive assets but into perfecting the art of securing aid money.

Second, establishing institutions of global distributive justice in this way once again means entrenching the power of the world's elites: those powerful states who would supply the funds and control their disbursement, with the help of elites in developing countries. The assumption here is that good will and sound institutional design will overcome the major difficulties and enable us to get closer to eliminating global inequality and securing justice. Past experience, however, suggests only that it will take us closer to global political inequality.[86]

VI. Conclusion

The fact of global poverty and the prevalence of oppressive regimes have provoked the call for attention to the problem of global injustice. The aim of this essay has not been to deny the existence of poverty or oppression; its aim has been to seek the appropriate response to these conditions. The main thesis it advances is that the solution does not lie in

[86] Much of Pogges's argument rests on the contention that global poverty and global inequality are increasing. While there is no doubt of the extent of global poverty, the claim of growing inequality is controversial. On this, see in particular the work of Surjit Bhalla, who has argued that, contrary to the received wisdom, inequality has been declining as a consequence of "globalization"—the lowering of trade barriers and the greater internationalization of commerce. See Surjit Bhalla, *Imagine Theres's No Country: Poverty, Inequality, and Growth in the Era of Globalization* (Washington, DC: Institute for International Economics, 2002). For criticisms of Bhalla, see Martin Ravallion, "Have We Already Met the Millennium Development Goal for Poverty?" Institute for International Economics, available at http:// www.iie.com/publications/papers/papers03.htm (accessed February 2005). For Bhalla's reply, see "Crying Wolf on Poverty: Or How the Millennium Development Goal for Poverty Has Already Been Reached," Institute for International Economics, available at: http:// www.iie.com/research/globalization.htm (accessed February 2005).

establishing or expanding political powers to address these problems. This promises neither to establish an acceptable understanding of justice, nor to do much more than provide another opportunity for political elites to pursue their own particular ends. However, it should also be made clear what is not being suggested here.

First, this is not a defense of realism in international politics. In Buchanan's account, realism recommends that states be guided at all times by a concern for their national interests. As a moral theory, this has little to commend it. The argument here is not that states should pursue their own interests but that we should not look for ways of increasing the power of political elites in the expectation that they will do anything but pursue their own interests. Contrary to what Buchanan and others suggest, the state and other political institutions are not instruments of moral progress. We should be more thoroughly cynical about political power, for justice is not its *raison d'être*.

Second, this is not a rejection of the importance of international law. What is rejected, however, is the idea that global justice demands sweeping reforms of international institutions, and the establishment of new structures.

Third, the argument here is not a rejection of cosmopolitanism, even though it criticizes the work of modest cosmopolitans such as Buchanan and Pogge. The main assumption of the essay in this regard is that the development of cosmopolitanism should not be the product of political reform. It may well be that there will be a convergence across the globe on common moral standards in the years to come. Unless that happens, however, we cannot even begin to think in terms of global justice.

Political Theory, University of Utah

THE LAW OF PEOPLES, SOCIAL COOPERATION, HUMAN RIGHTS, AND DISTRIBUTIVE JUSTICE*

By Samuel Freeman

I. Introduction

My aim in this essay is to discuss, and defend against some frequent objections, John Rawls's rejection of a global principle of distributive justice. As is well known, Rawls's *A Theory of Justice* argues for a principle of distributive justice, the difference principle, that is to be applied within different societies but not among them.[1] According to *A Theory of Justice*, each society has the duty to set up its economic and legal institutions in such a way that they make the least advantaged among its own members better off than the least advantaged would be if that society were structured according to any other distribution principle. But each society does *not* have a duty to structure its system so as to maximize the position of the least advantaged in the world at large. Though it is a universal principle that is to apply severally, or *within every society,* the difference principle is not global in reach, applying jointly to all societies simultaneously. To critics of many political persuasions, this seems a peculiar position. Why should principles of justice be domestically rather than globally applied?

Rawls's position in *A Theory of Justice* becomes even more complicated in *Political Liberalism* and *The Law of Peoples*, where he is guided by questions of political legitimacy, and feasibility (or "stability") of liberal regimes.[2] In *Political Liberalism* and later works,[3] Rawls appears to give up on the idea that a well-ordered society of justice as fairness is feasible (such a well-ordered society is one where every rational and reasonable citizen affirms, for moral reasons, justice as fairness, including the difference principle). The best we can expect of this world, he now seems to claim,

---

* I am grateful to K. C. Tan for many helpful discussions and criticisms of this essay. I am also grateful to the other contributors to this volume for their comments, and to Ellen Paul for her many helpful suggestions in preparing the final version of this essay.

[1] John Rawls, *A Theory of Justice* (Cambridge, MA: Harvard University Press, 1971; revised edition, 1999), cited as *TJ* in the text. References will be made to the 1999 revised edition.

[2] John Rawls, *Political Liberalism* (New York: Columbia University Press, 1993; paperback edition, 1996); John Rawls, *The Law of Peoples* (Cambridge, MA: Harvard University Press, 1999), cited as *PL* and *LP* respectively in the text.

[3] Here I have in mind particularly Rawls's last paper, "The Idea of Public Reason Revisited," in John Rawls, *Collected Papers*, ed. Samuel Freeman (Cambridge, MA: Harvard University Press, 1999).

---

are liberal and democratic societies in which all citizens recognize and accept the basic liberties and their priority, and the duty of society to provide a social minimum adequate to the exercise of the basic liberties. The social minimum need not be defined by the difference principle for liberal societies' economic systems to be politically legitimate, and their laws worthy of respect.

It is this conception of the legitimacy of liberal regimes and of their economic distributions that underlies Rawls's account in *The Law of Peoples* of a "reasonably just Society of Peoples." A just Society of Peoples is not (necessarily) a world in which all, or even any, of its member-nations structure their economies according to the difference principle. So long as a society provides for the basic needs of its citizens, respects their human rights, and is regulated by a common-good conception of justice, it is "decent" and has political legitimacy within the Society of Peoples, and is to be tolerated and respected by other peoples. There is no specific principle of distributive justice that must be met, either domestically or globally, within a just Society of Peoples. The difference principle simply drops out of the picture in Rawls's account of the Law of Peoples.

Oddly, perhaps, even within the Law of Nations that Rawls outlines in *A Theory of Justice*, Rawls held (or would have held) the same position. That is, even though, according to *A Theory of Justice*, each nation has a duty to realize the principles of justice in its basic institutions, the domestic justice of all member nations is not a condition of the justice of the well-ordered Society of Peoples. Moreover, Rawls still believed, when he wrote *Political Liberalism* and *The Law of Peoples*, that the difference principle defined the conditions of distributive justice for any and all societies; or at least it was for Rawls the ideal that societies should strive for. (This was part of his comprehensive liberal view.) However, being a just member of the Society of Peoples never meant for Rawls, even in *A Theory of Justice*, that a society must be fully just, especially not in its economic distributions of income and wealth among its members. For Rawls, it is simply not the role of peoples, individually or collectively, to enforce distributive justice anywhere except among their own peoples.

There are then two points of contention. First, Rawls, early and late, rejects the idea of a global principle of distributive justice, a principle of justice that is global in reach. The reference point for assessment of judgments of distributive justice is the "basic structure" of particular societies. This means we cannot know whether a person has his or her fair share of resources without knowing (at least) which society he or she is a member of, and details about the basic institutions of that society. Second, Rawls holds that a society can be in good standing in a "reasonably just Society of Peoples" without complying with requirements of distributive justice, or for that matter, even respecting basic liberties, so long as it respects human rights.[4] How can the Society of Peoples be just if all its members are not just?

Many different kinds of objections have been raised against Rawls's position. Utilitarians (R. M. Hare, Peter Singer, et al.), libertarians (Robert Nozick et al.), and others who reject the entire Rawlsian framework (Joseph Raz, John Finnis, et al.) claim that Rawls starts out by focusing on the wrong values and ideas. Then there are other critics who are more sympathetic to Rawls, insofar as they accept many of his ideas and the principles of justice. Their primary objection, in effect, is that Rawls goes astray by limiting the reach of the difference principle to the basic structure of society, thereby making membership within a particular society a condition for assessing claims of distributive justice. These critics contend that whatever reasons there are for applying a principle of distributive justice internally within a society must also justify its application to individuals all over the world. I want to limit my discussion here mainly to objections by these "Rawlsian cosmopolitans," as I call them. I cannot here defend the entire Rawlsian framework against its external critics. I do hope to argue, however, that the position is not guilty of some blatant or even subtle inconsistency, as Rawlsian cosmopolitans seem to suggest.

Finally, by way of introduction, many of the criticisms from all sides brought against Rawls assume current conditions, with all their injustices. For example, some critics claim that Rawls's Law of Peoples would allow for exploitation by private corporations of helpless people, or would permit conditions of peonage, apartheid, etc. Some also claim that it would allow for a government to impose egregiously unjust conditions on its people, such as ethnic cleansing, and anything short of slavery and forced servitude.[5] The problem with these sorts of objections is that they fail to recognize that the Law of Peoples is formulated to apply to ideal conditions (of a sort), among "well-ordered societies" all of whom are members of a "Society of well-ordered Peoples" (*PL*, 17–19). Well-ordered societies (both liberal and "decent") are societies where reasonable and

---

[4] For Rawls, the human rights all persons have under the Law of Peoples are a subset of the basic liberties all societies should provide. "Among the human rights are the right to life (to the means of subsistence and security); to liberty (to freedom from slavery, serfdom, and forced occupation, and to a sufficient measure of liberty of conscience to insure freedom of religion and thought); to property (personal property); and to formal equality as expressed by the rules of natural justice (that is, that similar cases be treated similarly." Rawls, *The Law of Peoples*, 65.

[5] See Simon Caney, "Cosmopolitanism and the Law of Peoples," *The Journal of Political Philosophy* 10, no. 1 (March 2002): 95–123, at 102, where he says: "Rawls's schema, thus, allows racial discrimination, the political exclusion of ethnic minorities, the forcible removal of members of some ethnic communities (that is, ethnic cleansing), the reduction of some to just above subsistence whilst other members of that society luxuriate in opulent splendor, and the perpetuation of grossly unequal opportunities and political power." None of these accusations is correct, for these practices are unjust, according to Rawls's principles of justice, wherever they occur. Moreover, some of them violate human rights, and all are difficult, if not impossible, to reconcile with any reasonable common-good conception, which is a condition of decency of peoples.

rational members generally accept the governing principles of justice and terms of cooperation of their society, and rely upon these principles and terms in their public reasoning about justice. Moreover, these terms of cooperation comply with a conception of the common good according to which all members of society are benefited, and the members of society generally endorse this conception of the common good. (In a liberal society, the conception of the common good is largely defined by a liberal conception of justice; in "decent hierarchical societies" [*PL*, 71], it is defined by some nonliberal moral conception.) These conditions virtually guarantee that apartheid, ethnic cleansing, and other egregious forms of discrimination will not be practiced in well-ordered decent societies. If Rawls's account of human rights does not prohibit such unjust practices (though I believe it does), then the implications of any common-good conception of justice conjoined with the general acceptability of terms of cooperation within decent societies should prohibit them. (I assume here that those who suffer from apartheid and ethnic cleansing would not endorse the treatment they endure. Even if they did, however, it is impossible to conceive of a feasible conception of the common good that incorporates terms of apartheid and ethnic cleansing directed toward those who are supposed to benefit from these very same terms.)

One question I consider is whether these conditions and restrictions will be adequate to prevent the economic exploitation of poorer peoples by richer peoples or multinational corporations. I contend that just as liberal societies will not permit economic exploitation of their own citizens since it presumably makes them worse off than many alternative terms of cooperation, so a decent society that domestically enforces a common-good conception of justice will not allow foreign or multinational corporations to take advantage of its members in exploitative ways. Moreover, there is plenty of room within Rawls's Law of Peoples for the Society of Peoples to limit exploitative economic dealings between private corporations and the political representatives of poorer peoples. Just because Rawls does not provide a principle of global distributive justice does not mean that unmitigated laissez-faire is the general rule of economic interaction within the Society of Peoples.

The Law of Peoples, then, is designed to apply in the first instance to hypothetical conditions, among well-ordered liberal and decent societies each of which has concern for the well-being of its own people and seeks their common good, and respects others as free and equal peoples. Rawls did not envision the Law of Peoples as the sole element of the terms of cooperation that apply among peoples "in our world as it is with its extreme injustices, crippling poverty, and inequalities."[6] Under current conditions, we are in the realm of nonideal theory and partial compliance. Just as Rawls regarded preferential treatment as permissible as a means of

---

[6] Rawls, *The Law of Peoples*, 117.

transition to a just liberal society, but as inappropriate under conditions of a well-ordered liberal society that is just, so too nations in the contemporary world are in less than ideal conditions and may require special remedies as a means to establishing a well-ordered Society of Peoples. Similar considerations apply to Allen Buchanan's claim that Rawls's Law of Peoples suffers from a failure to address questions of secession. The Law of Peoples is not a general theory of global justice that is designed to address all the problems that arise in the contemporary world. Rather, it is set forth as part of political liberalism, to provide the principles of foreign policy for a well-ordered liberal society (*LP*, 9–10). Questions of secession simply do not arise within this setting; they are, again, problems that arise within nonideal theory. It is no more a problem with Rawls's Law of Peoples that it fails to address issues of secession, than is its failure to address many other problems that arise within nonideal theory (for example, the problem of resolving boundary disputes, or a formula for deciding war reparations). Of course, it would have been wonderful had Rawls been able to tell us what he thought about rights of secession before he died, just as it would have been wonderful had he addressed many other political and moral issues. But Rawls's Law of Peoples cannot be dismissed or criticized for failing to address problems not within its intended purview.

II. Social Cooperation and Social Justice

The use of the term "distributive justice" to connote standards for assessing the distribution of income and wealth is relatively recent; it seems to have evolved out of the socialist critique of capitalism.[7] In *Anarchy, State, and Utopia*, Robert Nozick says that the term "distributive justice" is not neutral, since it suggests a central distribution mechanism that doles out a supply of resources to people and redistributes resources among people when their individual choices fail to match some principle.[8] Still, Nozick must have found the idea useful, since he entitles the central chapter in his book, covering eighty-three pages, "Distributive Justice." I will use the term "distributive justice" as neutrally as I can: namely, to designate moral standards for assessing ongoing methods of distribution of rights to income and wealth that are implicit in any economic system. It is the sense in which I believe that both Nozick and Rawls used the term. A principle or conception of distributive justice applies to all existing income and wealth within an ongoing system of production, exchange,

---

[7] The idea of "fair distribution" was current among nineteenth-century non-Marxian socialists. Marx himself disdained the French socialists' idea of fair distribution, along with the idea of "equal right," calling them "obsolete verbal rubbish." See Karl Marx, "Critique of the Gotha Program," in *Karl Marx: Selected Writings*, ed. David McLellan (Oxford: Oxford University Press, 1977), 569. Aristotle distinguished distributive justice from commutative justice, but the term was not used in the contemporary sense. For a discussion, see Samuel Fleischacker, *Distributive Justice* (Cambridge, MA: Harvard University Press, 2005).

[8] Robert Nozick, *Anarchy, State, and Utopia* (New York: Basic Books, 1974), 149.

and consumption. It specifies standards for deciding how and whether income and wealth are justly distributed among individuals—who should have rights to what and in exchange for what (if any) contributions. The difference principle, the principle of utility, and the equality principle are all distributive principles insofar as they cover all the economic resources that exist in any economic system. So too are Nozick's libertarian entitlement principles, according to which (very roughly) rights in things are fairly distributed only if they are transferred by market exchanges, gifts, bequests, gambling, or some other voluntary mode of transfer by the person who holds those rights. Such common-sense precepts as "To each according to effort," "To each according to contribution," and "To each according to need," when left unsupplemented, may not fit this definition of distributive principles. (For example, what if all needs are satisfied, or all efforts and contributions are rewarded, and there is still a remaining surplus?) Still, I presume these precepts can be made to fit the definition easily enough so long as we supplement each precept with some other (for example, the surplus remaining after all needs, efforts, or contributions are met might then be equally distributed, or distributed to maximize utility, etc.).

On this understanding, a people's duty to assist its own and other peoples so that their basic needs are met is not (by itself) a principle of distributive justice. For this duty, once satisfied, extends no further and establishes no further claim within the ongoing system of economic production and exchange. The same is true of duties to meet special needs of the handicapped; by themselves, these duties are not principles of distributive justice. In contrast, a principle of restricted utility which says "A society has a duty to provide a social minimum for all its citizens sufficient to meet their basic needs, and once basic needs are met, the economy is to be designed to distribute income and wealth so as to maximize utility" (or alternatively "to satisfy the principle of efficiency") *is* a distributive principle; for it applies to and enables an assessment of the justice of the distribution of all wealth within the economic system.

Rather than providing a specific global distribution principle, Rawls provides an account of human rights, coupled with the claim that the basic needs of all individuals in the world are to be met, partly as a matter of their human rights. This provides the basis for a duty of peoples to assist "burdened peoples" who are unable to meet the basic needs of all their members. The "target" of the duty of assistance is the capacity of a people to be economically independent so that they may at least meet all citizens' basic needs, and become bona fide members of the Society of Peoples.[9] At a minimum, a person's basic needs are those that need to be

---

[9] Principle number 8 of the Law of Peoples says: "Peoples have a duty to assist other peoples living under unfavorable conditions that prevent their having a just or decent political and social regime" (*LP,* 37). As a gloss upon this principle, Rawls says: "Certain

met to enable him or her to effectively exercise human rights. The human rights that Rawls mentions (initially) are: "the right to life (to the means of subsistence and security); to liberty (to freedom from slavery, serfdom, and forced occupation, and to a sufficient measure of liberty of conscience to ensure freedom of religion and thought); to property (personal property); and to formal equality as expressed by the rules of natural justice (that is, that similar cases be treated similarly)" (*LP*, 65).[10]

Here it is important to note that by "basic needs" Rawls is not just talking about subsistence needs that are protected by human rights—or what is needed so that people do not starve or perish from disease. In addition to human rights, Rawls intends that people should be able to "take advantage of the rights, liberties, and opportunities of their society," which would require institutional rights and liberties, and economic means, that go beyond what is needed to exercise one's human rights.

Given the role of Rawls's idea of human rights in determining the extent of the duty of assistance, it is important to emphasize the basis for Rawls's account of human rights. Rawls is often criticized for not including certain liberal and democratic rights among the human rights: primarily equal rights of political participation, freedom of speech and expression, and freedom of association, all of which are among the basic liberties that are part of Rawls's first principle of justice.[11] Many critics believe that Rawls's list of human rights, in addition to being truncated, is arbitrarily drawn, with no solid basis. Here one can add to this list of complaints that, in the case of the basic liberties, Rawls appealed to a conception of persons as free and equal democratic citizens with the two moral powers.[12] The basic liberties were regarded as fundamentally necessary to the exercise and development of the moral powers, and to enable democratic citizens to freely pursue a wide variety of permissible plans of life.[13] In the case of human rights, however, Rawls's list seems to

---

provisions will be included for mutual assistance among peoples in times of famine and drought, and, insofar as it is possible, provisions for ensuring that in all reasonable liberal (and decent) societies people's basic needs are met. [Note:] By basic needs I mean roughly those that must be met if citizens are to be in a position to take advantage of the rights, liberties, and opportunities of their society. These needs include economic means as well as institutional rights and freedoms" (*LP*, 38).

[10] Evidently, Rawls does not mean this list to be exclusive, for he says, "Among the human rights are . . ."—after which follows the quotation in the text above.

[11] See Charles Beitz, "Rawls's Law of Peoples," *Ethics* 110 (July 2000): 669–96, at 683–86; and Allen Buchanan, "Rawls's Law of Peoples: Rules for a Vanished Westphalian World," *Ethics* 110 (July 2000): 697–721, at 718–19 (on Rawls's "rather lean set of individual rights").

[12] The two moral powers are a capacity for a sense of justice (to understand, apply, and act from principles of justice) and a capacity for a rational conception of the good (to form, revise, and pursue a rational conception of the good). See Rawls, *Political Liberalism*, 19, 81, 103–4. Rawls calls these powers, respectively, the capacities to be reasonable and to be rational. They are, in effect, the capacities for practical reasoning as applied to matters of justice, which, Rawls believes, are necessary for social cooperation.

[13] See Rawls, *Political Liberalism*, lecture 8, "The Basic Liberties and Their Priority."

be without any such foundation. Isn't Rawls's account of human rights then simply an appeal to unfounded intuitions?

Rawls apparently does not provide a conception of the person to ground his account of human rights, and more generally the Law of Peoples, because there is no shared conception of the person that will provide a basis for the public reason of the Society of Peoples. Decent societies, in particular, rely upon comprehensive religious and philosophical doctrines that will conflict with almost any conception of the person that might be acceptable to liberal peoples and other decent peoples. This does not mean, however, that Rawls's list of human rights is conjured out of thin air. It is a list of rights that, he says, is not distinctly liberal, and that all liberal and decent peoples can agree to on the basis of their liberal and decent comprehensive views. Moreover, the list does not depend upon a particular religious or philosophical doctrine, not even (Rawls contends) upon liberalism. Rather, it has a substantial foundation that is part of the Law of Peoples itself. What is the basis, then, for Rawls's account?[14] Oddly, critics of Rawls rarely, if ever, discuss the substantial basis Rawls provides for his account of human rights: "What have come to be called human rights are recognized as necessary conditions of any system of social cooperation. When they are regularly violated, we have command by force, a slave system, and no cooperation of any kind" (LP, 68).

Rawls has nothing more to say about social cooperation in *The Law of Peoples*, but in *Political Liberalism* (*PL*, 16) he has this to say: First, social cooperation is by its nature voluntary, and involves an absence of forced servitude and other conditions that would prevent us from holding people responsible for their conduct. Second, social cooperation is to be distinguished from efficiently coordinated behavior, where people are working in a group, but their behavior is regulated simply for the sake of effectively achieving purposes that none of them may endorse. Prisoners in a work gang are not engaged in social cooperation, though they might work quite efficiently as a group (repairing roads, picking up trash, etc.). By contrast with efficiently coordinated behavior, the idea of social cooperation for Rawls assumes that each person has an idea of his or her good, and is benefited in some way that he or she would acknowledge by engaging in cooperation with others. Presumably, if a person's good were

---

[14] Thomas Pogge conjectures that Rawls's account of human rights is based in a concern to accommodate nonliberal peoples' rejection of liberal rights, in the hope that they can at least accept a smaller list of human rights. See Thomas Pogge, "An Egalitarian Law of Peoples," *Philosophy and Public Affairs* 23, no. 3 (Summer 1994): 195–224. This implies that the Law of Peoples is a *modus vivendi* between liberal and decent peoples, a claim that Rawls denies. Pogge's interpretation discounts the centrality of social and political cooperation to Rawls's account of human rights, and also to his account of distributive justice. Pogge's interpretation also ignores the fact that human rights are agreed to among liberal peoples themselves, as being among the conditions whose violation is necessary to justify intervention in the affairs of other liberal peoples. If respect for human rights is adequate for the ideal case of a Society of Liberal Peoples, then how can it be a compromise designed to accommodate decent peoples?

not in any way furthered by interaction, then his or her actions would not be rational or even voluntary. Finally, for Rawls social cooperation also involves an idea of reciprocity and fair terms of cooperation, which provide a sense of what is "reasonable." These are norms that members of the cooperating group rely upon and use to guide their conduct and regulate the distribution of benefits and burdens among themselves. Moreover, the members mutually recognize these fair terms and refer to them not only to regulate but to criticize and assess one another's conduct. These terms are, in this regard, public standards, not just strategic norms.

For Rawls, then, social cooperation incorporates a distinctly moral component—a notion of fair terms of cooperation, understood as "reciprocity," which provide standards of reasonableness. Rawls distinguishes reciprocity from mutual advantage, which can be explicated entirely in terms of a person's good and what is rational for her to do (the third aspect of social cooperation mentioned above). People who are engaged in social cooperation normally are not focused exclusively on their own good, in the sense that they are ready to take advantage of others and free-ride whenever circumstances permit. This does not mean that people have to be altruistic to cooperate with others; but they do normally have a sense of fairness or justice—a settled disposition to comply with terms of cooperation, and do their part, even on occasions when it is not to their benefit (so long as others manifest a like disposition). For Rawls, one thing that distinguishes "decent peoples" from "states" (as traditionally understood) is that they have moral motives and a sense of justice as a people, that enable them willingly to comply with their duties under the Law of Peoples, and not take advantage of weaker peoples whenever it seems favorable to do so.[15]

It is this sense of social cooperation that Rawls seems to rely upon in drawing up his list of human rights. The right to life, freedom from involuntary servitude, the right to hold and use at least some personal property, and other human rights that Rawls mentions are minimal reasonable terms necessary to social cooperation. The right to vote and the right to run for office, however central to democratic societies, are not necessary for social cooperation as such; other methods of decision making are compatible with social cooperation. Historically, most people in most societies have not enjoyed democratic rights, and even in societies where they do, these rights often willingly go unexercised. This option is not true of human rights generally. To contend that democratic rights of political participation are on a par with, and just as important as, the right to life, freedom from involuntary servitude, the right to hold personal property, and other human rights that Rawls mentions, is implausible and unreasonable. And while it may not be as unreasonable to say that *liberal*

---

[15] Cf. Rawls, *The Law of Peoples,* 17, 28–29: "A difference between liberal peoples and states is that just liberal peoples limit their basic interests as required by the reasonable" (ibid., 29).

freedom of association and freedom of speech are equally fundamental to
social cooperation, it is still far-fetched and unconvincing. Some degree of
freedom of speech and of association surely must be a human right, and
can be included under what Rawls calls the "right to liberty." For example, fundamentalist Muslim societies that punish women for just talking
with men who are not family members surely violate human rights. But
Rawls denies that among the human rights must be included *liberal* freedoms of speech and association, with all that they include (for example,
the right to defile or destroy national or sacred symbols, or enjoy por-
nography, or freedom of same-sex relations). To hold otherwise is not to
take the idea of human rights seriously.

The idea of social cooperation also is central to Rawls's account of
social justice. It underlies his distinction between "domestic justice" and
the Law of Peoples. Moreover, the idea of social cooperation informs
Rawls's account of the difference principle. What makes social cooperation possible for Rawls are the basic institutions that constitute "the basic
structure of society." [16] Here it is crucial that, for Rawls, political cooperation under the terms of a political constitution, including the legal system that it regulates, is a central aspect of the basic structure of society.
For Rawls, political cooperation is part of social cooperation; it makes
social cooperation according to the terms of other institutions (particularly economic institutions) possible and is necessary to those institutions.
(One important example: The institution of property is presupposed by
economic cooperation; property is largely a legal institution and cannot
exist—except perhaps in primitive form—in the absence of political cooperation according to the terms of a political constitution and a legal system.) When Rawls says that the political constitution is part of the basic
structure, he does not just mean the procedures that specify how laws are
enacted and that define offices and positions of political authority. He
means more or less the entire legal system, including most public and
private law, that is the product of the constitution in this procedural
sense. Modern legal systems, such as the federal system in the United
States, are made up of countless acts of legislation, administration, judicial precedent, and other legal rulings that are issued by the multiple legal
bodies with lawmaking authority. An economic system that is regulated
by the legal norms that are issued by the political constitution is also part
of the basic structure. Here, of course, the legal norms of property, contract, commercial law, intangibles, and so on that are essential for eco-

---

[16] The primary basic institutions that constitute the basic structure of society are the
following: the political constitution; the legal system of trials and other legal procedures it
supports; the institution of property; markets and the myriad laws and conventions making
economic production, exchange, and consumption possible; and the institution of the family,
which enables a society to raise and educate children and reproduce itself as an ongoing
system over time. See Rawls, *A Theory of Justice*, 6–7; and Rawls, *Justice as Fairness: A
Restatement*, ed. Erin Kelly (Cambridge, MA: Harvard University Press, 2001), sections 4, 15,
and 16.

nomic production and exchange are to be included in the basic structure. What makes possible the incredibly complicated system of legal norms that underlie economic production, exchange, and consumption is a unified political system that specifies these norms and revises them to meet changing conditions.

Nothing comparable to the basic structure of society exists on the global level. Moreover, if Rawls is correct—if a stable "world state" that assumes the primary functions of governments is not feasible—then nothing comparable to the basic structure of society can ever stably endure on a global level (see *LP*, 36, 48). This means that social cooperation is and must remain distinct from the kinds of relations that hold between different societies individuated by their own separate political systems. This does not mean that different societies do not cooperate; of course they do. But they do not engage in social cooperation in Rawls's sense of cooperation framed within the basic structure of society. Cooperation among peoples (to use Rawls's terms) is a qualitatively different kind of cooperation from social cooperation, and it has its own distinctive fair terms of cooperation. These terms ideally are the Law of Peoples, the terms of cooperation for the Society of Peoples. Some of Rawls's critics confidently claim that "there is a global basic structure,"[17] and argue that for this reason there must be principles of global distributive justice. This simply begs the question, however. Rawls does not need to deny a "global basic structure" in some sense, but clearly he would contend that it is very different from the basic structure of society. For Rawls, the global basic structure would just be the set of institutions that are needed to give effect to the Law of Peoples. Rather than "global basic structure" Rawls refers to "the basic structure of the Society of Peoples" (*LP*, 61). Whatever we call it, the important point is that these global institutions are very different—*qualitatively different*—from the basic structure of a society that makes social cooperation possible. It is only *because* there are societies, with their distinct basic structures of political, social, and economic institutions, that we can take seriously and regard as feasible any kind of "global basic structure." Global cooperation and global institutions are supervenient upon social cooperation and basic social institutions.

Why is the basic structure of society qualitatively different from the basic structure of the Society of Peoples, and from any other realistic and stable "global basic structure"? The Society of Peoples is not a *political society*, and thus has no *original political jurisdiction* or effective basic political power. (Here I use the terms "political society" and "political power" in John Locke's sense to include the idea of political authority, or having the right to rule.) The effective political power and jurisdiction that global

---

[17] Allen Buchanan asserts this and sees the existence of a global basic structure as sufficient grounds for a global distribution principle. See Buchanan, "Rawls's Law of Peoples," 705. As I argue in the text, this conclusion does not follow.

institutions exercise are possessed by these institutions only to the degree that they have been granted such power and jurisdiction by independent peoples. Global political authority (such as it is) then exists only as a result of the legal acts of independent peoples—"legal" insofar as these acts are authorized by their own constitutions. So long as independent peoples can withdraw or revise the grant of political power transferred to global institutions (granted there may be significant costs in doing so), global political power remains supervenient upon the political power of independent peoples. This is what it means to say that global political authority and jurisdiction is not "basic" or "original." Basic political authority resides only within the basic structure of societies. This is not a necessary truth, but it is a significant empirical truth, assuming that a world government would not be capable of any enduring stability (*LP*, 36). Basic political authority resembles the idea of political sovereignty, but it does not carry the connotations of absolute political power that reside with the idea of sovereignty. Of course, no political power is absolute *de jure*, not even the power of peoples. The legitimacy of all political power (not to mention its justice) is subject to respect for human rights and the other conditions that Rawls imposes upon a decent (hierarchical) society.

Thus, social cooperation, in Rawls's sense, is not the only kind of cooperation. There is cooperation among peoples, and there are also different kinds of cooperation that exist within families, universities, churches, and other associations and groups. Naturally, all cooperation is social in a sense, but cooperation among members of a society—that is, among people who share the same basic structure—is a distinct kind that Rawls calls "social cooperation." Then, to avoid confusion, he refers to the cooperation within groups in society as "associational cooperation." (Here we might provide each of these many different forms of cooperation with a distinct name, to distinguish them all from social cooperation—familial cooperation, religious cooperation, etc.) For each of these different kinds of cooperation, there are rules that specify the fair terms of cooperation among members of that cooperative institution. These are the rules of "local justice" for lesser associations that exist within the basic structure of society. To be just or fair, however, these rules need not all be the same. (For example, children should not have equal say with their parents; and employees need not have equal sway along with managers in order for the work rules internally regulating firms to be fair.)

Rawls says, "Justice as fairness starts with domestic justice—the justice of the basic structure. From there it works outward to the Law of Peoples, and inward to local justice."[18] What is distinctive about the basic structure of society is not simply that it exercises profound effects on individuals' aims, characters, and future prospects. The same can be said, of course, about the institution of the family, or the religious institutions that

[18] Rawls, *Justice as Fairness: A Restatement*, 11.

provide moral structure for many people's lives. It is the purportedly profound effects that global institutions and economic relations exercise on people's lives that advocates of a global difference principle or other global
distribution principle point to when they contend that there is nothing distinctive about the basic structure of a society. Rawls need not deny the significant (though not equally profound) effects of global cooperation to claim
that domestic justice, the justice of the basic structure, concerns a different
kind of institutional cooperation than does global justice, and that it therefore warrants its own principles of justice. Nor does Rawls even need to
deny that there are global principles of justice that regulate global cooperation in order to claim that domestic justice, the justice of the basic structure, has a kind of priority over other forms of justice. But it is part of Rawls's
"political constructivism" that terms of social cooperation must be worked
out first, independently of the principles of justice of other institutions,
whereas the principles of global and local associational justice presuppose
the principles of justice for the basic structure. Principles of social (or domestic) justice constrain or limit, but do not entirely determine, principles of
local justice. That is, we cannot fully specify the rights and obligations family members have to one another until we first work out the principles of
domestic justice. (For parents must respect the rights of their children,
spouses have certain duties of support owed not only to their children but
to each other, etc.) We can, however, specify the rights, duties, and obligations that citizens of a democratic society owe to one another without
first working out the terms of the Law of Peoples. What we cannot do is
decide the duties that different peoples owe to one another *as* peoples, and
how they are to act toward one another as peoples in their political relations, before the principles of domestic justice are decided. This is part of
what Rawls means by "political constructivism": the principles that appropriately regulate social and political relations depend upon the kinds of
institutions or practices involved, and are "constructed" on the basis of
ideas that are central to the functioning of those institutions or practices
and people's awareness of them.

Political constructivism is, I believe, integral to Rawls's rejection of
cosmopolitanism and a global principle of distributive justice. Cosmopolitanism, as a view about distributive justice, claims that "the content of
social justice cannot be arrived at by considering the individual society as
a closed system in isolation from all others."[19] As such, cosmopolitanism
is or at least involves an epistemological/methodological claim that denies
the possibility of political constructivism. Now what ultimately underlies
Rawls's political constructivism are his views regarding moral justification. The justification of principles of justice ultimately involves bringing
into a "wide reflective equilibrium" the considered convictions of justice

---

[19] See Samuel Scheffler, "Conceptions of Cosmopolitanism," in his *Boundaries and Allegiances* (Oxford: Oxford University Press, 2001), 116.

that we share regarding social institutions or practices. Practices and institutions each have their own rules that are constitutive of the practice or institution. So long as we do not question the existence of the institution itself, it is the role of a conception of justice to provide principles for the regulation of these rules constituting practices or institutions. Of course, it may be that as a matter of justice itself (the justice of society, or global justice), certain practices or institutions should not exist or should be radically revised. (Many people have raised questions regarding the institutions of marriage and the family, for example, arguing that for reasons of social justice they should be radically revised, and in the case of civil marriage, even eliminated.) Anarchists, of course, argue that the state, and political society among people, is inherently unjust and should not exist. Some cosmopolitans contend that the state or political society as traditionally conceived (as an independent and autonomous entity, with exclusive control over a territory) should not exist, and that justice requires a world government of some kind.

In response, Rawls's account of the Law of Peoples is based upon certain empirical assumptions and theoretical commitments that, taken together, require the existence of separate societies, each regulated by its own basic structure. Rawls assumes that justice and social cooperation too (at least under modern conditions) are not possible without governments and complicated legal systems, and that what social justice involves, in large part, are principles for structuring and defining the powers of political institutions. He also assumes that a politically autonomous world-state is utopian (i.e., a state that is capable of serving the functions that different peoples with their governments controlling their own territories now perform). For Rawls, this means that attempts to provide principles of justice on the assumption of conditions that could obtain only within (or that optimally obtain only within) a world-state are misguided, since in an important sense these principles are not compatible with human nature, the human good, or the possibilities of stable human society.

What does this mean? On the face of it, the practical impossibility of a world government might not seem to pose any problem in formulating global principles of justice. For example, a utilitarian would say that a just global distribution is one that maximizes the sum of global happiness. The utilitarian then might contend: "The fact that a world government is not feasible is not relevant to the justification of the principle of utility as a standard for global distributive justice (and everything else). It is, rather, a pragmatic consideration relevant to the application of the principle of utility to decide how institutions should be feasibly designed to achieve global justice. But the fact that one or another institution is not feasible has no bearing on *standards* for distributive justice, and whether they are to apply locally or are global in reach. Philosophical conceptions of justice should not be made hostage to contingencies, but are *a priori*, the product of (if you will) 'pure reason.' "

The role of empirical considerations and natural regularities in the justification of a conception of justice is a far more complicated question than can be addressed here.[20] This much should be said: For Rawls, our considered convictions of justice arise within the practices and institutions we live with, and are attuned to the structure and demands of those institutions. Our considered judgments regarding individual liberties and just distributions originate within the framework provided by the basic structure of society. Moreover, they primarily apply to those institutions (for example, what constitutional rights should people have? how should the system of property and taxation be structured? and so on). Our considered judgments regarding global distributive justice are more tentative and much less secure, since there are few global institutions that give rise to them or anchor them. For many reasonable persons, it is hard to know where to even begin in considering these issues.

Among our more abstract considered convictions of justice that a conception of justice must accommodate is, Rawls assumes, that principles of justice that regulate social and political relations should be *publicly knowable* and *reasonably acceptable* to people whose lives and relations these principles regulate. This is part of what it is to be a free person for Rawls—to know, understand, and be able to reason about the bases of social and political relations, and not be under any illusions about them. For Rawls, this suggests that principles of justice should be capable of serving as principles of practical reasoning and justification among people who conceive of themselves as free and responsible agents. It is also a requirement of democracy for Rawls that citizens be in a position to know the bases of their political relations; hence, a publicity condition is incorporated into political liberalism. To serve this public role, however, principles of justice have to be generally acceptable to reasonable people as a public basis for deliberation and justification. This is necessary to citizens' and a democratic people's political autonomy. Moreover, the institutions that these principles presuppose and support, if they are to be publicly acceptable among free persons, must be feasible and capable of enduring over time; and to meet these requirements, they must gain citizens' willing support. As Rawls says, institutions should be "stable for the right reasons," that is, acceptable to citizens on the basis of their sense of justice.

Now assuming that what we are looking for is a conception of justice that (1) fits with our considered convictions of justice, as reasonable persons, (2) is publicly acceptable to free and equal persons who are also reasonable, and can serve them as a basis for public justification, and (3) is feasible and will endure over time and across generations while serving

---

[20] G. A. Cohen challenges Rawls's reliance on facts in justifying the principles of justice. See G. A. Cohen, "Facts and Principles," *Philosophy and Public Affairs* 31, no. 3 (Summer 2003): 211–45.

this public role, then it should follow that (4) this public conception must be one that takes into account and is responsive to the permanent facts about human beings and their living together in social groups, including how they conceive of their good. To put the point another way: Assuming that we are concerned with achieving the freedom and equality of real persons in the world, given their nature and limitations as human beings, a conception of justice must be responsive to facts about human nature if it is to be stable by engaging people's sense of justice.

Consider now the fact that human beings are sociable creatures who develop within and are profoundly affected by the basic institutions of their society. Consider also that a world government and basic structure that includes all the world within one society, and is capable of enduring and remaining stable on reasonable terms over time, is not empirically feasible. For a variety of reasons, the existence of a number of different societies, each with their own political institutions, is a permanent fact about social life. If this is true—if there is no escaping the fact of independent societies each with their own basic structure—and if what we seek is a publicly acceptable conception of justice, then there is no escaping the need for an independent conception of social justice that applies domestically to regulate the basic structure of society. This is required, not simply because of considerations of stability of social groups, but because a conception of justice, for Rawls, has the role of providing a basis for public justification among people who regard themselves as free and as equals. (From the fact that a world-state is not feasible, it should also follow that there is no global conception of distributive justice that is acceptable as a basis for public justification among free and equal persons that is feasible and can remain stable across generations. But this separate issue will be addressed in the next section.)

Assuming all this is true (of course, many will contest it), the following problem arises: Once the conception of justice for the basic structure of society is in place, there is a further need for an account of how different societies are to interrelate with one another. An account of international justice, or "the Law of Peoples," is in this regard an *extension* (not a precondition) of an account of social justice, and presupposes it. This claim was already implicit in *A Theory of Justice*, where Rawls remarked on the need "to extend the theory of justice to the law of nations" in order to guide the foreign policy of a nation regulated by the principles of justice (*TJ*, 331–33). This claim is only slightly modified in *The Law of Peoples*, where Rawls says:

> I emphasize that, in developing the Law of Peoples within a liberal conception of justice, we work out the ideals and principles of the *foreign policy* of a reasonably just *liberal* people. This concern with the foreign policy of a liberal people is implicit throughout. (*LP*, 9–10, emphasis in original; cf. 83)

This is what Rawls means when he says the Law of Peoples arises "within political liberalism" (*LP*, 9). Since the Law of Peoples basically concerns the foreign policy of liberal peoples, questions of global justice are already confined to a narrow range of issues, relatively speaking, within the Law of Peoples. Many questions that occupy advocates of cosmopolitan justice do not even arise, having been preempted, in effect, by the problems that the Law of Peoples is designed to address. In the following section, I indicate in more detail how the question of global distributive justice is among these preempted issues.

III. Cosmopolitan Objections to the Law of Peoples

I turn now to more specific objections to Rawls's account in *The Law of Peoples*, especially those relevant to distributive justice. Rawlsian cosmopolitans (as I call them) criticize Rawls for failing to take into account a number of considerations in designing the Law of Peoples. Three of the main criticisms they make are the following:

1. With regard to Rawls's account of human rights: The parties to the original position among liberal peoples, where parties are representatives of (liberal) peoples, should carefully consider the list of human rights, and when they do, they will agree that the liberal rights that are a part of Rawls's first principle of justice, and are generally endorsed in all liberal societies, should be regarded as human rights enforceable over all the world by the Law of Peoples.[21] After all, what's good for the (liberal) goose should be good for the (nonliberal) gander. If so, then it is not at all clear that liberal societies will agree to tolerate decent (but nonliberal) societies in the way Rawls suggests.

2. Regarding natural resources: The representatives to the original position for liberal and decent peoples naturally should be concerned about the level of resources that their people respectively control. Not knowing this level, since they are behind the veil of ignorance, they should all insist that resource-poor nations be provided with resources from resource-rich nations. After all, as Rawls says in relation to domestic justice, no one deserves the resources he is born with, so no one deserves to be born rich or poor. By the same token, resource-rich nations do not deserve the natural resources that happen to be deposited by nature on their territory. These resources should be redistributed to resource-poor nations (or at least subject to a resource tax upon extraction) until those nations receive their fair share, and the rational representatives of liberal and decent peoples will insist on as much in the interest of those they represent.[22]

---

[21] See, for example, Pogge, "An Egalitarian Law of Peoples," 214–16; K. C. Tan, *Toleration, Diversity, and Global Justice* (State College, PA: Penn State Press, 2000), 28, 79–80.

[22] See Pogge, "An Egalitarian Law of Peoples," 199ff.; and Charles Beitz, *Political Theory and International Relations* (Princeton, NJ: Princeton University Press, 1979; 2d edition, 1999), 138, 141.

3. Regarding distributive justice: Since representatives of peoples behind the veil of ignorance are ignorant not only of natural resources, but also of the level of talent, knowledge, technology, capital, and culture their people enjoy, they should want to protect themselves not just against resource poverty, but also against occupying globally less-advantaged positions. As a result, and for the same reasons as the parties in the domestic original position, they should choose a principle of global distributive justice. Here, some critics argue that for the same reasons that parties agree to it in the domestic original position, the global principle of distributive justice should be the difference principle. (Charles Beitz, Thomas Pogge, Brian Barry, David Richards, K. C. Tan, and others make this argument.) Others contend that Rawls's argument for the difference principle is mistaken and the global distribution principle should be another principle of justice. (Allen Buchanan makes this argument.) A third group contends that the difference principle should domestically apply within nations, subject to the requirements of a different global distribution principle which determines the share that each nation receives and to which they are to apply the domestic difference principle. (Pogge and Tan have suggested this position in conversation.)

One feature that is common to all three of these main criticisms is that they seem to assume that Rawls has made a mistake in applying the terms of his own argument from the original position. I do not think this assumption is warranted. In this section, I address the first two criticisms. In Section IV, I turn to the criticism regarding Rawls's rejection of a global difference principle or other global distribution principle.

A. Why liberal rights are not incorporated into the Law of Peoples

1. Human rights. In response to the first main criticism, the claim that liberal rights should be human rights, I have already discussed in Section II the connection Rawls forges between human rights and the minimally necessary conditions for social cooperation. To defend his distinction between human rights and liberal rights against the cosmopolitan argument that it would not be accepted by liberal peoples within the original position, it is important, first, to see how Rawls sets up the original position in his discussion of the Law of Peoples. For simplicity's sake, I will call this the "original position among (liberal or decent) peoples," to be distinguished from the "global original position" among representatives of all world-inhabitants that is argued for by Rawlsian cosmopolitans. The first original position among peoples consists of representatives of liberal peoples (not representatives, one for each person in the world, like a global original position), with all peoples regarded as equals regardless of the size of their populations. These representatives of liberal peoples are subject to a veil of ignorance; they do not know specific contemporary or historical facts about their own and other societies (their population, resources, wealth, and so on). They do know, however, that they are regulated by a conception of liberal justice—if not specifically justice as fairness then some other liberal conception that guarantees the basic liberties and their priority, and an adequate social minimum. Importantly, and as in the case of Rawls's domestic original position, the representatives of liberal peoples are concerned *solely* with promoting the "fundamental interests" of the individual society that each one represents. Unlike the parties to the domestic original position, however, these representatives are not moved only by a purely rational motive, to procure a greater share of the primary goods. Rather, their main aim is to obtain terms of cooperation among peoples that best guarantee liberal justice within their *own* society and among their *own* people (*LP*, 33, 40). But while the parties are moved by a concern for justice for their own peoples, they are not moved by benevolence toward other peoples or even by a concern that liberal justice be done to them for its own sake. They are mutually indifferent in this regard. In this respect, the original position among liberal peoples does not differ from the domestic original position.[23]

[23] Here there is an important point of interpretation. Earlier in section 2.3 of *The Law of Peoples*, Rawls sets forth four fundamental interests of liberal peoples: "They seek [1] to protect their territory, [2] to ensure the security and safety of their citizens, and [3] to preserve their free political institutions and the liberties and free culture of their civil society. Beyond those interests, a liberal people [4] tries to assure reasonable justice for all its citizens and for all people" (*LP*, 29). In section 3.3 Rawls adds a further interest, [5] "a people's proper self-respect of themselves as a people" (*LP*, 34). It is important to my argument above (and, I believe, to Rawls's argument as well) that a distinction be drawn between the fundamental interests of liberal peoples, and the motivations of their representatives in the original position. It is a fundamental interest of liberal peoples "to assure reasonable justice . . . for all people"; this is what it means for a people to "have a moral nature." But as for the representatives of peoples in the original position, they are not moved by this moral motive. Like the parties to the domestic original position, they are "modeled as rational" in Rawls's sense (*LP*, 32, 33), which means they are not morally motivated and are indifferent toward the interests of other parties and peoples they do not represent (except insofar as it promotes the fundamental interests of their own people). This motivational assumption of mutual indifference of the parties is necessary for the structure of the original position, in order for it to do the work Rawls assigns to it: namely, to regulate rational judgments (regarding the interests of those one represents) by reasonable constraints (the veil of ignorance and other constraints of right). Nevertheless, the fact that the parties' representatives are modeled as purely rational and indifferent to one another and other peoples does not by any means imply that liberal peoples themselves are purely rational and indifferent. Indeed, Rawls is careful to emphasize in section 9 that what primarily distinguishes peoples from states is that peoples have a moral nature; thus, they are not moved solely by their own interests and are not indifferent to one another, but do seek "to assure reasonable justice . . . for all peoples" (*LP*, 29).

The reason this is an important point of interpretation is that, if the parties to the original position were motivated to do justice, not just for their own people, but for all peoples, then this would open the way for the argument that the representatives of liberal peoples should also be concerned that nonliberal peoples accept liberal justice, including all the liberal basic liberties. If so, then liberal peoples would not have reason to tolerate nonliberal decent peoples, at least not for the reasons Rawls suggests. K. C. Tan, among others, has made this argument, and my remarks here are intended as a response to him. See Tan, *Toleration, Diversity, and Global Justice*, chap. 2.

Given this concern for liberal justice among their own people, and assuming that other liberal peoples already recognize the basic liberties and their priority, there is *no reason* for a liberal people to agree to enforce liberal rights against other liberal peoples. To begin with, other liberal peoples already accept and domestically enforce requirements of liberal justice—this is what entitles them to take part in the agreement among liberal peoples. Moreover, even if an injustice is done by another liberal government against one of its own people (suppose, for example, that a liberal people falsely convicts a member of a minority group that is widely disliked), this poses no danger of injustice to other liberal peoples. Given their interests in liberal justice in their own societies, there is insufficient reason for the representatives of liberal peoples to incorporate liberal basic liberties into the Law of Peoples that regulates their foreign relations with one another.

What about liberal peoples' relations with nonliberal peoples? Here Rawls invokes the original position a third time, and imagines an agreement, not among liberal peoples and decent peoples, but only among decent hierarchical peoples themselves. They too, Rawls contends, would agree to the same Law of Peoples as would liberal peoples, including respect for everyone's human rights. For this reason, Rawls concludes that liberal peoples should tolerate decent hierarchical peoples and accept them as equal members in the Society of Peoples (*LP*, 84). The apparent reason for this claim is that liberal peoples have nothing to fear from a people if the latter endorses the Law of Peoples. For a people that endorses this Law respects other peoples' integrity and political autonomy; moreover, it also respects the human rights of its own members and of other individuals, and seeks to realize a common-good conception of justice among its own people. Decent peoples, then, do not present a threat to liberal peoples, or to anyone else, so there is no reason for the representatives of liberal peoples to refuse to tolerate decent peoples and recognize them as equals.

Here enters the objection (posed by Beitz, Tan, and others) that if a liberal people is genuinely concerned about enforcing liberal rights among its own citizens, then it should also be concerned about enforcing the same rights among nonliberal peoples. As we have just seen, however, the representatives of liberal peoples in the original position have no motivation to enforce liberal rights among nonliberal peoples. This is not their assigned role. This is not to say that as individuals, representatives of liberal peoples do not care about the extension of liberal rights—they may care quite a lot that all the world adopt liberalism. But in their capacity as the legal representatives of their peoples' own interests, they are not motivated to enforce liberal rights around the world. Instead, they seek a Law of Peoples that secures the conditions of liberal justice for their *own* people. It is not their responsibility, charge, or jurisdiction to agree on a cosmopolitan conception of justice providing liberal rights for all peoples (any more than it is any other trustee's or legal representative's charge or responsibility to concern himself with the rights and interests of third parties or the general population as a whole). So long as nonliberal peoples can accept and respect the Law of Peoples, and thus respect the integrity of other peoples and their human rights, there is no need for them also to accept liberal rights for their own people; such acceptance is not necessary to secure the conditions of liberal justice for a liberal people.

The general point is that there is no room in the original position for the argument that nonliberal people should not be tolerated because they do not accept liberal rights. That question simply does not arise. Of course, here it might be objected that this is arbitrary, due simply to the artifice of the original position and how the interests of the parties are defined by Rawls. But that is a different objection from the one we have been considering, namely, that Rawls's argument from the original position fails and is inconsistent since it fails to address certain legitimate concerns the parties may have.

In response to this defense of Rawls, it may be said that if the representatives in the original position were only concerned about justice among their own peoples, why would they agree to tolerate only decent peoples? For there are many "outlaw" and "burdened" states whose rulers do not respect the human rights of their own people, but nonetheless present no danger to liberal peoples (for example, the rulers of many African states). Why not tolerate these "harmless outlaws" too, so long as they present no threat to one's own security?[24] This suggests that Rawls, by his own arguments, puts himself into the position of having to accept a realist foreign policy, in spite of his efforts to do otherwise, and must tolerate gross injustices and violations of human rights by some nations so long as they do not jeopardize other nations' security.

One reply to this argument is that liberal people do indeed have a good deal to fear from a state that has no respect for human rights or other principles of the Law of Peoples.[25] One only has to look at the dislocation of individuals and the disruption and war among neighboring nations that is caused by violations of human rights in Africa today. Behind the veil of ignorance, a representative does not know whether a neighboring country is liberal, decent, or an outlaw regime, nor does he know its relative size or strength in comparison with other peoples. Moreover, putting the original position and the motivations of its parties aside, the fact is that liberal peoples themselves do value human rights for their own sake, and seek "reasonable justice . . . for all peoples" (*LP*, 29). Peoples as peoples have a moral nature, and as such they have a sense of justice and are concerned with respect for human rights for their own

---

[24] Charles Beitz raises considerations along these lines in "Rawls's Law of Peoples," 685.
[25] Rawls says, "Liberal and decent peoples have extremely good reasons for their attitude. Outlaw states are aggressive and dangerous; all peoples are safer and more secure if such states change, or are forced to change, their ways. Otherwise they deeply affect the international climate of power and violence" (*LP*, 81).

sake. (They are also concerned with respect for liberal rights for their own sake, with the important qualification that people who enjoy them conceive of themselves as free and as equal citizens.) The objection stems from focusing on the motivations of the parties to the original position. Just because, from the point of view of the parties to the original position, respect for human rights by other peoples is important for instrumental reasons, does not mean that the Law of Peoples regards human rights purely instrumentally or from a self-interested perspective. (The parallel here is with citizens in a well-ordered society of justice as fairness, who value justice for its own sake, and their representatives in the original position, who are not motivated by considerations of justice in the original position.) To say that Rawls's justification of human rights is purely "instrumental" is to fail to see that the parties in the original position are only part of a larger argument. They are not real people, but merely embody rational considerations regarding the good of those they represent, whose interests are then subjected to the moral constraints of the original position, and the moral nature of free and equal people.

Here it bears emphasizing that the parties' toleration of nonliberal decent peoples, and their failure to include liberal rights in the list of human rights that the Law of Peoples protects, does not mean that liberal citizens or liberal societies do not regard liberal rights as universally applicable or as an ideal all societies ought to aspire to. Clearly, most liberal citizens do, as do most liberal government officials. Nevertheless, as a people (if not individually), they also respect well-ordered decent peoples as free and equal peoples, and as politically autonomous, capable of self-determination, and capable eventually of coming to an acceptance of liberal rights themselves. Recall that in a well-ordered decent hierarchical society, all reasonable and rational members of society accept its nonliberal terms of cooperation, and likely accept too the nonliberal comprehensive doctrine that is used to justify these terms of cooperation. To regard all liberal rights as human rights and insist they should be enforced by the Law of Peoples is to impose upon nonliberal but decent peoples, for reasons they cannot accept, terms of cooperation that are universally at odds with the moral and political views of nearly everyone in that society. There is no justification within the public reason of the Society of Peoples for such measures. Moreover, such measures would fail to respect decent peoples as politically autonomous, both as individuals and as a people. Finally, there is the practical consideration that nonliberal decent peoples will not come to accept and endorse liberal rights under coercive terms, or if they are made to feel that they and their own comprehensive views are disdained and not worthy of respect by liberal peoples.

2. The duty of assistance. Since liberal peoples have reason to care about reasonably just institutions and practices, including human rights, for their own sake, and not simply because they are themselves benefited, we can see why Rawls argues for a duty of assistance for burdened peoples.

To begin with, for Rawls, the human right to life includes a "basic right" to the means of subsistence as well as security (*LP*, 65). Subsistence includes "minimum economic security" (*LP*, 65 n. 1). To justify a basic right to minimum economic security, Rawls says that "the sensible and rational exercise of all liberties, of whatever kind, as well as the intelligent use of property, always implies having general all-purpose economic means" (*LP*, 65). The question is, who has the duty to see to it that this right is satisfied? Clearly, the government that is the agent responsible for a people has the primary duty to provide the means of subsistence for its members.[26] But when a government is incapable or refuses to provide economic means sufficient to meet its members' subsistence needs (and basic needs as well?), it falls to the Society of Peoples to fill this duty. The eighth Law of Peoples says: "Peoples have a duty to assist other peoples living under unfavorable conditions that prevent their having a just or decent political and social regime" (*LP*, 37). Here it appears that the duty of assistance requires more than simply providing for the subsistence needs of a burdened people, which is a human right they have. For Rawls's gloss on the eighth Law of Peoples refers to "basic needs," which is clearly a broader category than subsistence needs since it includes "those [needs] that must be met if citizens are to be in a position to take advantage of the rights, liberties, and opportunities of their society. These needs include economic means as well as institutional rights and freedoms" (*LP*, 38 n. 47). The duty of assistance is keyed to this broader concept of basic needs, and this suggests that the duty of assistance extends beyond meeting a burdened peoples' subsistence needs.[27] The

---

[26] Rawls says that for a government to allow its people to starve when starvation is preventable reflects a "lack of concern for human rights" (*LP*, 109).

[27] It is fairly clear that Rawls sees the duty of assistance as providing more than basic means of subsistence for people. He says that the aim of the duty of assistance "is to help a people manage their own affairs reasonably and rationally" (*LP*, 111), and to help them "to be able to determine the path of their own future for themselves" (*LP*, 118). "When the duty of assistance is fulfilled, and each people has its own liberal or decent government . . . each people adjusts the significance and importance of the wealth of its own society for itself. If it is not satisfied, it can continue to increase savings, or, if that is not feasible, borrow from other members of the Society of Peoples" (*LP*, 114). Either alternative assumes that a people is in a position to create wealth well above what is needed to provide means of subsistence for all its members. Here again, the argument cannot be made that Rawls's reliance on a duty of assistance and his rejection of a global distributive principle allows corrupt governments to borrow money and saddle their people with poverty for generations. This criticism, based on contemporary practices by corrupt regimes and their relations with affluent nations, refuses to acknowledge that the Law of Peoples is formulated for the ideal feasible case of well-ordered decent societies governed by a common-good conception of justice. Nothing in the Law of Peoples implies that peoples now should tolerate the exploitation of less-developed peoples either by their own governments or by multinational corporations. Quite the contrary: since the aim of the Law of Peoples is that all peoples should be members of a well-ordered Society of Peoples, the implication is that historical practices of exploitation of one people by another or by private interests should be prohibited, since such practices impede the development and independence of burdened peoples.

implication is that while it is not a human right to have all one's "basic needs" met, as defined, still the Society of Peoples has a duty of assistance to meet basic needs until burdened peoples can provide for all their members themselves and become self-sustaining members of the Society of Peoples. Rawls says that the "target" of assistance is to enable "burdened societies to be able to manage their own affairs reasonably and rationally and eventually to become members of the Society of well-ordered Peoples" (*LP*, 111). The "final aim of assistance" is "freedom and equality for the formerly burdened societies." Particularly important, as we will see, is his claim that the purpose of the duty of assistance is to "assure the essentials of *political autonomy*" or the capacity of a people "to determine the path of their own future for themselves" (*LP*, 118).

This duty of assistance can be quite extensive, then, especially if it is made contingent upon both a society's capacity for political autonomy and also the culture of particular societies and the resources needed to take advantage of the opportunities they offer. It would suggest, for example, a duty to provide in some way for the educational needs of a burdened people, so that they can find employment and be economically self-sufficient, and can actively participate in the life of their culture. Rawls has too little to say here. He does say that what the representatives of peoples discuss in the original position, instead of competing conceptions of the Law of Peoples, are different formulations and interpretations of the eight principles of the Law of Peoples (*LP*, 40). This seems to leave it open for further determination that the duty of assistance might impose rather exacting demands upon members of the Society of Peoples, to assist burdened peoples. This is an important point in responding to the argument against Rawls for his failure to provide for a principle of global distributive justice (a subject I will return to in Section IV).

B. A resource redistribution principle?

Still, the duty of assistance has both a "target" and a "cutoff," and does not amount to an open-ended principle of distributive justice (as Rawls uses that term). Once peoples' basic needs are met and they are self-sustaining members of the Society of Peoples, the duty of assistance to other peoples is fully satisfied by other members of the Society of Peoples. There is no further duty arising from a principle of distributive justice to continually provide once-burdened societies with resources. The implication of this lack of a distribution principle is that no real limit is imposed on the degree of inequality that can exist among peoples (other than the limit implied by the duty of assistance).

Here it is objected (by Beitz, Pogge, Martha Nussbaum, and others) that Rawls is guilty of (yet another) inconsistency in his argument. In his argument for principles of domestic justice, Rawls makes much of the fact that people do not deserve either the greater natural talents or the social position with which they are born.[28] But if no person deserves his starting position in life, or to be born with greater (or less) natural and social advantages than anyone else, then surely it must also be true that no nation or people deserves to be "born" with greater or less natural resources than other peoples either. Charles Beitz says, "Like talents, resource endowments are arbitrary in the sense that they are not morally deserved."[29] But the natural resources a people controls contribute decisively to the level of income and wealth its members enjoy and their comparative (dis)advantages.

In his earlier work, Beitz argues that the parties to an international original position would insist on a resource redistribution principle; they would do this, not simply because it is fair, but to protect their own interests. "Not knowing the resource endowments of their own societies, the parties would agree on a resource redistribution principle that would give each society a fair chance to develop just political institutions and an economy capable of satisfying its members' basic needs."[30] Is Beitz's claim true when applied to the original position among peoples that Rawls sets forth in his discussion of the Law of Peoples, which involves separate agreements among liberal peoples and among decent peoples? Why wouldn't liberal peoples (and then decent peoples) agree at least among themselves to redistribute resources, in order to protect themselves from the eventuality that they may represent resource-poor peoples? Here, surely, we have a different case from the preceding one, where liberal peoples had insufficient reason to agree to enforce liberal rights globally.

If we focus just on the artifice of the original position, I think it must be said once again (though here the argument is not as conclusive) that the original position is structured so that the question of redistributing resources does not arise. The purpose of the agreement within the original position is to establish principles of foreign policy among liberal peoples; its purpose is not to arrive at principles of compensation or at a conception of cosmopolitan justice. Of course, the parties might be concerned with the level of natural resources that they have. But would their concern lead them to insist upon redistributing natural resources among

---

[28] Here is it important to emphasize that Rawls does *not* say that people do not deserve their natural talents. This is a common misreading, and it leads to much criticism of Rawls (e.g., claims to the effect that Rawls rejects natural rights to one's own talents and abilities). What Rawls in fact says is that we do not deserve to be "better endowed" than others (*TJ*, 13), and that "[i]t seems to be one of the fixed points of our considered judgments that no one deserves his *place in the distribution of natural endowments,* any more than one deserves his initial starting place in society" (*TJ*, 89, emphasis added; see also 274, where Rawls repeats this claim). He means here simply that people do not deserve the *differences* in natural talent or social position they are born with. No one deserves to be born smarter or richer than anyone else. This seems obvious to Rawls, a "fixed point in our considered judgments" (*TJ*, 274). It is a very different claim from the one often falsely attributed to Rawls, namely, that no one deserves his or her natural talents.

[29] Beitz, *Political Theory and International Relations,* 139.

[30] Ibid., 141.

peoples as a condition of cooperating as peoples? (Or, we might ask, would it lead them to insist upon a global resource tax, as Pogge argues?) Here they would need to take into account the burdens and the degree of interference with their independence that may be involved in redistributing natural resources discovered in their territory. (Is it to be done in kind? If so, who is responsible for extracting resources? If instead of going to the enormous trouble of redistributing resources in kind, poor peoples are to be compensated monetarily, then where is this money to come from and what is the periodic rate of payment? Are the peoples of resource-rich countries to be taxed, and can they afford this? Or is a resource-rich country to flood the world market with its resources—thus driving down the price—to raise money to pay compensation to resource-poor nations?) Many questions like these arise, which might give representatives of peoples pause in considering the wisdom of a resource redistribution principle.[31] Just as the representatives to Rawls's domestic original position do not agree to a resource redistribution principle per se, or a principle that compensates people proportionately for the degree of their disadvantage, but instead agree to a principle of distributive justice that structures the economy so as to maximally benefit the worst off, so it would seem to be more rational for the parties to the extended original position to simply agree to a principle of distributive justice to deal with issues of resource inequality.

Nevertheless, even dealing with the problem that way might be questionable, for reasons Rawls himself suggests. Rawls gives short shrift to the resource redistribution argument. Basically, he denies its claim that the natural resources a people controls determine its members' income and wealth. Pointing to the people of Japan and other resource-poor but still well-to-do peoples (and also to the people of Argentina and other resource-rich but still poor peoples), he says that how a nation fares has much more to do with its political culture than with the natural resources it controls within its boundaries:

> There is no society anywhere in the world—except for marginal cases—with resources so scarce that it could not, were it reasonably and rationally organized and governed, become well-ordered. . . . [T]he crucial element in how a country fares is its political culture—its members' political and civic virtues—and not the level of its resources. (LP, 108, 117)

Given the centrality of political culture to a society's well-being, Rawls says, "the arbitrariness of natural resources causes no difficulty" (LP, 117).

---

[31] Here it might be said that these are simply questions of the application of a global resource principle. However, if we accept the publicity condition on principles, then I think that more is involved here than simply the application of a vague principle. Why should representatives of peoples want to accept a principle that inevitably will give rise to interminable disputes among peoples?

I think an important assumption underlying Rawls's argument here is that, on Rawls's view, the duty of assistance should be set at a level that assures political autonomy, the capacity of a people "to be able to determine the path of their own future for themselves" (*LP*, 118). It is only once the political autonomy of a people is procured that the level of wealth a country enjoys can become largely a matter of its political culture (as opposed to being a matter of the natural resources it has on hand). (See *LP*, 117–18.) Here, again, it is important to emphasize that Rawls's argument applies to well-ordered societies in a well-ordered Society of Peoples. It is under those circumstances, where there is an absence of internal political corruption and external exploitation by other peoples and by multinational business interests that a people's level of well-being will largely be decided by its political culture, and the natural resources it controls will not be such a significant factor.

We can assume that the parties to Rawls's original position have this general knowledge. Thus, if Rawls's argument is convincing, then it is questionable whether it is rational for the representatives of peoples to be worried about instituting a resource redistribution principle or about compensating the resource-poor at all, especially given all the potential problems that arise with administering such a principle.

One response to Rawls's argument is this: Why should the inhabitants of poor countries have to take responsibility for the miserable political and social culture they are born into any more than they should have to take responsibility for the level of resources they are born with? From the perspective of individuals, it is just as arbitrary for one to be born into a culturally impoverished country as it is for one to be born into a resource-poor country. This raises the question of the need for a global distribution principle (as opposed to a global resource redistribution principle), a subject that will be considered in the next section. For his part, Beitz in his response to Rawls says that the question of the degree to which political culture, natural resource endowments and the lack thereof, technology and human capital, and other factors contribute to economic backwardness is in dispute; moreover, it may not even be an intelligible question, given developing societies' enmeshment in a world economy.[32] I would argue, however, that to refute Rawls's position, one would have to make a more convincing empirical case that political culture *cannot* be relatively independent and self-determining even under ideal conditions. In any case, Beitz in later works seems to drop his earlier insistence on a resource redistribution principle, and resolves problems of differences in natural resource endowment with a global principle of distributive justice.

Here, again, it has to be kept in mind that Rawls is focused on the possibility of political autonomy and a people's control over its political and social culture under conditions of well-ordered societies, all of which

---

[32] Beitz, "Rawls's Law of Peoples," 690.

are members of the Society of Peoples. The importance of this point will be emphasized again in the next section in my discussion of a global principle of distributive justice. But the main point I want to make here is that these criticisms of Rawls's position—for failure to include a resource redistribution principle and perhaps a principle of distributive justice also—indicate the degree to which the cosmopolitan position depends (frequently, if not always) upon what is often called "luck egalitarianism," or the idea that it is the role of a conception of justice to correct for and equalize the effects of natural and social chances and accidents. The degree to which many of Rawls's cosmopolitan critics are luck egalitarians is evident when they suggest that Rawls is inconsistent in this argument.[33] They claim that if Rawls is bothered by the luck of the draw in the natural and social lottery in the domestic case, he should also be bothered by the luck of the draw among peoples in the "resource lottery." This contention underlies many arguments for the resource redistribution principle, and for a global distribution principle. For Beitz and others who advocate a resource redistribution principle, being engaged in a cooperative endeavor is not a condition for the application of this principle. Indeed, a cooperation requirement would be contrary to the purpose of the principle, since the opportunity for cooperation is itself nearly as dependent upon arbitrary factual contingencies as other facts that influence distributions of benefits. Why should the natural resources a country has at its disposal depend upon whether it cooperates (economically, politically, etc.) with other nations? After all, the lack of natural resources has a direct bearing upon an impoverished people's inability to cooperate.

Luck egalitarians, who include the Rawlsian cosmopolitans, often refer to Rawls's claim that no one deserves greater natural talents or his starting position in society, and that the outcome of the natural lottery "is arbitrary from a moral perspective" (see *TJ*, sec. 12), and contend that there is an inconsistency in Rawls's argument. They use the same idea to support their position that the consequences of chance should be equalized or at least neutralized in the distribution of natural resources among peoples. Here it is relevant that, when Rawls says in *A Theory of Justice* that no one deserves his place in the distribution of native endowments (*TJ*, 89) and that this natural distribution is morally arbitrary (*TJ*, 64), he is making this point within the context of an argument for principles of justice that apply to societies' basic structures, as ongoing socially cooperative endeavors. The inference he draws is not that a society should seek to equalize distributions that are the consequences of chance. It is, rather, that the natural (or social) endowments one is born with should not be allowed to determine one's place in the distribution of income and wealth; instead, some other principle should. This principle is the difference principle, as Rawls goes on to argue. The difference principle is not

---

[33] Cf. Beitz, *Political Theory and International Relations*, 137–38.

a luck egalitarian principle, or, as Rawls says, it "is not the principle of redress" (*TJ*, 86–87). That is not its point. It does not try to equalize the results of birth, social class, and other contingencies, or compensate the disadvantaged for their unfortunate circumstances. Rather, it is a principle that "distributes" the benefits and burdens that result from natural and social differences, regardless of whether they are the product of chance, so as to maximally benefit the least advantaged. As I discussed earlier, the difference principle presupposes, and is designed to apply to, the basic institutions constituting the basic structure of society. Rawls's point is not that luck or natural facts should *never* determine or affect distributions of income and wealth of any kind. (How could that be possible? No matter what we do, morally arbitrary natural facts are going to affect distributions of assets in some way.) It is rather that, *within socially cooperative frameworks*, the distribution of natural assets should not be allowed to determine the distribution of income and wealth, *unless* it also maximally benefits the least-advantaged members of society. It does not follow that one may generalize this point, and apply it globally, where there is an absence of socially cooperative frameworks and a shared basic structure. Such a move rejects Rawls's position that social cooperation and the special political and social relationships of a shared basic structure matter to distributive justice. I conclude that Rawls is not guilty of the inconsistency he is accused of on this point.

The luck egalitarianism presupposed by cosmopolitans invokes larger issues that cannot be discussed here. Briefly, however, a problem with the luck egalitarian position—that the results of natural and social contingencies should be equalized or at least neutralized—is that it has no clear stopping place in the following sense. Luck egalitarians want to draw a sharp distinction between events that result from chance and those that result from people's choices. Differences in distributions should only reflect people's free choices, after everyone has been compensated (or taxed) for the unfavorable (or favorable) circumstances he or she starts out with. But our capacities for choice, our occasions for choice, and the alternatives for choice we confront are also influenced by chance circumstances (by our natural talents, our upbringing, others' talents, upbringing, and choices, our social connections, etc.); so it is hard to say when a choice is not itself the result of "brute luck." Moreover, for the strict determinist, nothing is left undetermined by nature; thus, our choices are themselves as much a matter of our circumstances as are our starting positions in life. The point is not that the choice/chance distinction does not have its place within our practices of holding people responsible and in deciding particular questions regarding fair distributions. Rather, it is that, because the distinction is so uncertain in so many cases, it is an unsuitable foundation for a conception of distributive justice.[34]

---

[34] On this issue, see Samuel Scheffler, "What Is Egalitarianism?" *Philosophy and Public Affairs* 31, no. 1 (Winter 2003): 5–39. For a more general discussion, see Susan Hurley, *Justice, Luck, and Knowledge* (Cambridge, MA: Harvard University Press, 2003).

IV. Problems with a Global Distribution Principle

The argument is frequently made that Rawls's difference principle, or some other principle, should globally apply to determine the distribution of income and wealth.[35] In this section, I discuss some potential problems with the idea of a global difference principle and, more generally, some reasons why Rawls rejects the idea of global distributive justice.

It is sometimes suggested that, in rejecting a global distribution principle, Rawls wrongly assumes that laissez-faire among peoples is the default position for global economic distribution. Thomas Pogge, for example, says that Rawls in effect gives a Nozickian reply to arguments for a global difference principle. For Rawls, "It is somehow natural or neutral to arrange the world economy so that each society has absolute control over, and unlimited ownership of, all natural resources within its territory."[36] However, Pogge claims, Rawls gives no reason for this assumption, nor does he show why the opposite assumption should not be made, namely, that the difference principle or some other distributive principle should be the default position and should apply globally.

I would argue, however, that Rawls does not assume that the difference principle globally applies for the simple reason that he believes that claims of distributive justice are already settled at the domestic level. For reasons I will discuss momentarily, it would make no sense to argue that the difference principle should apply a second time, before or after it is domestically applied. Moreover, the disanalogies with Nozick's libertarianism are too numerous for Pogge's comparison to be of critical value. Rawls does not assume absolute property rights or laissez-faire economic relations among peoples. For Rawls, the duty of assistance to burdened societies is a condition upon a society's use of its resources; by contrast, in Nozick's libertarianism there is no political duty to assist anyone in need. Moreover, on Rawls's view, the Society of Peoples has requisite authority to restrict or regulate nations' and corporations' detrimental uses of resources in ways that would not be recognized by libertarians. Finally, the analogy between a people's independent control of a territory and an

[35] For example, Thomas Pogge says: "Taken seriously, Rawls's conception of justice will make the life prospects of the globally least advantaged the primary standard for assessing our social institutions." Thomas Pogge, "Rawls and Global Justice," *The Canadian Journal of Philosophy* 18, no. 2 (1988): 227–56, at 233. And Charles Beitz has said: "It seems obvious that an international difference principle applies to persons in the sense that it is the globally least advantaged representative person (or group of persons) whose position is to be maximized." Beitz, *Political Theory and International Relations*, 152. T. M. Scanlon also once suggested that the difference principle should apply globally. See T. M. Scanlon, "Rawls' Theory of Justice," in *Reading Rawls*, ed. Norman Daniels (Palo Alto, CA: Stanford University Press, 1989), 202.

[36] Pogge, "An Egalitarian Law of Peoples," 212–13. See also Pogge, "Rawls and Global Justice," where he says that Rawls leaves international economic interactions up to "libertarian rule-making" (250) and that "[t]he economic order of Rawls's utopia . . . is shaped by free bargaining" (252).

individual's rights over property (however extensive) is unfitting. By exercising political jurisdiction over a territory, a people establishes a system of property, which is a complicated system of rules and inter-dependent expectations. By contrast, individuals do not establish systems of property; rather, they hold and use possessions within property sys-tems, subject to the systems' legal rules and expectations. A people's control over a territory is not a kind of property; it is the condition for the existence of the social institution of property. More generally, it is a con-dition for social and political cooperation and the very existence of a political people.

Why does Rawls reject the global application of the difference princi-ple? There are several reasons:

1. Rawls regards the difference principle as a principle of reciprocity, designed to apply under conditions of social cooperation to the basic structure of society, where the members of society are regarded as engag-ing in a complex web of political and social institutions that make up the basic structure. People engaged in social cooperation in a common basic structure of institutions are confronted with a crucial question: How are the terms of cooperation to be structured among themselves as they each pursue their individual purposes and conceptions of the good? The dif-ference principle is designed to express the idea of reciprocity from a benchmark of equality that (for Rawls) defines the terms of social coop-eration among free and equal democratic citizens. Assuming that the members of a democratic society are engaged in a common social and political endeavor, advances in the position of those better off should not at any point come at the expense of the worse off; rather, the worse off should consistently benefit from changes in the terms of cooperation that benefit the more advantaged members of society.[37]

To say that the difference principle should apply globally, and regard-less of the kind of cooperation that exists among people, implies that there is nothing special about social and political cooperation within the basic institutions of society; moreover, it implies that democratic social and political cooperation is of no consequence to questions of distributive justice. This is explicit in the objection of those luck egalitarians who argue that the difference principle should apply globally since people cannot control which society they are born into or whom they are des-tined to cooperate with. The luck egalitarian will say: "If cooperation and whom you cooperate with are just as arbitrary as are the talents and social position you are born with, then the fact of cooperation should not act as a limit upon the application of the difference principle."[38] But if society

---

[37] I refer here to Rawls's graphical depiction of the difference principle in *A Theory of Justice*, sec. 13, figure 6, and in *Justice as Fairness: A Restatement*, sec. 18, p. 62, figure 1.

[38] As K. C. Tan argues: On Rawls's account of distributive justice, "Citizens of disadvan-taged countries are *collectively* held accountable for their country's unsound domestic pol-icies, even when a majority of them had no part in the making of these policies. And this is

is to be possible at all among individuals, there must be special terms of cooperation that apply to members of the group that do not apply to those who are not members. Among these, Rawls contends, are principles of distributive justice based on the idea of reciprocity.

2. Luck egalitarianism is one basis for a global distribution principle. Another potential basis is more Rawlsian: it is the claim that global cooperation and a global basic structure exist, particularly in economic relations, and that by Rawls's own criteria a global distribution principle is appropriate in order to reward all those poorer peoples who do their part in global economic production. Allen Buchanan, among others, argues that "it is unjustifiable to ignore the global basic structure in a theory of international law," and that if Rawls had recognized the influence of the global basic structure on individuals' and peoples' prospects, he would have accepted a global distribution principle. Constituting the global basic structure for Buchanan are the following institutions:

> [R]egional and international economic agreements (including the General Agreement on Tariffs and Trade, North American Free Trade Agreement, and various European Union treaties), international financial regimes (including the International Monetary Fund, the World Bank, and various treaties governing currency exchange mechanisms), an increasingly global system of private property rights, including intellectual property rights that are of growing importance as technology spreads across the globe, and a set of international and regional legal institutions and agencies that play an important role in determining the character of all the preceding elements of the global basic structure.[39]

If this is what Buchanan means by "global basic structure," it is incorrect to suggest that Rawls ignores it. For Rawls, institutions like these are an integral part of the Society of Peoples, but he refuses to regard them as a global basic structure of the kind that warrants principles of distributive justice. Buchanan and others put greater emphasis on these international institutions since they believe they affect people's future prospects just as a domestic basic structure does.[40] But there is really no comparison between the basic structure of society and the effect of global institutions. The difference is not simply a matter of the (far) greater degree to which

---

clearly inconsistent with Rawls's own moral individualism. On Rawls's own reasoning, a person born into a society with poor population control and economic policies cannot be said to deserve her fate any more than another born into more favorable circumstances deserves her[s]. These are mere accidents of birth, and are as morally arbitrary as is being born into wealth or poverty in the domestic context." K. C. Tan, "Critical Notice of John Rawls, *The Law of Peoples,*" *Canadian Journal of Philosophy* 31 (March 2001): 113–32, at 122.

[39] Buchanan, "Rawls's Law of Peoples," 706.

[40] Ibid.

domestic institutions affect people's lives. Nor is it simply that international institutions are supervenient upon national ones: they presuppose the complicated basic institutions (the many systems of property and contract, for example) of the basic structures of the many societies whose practices they regulate. Rather, it is also that these international institutions are the product of independent peoples' exercise of their original political jurisdiction as members of the Society of Peoples, which they agree to in order to maintain their own basic structure of society, over which they exercise political autonomy. Simply put, there is no global basic structure *mainly* because there is no world-state, with all it would entail. (For example, as I discuss below, since there is no world-state, there is no independent global property system to apply a principle of distributive justice to, such as the difference principle; international property conventions presuppose and are confined by the terms of the rules of property systems of politically independent peoples.) There is, then, a fundamental difference between Rawls's and his cosmopolitan critics' assumptions regarding the conditions of social cooperation and distributive justice.

3. Rawls regards the difference principle as a political principle in the sense that it is to guide legislators in defining and regulating the uses of property, setting commercial policies, specifying schemes of taxation, regulating securities and negotiable instruments, defining conditions for copyrights, patents, royalties, and other forms of intellectual property, and establishing the other indefinitely many laws and regulations that structure an economy. (Compare Rawls's remarks regarding application of the difference principle at the legislative rather than the constitutional stage [*PL*, 229–30].) Strictly applied, the difference principle would require legislators and other officials to consider the effect of laws and regulations upon the prospects of the worst-off members of society. While they may not need to scrutinize each decision to determine if it maximizes the prospects of the worst off, governing officials should at least determine that the least advantaged are not disadvantaged indirectly by decisions made, and that any benefits created by political and economic policies also redound to an appropriate degree to the benefit of the worst off.

There are an enormous number of laws, regulations, legal precedents, and conventions that structure property and economic systems (literally millions in the U.S. federal system). In the absence of political authority and political cooperation, it is hard to see how the difference principle could be applied to influence, much less determine, these innumerable laws, rules, and social practices. The primary practical problem with the cosmopolitan suggestion that the difference principle should be globally applied is that, in the absence of a world-state, there is no political agent with authority to apply it on a global level. Here it might be suggested that each government representing the world's many peoples should apply the difference principle, if not jointly then at least severally. This

would require that each nation calculate the effects of its many decisions
upon the worst-off members of the world. This is not feasible, nor would
it have the desired (or even desirable) effects. The coordination problems
of many nations separately trying to tailor their many decisions to affect
peoples in distant lands over whom they have no political authority seem
insurmountable in the absence of a world-state.

This does not mean that, in making their laws regulating economic
institutions, societies should not take into account the adverse effects of
their economic policies and property norms upon other peoples, particularly less-advantaged peoples. But this would not be equivalent to instituting the difference principle on a global scale, since it would not require
governments to choose only those policies that *maximally* benefit the
(world's) least advantaged. Moreover, there is no need for a global difference principle, or a global distribution principle of any other sort, to
induce governments to take into account and restrict the adverse effects
of their policies on the world's least-advantaged nations. The duty of
assistance already implies a duty to consider and rectify adverse effects of
economic policies upon burdened peoples. Moreover, in reference to the
"guidelines for setting up cooperative organizations," "standards of fairness for trade," and "provisions for mutual assistance," Rawls states:
"Should these cooperative organizations have unjustified distributive
effects, these would have to be corrected in the basic structure of the
Society of Peoples" (*LP*, 115). Presumably he means here the "Confeder-
ation of Peoples" and international economic institutions with regulatory
oversight duties over economic agents as they engage in trade, international investment, and other economic transactions (see *LP*, 42–43, sec.
4.5 on cooperative organizations). Nothing Rawls says implies that standards for fairness of trade and "distributive effects" are to be decided (as
Pogge and other critics suggest) at the global level by a doctrine of unmitigated laissez-faire or libertarian entitlement principles. On the contrary,
the implication is that economic relations among peoples are to be regulated with the aim of rendering them all independent and self-sustaining
members of the Society of Peoples, each of whose individual members'
basic needs are met so that all persons are able to actively participate in
their particular society and take advantage of the rights, liberties, and
opportunities it offers them (cf. *LP*, 38 n. 47).

4. It has been suggested (by Pogge, K. C. Tan, et al.) that since there is
global economic cooperation, the difference principle should doubly apply,
both at the global and at the national level. The thought here seems to be
that just as the members of a family can distribute their resources according to principles of local justice once they obtain their fair share under the
difference principle in their (liberal) society, so too a society can apply the
difference principle to distribute its fair share of the global product once
the global difference principle has been satisfied. But the difference principle is not like a principle that applies to a fixed allocation of goods—it's

not as if the total global product is like a big cake that we can keep slicing into shares at the global, domestic, and then familial levels. The difference principle can apply only once to structure economic and property institutions, either globally or domestically. It cannot apply to both. (Among other reasons, we can seek to maximize the position of the globally least advantaged, or the domestically least advantaged, but not both, for we can maximize only one thing.) In this way, the analogy between the dual application of the difference principle at the global and domestic levels differs from the dual application of the difference principle first domestically and then within the family. The economy and the family are two different kinds of social institutions, whereas domestic and global economic relations are not. It is not clear what sense could be given to the idea of first structuring economic institutions so that they maximize the position of the worst off in the world, then structuring domestic economic and legal institutions so that they maximize the prospects of the domestically worst off within each society.

5. Not only is there the problem (mentioned in item 3 above) of *who* is to apply a global difference principle to achieve its intended effects, but there is also a problem regarding just what a global difference principle is supposed to apply *to*. In the absence of a world-state, there is no global legal system regulating relations among individuals. To take one important example, one role of the difference principle is to specify rights and permissible uses of property interests, and to regulate transactions involving property. However, there is no global property system to apply a global difference principle to. There are economic relations among peoples and members of different peoples. But even here, in the case of international trade, it is (in the absence of treaties setting out specific rules) the property and contract laws of one or another country that apply to regulate economic transactions and to decide disputes about rights when they break down. There is very little international property law that applies to international trade, and the international law that does exist is largely the result of treaties among peoples, and is dependent in many ways upon existing laws in various countries.

6. Let us suppose, however, that we can make sense of the idea of a global difference principle, independent of a basic structure of society and a world-state (and leaving aside questions of how it is to be implemented among nations, and whether it can practicably serve as a public conception of justice that guides the actions of independent peoples or individuals). Rawls's explicit reason for rejecting a global difference principle, or any other global principle of distributive justice, is that since a global distribution principle would continuously apply to all wealth without a cut-off point, it would be unfair to politically independent peoples. He gives two examples, both of which assume the ideal case of well-ordered societies that are members of the Society of well-ordered Peoples. The first example involves two societies beginning with the same level of

wealth, one of which saves and invests its resources in industrialization and over time becomes wealthier, the other of which prefers to remain "a more pastoral and leisurely society" of modest means. It would be "unacceptable," Rawls says, to tax the incremental wealth of the richer society and redistribute it to the poorer nation. The second example runs parallel to the first, but assumes a rather high rate of population growth. One society undertakes population control measures to restrain the high rate of growth and achieves zero-growth, while the other society, for religious and cultural reasons "freely held by its women" does not. (Rawls's example here presupposes "the elements of equal justice for women as required by a well-ordered society" [LP, 118].) Over time, the per-capita income of the society practicing population control is higher. Again, it "seems unacceptable" to tax the wealth of the richer nation and redistribute it to the poorer nation that has freely chosen to maintain its population at higher levels for religious reasons (LP, 117–18).

Importantly, Rawls's rejection of a global distribution principle rests upon the assumption that it is possible for a well-ordered people to exercise political autonomy, that its members are economically self-sufficient (relatively speaking) and not subject to manipulation by external forces beyond their control, and that they can control their level of wealth through savings, investment, population control, and other measures. (See The Law of Peoples, 117 and 118, where Rawls indicates that well-ordered liberal and decent peoples are "free and responsible and able to make their own decisions," and "able to determine the path of their own future for themselves.") Rawls's critics seem to question this crucial assumption of the independence of peoples under ideal conditions of a well-ordered Society of Peoples. It has been said, for example, that the inequalities of resources that Rawls's account allows for will inevitably lead to political corruption and the exploitation of less-developed peoples by richer peoples. "In a world with large international inequalities, the domestic institutions of the poorer societies are vulnerable to being corrupted by powerful political and economic interests abroad."[41]

Again, it is important to recall that the Law of Peoples is drawn up for the ideal case of well-ordered societies joined into a well-ordered Society of Peoples. The Law of Peoples includes a duty of peoples to provide for material and other conditions that enable all peoples to be politically autonomous and independent. These and other requirements should protect less-advantaged peoples from "being corrupted by powerful political and economic interests abroad." If critics claim that such corruption is nonetheless inevitable so long as inequality exists, then clearly Rawls is

[41] See Pogge, "An Egalitarian Law of Peoples," 213. Pogge further argues against the inequality of wealth allowed by Rawls's account, saying that "[r]elative poverty breeds corruptibility and corruption," and that "[i]t is entirely unrealistic to expect that such foreign-sponsored corruption can be eradicated without reducing the enormous differentials in per capita GNP" (ibid., 213, 214).

more sanguine here than his critics are regarding human nature and the possibilities for a "realistic utopia" of politically autonomous and independent well-ordered peoples. Let us put this dispute aside, since it involves largely empirical conjectures about the capacity for political autonomy and the workings of an economy, both domestically and worldwide, under conditions of a well-ordered Society of Peoples. What I want to focus on instead is Rawls's claim that the argument for a global distribution principle made by cosmopolitans is grounded in concern for "the well-being of individuals and not the justice of societies." What are the origins of this claim? I believe we can understand its origins by examining the two examples I discussed earlier, involving rich and poor societies. A global distribution principle would require that wealth be transferred from richer peoples to poorer peoples in these two examples, even though the relative levels of wealth were (we are assuming) the result of each well-ordered people's free decisions. The insistence that such redistribution should nonetheless be effected can only be based in an ultimate concern for the well-being of individuals, independent of the choices made by their own political culture (and even by themselves, assuming they agree with the decisions of their political culture). This goes beyond my earlier suggestion, that cosmopolitan accounts of distributive justice are ultimately guided by a kind of luck egalitarianism, or the idea that distributions of income and wealth should not in any way reflect outcomes due to chance. It says that transfers of wealth should occur from richer to poorer without regard to either chance or choice, and should be decided purely on the basis of comparative welfare.

Rawls's rejection of welfarism is integral to his rejection of a global distribution principle. In the domestic case, the end of social justice is not individual welfare, but the freedom and equality of citizens. Similarly, in the international case, the end of the Law of Peoples is not the total welfare of a people. (It is not even the welfare of its least-advantaged individuals, though all individuals' basic needs are to be met so that they can participate in the social and political life of their culture.) The end of the Law of Peoples is equal political autonomy, or "the freedom and equality of a people as members of the Society of well-ordered Peoples" (cf. *LP*, 118). Essential to this is that a society should be in a position to meet the basic needs of all its members so that they can participate in the social and political life of their culture. Recall that this is the basis for the duty of assistance, as opposed to a principle of distributive justice. Here again, however, cosmopolitans may object that, if not welfare, then at least the freedom and equality of *individuals*, and not of peoples, should be the aim of an account of international justice. But Rawls focuses on peoples rather than individuals in the global case, we have seen, because of the priority he assigns to the basic structure of society and the central role that political cooperation, political culture, and political autonomy play in his account of social justice.[42] This focus is precisely the result of his concern for the freedom and equality of individuals, which is in the background throughout in *The Law of Peoples*. (Recall that the book's purpose is to "work out the ideals and principles of *foreign policy* of a just *liberal* people" [*LP*, 10, emphasis in original].) A condition of the freedom and equality of individuals, as Rawls conceives these basic democratic values, is *politically autonomous citizenship* within the basic structure of a democratic society that itself exercises political autonomy (that is, its citizens are "able to make their own decisions" and "able to determine the path of their own future for themselves" [*LP*, 118]). In the end, Rawls's rejection of a global distribution principle does not rest simply upon the assumption that a people can exercise political autonomy, that its members can be economically self-sufficient (relatively speaking) and not subject to manipulation by external forces beyond their control, and that they can control their level of wealth through savings, investment, population control, and other measures. It also rests upon his ideal conception of the freedom and equality of democratic citizens, and the social and political conditions that must hold if that ideal of the person is to be realized.

7. Finally, there is an issue that requires more discussion than I can give it here:[43] Rawls envisions the difference principle as a principle that structures property institutions so as to encourage (when conjoined with fair equality of opportunity) widespread ownership and control of the means of production, either in a "property-owning democracy" or in a liberal socialist economy. Like John Stuart Mill, Rawls believed that for workers to have realistically available to them only the option of a wage relationship with capitalist employers undermines individuals' freedom and independence, blunts their characters and imaginations, diminishes mutual respect among members of different income classes, and leads to the eventual loss of self-respect among working people. For this and other reasons, Rawls was attracted by such ideas as a "share economy" (where workers have part ownership of private capital), workers' cooperatives, public provision of capital to encourage workers to become independent economic agents or to start up small businesses, and other measures for the widespread distribution of control over the means of production.[44]

Because there is no global basic structure, advocates of a global difference principle are required to envision the difference principle as a re-

---

[42] Cf. Rawls's claim: "It is surely a good for individuals and associations to be attached to their particular culture and to take part in its common public and civic life. . . . This is no small thing. It argues for preserving significant room for the idea of a people's self-determination" (*LP*, 111).

[43] For a more in-depth discussion of this issue, see my "Distributive Justice and the Law of Peoples," in *Envisioning a New International Order: Essays on Rawls's "The Law of Peoples,"* ed. Rex Martin and David Reidy (Oxford: Basil Blackwell, 2006).

[44] See, for example, *Justice as Fairness: A Restatement,* 176, where Rawls endorses Mill's idea of worker-owned cooperatives as part of a property-owning democracy. On Mill, see also *LP*, 107n.

allocation principle, where the income and wealth of more-advantaged societies are reallocated to less-advantaged peoples. But since this principle does not apply to any substantial basic structure to shape property and other economic relations, and is not conjoined with a principle of fair equality of opportunity, the allocative model of the global difference principle can do little to further Rawls's primary aims. Rawls writes:

> The intent [of the difference principle] is not simply to assist those who lose out through accident or misfortune (although that must be done), but rather to put all citizens in a position to manage their own affairs on a footing of a suitable degree of social and political cooperation. . . . The least advantaged are not, if all goes well, the unfortunate and unlucky—objects of our charity and compassion, much less our pity—but those to whom reciprocity is owed as a matter of political justice among those who are free and equal citizens along with everyone else.[45]

This is not to say that the difference principle, when applied domestically, does not also have an allocative role (primarily in the form of income supplements for workers who earn too little to achieve economic independence [*TJ*, 252]). As Rawls makes clear, however, the difference principle specifically, and distributive justice more generally, should not be confused with measures for alleviating poverty or misfortune; nor is its purpose to assist those with special needs or handicaps, or to compensate the unfortunate for bad luck, natural inequalities, and other accidents of fortune. Any number of principles, domestic and global, can provide a decent social or global minimum and serve the role of poverty alleviation and meeting special needs. There is no need to appeal to a dysfunctional "global difference principle" for these purposes. Rawls's duty of assistance to meet basic needs is already sufficient to serve the role of addressing global poverty and special needs.

The general point, then, is that Rawls does not regard distributive justice in terms of the alleviation of poverty or misfortunes; rather, he transforms the issue from a narrow question of the allocation of a fixed product of wealth in order to address a larger set of issues. Distributive justice is made part of the larger question about how to fairly structure economic and property relations among productive, socially cooperative agents, who regard themselves as free and equal, and each of whom does his or her fair share in creating the social product. In effect, Rawls incorporates the question of distributive justice into the tradition of Mill and Marx, where the primary focus is on how to fairly structure production relations in a way that affirms the dignity, freedom, and equality of socially productive agents. The robust conception of reciprocity implicit in the

---

[45] Rawls, *Justice as Fairness: A Restatement*, 139.

difference principle is a response to this general issue. It is not the proper response to the problem of global poverty, or to the other alleviatory issues I have mentioned (meeting handicaps and special needs, redressing misfortune, etc.). These are specific problems to address in nonideal theory, by reference to moral duties of assistance, mutual aid, and so on, and are to be determined by citizens' democratic deliberations, on the basis of their knowledge of available resources once the demands of distributive justice are in place and satisfied. These alleviatory problems of nonideal theory raise issues that are separate from the question in ideal theory of determining appropriate standards for just distributions among socially productive democratic citizens who are cooperative members of a well-ordered society.

V. Conclusion

A central theme running through this essay is the centrality of political cooperation and political autonomy to Rawls's account of distributive justice, human rights, and the Law of Peoples. Political autonomy is essential to his idea of social cooperation and the basic structure of society. It accounts for his position regarding distributive justice as a requirement of domestic rather than global justice. Finally, political autonomy provides the basis for his account of the Law of Peoples. We would, perhaps, be making too strong a claim if we said that, for Rawls, political autonomy of individuals and well-ordered societies would not be possible if there were a global principle of distributive justice. But given the centrality of the difference principle to his account of domestic justice and the task of democratic legislation, the claim is not too far off the mark. For this reason, I conclude that the dilution of political autonomy of a (democratic) people that is required by a global distribution principle entails the dilution of the ideal of free and equal democratic citizens around which Rawls's account of justice and political liberalism is constructed.

Philosophy and Law, University of Pennsylvania

INTERNATIONAL AID: WHEN GIVING
BECOMES A VICE*

By Neera K. Badhwar

I. Introduction

A. The Singer-Unger thesis

Is giving up all one's "unnecessary" pleasures, all one's luxuries, in order to help the hungry and naked of the world essential to leading a morally decent life, or even the ideally moral life? Peter Singer and Peter Unger would have us believe that it is.[1] According to these two theorists, moral decency requires that the affluent—and nearly all residents of affluent countries count as affluent—donate all their surplus to relieving poverty and its consequences. Although Singer also calls for higher levels of government-to-government aid, his main concern, like Unger's, is to exhort us as individuals to give more.

Despite the clash of this view with common sense and common (almost universal) practice, it seems to have strong popular and philosophical appeal. Singer's provocative 1972 article "Famine, Affluence, and Morality," written at the time of the civil war in East Pakistan, led to the establishment of Oxfam America[2] and spawned dozens of articles and comments, both supportive and critical.[3] Since its original publication, Singer's article has been reprinted in over two dozen books. It also inspired Unger to write *Living High and Letting Die* in the hope of providing a

* I am grateful for helpful comments on this paper from Ellen Frankel Paul, Larry White (who commented on the paper at the 2005 conference of the Association for Private Enterprise Education), David Blumenfeld, and Garrett Cullity (whose comments from Australia were a wonderful example of voluntary international aid to a stranger). I would also like to thank Georgia State University, Bowling Green State University, and the Association for Private Enterprise Education for inviting me to present this paper, and the audiences at these presentations for their helpful discussion. Finally, I would like to thank Harry Dolan for his expert copyediting, which saved me from some embarrassing mistakes and infelicities.

[1] See Peter Singer, "Famine, Affluence, and Morality," *Philosophy and Public Affairs* 1, no. 3 (1972): 229–43, revised version at http://www.petersingerlinks.com/famine.htm; Singer, *Practical Ethics,* 2d ed. (Cambridge: Cambridge University Press, 1993), 230; Singer, *One World: The Ethics of Globalization* (New Haven, CT: Yale University Press, 2002); Singer, "The Bread Which You Withhold Belongs to the Hungry: Attitudes to Poverty," http://www.iadb.org/etica/documentos/dc_sin_elpan-i.htm (2003); Peter Unger, *Living High and Letting Die: Our Illusion of Innocence* (New York: Oxford University Press, 1996). All further references to Singer's "Famine" are to the revised version.

[2] Oxfam is an abbreviation for the Oxford Committee for Famine Relief.

[3] See, e.g., the essays in Dale Jamieson, ed., *Singer and His Critics* (Oxford: Blackwell Publishing, 1999).

stronger and more detailed defense of Singer's thesis against actual and possible objections. Unger's book also generated intense discussion in philosophy journals, and Singer himself has written on the topic several times since his 1972 article and has talked about it in interviews in the print media.[4]

One reason for the persuasive power of the Singer-Unger thesis, as I shall call it, is that the ideology of aid to the poor, especially poor children, has long been revered and, like all ideologies, rather uncritically so. Thus, politicians who launch new programs that claim to help the needy are hailed by people of different political and religious persuasions (whatever the politicians' motives or the actual results of their programs), and those who claim to love "the poorest of the poor" are everywhere hailed as saints (no matter how weak the evidence for their claim).[5] Even totalitarian leaders who have committed mass murder in the name of "justice for the poor," such as Mao Tse-tung, have been admired the world over

[4] See, for example, Peter Singer, "Should We Let Them Starve?" *New Humanist*, June 1974; Singer, "The Right to Be Rich or Poor," *The New York Review of Books*, March 6, 1975; Singer, "Greed Is Stupid," *Australian Business Monthly*, March 1992, 78–81; Singer, "Not What You Produce, But How Much You Spend," *Modern Times*, March 1992, 16–17; and Singer, "The Drowning Child and the Expanding Circle," *New Internationalist*, April 1997, 28–30.

[5] "Compassionate" conservatism in the United States seems obviously to be a response to the public adulation of "generous" politicians; and the belief in the "saintliness" of Mother Teresa, based almost entirely on uncritical acceptance of her own claims and those of a few hagiographers, persists despite the vast evidence for the fact that very little of the tens of millions she received in donations every year worldwide was spent on the care of the poor. Instead, nearly all of it was spent either directly on missionary work or repatriated to the Vatican for its missionary work. The evidence comes from former nuns, lay helpers in her missions, and the poor of Calcutta, including those in the immediate vicinity of her homes in the city. The results are reported and discussed in books and articles based on years of research. See, in particular, Aroup Chatterjee, *Mother Teresa: The Final Verdict* (Kolkata, India: Meteor Books, 2003), http://www.meteorbooks.com/index.html; Christopher Hitchens, *The Missionary Position: Mother Teresa in Theory and Practice*, reprint ed. (New York: Verso, 1997); Hitchens, "Less than Miraculous," *Free Inquiry* 24, no. 2 (2004), http://www.secularhumanism.org/library/fi/hitchens_24_2.html; Susan Shields, "Mother Teresa's House of Illusions," *Free Inquiry* 18, no. 1 (1997/1998), http://www.secularhumanism.org/library/fi/shields_18_1.html; and Walter Wuellenweber, "Mother Teresa: Where Are Her Millions?" *Stern*, September 10, 1998 (English translation available at http://are.berkeley.edu/~atanu/Writing/teresa.html and http://members.lycos.co.uk/bajuu). Before the publication of Chatterjee's book, Christopher Hitchens and Tariq Ali produced a documentary based on Chatterjee's research called *Hell's Angel* for Britain's Channel 4. Hitchens also accused Mother Teresa of celebrating suffering instead of alleviating it. A nice summary of the findings in these works and in the works of other investigators may be found online at "Missionaries of Charity," http://en.wikipedia.org/wiki/Missionaries_of_Charity, and "Mother Teresa," http://en.wikipedia.org/wiki/Mother_Teresa. A somewhat different perspective is provided by Clifford Orwin in "Compassion and Christian Charity: Princess Diana versus Mother Teresa," in Amy L. Kass, ed., *The Perfect Gift: The Philanthropic Imagination* (Bloomington: Indiana University Press, 2002), 188–211. Orwin argues that although it is true that Mother Teresa did not do much to help relieve suffering, and thus was not charitable in the modern meaning of the term, she did help sufferers see Christ in their suffering and take joy in it as a path to redemption, and thus was charitable in the original meaning of the term. This, however, does not exempt her from criticism. When a person refuses to relieve the suffering of another because, according to her own beliefs and wishes, not those of the sufferer, suffering will bring the sufferer closer to Christ, her "charity" is cruel and immoral.

by many people, educated and uneducated alike.[6] Hence, it is not surprising that many philosophers accept the idea that if donating all one's
surplus would help the poor, it would be a worthy ideal.[7] And indeed,
when one thinks of the condition of those who live in "absolute poverty"
(as Robert McNamara, former president of the World Bank, called it),[8]
poverty that reduces people to an existence on the margins, it can seem
that there is no justification for not giving one's entire surplus to the poor
if doing so would relieve poverty.

[6] Of course, in all these cases the motivations for the praise are more diverse than I have
described them here, including both self-interest or envy (on the part of the worse-off) and
guilt (on the part of the better-off).

[7] See, for example, Richard Arneson, "Moral Limits on the Demands of Beneficence?" in
Deen K. Chatterjee, ed., *The Ethics of Assistance: Morality, Affluence, and the Distant Needy*
(Cambridge: Cambridge University Press, 2004), 33–58; Thomas W. Pogge, "Real World
Justice," *Journal of Ethics* 9, nos. 1–2 (2005): 29–53, reprinted in an abbreviated form as "A
Cosmopolitan Perspective on the Global Economic Order," in Harry Brighouse and Gillian
Brock, eds., *The Political Philosophy of Cosmopolitanism* (Cambridge: Cambridge University
Press, 2005), 92–109; and Thomas W. Pogge, *World Poverty and Human Rights: Cosmopolitan
Responsibilities and Reforms* (Malden: Blackwell Publishers, 2002). Pogge's main theme in
these works, however, is not the positive duty to aid but the negative duty to change the
global economic order which, he argues, is unjust and partly responsible for much of the
poverty of the developing world. In "Duties to the Distant: Aid, Assistance, and Intervention in the Developing World," *Journal of Ethics* 9, nos. 1–2 (2005): 151–70, Dale Jamieson
argues that aid, both governmental and private, has been harmful overall to its recipients,
but takes pains to state that if this were not the case, he would accept Singer's view of the
duty to assist. In "Famine Relief: The Duties We Have to Others," in Andrew I. Cohen and
Christopher H. Wellman, eds., *Contemporary Debates in Applied Ethics* (Oxford: Blackwell,
2005), 313–25, Christopher Heath Wellman defends Singer's "less demanding principle"
that we have a positive duty to give to famine relief "until we sacrifice something 'morally
significant'," but rejects the "more demanding principle that we ought to contribute until we
are sacrificing something 'morally comparable'" (323 n. 1). In *The Moral Demands of Affluence*
(Oxford: Clarendon Press, 2004), Garrett Cullity argues that beneficence requires giving of
one's time or money to the cause of global poverty or some other comparable philanthropic
cause, but rejects the view that its demands are as high as Singer and Unger claim. (Unfortunately, the book came out too late for me to take its arguments into account.) In his review
of Unger's *Living High and Letting Die* ("Sacrificing for the Good of Strangers—Repeatedly,"
Philosophy and Phenomenological Research 59, no. 1 [1999]: 177–81), Brad Hooker argues that
we face a dilemma: accepting an endless duty to give to the world's needy can seem
counterintuitively demanding, but rejecting it "can seem counterintuitively mean" (181).
Among those who have questioned the ideal qua ideal are Fred Feldman, "Review of
Unger's *Living High and Letting Die: Our Illusion of Innocence*," *Noûs* 32, no. 1 (1998): 138–47;
Feldman, "Comments on *Living High and Letting Die*," *Philosophy and Phenomenological Research*
59, no. 1 (1999): 195–201; David Schmidtz, "Islands in a Sea of Obligation: Limits of the Duty
to Rescue," *Law and Philosophy* 19 (2000): 683–705; Raziel Abelson, "A Middle View," in
Raziel Abelson and Marie-Louise Friquegnon, eds., *Ethics for Modern Life*, 6th ed. (Boston:
Bedford/St. Martin's, 2003), 341–47; John Arthur, "Famine Relief and the Ideal Moral Code,"
in Hugh LaFollette, ed., *Ethics in Practice: An Anthology*, 2d ed. (Oxford: Blackwell Publishers, 2002), 582–90; and Andrew I. Cohen, "Famine Relief and Human Virtue," in Cohen and
Wellman, eds., *Contemporary Debates in Applied Ethics*, 326–42. There are several points of
overlap between some of my arguments and some of the arguments offered by these critics,
but I develop my arguments differently and offer a different conception of the role of
beneficence in a morally good life.

[8] Cited in Singer, *Practical Ethics*, 218. Robert McNamara, who served as secretary of
defense under presidents Kennedy and Johnson, was president of the World Bank from 1968
to 1981.

These ideological and moral reasons are not, however, the only reasons for the wide acceptance of the ideal put forward by Singer and Unger. Another is that, although their ideal is counterintuitive, their argument for it is thought by many philosophers to be rationally compelling or, at least, hard to refute.

B. A doubly flawed argument

The failures of most governmental aid programs to date—indeed, even their long-range harmful effects—are by now well-documented.[9] The net effect of private aid programs, according to some former aid workers, is almost as disastrous, though some would disagree or offer a mixed view.[10] Singer acknowledges that if aid were harmful, or even if it were not efficacious, we would not be obligated to give.[11] But he usually assumes, as do Unger and other advocates of aid, that both private and (at least in recent times) governmental aid *are* efficacious, and continues to exhort people to give more.[12]

I will not be concerned to settle the practical issue here, other than noting that, however efficacious, aid cannot be a big part of the solution or its lack a big part of the problem. If it were, it would be a mystery how

[9] See Peter T. Bauer on the history of harmful or wasted foreign aid, in Bauer, *The Development Frontier* (Cambridge, MA: Harvard University Press, 1991), 38–55. In "The New Approach to Foreign Aid: Is the Enthusiasm Warranted?" Cato Foreign Policy Briefing No. 79 (September 2003), http://www.cato.org/pubs/fpbriefs/fpb-079es.html (accessed March 11, 2005), Ian Vasquez questions many of the positive claims the World Bank makes in its book *Assessing Aid: What Works, What Doesn't, and Why* (Oxford: Oxford University Press, 1998), www.worldbank.org/research/aid/aidpub.htm, and the claims made in the essays in Roger D. Cowe, ed., *A Case for Aid: Building a Consensus for Development Assistance* (Washington, DC: World Bank Publications, 2002). The *World Development Report 2005*, released on September 29, 2004, accepts the main points long made by the World Bank's critics, namely, that the way out of poverty is private investment, not aid, either private or (especially) governmental, and that the way to invite private investment into a country is for governments to define and enforce private property rights and end corruption. See *World Development Report 2005: A Better Investment Climate for Everyone* (Washington, DC: World Bank Publications, 2004). Another World Bank publication, *Doing Business in 2005: Obstacles to Growth* (Washington, DC: World Bank Publications, 2004), cites weak property rights and too many regulations creating barriers to doing business as two of the main obstacles to growth in poor countries, and argues that these barriers hurt the poor (unskilled workers, women, and the young) most of all.

[10] For a criticism of aid agencies' work and many aid workers' motives, see Michael Maren, *The Road to Hell: The Ravaging Effects of Foreign Aid and International Charity* (New York: Free Press, 1997); interview with Maren, "A Complete Waste of Money That Succeeds Primarily at Keeping Westerners Employed," *Might Magazine*, March/April 1997, http://www.netnomad.com/might.html. For a mixed view, see David Rieff, "Charity on the Rampage: The Business of Foreign Aid," review of *The Road to Hell*, in *Foreign Affairs*, January/February 1997, http://foreignaffairs.org/19970101fareviewessay3744/david-rieff/charity-on-the-rampage; and Mary Andersen, "Some Moral Dilemmas of Humanitarian Aid," in Jonathan Moore, ed., *Hard Choices* (Lanham, MD: Rowman and Littlefield, 1998), reprinted in James P. Sterba, ed., *Morality in Practice*, 6th ed (Belmont, CA: Wadsworth, 2001), 104–10.

[11] Singer, "Famine, Affluence, and Morality," 9.

[12] Singer, *One World*, chap. 4.

the East Asian Tigers—Taiwan, Hong Kong, Singapore, and South Korea—ever became rich. Rather, I will focus on the question of whether the Singer-Unger ideal would be a worthy ideal even *if* private aid were beneficial overall.[13] Hence, we need to be clear about the implications of this ideal. If Singer and Unger are right about what is required for moral decency—or even for the ideally moral life—then practically no one is morally decent, and certainly no one even approaches the moral ideal. Moreover, a well-off person who gives *nothing* to help alleviate the desperate poverty of fellow human beings in distant lands (or in her own land, if she lives in a poor country) is positively indecent. It little matters, on this view, what else is true of this person's character or actions, including how beneficent or charitable she might be in other respects, let alone how honest, just, courageous, generous with her friends, and so on. Indeed, on Unger's view, other forms of moral decency—such as honesty or respect for what are usually called negative rights, especially property rights—are utterly dispensable if they stand in the way of helping the desperately poor.[14]

Any thesis with such radically counterintuitive implications had better be supported by very strong arguments, especially since both Singer and Unger claim that their thesis and arguments are addressed to everyone, and not only to utilitarians. I will argue that Singer's and Unger's central argument, though initially seductive, is doubly flawed. Their central argument is an argument by analogy with a life-threatening emergency. If the analogy they rely on turns out to be weak—and I will argue that it does—they are left without solid ground for their thesis. Moreover, their thesis is subject to four independent, but related, moral objections (which I will discuss in subsection C). If, however, we assume for the sake of argument that the analogy is strong, then it proves too much, for it shows that the relief of global poverty does not occupy a privileged moral status. This means that Singer and Unger must modify their thesis; but the modified thesis, I will argue, is even more vulnerable to the moral objections than the unmodified thesis.

C. Four moral objections

First, the thesis is monomaniacal. The world offers a rich variety of values that can make a life morally good: many goals and activities worth pursuing, many moral personalities worth developing, many ideals worth

---

[13] For an impressive attempt to assess the case for private aid, see Cullity, *The Moral Demands of Affluence.*

[14] Unger, *Living High and Letting Die,* 62–63. And Singer makes it clear that giving away all our surplus would not be "charitable, or generous" or "supererogatory," since this implies that to do so would be to go beyond the call of duty and, therefore, not wrong not to do ("Famine," 4). His view is that we *owe* our surplus to the poor, and that therefore withholding it is simply wrong. I disagree with Singer on both points here: we do not "owe" what we have justly acquired to the needy, and certainly not all our "surplus"; nevertheless, withholding charity is wrong if it comes from a deficiency or lack of concern for others.

cherishing and emulating.[15] A good person must be beneficent—this is true on practically all conceptions of morality, and certainly on the everyday common-sense conceptions most people endorse. However, beneficence need not take the form of big contributions of time or money to aid agencies for the prevention or relief of absolute poverty—or, for that matter, of *any* great evil.

Second, if taken seriously, the Singer-Unger ideal is deeply misanthropic, because, with rare exceptions, it is incompatible with that which makes life worth living: the pursuit of happiness, by which I mean the attempt to forge a life that is both objectively meaningful or worthwhile, and meaningful and enjoyable to the individual concerned.[16] By "rare exceptions" I have in mind people who have a special interest in the relief of poverty, as some people have a special interest in, say, fighting fires or rebuilding houses destroyed by tornadoes—or, for that matter, in *studying* tornadoes. For people with a special interest in the relief of poverty, devoting most of their spare time and money to the cause of poverty relief, whether over their entire lives or during a period of their lives, is not only compatible with, but necessary for, making their lives truly rewarding.[17] And it is necessary because it is dictated by their own particular interests and aptitudes, and not by the (as I will argue, mistaken) belief that this is what a one-size-fits-all morality requires of them, or by a desire to prove their worth or assuage their guilt.[18]

The problem is that the Singer-Unger ideal claims allegiance from all of us, regardless of our vocations, moral personalities, individual histories, or the effect of adopting such an ideal on our lives. To put it differently, it fails to recognize the variety of moral ideals and of individual personalities and vocations, arbitrarily putting relief or prevention of absolute

[15] Feldman makes a similar point about there being other goals worth pursuing in "Comments on *Living High and Letting Die*," calling Unger's view fanatical. Unger rejects this characterization in his reply, but without addressing the point that there are other goals worth pursuing ("Replies," *Philosophy and Phenomenological Research* 59, no. 1 [1999]: 203–16).

[16] I have defended this "objectivist" conception of happiness in my "Happiness as the Highest Good," unpublished manuscript.

[17] What I have in mind here is charity, that is, voluntary work for the poor motivated by beneficence, and not a career in poverty relief or prevention. A career in poverty relief is no more charity than, say, a career in medicine. Nor can we assume that everyone or even most people involved in aid work as a career must have a stronger-than-usual sense of beneficence. See Maren, *The Road to Hell*.

[18] For an example of someone whose obsessive giving has been motivated by all these reasons, see the story of Zell Kravinsky as told by Ian Parker in "The Gift," *The New Yorker*, August 2004, 54–63. Kravinsky started by giving away his millions, went on to donate a kidney, and at the time of his interview for "The Gift" had graduated to unhappily obsessing about giving his other kidney away and living on dialysis, or even giving his entire body away to be harvested for his organs. Predictably, Peter Singer has called him a "remarkable" and admirable person, while allowing that we shouldn't blame people who don't go as far as Kravinsky in their self-sacrifice (Singer, quoted in "The Gift," 63). A nondirected live donation of a kidney (the name for the kind of donation Kravinsky made) can, of course, be motivated by perfectly good reasons, such as the desire to relieve suffering or, more positively, to share with others one's good fortune and joy in living. See Marc Ian Barasch, "Extreme Altruists," *Psychology Today* 38, no. 2 (March/April 2005): 78–82, for stories of live donors motivated by such reasons.

poverty through massive sacrifice at the top of the "right" hierarchy of values. As a result, the Singer-Unger ideal effectively denies that we are entitled to use our time and resources to lead a worthwhile life that we find meaningful and enjoyable. But this, I will argue, also makes their ideal of self-sacrificial giving pragmatically self-defeating.

Third, because most of us feel entitled to pursue our happiness, regardless of what our theories tell us we *ought* to feel, and because the Singer-Unger ideal is incompatible with happiness for most of us, endorsing this ideal leads to doublethink and doublespeak. Its endorsement is, thus, incompatible with integrity for most of us. Regard for individuals' integrity, concern for their happiness and, indeed, a proper understanding of beneficence itself, require recognition of the fact that our moral ideals must respect the constraints of human nature and the variety of humanly worthy pursuits. In particular, our ideals must recognize the importance of creativity or productivity in human life, acknowledging that creating wealth, whether material, intellectual, or artistic, is more fundamental in happiness and the formation of individual identity than receiving wealth, and that beneficence itself aims, in the final analysis, to make people independent creators of wealth. The Singer-Unger ideal seems to value the creation of wealth only as a means to giving it away.

Fourth, even if the activities of aid agencies in themselves were beneficial overall, if most of us did start living by the Singer-Unger ideal, the effects of giving away all our "spare" money instead of investing it in worthwhile enterprises or spending it on "luxuries" would push even more people into the ranks of the absolutely poor. Although Singer and Unger offer extensive empirical data about the incidence of absolute poverty and its rise or fall over the years, their arguments are striking in their neglect of, or only cursory attention to, some fundamental commonsensical economic principles.

My discussion in the remainder of this essay will proceed as follows. I will begin, in Section II, with my first objection to the Singer-Unger ideal, namely, that it is monomaniacal, and the problems I see with the life-saving analogy that Singer and Unger employ. In Section III, I will go on to argue that their ideal is misanthropic. In Section IV, I will contend that (for reasons related to its misanthropy and its disregard of the constraints of human nature and the importance of wealth-creation) endorsement of the Singer-Unger ideal is incompatible with integrity for most of us. Finally, in Section V, I will argue that if most of us did start living by this ideal, the effects would be disastrous for everyone, including the poor.

II. Moral Monomania and the Life-Saving Analogy

A. Moral monomania

The Singer-Unger ideal is monomaniacal for the simple reason that positive aid for the prevention or relief of absolute poverty is not the only, or even the highest, goal worth pursuing. Almost anyone would agree that a morally decent person must be beneficent as well as just and, therefore, must have *concern* for those living in absolute poverty—as she must for the victims of other misfortunes, such as the thousands of prisoners of conscience in the jails of despots, or the millions living in absolute unfreedom (many of whom also live in absolute poverty, such as in North Korea). And to the extent that her country's policies perpetuate poverty in poor countries through such mechanisms as tariffs or subsidies or restrictions on "outsourcing," her concern must lead her to refrain from supporting these policies, directly or indirectly. Indeed, that we thus refrain is a requirement of justice, which tells us to do no harm to the innocent, and justice is presupposed by beneficence, which tells us to help those in need.[19] A beneficent person may also spend a portion of her time or money on trying to prevent harmful policies by actively supporting programs or organizations that work against them, or she may lend her support to organizations that try to bring hope to prisoners of conscience or to relieve poverty. But she does not fail in beneficence or, therefore, in moral decency, by not giving time or money to institutions that help relieve absolute poverty, such as UNICEF or Oxfam. This is the case not only because there are many well-fed, well-sheltered people just as worthy of help, both in one's home country and abroad, but also because one can be sufficiently beneficent even if one's contributions to institutionalized charity are small or occasional.

B. Beneficence

What *is* essential to being fully beneficent—that is, to having the virtue of beneficence—is being the kind of person who habitually wishes others well for their sake, is pleased to see them do well, and thus gladly but wisely uses her (own) resources to help them in a variety of situations for their sake. This definition of beneficence presupposes a basically Aristotelian conception of virtue, which I have defended elsewhere and will explain briefly here with reference to beneficence.[20]

Like any morally worthy act, a beneficent act must be done *voluntarily* and for the *right reasons,* that is, for the other's benefit rather than, say, out of guilt or fear of God, or as a mere means to a further end. It must be done *wisely,* because giving without due thought to the possible harmful consequences to one's intended beneficiaries, to oneself, or to third parties, falls short of the rational self-concern and other-concern required of a morally worthy act. Hence, a beneficent person will try to learn the

---

[19] Someone who liked to help the needy but cared little about harming the better-off would be lacking in the concern that is the common root of both justice and beneficence. Whatever her configuration of motives, then, they could not count as beneficent on my conception of beneficence.

[20] See Neera Badhwar, "The Limited Unity of Virtue," *Noûs* 30, no. 3 (1996): 306–29.

relevant facts before lending her support to programs or policies that claim to "help the poor" or bring "social justice" to the poor.[21] Beneficence requires giving *of one's own resources* and not those of others, because if one is merely distributing what others have given for the purpose, then the beneficence is theirs, not one's own.[22] Worse, if one is merely distributing what has been taken forcibly from others, then one's act partakes of injustice, and no act that requires an act of injustice or some other vice can count as morally worthy.

An act that meets these conditions counts as a beneficent act, and a person whose giving typically meets these conditions counts as a beneficent person. To exemplify the excellence of a full-fledged (Aristotelian) virtue, however, a further condition must be met: the act must be wholehearted, and the person must typically give wholeheartedly.

On this conception of beneficence, any beneficent person must be disposed to do what I shall call small-scale acts of beneficence. Examples of such acts include giving money or time to organizations in times of emergency if the costs to oneself are small, as well as directly helping people in emergencies when the risk to oneself is small. Someone who cared naught about letting a child drown in front of his eyes, or not enough to get his pants muddy, would be seriously deficient in, if not altogether devoid of, the empathy that is necessary not only for beneficence, but for moral agency itself.[23] Such a person, we would be justified in suspecting, would merrily drive over an errant pedestrian if there were no laws waiting to get him.

Other examples of small-scale beneficence include the myriad small acts that make everyday coexistence pleasant rather than burdensome, such as holding a door open for someone who is loaded down with books, giving directions to someone who is lost, helping someone who has just fallen down, going beyond the requirements of the job to respond to a colleague's or student's occasional need for help, and so on. Someone who *never* found reason to do any of these things would also be seriously deficient in empathy.

[21] Such as, for example, the Soviet-inspired socialist policies adopted by India under the leadership of Jawaharlal Nehru, policies that persisted despite strong evidence of their poverty-creating power.

[22] A government's foreign aid or domestic welfare programs, then, cannot count as a measure of that country's—much less that government's—beneficence, politicians' claims and the popular view notwithstanding. With respect to those who do not consent to the taxation that funds one or another of these programs, the money taken from them is taken forcibly. With respect to those who do consent to the taxation, their consent may be an instance of their beneficence if they are motivated primarily by genuine good will rather than, say, guilt or fear of God, and if they have rational (even if mistaken) reasons for believing that these programs help their intended beneficiaries without unjustly harming anyone else.

[23] For empirical evidence that empathy is necessary for moral agency, see Hervey Cleckley, *The Mask of Sanity* (St. Louis, MO: C. V. Mosby, 1964). I have argued for this in "Self-Interest and Virtue," *Social Philosophy and Policy* 14, no. 1 (1997): 226–63, and in "The Rejection of Ethical Rationalism," *Logos* 10 (1989): 99–131.

On my conception of beneficence, however, a beneficent person need never have engaged in large-scale beneficence—"munificence"—such as devoting a major part of her free time or money to the cause of the poor or to some other philanthropic purpose. For, as I will argue, she might have other (nonbeneficent) worthwhile uses for her time or money. I will say more about beneficence and other worthwhile uses of time or money in Section IV below.

C. The life-saving analogy

Singer and Unger, however, would reject the distinction I have drawn between small-scale and large-scale beneficence. They would do so because, according to their argument, giving all one's surplus wealth to help the global poor is strictly analogous to saving a drowning child from a shallow pond. They argue that just as it is wrong not to save a drowning child if you can do so without serious risk to your own life or health, so it is wrong not to save as many people from absolute poverty and its systemic consequences as you can without serious risk to your own life or basic welfare. The general principle at work in both cases, according to Singer, is that it is wrong not to prevent something very bad from happening if we can do so "without sacrificing anything of comparable significance."[24] Serious risk, then, is risk to something that has comparable or greater significance. Singer thinks that this principle (henceforth "Singer's Principle") should be acceptable to both consequentialists and nonconsequentialists, because it does not call for the unconstrained maximization of the good, and hence does not require the violation of rights or other principles that nonconsequentialists regard as having comparable moral significance.[25]

Nevertheless, despite this principle's innocuous appearance, Singer observes correctly that, if it were taken seriously, it would change our lives "fundamentally."[26] For it requires giving up far more than clean pants or a passing enjoyment. Among the things that do not compare in significance to the prevention or relief of absolute poverty—and that, therefore, we ought to be willing to sacrifice—are "stylish clothes, expensive dinners, a sophisticated stereo system, overseas holidays, a (second?)

[24] Singer, "Famine," 2; Singer, *Practical Ethics*, 230.

[25] Singer, *Practical Ethics*, 230.

[26] See ibid.; and Singer, "Famine," 2. Sometimes Singer says that it is wrong not to prevent something very bad from happening if we can do so without sacrificing anything "morally significant" ("Famine," 2). This has been interpreted by some as a weaker principle than the "comparable significance" thesis. But Singer himself thinks it makes no practical difference. In his own words, if the principle "were acted upon, even in its qualified form, our lives, our society, and our world would be fundamentally changed" (2). And indeed, it is hard to see how the "morally significant" formulation will allow us to hang on to movies, art, music, etc.—anything that is not needed to satisfy our basic needs and earn a living. For these things have little moral significance compared to saving the lives of the destitute—if saving their lives is like saving a child drowning in front of our eyes.

car, a larger house, private schools for our children, and so on."[27] Indeed, it is hard to see how *anything* over and above the minimum needed for living a normal lifespan (presumably, by Western standards) and earning a living could be seen as having significance comparable to the relief of absolute poverty, or how the loss of anything above this minimum could be seen as constituting a serious risk to our lives or welfare. As Singer states, to save "every life we could," we would have to give till we had reached the "minimum level compatible with earning the income which, after providing for our needs, left us most to give away."[28] Although he does not say so explicitly, his principle entails that all "unnecessary" things—"unnecessary" movies, books, art, music, toys, gardens, sports, air-conditioning—must go.

Onora O'Neill supports Singer's Principle from a Kantian perspective, arguing that even if we assume that we have acquired all our wealth justly (a point she disputes), not saving the world's poor by sharing our surplus with them is akin to killing them.[29] O'Neill's argument asks us to imagine that we are in a lifeboat to which we have a special claim, and which we have stocked with food that is more than enough for our own needs. Then we discover stowaways on our lifeboat. If we withhold our surplus food from them and they die, we have killed them, even though it is not our fault that they did not have their own lifeboat or their own supplies. So, even if the poor of "lifeboat Earth" are in the same position as these stowaways, if we withhold our surplus from them and they die, we are guilty of killing them (although not, as O'Neill is careful to point out, of murdering them).

Those who have rejected these life-saving analogies between the drowning child or the starving stowaway, on the one hand, and the world's poor, on the other, have done so on two main grounds. One is that we can identify relevant differences between emergencies and ongoing evils, such as the fact that in the former but not the latter the individual to be rescued is close to us, or he is identifiable, or the need is urgent and immediate, or we can save him directly, or there is a particular individual we save.[30] The other ground for rejecting the analogy is methodological: if we must take seriously the intuitive response that failing to rescue a child drowning in front of our eyes is wrong, then we must also take seriously the intuitive response that failing to save people from chronic hunger or disease is *not* wrong, even if we cannot identify relevant differences between the two cases. There is no justification for privileging one intuition over another.

[27] Singer, *Practical Ethics*, 232.

[28] Ibid., 223 n. 1.

[29] Onora O'Neill, "Life-Boat Earth," in Charles R. Beitz, Marshall Cohen, Thomas Scanlon, and A. John Simmons, eds., A *"Philosophy and Public Affairs" Reader* (Princeton, NJ: Princeton University Press, 1985), 262–81.

[30] See Garrett Cullity, *The Moral Demands of Affluence*, for a useful summary of the differences usually adduced in rejecting the analogy (20–27). The term "methodological" for the second kind of objection addressed in the next sentence is also from Cullity.

In his book *Living High and Letting Die,* Unger seeks to meet both sorts of objections by arguing that the second intuitive response is based on *"distortional* dispositions," dispositions that lead us to think that there are relevant differences between emergencies and ongoing evils when, in fact, there are not.[31] His strategy is to create a dazzling array of imaginary cases and examine a variety of common responses to them for these distortions. He claims that in the case of "The Shallow Pond," when we say that it would be wrong not to save the drowning child, we are reflecting our "primary values" and "the true nature of morality." By contrast, in "The Envelope," when we say that it is not wrong to refuse the appeal from UNICEF to make a $100 contribution, even though thirty more children will die as a result, we are reasoning badly as a result of these distortional dispositions and reflecting only our "secondary values." Indeed, even if we think that we may throw away the envelope because we have already sent $100 to UNICEF, we are reasoning badly. We do wrong not only in not helping these distant children, but also in not giving everything over and above what is necessary for our basic needs (where this includes the trappings needed for earning our living). To support this, Unger produces another example.[32] Suppose that you spend the morning saving trespassers with wounded legs from bleeding to death, and then in the afternoon come upon another such trespasser. Would you be entitled to say, "[H]oly moly, enough is enough!"? Surely not. Similarly, it is not enough to give only a small percentage of your income to an aid agency. You must give everything not necessary for your basic needs.

Unger is right that some of our intuitive responses to "The Envelope" and the trespasser case are based on fallacious reasoning.[33] There is, for instance, the "futility thinking" that leads us to say, "What's the point of doing anything about the poor? There are *so many* of them."[34] As Unger rightly reminds us, however, the child drowning in front of our eyes (in "The Shallow Pond") is also one of many such children in the world. Just as that is no reason to let this one drown, so the fact that the world is full of starving children is no reason to save none of them. Nor is it some shapeless, identity-less multitude that we will be spending our money to save if, for example, we send money to UNICEF; we will be spending it to save some particular child or children.

However, there is a fundamental, relevant disanalogy between "The Shallow Pond" and "The Envelope" that can explain and justify our conviction that throwing away the envelope is not (necessarily) wrong. To

---

[31] Unger, *Living High and Letting Die,* 13.

[32] Ibid., 60–61.

[33] But see Frances Kamm for a dissenting view in her review of Unger's *Living High and Letting Die* in *The Philosophical Review* 108, no. 2 (April 1999): 300–305.

[34] Unger, *Living High and Letting Die,* 75–76. The words in quotation marks are a paraphrase of what Unger says there.

paraphrase Bernard Williams's well-known words, those who use the life-saving analogy (Singer, Unger, and O'Neill) rely on one thought-experiment too few.[35] Had they come up with an emergency situation that was genuinely analogous to the problem of chronic global poverty, they would have seen that the intuitive response was no different in the two cases.

D. The life-saving (dis)analogy

The crucial disanalogy between an emergency and the chronic problem of absolute poverty is that emergencies, by definition, are short-lived events that come to an end, whereas chronic poverty (or other chronic horrors), by definition, are enduring. To save a life in an emergency, we may be willing to give up quite a lot—we may even have a duty to give up quite a lot—because when the emergency comes to an end, so does the giving. However, if we accept the claim that the moral requirements in the two cases are the same, then our duty to give must be endless. Most of us intuitively reject this claim because we do not believe in an endless duty to give.[36]

Nevertheless, it is precisely this response that Unger's counterexample of the wounded trespasser is designed to undermine.[37] Most of us would agree that the fact that we saved someone in the morning does not mean it's hunky-dory to let someone else bleed to death in the afternoon. But Unger's counterexample is not truly analogous to chronic evils and hence not truly a counterexample. A truly analogous situation would exist only if what we think of as emergencies became everyday phenomena.[38] But if we came across someone drowning or bleeding to death every time we stepped out, how long would we continue to be good samaritans? Could anyone plausibly argue that a requirement of living a morally decent life was sacrificing all one's aspirations and projects to the task of saving people? And if it was, how many of us would have reason to live a morally decent life? I will have more to say about plausible requirements for a morally decent life later (in Section IV). My point here is that Singer and Unger are not entitled to draw an analogy between emergencies and ongoing evils to reach their conclusion. If emergencies were truly like chronic evils in being an ongoing feature of life, who would not say that

[35] In "Persons, Character, and Morality," reprinted in his collection, *Moral Luck* (New York: Cambridge University Press, 1981), Bernard Williams criticizes the rule utilitarian for having "one thought too many" when he tries to give an impartial justification for saving his drowning wife over a drowning stranger: "*This* [rule utilitarian] *construction provides the agent with one thought too many: it might have been hoped by some (for instance, by his wife) that his motivating thought, fully spelled out, would be the thought that it was his wife, not that it was his wife AND in situations like this it is permissible to save one's wife*" (18, italics in the original).

[36] Others who take this position are cited in note 7 above.

[37] Unger, *Living High and Letting Die*, 60–61.

[38] Cf. the works by Schmidtz and Hooker cited in note 7 above.

although drowning children were tragic, there was nothing wrong in not spending one's life saving them? And even if some people did not *say* that, who would not *live* like that, other than those whose job or vocation it was to save drowning children? Just as children die every day from absolute poverty in distant lands, we might say, so children die every day from drowning in front of our eyes. A terrible thing, yes, but what can one do? We all have our own lives to lead: we can at best save a few from drowning every year; it's the system that leads to drowning children that needs to be fixed.

It might be thought that this recurring-emergency situation is not analogous to chronic poverty, because what recurring emergencies demand is one's time, whereas chronic poverty merely demands giving money to international agencies. Spending every day saving people's lives requires giving up one's entire life; spending money on aid agencies leaves a major part of one's life—one's work life—intact (although even this may be in danger if we adopt Unger's moral vision, as I explain in Section III below). Let us therefore suppose that every time we stepped out we found an emergency aid agency attending to an emergency, so that we were required to do no more than hand over all the money we could spare to save the victims. Or suppose that emergency aid agencies solicited donations on a monthly or yearly basis so that we didn't even have to stop to make a donation every time we stepped out; all we were required to do for these ubiquitous emergencies was donate everything not necessary for our basic needs. Would we not have the same reaction as we did in rejecting the inference from emergencies to chronic poverty: "Just as children die every day from absolute poverty, so children die every day from drowning. It's terrible, yes, but we all have our own lives to lead"? Our attitudes may shift from a mixture of compassion, pity, guilt, and despair to indifference and then to irritation at "those people" who can't keep their children from drowning. More reflectively, we might feel anger at the system that allows children to drown every day and attempt to fix it. But we would not think we had a duty to spend all our "surplus" wealth on emergency aid agencies.

Similar considerations apply to O'Neill's contention that not giving our surplus to the poor of the world is akin to killing them, even if their poverty is no fault of ours. If so-called lifeboat Earth were like a real lifeboat, with solid ground in sight, most of us would happily share some of our surplus with the destitute—as, indeed, we do in times of famines or natural disasters. The most recent example of this is the more than $990 million raised in private aid in the United States alone (on top of $350 million in government aid) for the victims of the December 2004 tsunami.[39] Indeed, if we were convinced that giving *all* our surplus money

---

[39] See *The Chronicle of Philanthropy Update* (March 10, 2005), http://philanthropy.com/temp/email.php?id=cdg9ot6g1sfirlqewkyu7df2aid62x1v.

would magically end global poverty once and for all, the vast majority of us might happily give it.[40] Conversely, if we had to spend our entire lives on a lifeboat, with no end in sight, and the ocean was full of people in dire straits (as in the real world), we would come to regard it as an ongoing tragedy about which we could, unfortunately, do little, other than not contributing to it directly or indirectly.

My hypothesis about how our attitudes toward emergencies would change if emergencies became a daily feature of life is supported in part by its intuitive plausibility. But it is also supported by first-hand knowledge of the actual attitudes of people in poor countries, such as India, toward the poor. These attitudes are shared both by people who, though not destitute themselves, live cheek-by-jowl with the destitute, and by people who, being relatively well-off or rich, live physically removed from the destitute but within daily sight of them. Indeed, I expect these attitudes are shared even by the destitute, who do not think (at least until they are taught to do otherwise) that the better-off do wrong not to share their surplus with them. If recurring emergencies became part of everyday life, we should expect the same processes of habituation and the same sense of entitlement to a life of one's own to give rise to the same attitudes.

To summarize the discussion so far: We cannot extrapolate what we ought to do in the face of global poverty from what we ought to do in the face of an emergency because there is a crucial disanalogy between the two. Emergencies are short-lived and rare events, global poverty is chronic. If emergencies became recurring phenomena, common attitudes toward them and our judgments of right and wrong behavior would be no different from common attitudes toward chronic poverty. Of course, these attitudes might still be *wrong*, but if they are, we have so far been given no good reason to think so, since the only game in town—the argument from the so-called life-saving analogy—fails to do the job.

Let us suppose, however, that Singer and Unger are right that chronic poverty is analogous to a life-threatening emergency. Then, I will argue, their strategy proves too much and cannot be used to show that we ought to make eradication of global poverty the primary object of our beneficence. For extreme poverty and its systemic consequences are not the only tragic, chronic life-threatening situations analogous to a life-threatening emergency. Nor do life-threatening situations occupy a special moral status: some non-life-threatening situations, emergency situations as well as chronic ones, may be far more tragic and equally or more worthy of intervention. Let us consider some examples of both life-threatening and non-life-threatening situations that are not examples of extreme poverty.

---

[40] Thanks to David Blumenfeld for suggesting this idea.

E. If the life-saving analogy proves anything, it proves too much

Imagine that you see a young woman in a parked car having a heart attack. You are a heart patient too and you could save her from certain death by administering cardiopulmonary resuscitation on her. Wouldn't it be monstrous of you to just shrug your shoulders and keep going? Of course it would. But according to the Centers for Disease Control and Prevention, in the decade ending in 2001, death from cardiac arrest in young American women—women in the prime of youth—went up by 32 percent, and in young men by 10 percent.[41] If you think about it seriously, you have to acknowledge that the waste of lives is shocking—lives so full of promise, so worth living from the point of view of both the victims and society. If anything is very bad, surely this is. In addition, about 1 percent of infants are born with heart disease.[42] So if you throw away the envelope the American Heart Association (AHA) has sent you for a donation, you are no better morally than someone who just walks by the woman having a heart attack in her car. You ought to give everything you don't require to meet your basic needs to the AHA.

This argument can be repeated for other life-threatening emergencies. Think of the children all over the world who attempt suicide because of abuse by their caretakers. Think, too, of the tens of thousands of people, most of them between fifteen and forty-four, who commit suicide every year owing to mental illness or depression.[43] If you saw a child being abused whom you could rescue at small cost to yourself, wouldn't it be wrong to turn away? If you saw someone about to commit suicide and you could prevent it, wouldn't it be wrong not to do so?[44] If you could lessen someone's pain by extending a hand of friendship, wouldn't it be wrong to refuse? Thus, if you fail to donate everything above your basic needs to the Samaritans or the "befriending centers"[45] around the world whose mission it is to help potential suicides, you are no better morally than someone who just walks by a distraught individual about to throw himself off the Golden Gate Bridge.

Untimely threats to life, however, are not the only great evils in the world. Consider this scenario. You are passing an alley where you see

[41] See "Sudden Death Becoming More Common in the Young," http://heartdisease.about.com/library/news/blnws01044.htm (March 5, 2001).

[42] See "Reducing Heart Failure in Infants," http://www.heartinfo.org/ms/news/8008856/main.html (last updated June 23, 2004). There was no information about which countries, other than the United States, formed the basis of these figures.

[43] The World Health Organization estimates that about 873,000 people commit suicide every year and that mental illness is a source of great suffering (http://www.who.int/mental_health/en).

[44] The act of trying to prevent someone from committing suicide cannot be criticized as paternalism if you do so on the well-founded assumption that most attempted suicides are cries for help, and that even if you are wrong about this particular one and the potential suicide truly wanted to die, he can still kill himself later.

[45] See the Befrienders International website, http://www.befrienders.org/aboutus/about.htm.

someone torturing a handcuffed man. You overhear the torturer muttering threats that reveal that the torture has been going on for quite some time and will continue indefinitely. The torturer is a sadist. You have a gun; the torturer has only a knife. All you need do is threaten him with your gun to scare him off. Of course, you might then have to take responsibility for seeing the victim to a hospital and giving a report at a police station, thus losing valuable time; but this is small potatoes compared to saving a man from torture. However, if leaving this man to his fate is wrong, then so is doing nothing for the tens of thousands of people in the torture chambers of despots all over the world. Their lives are living hells, hells that make the prospect of death seem like a blessing to many of them—except that the lack of freedom to kill themselves is part of their hell. To suppose that it is all right to leave them to their fate is to succumb to what Unger calls our "distortional dispositions." We ought to give as much of our thought, time, and money to saving them as we can spare after meeting our basic needs.

If the single-minded focus on saving a person from death, torture, or some other form of abuse in an emergency situation is the proper model for right behavior in a non-emergency, then we ought to distribute everything over and above what is required for our basic needs among all or some of these causes and many others to boot. Thus, Singer, Unger, and like-minded theorists have to admit that their life-saving analogy does not single out relief of absolute poverty and its systemic consequences as the only cause worth supporting.

This broadened conception of the causes that are worth supporting makes the Singer-Unger thesis less demanding in one respect, since a decent person now has a choice about which cause or causes she may give all her "surplus" to, and hence has a higher chance of reconciling her charitable giving with her interests and, thus, her happiness. In another respect, however, the thesis becomes more demanding. For even if all the currently existing rapacious regimes and poverty-producing economic and political policies were to be reformed overnight—and it is now widely admitted that most or much of absolute poverty is due to such regimes and policies[46]—and even if judiciously targeted aid followed by trade enabled the people of those countries to lift themselves out of absolute poverty in the near future, it would not mean an end to continuing immense self-sacrifice. So long as human beings are human beings, there will be new tyrants who reduce their people to poverty, new politically

[46] See, for example, the essays in James A. Dorn, Steve H. Hanke, and Alan A. Walters, eds., *The Revolution in Development Economics* (Washington, DC: Cato Institute, 1998); P. T. Bauer, *Rhetoric and Reality: Studies in Economic Development* (Cambridge, MA: Harvard University Press, 1986); John Rawls, *The Law of Peoples* (Cambridge, MA: Harvard University Press, 2001); World Bank, *Doing Business in 2005: Obstacles to Growth*; Pogge, *World Poverty and Human Rights*; and Hernando de Soto, *The Mystery of Capital: Why Capitalism Triumphs in the West and Fails Everywhere Else* (New York: Basic Books, 2000).

induced famines and civil wars, and maybe even new forms of demo-
cratically elected poverty if democratic countries gradually destroy their
wealth-creating capacity through hostility to economic freedom. Moreover, there will always be accidents and relative poverty (which can also
kill), sadists and abusers, depression and mental illness, earthquakes and
hurricanes, and diseases both old and new. And as long as people are
unequal in their capacities, achievements, and misfortunes, there will be
many who need help from others. (As if to prove the point, even as I was
writing this paragraph, I received an email appeal from the American Red
Cross for help with the August 2004 hurricane victims in Florida. Over
the course of writing this essay, I received dozens of appeals from various
organizations, by email, mail, and telephone.) Moreover, if we redescribe
the torture scenario in more general terms as a case of severe abuse and
injustice, we must add all forms of serious abuse and injustice to the list
of evils for which we must sacrifice.

Whatever support the Singer-Unger thesis might derive from the
suggestion that the self-sacrifice it calls for is temporary, considered in
historical terms, is undermined by these considerations.[47] If the Singer-
Unger thesis is justified, every generation—or rather, the morally conscientious of every generation—will have to bear an immense burden of
sacrifice, since only the morally conscientious will act on their obligations
and the morally conscientious are relatively few. Thus, whatever sense of
meaning and fulfillment they may derive from the thought that their
sacrifice has a definite, reachable goal must also be undermined. For most
people who accept the Singer-Unger thesis, then, doing the right thing
means giving up the prospect of happiness.

Singer and Unger might say that if we have the right values and focus,
the right commitments, we can find meaning and enjoyment in a life of
extreme self-sacrifice for the prevention or alleviation of poverty (or whatever serious ills we choose to address). But even if they are right that such
a life of self-sacrifice is what moral rectitude requires of us—and in this
section I have assumed for the sake of argument that the life-saving
analogy provides a reason for thinking that it is—it does not follow that
if we commit ourselves to living morally, we will be happy. Happiness

[47] Singer and others who believe in massive infusions of aid, both private and governmental, sometimes talk as though properly targeted aid could end global poverty once
and for all. The Millennium Challenge Account proposed by U.S. president George W. Bush
in 2002 (speech at the Inter-American Development Bank, March 14, 2002, http://www.
whitehouse.gov/news/releases/2002/03/20020314-7.html) and the call by James Wolfensohn,
former president of the World Bank, to double the total amount of development aid are
motivated by this belief (James Wolfensohn, "A Partnership for Development and Peace,"
speech delivered at the Woodrow Wilson International Center, Washington, DC, March 6,
2002). Ian Vasquez points out, however, that the claims for the effectiveness of selective aid
made by the World Bank are based on research that is "difficult or impossible to reproduce
by outside researchers," and that "the few attempts to reproduce the Bank's findings using
its own data and methodology have contravened the Bank's findings" (Vasquez, "The New
Approach to Foreign Aid," http://www.cato.org/pubs/fpbriefs/fpb79.pdf).

requires not only that an individual's pursuits be objectively meaningful and capable of being enjoyed, but also that they be meaningful and enjoyable *to the individual in question;* and what is meaningful and enjoyable to an individual depends on her personality and interests. It is a rare individual who will find enjoyment and meaning in living by the Singer-Unger ideal; most people who try to live by it will have to sacrifice not only their money but also their happiness. In shrugging off this fact, the ideal shows itself to be misanthropic. This provides a reason for thinking that the Singer-Unger ideal is immoral, whether or not the life-saving analogy provides a reason for thinking otherwise. Indeed, if emergencies really are analogous to chronic poverty and other ills, then the Singer-Unger view of what morality requires is even more misanthropic than it first seemed, because the sacrifices it calls for are not temporary even in historical terms.

As I have already argued, however, emergencies are not analogous to chronic ills, and thus proper behavior in response to an emergency does not provide the right model for proper behavior in response to chronic ills.

III. A Misanthropic Ideal

I have tried to imagine how Singer and Unger might try to reconcile their thesis about what morality requires with the possibility of happiness. In fact, however, they do not seek to show that their view is compatible with people's happiness. Singer does remark that the philosopher who starts trying to live by his ideal can at least "find compensation in the satisfaction of a way of life in which theory and practice, if not yet in harmony, are at least coming together."[48] But satisfaction in the coming together of theory and practice may not make up for the loss of other sources of meaning and enjoyment, at least when the philosopher comes anywhere close to meeting the requirements of Singer's theory. In any case, for the most part Singer seems unconcerned about happiness, and proceeds as though he thinks that our happiness is unimportant so long as there are desperately poor people in the world.

Unger goes further: he explicitly calls for the sacrifice of both enjoyment and sense of meaning. Recognizing that most of us academics are in the academy because we enjoy our work rather than for the money, he argues that those of us who are capable of earning higher salaries in occupations outside the academy ought to give up our university posts for these more remunerative occupations, so that we will have more to give away.[49] Since we will still be better off than the many millions who need our help, it is "seriously wrong" for us not to do so. But what about

[48] Singer, "Famine," 8.
[49] Unger, *Living High and Letting Die,* 151.

those who are too old to learn new skills? Unger assures his readers with some relish that they too will suffer: the "old philosopher" will "have to change the focus of his work so enormously that, in short order, he'll enjoy little intellectual satisfaction."[50] Thus, for example, the "old philosopher" must give up metaphysics for applied ethics, and even here, he must aim for writing that is "socially beneficial" rather than "philosophically revealing."[51]

Let us leave aside for now the assumption that even if there were a rush on high-paying jobs, they would continue to pay the same high salaries. Let us also leave aside the assumption that high-paying jobs would remain plentiful even if we followed Singer's and Unger's advice and gave up all luxuries (that is, everything that doesn't count as a basic need). The question I want to raise for them is this: If our pursuit of happiness is unimportant in the face of others' misery, then how important can the happiness of those we save from poverty be? After all, there will still be plenty of others needing to be rescued from poverty and misery. But if the happiness of those we save from poverty is unimportant, how important can it be to save them?

Singer and Unger might say that escape from dire poverty means escape from utter misery, and thus those we rescue are at least better off than before. But if the rescued had to accept that pursuing their own happiness with honesty and justice but only small-scale beneficence was morally wrong because the "surplus" of their time and money belonged to the poor (or, more generally, to the needy or oppressed), why suppose that they would not be miserable? Misery does not visit only those living in absolute poverty, as the prevalence of antidepressants and depression counseling in the developed world shows. Indeed, the feeling that it is wrong to seek happiness, even if this happiness comes from humanly worthy activities, is a common source of depression and unhappiness. This, however, is precisely what adopting the Singer-Unger ideal would imply for most of us—explicitly in Unger's theory, and implicitly in Singer's.

Perhaps Singer and Unger would say that so long as those we rescue from absolute poverty do not become affluent (and the empirical literature gives no reason to think that they will), they don't have to worry about the very poor and are free to live their own lives. Like George Orwell's proles in 1984, the relatively poor are free of the strict moral discipline imposed on the relatively well-off and the rich. But this is arbitrary. If the life-saving analogy works, it applies to the relatively poor as much as to anyone else. The relatively poor are not morally permitted to let a child drown because, for example, the delay might lead to the loss of their day's wage or, for that matter, the loss of their job. Besides, even

[50] Ibid., 152–53.
[51] Ibid., 152.

the relatively poor may have more than they require to meet their basic needs, partly, no doubt, because their basic needs, on their own conception of the matter, are far fewer and far cheaper to meet than those of the affluent.[52] Even the relatively poor occasionally spend money on trinkets and baubles of various kinds, the sorts of things Singer regards as trivia (which is not to say that there is no such thing as trivia; I say something about this below, in Section IV). Thus, even the relatively poor must be required to see whatever they have left after meeting their basic needs as rightfully belonging to the destitute who surround them, and their own happiness as unimportant in the face of others' unhappiness. Indeed, in "Famine, Affluence, and Morality," Singer goes so far as to say that the principle which requires us "to prevent bad things from happening unless in doing so we would be sacrificing something of comparable moral significance" requires that "we ought to give until we reach the level of marginal utility—that is, the level at which, by giving more, I would cause as much suffering to myself or my dependents as I would relieve by my gift," and that this means reducing "oneself to very near the material circumstances of a Bengali refugee."[53]

This makes the task of saving people from dire poverty far less important than it would otherwise be. The thought that you ought to make a great sacrifice for the sake of saving people who, in turn, ought to make a great sacrifice for the sake of saving people who, in turn, ought to make a great sacrifice ... is both pragmatically self-defeating and rationally unpersuasive. Replacing the misery of absolute poverty with the misery of sacrificing all prospects of happiness is hardly an improvement. Whatever rational force the Singer-Unger thesis derived from the supposition that the sacrifice of a few would enable many to achieve happiness is now lost. In its casual disregard of the importance of happiness in people's lives, the Singer-Unger thesis is not only misanthropic but also pragmatically self-defeating and lacking in rationality. It is also, I will argue, incompatible with integrity.

IV. Integrity, Human Nature, and Happiness

A. Integrity

Regardless of what our theories tell us, most of us feel entitled to pursue our happiness, seeing the prospect of happiness as the thing that

---

[52] For example, what most of us would count as a basic necessity, namely, privacy, is regarded as less important (no doubt out of economic necessity) than many other things by many poor people in India. Thus, it is not uncommon for a poor but far from destitute family of four to live in one or two rooms that serve as bedroom, kitchen, and living room, and to use the savings to buy stylish clothes, cosmetics, a TV, a radio, arts and crafts, a scooter, and a couple of bikes. I don't know if a radio or TV counts as a basic necessity, but clearly stylish clothes and cosmetics cannot on the Singer-Unger austerity program. Yet equally clearly, they play an important role in their consumers' enjoyment of life.

[53] Singer, "Famine," 7.

makes life worth living. At the very least, we regard a sense of meaning, which is an important component of happiness as I have been using the word, as being crucial to making life worth living. A sense of meaning can, to some extent, make up for the misfortunes or failures that undercut enjoyment of life. However, since most of us can find neither a sense of meaning nor enjoyment in living by the Singer-Unger ideal, endorsing it is incompatible with integrity. For it divides us against ourselves by creating a dichotomy between what we think we *ought* to cherish and what we *do* cherish. In the absence of any independent, overriding reason to accept this ideal (and even if, contrary to my argument, the life-saving analogy does provide a reason, it does not provide an overriding reason, since it is countered by the misanthropy objection), the fact that the ideal is incompatible with integrity for most of us constitutes another moral objection to advocating it as a universal requirement of moral decency.

My claim that the Singer-Unger ideal divides us against ourselves is supported by the fact that even its most passionate defenders—Singer and Unger themselves—evidently cannot live up to it. Singer's actions make it obvious that he is sincere in his advocacy and tries to live up to his ideals. He gives away far more of his income than almost anyone—between 20 percent and 25 percent, according to various sources.[54] But this is a far cry from what he thinks people *should* give: everything they don't require for their own or their family's basic needs. Singer suggests that he would give more if others did, but this is a feeble excuse. It is precisely when others are giving too little that his giving more is more needed, as he himself urges in response to those who object that they should not have to do more than their "fair" share just because others are doing less.[55]

Unger, for his part, cheerfully admits that he does not "even come close to satisfying" his theory's requirements in terms of how much he gives to aid organizations. His website reveals that he also does not satisfy the requirement that the "old philosopher" give up "philosophically revealing" philosophy for "socially beneficial" philosophy, for it tells us that Oxford University Press is publishing his "most substantial book, by far,

---

[54] See the interview with Singer conducted by Ronald Bailey, "The Pursuit of Happiness," in *reasononline*, http://reason.com/0012/rb.the.shtml (December 2000). Bailey comments that Singer stated that he gives 20 percent of his income for famine relief and "hinted" that he would give more if others gave more. A *New York Times* article reports him as saying that he gives 25 percent. See "The Singer Solution to World Poverty," *The New York Times on the Web* (September 5, 1999), posted on http://people.brandeis.edu/~teuber/singermag.html (accessed September 26, 2004). Reportedly, Singer also lives in the very style he condemns by maintaining two residences: a house in Princeton and an apartment in New York City (Bailey, "The Pursuit of Happiness"). Of course, his family's "basic needs" might require two residences, but if so, Singer should at least acknowledge that basic needs can vary and make it permissible for *others* to have "a (second?) car, a larger house, [or] private schools for . . . [their] children" (Singer, *Practical Ethics*, 232).

[55] Singer, "The Bread Which You Withhold Belongs to the Hungry," 3.

All the Power in the World"—a book not on, say, the power of international aid, but rather on central problems in metaphysics.[56]

Ad hominems are usually both poor in taste and poor as arguments, but these are relevant to seeing how deeply the Singer-Unger ideal cuts against the grain. Moreover, the ideal is contrary to integrity not only in the sense that it divides those who adopt it against themselves, but also in the sense that it creates in them a tendency to doublethink and doublespeak. The trouble starts with the very effort of its chief advocates to sell their ideal to the masses. Both Singer and Unger write that although they believe that we ought to give everything not required for our basic needs for the relief of poverty, it is expedient to publicly advocate the giving of a much smaller sum. (Of course, this cannot apply to people who are reading their work or sources that discuss their work.) Singer and Unger justify this violation of the "publicity condition," as John Rawls calls it,[57] on the grounds that telling people the truth about what they really ought to give might discourage them and prevent them from giving even a little. As a sop to flawed human nature, in *Practical Ethics* Singer is willing to tell people that giving 10 percent is the minimum necessary for moral decency, even though he clearly thinks that the minimum is much higher.[58] Later, in *One World*, he makes a bigger compromise by revising this figure down to 1 percent, while clearly disapproving of people for failing to give more.[59]

Singer's claim that these figures are compromises suggests that at least some people are "good" or "strong" enough (as he sees it) to accept the truth about what they ought to do and live up to it. It is natural to think that those who advocate this demanding ideal would be among them, but as we have seen, they are not. Moreover, nowhere in his many admonishments to those who fail to meet his standards does Singer once admit that he himself fails to meet them. If his silence on the topic in the course

[56] Unger, *Living High and Letting Die*, 156. Unger's website can be found at http://philosophy.fas.nyu.edu/object/peterunger (accessed May 8, 2005).

[57] John Rawls, *A Theory of Justice* (Cambridge, MA: Harvard University Press, 1971).

[58] Singer, *Practical Ethics*, 246. In "The Bread Which You Withhold Belongs to the Hungry," Singer says, "In most communities, rich people who give, say, 10 percent of their income to help the poor are so far ahead of virtually all their equally rich counterparts that I wouldn't go out of my way to blame them for not doing more . . . [even though] in some sense, they really should be doing more" (4).

[59] His criticism is especially directed at the United States. Ironically, according to *Giving USA 2004* (AAFRC Trust for Philanthropy, Center on Philanthropy, Indiana University, 2004), Americans voluntarily gave 2.2 percent of the U.S. gross domestic product (GDP) to private philanthropy in 2003 (a staggering $241 billion), and have been giving 2 percent or more every year since 1998, after over two decades of giving somewhat less than 2 percent. Clearly, then, Americans could allocate or permit 50 percent of their total giving (1.1 percent of GDP) to go toward international aid if they saw good reason to do so, instead of the 12.2 percent (0.26 percent of GDP) they currently do (although another 10 percent is left unallocated and could, in principle, be used for international aid). The figures I cite are available at http://www.aafrc.org/press_releases/trustreleases/americansgive.html (accessed May 8, 2005).

of advocating his ideal is to be seen as justified on his own terms, we must suppose that it is due to his desire to serve the goal of getting people to accept his ideal as realizable and worth striving for: admitting his own failure would stand in the way of achieving that goal. It is in the interest of his own ideal, then, that he violates the requirements of integrity, both in misleading people about what morality requires and in allowing people to believe, falsely, that he himself lives up to his ideal. In other words, it is his ideal that leads him to this double violation of integrity. And this is a third strike against his ideal.

Whereas Singer's compromises with reality are at least understandable, both theoretically and psychologically, this cannot be said for Unger's. His compromises in the last chapter of *Living High and Letting Die* bafflingly take back everything he advocates in the first six chapters in a breathtaking display of doublespeak and doublethink. In chapter six of his book, Unger formulates what he calls *"A Pretty Demanding Dictate,"* which states:

> On pain of living a life that's seriously immoral, a typical well-off person, like you and me, must give away most of her financially valuable assets, and much of her income.[60]

This is a good summary statement of where his argument has been heading in the first six chapters of the book. In the last chapter of the book, however, he gives what he calls a "multi-dimensional context-sensitive semantics" to show that this dictate holds only in very demanding, unusual contexts—ideal contexts, for short.[61] The ideal context is the context defined by our primary values, whereas the nonideal or everyday context is the context defined by our secondary values.[62] In the latter context, we do nothing wrong when we fail to conform to this dictate (even though it is only *pretty*, and not *very*, demanding—presumably, in the ideal context). But when are we in each of these contexts? Unger thinks that we can set the context ourselves for our discussions. Apparently, then, when we do moral philosophy (or, at least, ideal moral philosophy), we are in an ideal context, whereas when we cease to philosophize, we enter the ordinary context. The upshot seems to be that as moral philosophers we ought to argue (sincerely?) that our readers (mostly other moral philosophers) should give away most of their income and assets; but when we shut down our computers and close our books, we

---

[60] Unger, *Living High and Letting Die,* 134.

[61] Ibid., 162ff. For a thorough analysis of what Unger is doing in this chapter in the light of an earlier paper on contextual ethics, see Fred Feldman's review of the book in *Noûs* (cited in note 7 above). Feldman makes a detailed attempt to reconcile this last chapter with the rest of Unger's book, but ultimately gives up.

[62] Unger, *Living High and Letting Die,* 160.

can enjoy that beer or go on that cruise without giving the argument another thought.

Presumably, then, we also needn't worry about giving up the philosophy we love for better-paying jobs in, say, Hollywood or Bollywood, or about making that move from "philosophically revealing" to "socially beneficial" philosophy. It is only in the philosophical context that we are obligated to advocate leaving philosophy for Hollywood/Bollywood; indeed, it is only those who do "socially beneficial" philosophy who are obligated to advocate leaving, say, philosophy of film for work in the film industry or, at least, for "socially beneficial" philosophy. When "socially beneficial" philosophers shut down their computers and close their books, they enter a different context, and so they can get together with colleagues in philosophy of film without preaching at them. Likewise, since the latter are also in a different context, they need pay no attention to the arguments for leaving their fields in favor of "socially beneficial" moral philosophy, much less actually acting on those arguments. Indeed, even those who currently do "socially beneficial" philosophy can stop doing it and start doing, say, metaphysics instead, since by that act they will have entered a different context. A look at Unger's website shows that he is following his contextual semantics (David Schmidtz aptly calls it "Orwellian semantics"),[63] having gone back, as I noted earlier, to writing about central problems in metaphysics.

B. The "problem" of human nature

The Singer-Unger ideal manifests the same flaw that all ideals of universal, unconditional love and concern, whether in their religious or their secular (Marxist) form, have manifested: it refuses to accept the constraints of human nature, instead seeing human nature as the fault in human existence that must somehow be corrected. In a *New York Times* article, Singer states:

> Now, evolutionary psychologists tell us that human nature just isn't sufficiently altruistic to make it plausible that many people will sacrifice so much for strangers. On the facts of human nature, they might be right, but they would be wrong to draw a moral conclusion from those facts. If it is the case that we ought to do things that, predictably, most of us won't do, then let's face that fact head-on.[64]

But if our "oughts" ought not to take into account the basic facts of human nature, then in what sense is our ethics *practical* and in what sense is it concerned with the *human good*? The human good has to be the good

---

[63] Schmidtz, "Islands in a Sea of Obligations."
[64] Singer, "Singer Solution to World Poverty."

for humans as they are, defined in terms of their most fundamental needs and capacities, not as some philosopher might prefer that they be.[65] To be sure, human nature is highly variable and plastic, allowing for a great variety in humanly good lives, but it is not infinitely variable or plastic. For the requirements of survival impose certain limits on the ways we can be, as does the fact that we are finite beings with limited resources. One of the limits imposed by these facts is a limit on our capacity for love and effective other-concern. Unlike God's love and concern, human love and concern are strongly preferential. Hence, in allocating our time, attention, or money, we give strong preference to the needs and happiness of those we love, including ourselves. Given the importance of such preferential love and concern, and of happiness, in survival and in making us the individuals we are, it is not surprising that preferential love and happiness are fundamental goods in human life. Hence, any naturalistic or this-worldly ethics must give an important place to preferential love and concern and to happiness in its conception of the intrinsic good—as Singer's and Unger's ethics do not. Of course, they allow that we should meet our own and our families' basic needs before we try to help the poor, but no more than that, and even this limited partiality seems to be allowed only as a means to optimizing our ability to help. But if Singer and Unger think that the fundamental needs and tendencies of human nature can be dispensed with in constructing and justifying our ideals, what grounds do they have for thinking that we should accept *their* ideal rather than, say, the erstwhile Taliban's theological ideal, or another Pol Pot's collectivist ideal?[66]

Singer does sometimes take biological facts into account—at least, provisionally. In *A Darwinian Left: Politics, Evolution, and Cooperation,*[67] Singer argues that the Left ought to replace Marx with Darwin and realize that, given the hierarchical nature of human beings, we cannot have both perfect equality and perfect liberty. In an interview in an online magazine,

---

[65] My point is not that there is *no* human feature that we would be better off without; clearly, if power-lust or blind hatred or blind obedience or cold-heartedness could be done away with, we would be much better off in terms of survival and happiness. It is not clear, however, that these features could be done away with without also doing away with capacities necessary for survival, for they may be developments—or perversions—of underlying capacities we need for survival. My complaint against Singer and Unger is that their "oughts" ignore capacities, needs, and tendencies fundamental to human survival and happiness.

[66] Thanks to Clifford Orwin for pointing out this problem with Singer's and Unger's disregard of the facts of human nature. In the last section of his act-consequentialist defense of the Singer Principle in "Moral Limits?" (cited in note 7 above), Arneson also assumes that we can ignore human nature in constructing our standards of right and wrong—although we must take it into account in praising or blaming people, as it would be "priggish" to think that, given human nature, it is a "great sin" to fail to live by the Singer ideal. Arneson does not explain why it is not priggish—or irrational—to not take human nature into account in constructing our standards of right and wrong.

[67] Peter Singer, *A Darwinian Left: Politics, Evolution, and Cooperation* (New Haven, CT: Yale University Press, 2000), cited in Bailey, "The Pursuit of Happiness" (*reasononline* interview).

he goes so far as to say that the pursuit of equality "has undoubtedly been the source of significant amounts of suffering."[68] Nevertheless, like many a utopian before him, he still seems to harbor the hope that since his ideals are not based on human nature, it will someday become possible to base human nature on his ideals. After conceding that the Left is wrong in thinking that human nature as it exists is malleable, he states that genetics offers the hope that it can *become* malleable (and he is not averse to government subsidies for those who cannot afford to change their offsprings' nature).[69]

The solution to our troublesome human nature, then, is not the old Left's social engineering, but genetics. Singer seems not to realize that state-subsidized eugenics might be in the hands of the same sorts of governments that carried out the old Left's social engineering programs in European and Asian countries, governments that sought to kill not only the capacity for preferential love, but also the capacity for independent thought and creativity. But the importance of our creative or productive capacity in survival and in the creation of our individual identities (and, thus, in happiness) is also not something that Singer or Unger seem to recognize. Their ideal devalues creativity by seeing moral decency entirely in terms of helping the needy, thus making impermissible all investments of time, energy, or money in creative activities that cannot be justified in terms of their poverty-relieving potential. Singer's and Unger's devaluation of creativity is, of course, of a piece with their devaluation of the individual's integrity and happiness, since creative engagement, like love, is a major source of both our identity and our happiness.

In the next subsection, I will argue that a morality that takes the human good seriously must recognize the moral importance of creativity, and that only if it does so can it have a sound view of the importance of beneficence in human life.

C. Creativity and beneficence

In Section II, I argued that although a good person must be beneficent in her attitudes and habitual actions, large-scale beneficence is morally optional. Moreover, if we choose to exercise large-scale beneficence, it is optional which cause we choose to support—and it is far from obvious that the cause Singer and Unger support is the most worthwhile. For example, saving children from certain death in poor African villages simply to enable them to live a few more years, regardless of the quality of those years, is not obviously better than giving hope to a prisoner of conscience in an African despot's jail. Indeed, on grounds of quality of life, as well as of admiration for courage and justice, the latter is a far

---

[68] Singer, quoted in Bailey, "The Pursuit of Happiness."
[69] Ibid.

worthier object of our beneficence than the former. Again, giving time or money to bring hope to a prisoner of conscience in an African despot's jail is not obviously better than giving it to defend the victims of unjust takings here in the United States.[70] Indeed, on grounds of results and special responsibilities to fellow citizens, the latter is better. However, giving our time or money to defend victims of unjust takings in the United States is not obviously better than giving it to support organizations that spread ideas of economic, political, and civil freedom in the U.S. and abroad, thereby helping to protect or promote the conditions for prosperity.[71] Finally, giving our time or money to support organizations that spread ideas of freedom is not obviously better than investing it to create worthwhile enterprises that employ people in our own country or abroad, thereby bringing about the self-reliance that is the ultimate goal of beneficence.

This last example is of a profit-making project whose motive and aim is mutual benefit, not charity. It is, however, at least as worthy as any project of beneficence, for like the latter, a worthwhile business project protects, promotes, or expresses something important in human life, something that plays an enabling or constitutive role in human happiness. Moreover, for a variety of reasons, genuine beneficence must recognize the importance of wealth-creation in human life.

To begin with the last point: Consider, first, that beneficence not only depends upon the creation of wealth, it aims at creating or restoring the conditions that enable its beneficiaries to become, so far as they are able, self-sufficient creators themselves—creators of wealth and of meaningful and enjoyable lives. Hence, genuine beneficence implies an appreciation of the role in human happiness of the ability to create wealth in all its forms, material, intellectual, and artistic, as well as to enjoy the wealth one creates. Someone who gives vast quantities of cash to aid organizations, or spends hours doing volunteer work for them, but cares little about the role of creating and enjoying wealth in human happiness, may well be self-sacrificial, but he is not beneficent, not even if he is filled with compassion for the poor.

By contrast, a highly creative person who lives justly and honestly, plays no role in the perpetuation of poverty or suffering, invests all his

[70] The not-for-profit Institute of Justice in Washington, DC, defends victims of eminent domain abuse as well as victims of regulations that benefit established businesses at the expense of new entrants or would-be entrants into the field.

[71] In the absence of these conditions, no amount of humanitarian or development aid can do much good and, indeed, has often done much harm. See, in particular, *World Development Report 2005* and other sources cited in note 9 above.

The organizations I have in mind include the Cato Institute, which has held several conferences on limited government, free trade, and the rule of law in China; the Institute for Humane Studies, which offers scholarships and educational seminars in ideas of liberty and the rule of law for students; and Atlas Economic Research Foundation, which provides seed money and technical and intellectual assistance for setting up think-tanks devoted to spreading these ideas in countries from India to Kenya.

resources in the creation of worthwhile enterprises, and engages only in small-scale beneficence, is sufficiently beneficent. Moreover, the life he leads is at least as worthy as, say, the life of someone equally just and honest whose talents or interests lead him to invest some of his resources in (well-administered) large-scale beneficence. For given his talents and interests, the highly creative person is doing the best he can in terms of his own happiness and that of others. What we admire in people like Marie Curie or Burt Rutan is their love of their work as scientists or inventors and businessmen, and the value they seek to create for generations to come. We do not even think to ask if they spent some of their surplus resources on large-scale beneficence, and rightly so. Indeed, it would be a perverse morality that held that Burt Rutan should have given up his vision and invested his time and money not in designing and developing SpaceShipOne (whose utility for poverty relief is dubious) but on charity.[72] Whereas our capacity for beneficence bids us to stretch out a hand to those in need, our capacity for creation bids us to reach for the stars. Both capacities are central to our humanity.

D. Lack of beneficence

What if our resources exceed our ability to use them profitably for our work, needs, and enjoyment, yet we refuse to use them for large-scale beneficence because the thought of giving something for nothing is painful, or at least insufficiently motivating? Clearly, then, we lack the spirit of charity. We look for ways to spend our money on meaningless activities or trifling pleasures. We buy too much and leave it unused or let it go to waste because we already have more than we can enjoy. What we cannot spend we invest in risky, profitless endeavors. Or perhaps we have a lot of time to spare, and are aware of the need for volunteers in some worthwhile endeavor. Nevertheless, ignoring calls for volunteers, we spend our time on gossip or other amusements that mean little or nothing to us in terms of worth or enjoyment. In these cases, our lack of beneficence is coupled with—and may be the result of—greed, an inordinate attachment to our time or possessions which takes the form of wanting to have more than we can really enjoy. A lack of beneficence may also come from miserliness, which leads us to hoard our money, neither investing it nor spending it on anyone, either ourselves or others. Or it may come from an unjustified contempt for or indifference to the needy, a contempt or indifference that fails to recognize the role of luck in human life.

---

[72] SpaceShipOne, the first privately-funded manned spacecraft to reach space, was the winner of the Ansari X-prize in 2004 for twice reaching an altitude of more than 100 kilometers within a week. Burt Rutan's dream is to make space-tourism possible by finding cheaper ways of launching into space. Much of the funding comes from billionaire Paul Allen, the former Microsoft cofounder.

Whatever the explanation for the lack of beneficence, the uncharitable person violates what I will call a neo-Lockean proviso: that we acquire or keep for ourselves and those we love as much, but only as much, as we can use or invest meaningfully or enjoyably, now or in the long run.[73] The uncharitable person wastes her possessions by neither enjoying them nor investing them in any productive way, and shows a lack of regard for others by refusing to give her possessions to those who *could* use them in profitable ways.[74]

In the final analysis, both the creation and proper enjoyment of material, intellectual, and artistic wealth, and the beneficent sharing of this wealth with others, come from love of the world and love of life. Indeed, on a humanistic, naturalistic ethics, as well as on many religious ones, it is hard to conceive of any virtue, either self- or other-regarding, for which such love is not a necessary condition. If this is right, then the uncharitable person, as much as the profligate one, leads a life that is less meaningful, and often less enjoyable, than the beneficent person.

The Singer-Unger thesis, unfortunately, shows little appreciation, if any, for the role of either the creation of wealth or its enjoyment in a good human life; the thesis views wealth-creation entirely as a means to the end of poverty-relief. If we started living as the thesis says we should, it would be bad not only for the givers, but also, as I argue in the next section, for the recipients and for third parties.[75]

V. Disastrous Effects

Let us suppose that we have identified efficacious aid agencies and, in our new commitment to personal austerity, we (that is, most affluent people) decide to forgo that new sophisticated stereo or DVD system with surround sound. Neither counts as a basic need, especially if we already have a radio, TV set, and VCR (and surely even the TV set and VCR are luxuries that we are not justified in replacing after they quit working—all the news that's fit to hear or see is available on radio or online). But those DVD systems (and TV sets and VCRs) are manufactured in Chinese and South Korean factories, employing people who would be thrown out of

---

[73] This neo-Lockean proviso is derived from John Locke's non-waste condition on the acquisition of property: Locke argues that it is wrong to acquire more than one can use before it is destroyed. See John Locke, *Second Treatise of Government* (1698), in *Two Treatises of Government*, 3d ed. (Cambridge: Cambridge University Press, 1988), chap. 5, para. 33.

[74] Of course, wasting or hoarding instead of giving are not the only expressions of a lack of due regard for others. Another is systematically failing to notice occasions for beneficence. It is probably impossible to give a list of necessary and sufficient conditions for lacking beneficence, but it is safe to say that someone who spends money easily for his own pleasures but almost never for beneficent causes is lacking in beneficence.

[75] In "Islands in a Sea of Obligations," Schmidtz imagines the disastrous effects for Western economies if we started following the Singer-Unger thesis; I imagine these effects for the global market and the global poor.

work if we stopped buying DVD systems for the sake of saving the money for prolonging the lives of some poor children in Ethiopia.

We decide to stop going out for expensive dinners. But expensive dinners are often served up by restaurants owned by refugees fleeing from political repression and poverty, including the very Ethiopians whose relatives back in Ethiopia we want to help with our savings (and who are currently repatriating some of their profits to help their relatives at home).

We decide to stop buying expensive, stylish clothes so we can prolong the lives of some children in India or teach Nepalese villagers to become entrepreneurs. But these clothes are tailored by the parents of children in India and China who will join the ranks of those we will then need to help if we stop buying these clothes.[76]

We decide to forgo those beautiful Afghan rugs in order to send the savings to UNICEF for saving the lives of some poor children in Afghanistan. But by doing so we reduce to destitution and dependence a whole village of self-sufficient Afghan families.

Needless to say, my point is not that we should increase our spending on imported goods for the sake of preventing the relatively poor from joining the ranks of the absolutely poor. As my example of the greedy person shows, trying to consume more than we can enjoy or use meaningfully is as much a waste as depriving ourselves of enjoyment or meaning because we think our lives belong to the poor. My point is simply that the alleviation of absolute poverty should not be the single or primary determinant of how to dispose of our resources one way or the other, even if the alleviation of poverty is one of our goals. If we have good reason to spend money on a meal or a rug—if, that is, it is worthwhile in terms of our overall goals and resources—we should not refrain from doing so simply for the sake of sending the money we would thereby save to a charitable organization. Not only is trying to live by this single rule morally arbitrary and bad for us, it would also be bad for the poor and for everyone in between if most people tried to live by it. For doing so would destroy the reciprocal relations of trade and productive cooperation that constitute the global market, and would push into absolute poverty many who are currently self-sufficient thanks to this network of productive relations.

Unger's recommendation that we give away most of our "financially valuable assets" is even more drastic.[77] What this recommendation amounts to is that we give away our very seed corn—the source of our economy's future productivity and, thus, of continued aid for the poor. In "Famine,

---

[76] Many stylish, expensive clothes are manufactured in China or India and, thanks to a 1995 World Trade Organization (WTO) agreement to strike down trade barriers, from 2005 on such clothes are expected to come largely from these two countries. For information on the WTO agreement, see http://www.wto.org/english/tratop_e/texti_e/texintro_e.htm (accessed May 8, 2005).

[77] Unger, *Living High and Letting Die*, 134.

Affluence, and Morality," Singer does consider the possibility that "if we gave away, say, 40 percent of our Gross National Product, we would slow down the economy so much that in absolute terms we would be giving less than if we gave 25 percent of the much larger GNP that we would have if we limited our contribution to this smaller percentage."[78] However, he does not consider the possibility that slowing down our economy might also slow down the global economy that produces much of the wealth in poor countries. Nor does his hesitation here prevent him from stating again in a later article that those earning annual incomes of $50,000 to $100,000 ought to give away 40 to 70 percent of their income, respectively, because their basic needs can be met with $30,000.[79] This recommendation to consume—or have the poor consume—our seed corn is the unsurprising result of an ethics that advocates the profligate giving away of wealth to prolong lives, while failing to appreciate what makes life worth living.

VI. Conclusion

I have argued that the so-called analogy that Singer and Unger invoke to support their thesis does not really support it, because it is not really an analogy. If, however, we accept the analogy, it proves too much, so that the alleviation of poverty becomes only one of many worthy causes an individual may choose to support with her time or money. I also make four moral objections to the Singer-Unger thesis. First, it is monomaniacal. A good person must be beneficent, but beneficence need not take the form of large contributions of time or money to aid agencies for the prevention or relief of absolute poverty—or, for that matter, of *any* great evil. The world offers a rich variety of values that can make a life morally worthy. Second, if taken seriously, the self-sacrificial ideal that Singer and Unger advocate is deeply misanthropic, because (with rare exceptions) it is incompatible with that which makes life worth living: the pursuit of happiness. Third, because trying to live by this ideal is incompatible with the pursuit of happiness, yet most of us feel entitled to our happiness, the endorsement of this ideal is incompatible with integrity. The Singer-Unger ideal manifests the same flaw that all ideals of universal love have manifested: it refuses to accept that our moral ideals must be based on certain fundamental facts of human nature. Accordingly, the Singer-Unger ideal also devalues the importance of creativity in human life. Fourth, even if the activities of aid agencies for poverty relief or prevention were in themselves beneficial overall—and this premise is disputable—if most of us did start living by the Singer-Unger ideal, the effects of giving away all our "spare" money instead of investing it or

[78] Singer, "Famine," 7.
[79] Singer, "Singer Solution to World Poverty."

spending it in ways that make our lives meaningful and enjoyable would be disastrous for the global economy, pushing into poverty many who are currently self-sufficient thanks to this productive economy.

The Singer-Unger ideal advocates not the virtue of beneficence, but the vice of profligacy. A proper understanding of beneficence implies an understanding of the role of wealth-creation in human life and happiness, and the role of happiness in making life worth living; for beneficence itself aims, as far as possible, to create or restore the conditions that will enable its recipients to lead meaningful and enjoyable lives as creators of wealth.

Philosophy, University of Oklahoma

RESPONSIBILITY AND GLOBAL JUSTICE: A SOCIAL CONNECTION MODEL*

By Iris Marion Young

I. Introduction

In this essay, I clarify the status of claims about global justice and injustice that are increasingly voiced and accepted in our world. Such claims present a problem for political philosophy because until recently most philosophical approaches to justice assumed that obligations of justice hold only between those living under a common constitution within a single political community. I will argue that obligations of justice arise between persons by virtue of the social processes that connect them; political institutions are the response to these obligations rather than their basis. I develop an account of some of these social processes as structural processes, and I argue that some harms come to people as a result of structural social injustice. Claims that obligations of justice extend globally for some issues, then, are grounded in the fact that some structural social processes connect people across the world without regard to political boundaries.

The second and more central project of this essay is to theorize about the responsibilities moral agents may be said to have in relation to such global social processes. How ought moral agents, whether individual or institutional, conceptualize their responsibilities in relation to global injustice? I propose a model of responsibility based on social connection as an interpretation of obligations of justice arising from structural social processes. I begin, in Section II, with an examination of various views on the extent of obligations of justice. In Section III, I turn to a discussion of justice in the transnational processes of production, distribution, and marketing of clothing, which I use as an example to illustrate the operations of structural social processes that extend widely across regions of the world.[1]

The "social connection model" of responsibility says that all agents who contribute by their actions to the structural processes that produce

* Thanks to David Alexander, Daniel Drezner, David Owen, and Ellen Frankel Paul for comments on an earlier version of this essay. Thanks to David Newstone for research assistance.
[1] I have begun analysis of global labor justice, focusing on the anti-sweatshop movement, in two previous papers: Iris Young, "From Guilt to Solidarity: Sweatshops and Political Responsibility," in *Dissent*, Spring 2003: 39–45; and Iris Marion Young, "Responsibility and Global Labor Justice," *Journal of Political Philosophy* 12, no. 4 (2004): 365–88.

injustice have responsibilities to work to remedy these injustices. I discuss the notion of "structural injustice" in Section IV. In Section V, I distinguish the social connection model from a more standard model of responsibility, which I call a "liability model." I specify five features of the social connection model of responsibility that distinguish it from the liability model: it does not isolate perpetrators; it judges background conditions of action; it is more forward-looking than backward-looking; its responsibility is essentially shared; and it can be discharged only through collective action. In Section VI, I sketch four parameters of reasoning that agents can use for thinking about their own action in relation to structural injustice.

II. GLOBAL CONNECTIONS AND OBLIGATIONS OF JUSTICE

A widely accepted philosophical view continues to hold that the scope of obligations of justice is defined by membership in a common political community. On this account, people have obligations of justice only to other people with whom they live together under a common constitution, or whom they recognize as belonging to the same nation as themselves. In all of his writing on justice, for example, John Rawls assumes that the scope of those who have obligations of justice to one another is a single relatively closed society.[2] The members of each such society are mutually bound by obligations of justice they do not have to outsiders. This is not to say that insiders have no moral obligations to outsiders. There are some moral obligations that human beings have to one another as human; these are cosmopolitan obligations or obligations to respect human rights. In *The Law of Peoples*, Rawls reiterates that principles of justice as fairness mutually oblige the members of a given society to one another, yet do not apply to the moral relationships among people belonging to different societies across the globe. The law of peoples—which does apply across societies—is broader and thinner than justice as fairness.[3]

Philosopher David Miller also conceives principles of justice as having in their scope only relations among those persons who dwell together within the same nation-state. Obligations to organize coercive institutions to ensure distributive fairness according to need, desert, and equal respect obtain only between persons who belong together in the same nation-state and who live under a single political constitution.[4] Miller worries that a globalizing world is making state sovereignty more porous and liable to being affected by and affecting persons and circumstances outside these nation-state borders. He concludes from this undeniable fact

[2] John Rawls, *A Theory of Justice* (Cambridge, MA: Harvard University Press, 1971/1999), 7–8.

[3] John Rawls, *The Law of Peoples* (Cambridge, MA: Harvard University Press, 1999), sec. 1, pp. 11–22.

[4] David Miller, *On Nationality* (Oxford: Oxford University Press, 1995).

not that principles of justice should follow these globalizing trends, but rather that social justice itself may be a historically specific idea and set of practices whose time is past.[5]

As I understand the logic of this position, it holds that obligations of justice presuppose the existence of shared political institutions. It is incoherent to say that relationships between people are unjust or just, on this interpretation, in the absence of shared institutions for adjudicating such claims or regulating people's relations. Some more general and less stringent obligations obtain between persons across political jurisdictions just because they are human, but these are not obligations of justice.

A contrary position about moral obligation is one that I will call the "cosmopolitan-utilitarian model." On this view, nation-state membership or any other sort of particularist relationship among persons is irrelevant to assessing the nature, depth, or scope of obligations they have to one another. Moral agents have identical obligations to all human beings and perhaps to some nonhuman creatures. There is a moral imperative to minimize suffering, wherever it occurs. Every agent is obliged to do what he or she can to minimize suffering everywhere, right up to the point where he or she begins to suffer. Membership in a political order, either on the part of the agent or the sufferers, is relevant only instrumentally as providing efficient means of discharging obligations and distributing particular tasks. Much about global relationships, however, can override this issue of convenience. Peter Singer and Peter Unger are two prominent examples of theorists who hold this view.[6]

I think that each of these accounts is wanting. Critics of the cosmopolitan-utilitarian model argue that it is too demanding.[7] It flies in the face of moral intuition, moreover, to suggest that all moral agents have exactly the same duties to all other agents and no special obligations to some subset of persons with whom an agent has a special relationship. While the basic moral respect owed to all persons grounds the cosmopolitan obligations that Immanuel Kant calls hospitality,[8] obligations of justice require more and are based on more than common humanity.

Nevertheless, critics of the position that limits the scope of obligations of justice to members of a common political order are right to argue that it is arbitrary to consider nation-state membership as a source of obligations of justice. Political communities have evolved in contingent and

---

[5] David Miller, *Principles of Social Justice* (Cambridge, MA: Harvard University Press, 1999), chap. 1.

[6] See Peter Singer, *Practical Ethics* (Cambridge: Cambridge University Press, 1993), chaps. 2 and 9; and Peter Unger, *Living High and Letting Die: Our Illusion of Innocence* (New York: Oxford University Press, 1996).

[7] See, for example, Samuel Scheffler, *Boundaries and Allegiances: Problems of Responsibility and Justice in Liberal Thought* (Oxford: Oxford University Press, 2001); and Neera K. Badhwar, "International Aid: When Giving Becomes a Vice," elsewhere in this volume.

[8] Immanuel Kant, "To Perpetual Peace: A Philosophical Sketch" (1795), in Ted Humphrey, trans., *Perpetual Peace and Other Essays* (Indianapolis: Hackett Publishing, 1983), 107–44.

arbitrary ways that are more connected to power than to moral right. People often stand in dense relationships with others prior to, apart from, or outside political communities. These relationships may be such that people's actions affect one another in ways that tend to produce conflict. Or people may cooperate with numbers of others in ongoing practices and institutions that meet some shared objectives. In such social relations, we expect fair terms of conflict-resolution and cooperation. Thus, in contrast with the cosmopolitan-utilitarian position, I believe that some account needs to be offered of the nature of social relationships that ground claims that people have obligations of justice to one another. It is not enough to say that the others are human.

The nation-state position, however, makes prior what is posterior from a moral point of view. Ontologically and morally, though not necessarily temporally, social connection is prior to political institutions. This is the great insight of social contract theory. The social connections of civil society may well exist without political institutions to govern them. A society consists in connected or mutually influencing institutions and practices through which people enact their projects and seek their happiness, and in doing so affect the conditions under which others act, often profoundly. A social contract theory like that of John Locke argues that the need and desire for political institutions arises because socially connected persons with multiple and sometimes conflicting institutional commitments recognize that their relationships are liable to conflict and inequalities of power that can lead to mistrust, violence, exploitation, and domination. The moral status of political institutions arises from the obligations of justice generated by social connection: such institutions are instruments through which these obligations can be discharged.

In his landmark work *Political Theory and International Relations,* Charles Beitz challenged Rawls's assumption that the scope of obligations of justice extends only among members of a single political community by arguing that there exists an international *society* even in the absence of a comprehensive political constitution to regulate it. Ongoing economic processes of production, investment, and trade connect people in diverse regions of the world, and these relationships are often unequal in power and material resources. People move across borders, and institutions of expression and communication are increasingly global in their reach. The activities of many religious, artistic, scientific, legal, and service-providing institutions and networks extend to many parts of the world without too much regard for nation-state membership and boundaries. Beitz concludes that principles of justice like those Rawls argues for apply globally because there are dense global social and economic relationships.[9] A need for political institutions wide enough in scope and sufficiently strong to

---

[9] Charles Beitz, *Political Theory and International Relations* (Princeton, NJ: Princeton University Press, 1979).

regulate these relationships to insure their fairness *follows from* the global scope of obligations of justice, rather than *grounding* those obligations.

Onora O'Neill argues somewhat differently to reach a similar conclusion. The scope of an agent's moral obligation extends to all those whom the agent assumes in conducting her or his activity. Each of us pursues our interests and goals within the frame of specific institutions and practices, and within which we know others do the same. Our actions are partly based on the actions of others, insofar as we depend on them to carry out certain tasks, and/or insofar as our general knowledge of what other people are doing enables us to formulate expectations and predictions about events and institutional outcomes that affect us or condition our actions. In today's world of globalized markets, interdependent states, and rapid and dense communication, the scope of the actors we implicitly assume in many of our actions is often global. The social relations that connect us to others are not restricted to nation-state borders. Our actions are conditioned by and contribute to institutions that affect distant others, and their actions contribute to the operation of institutions that affect us. Because our actions assume these others as a condition for our own actions, O'Neill argues, we have made practical moral commitments to them by virtue of our actions. That is, even when we are not conscious of or when we actively deny a moral relationship to these other people, to the extent that our actions depend on the assumption that distant others are doing certain things, we have obligations of justice in relation to them.

It is not possible to trace how each person's actions produce specific effects on others because there are too many mediating actions and events. Nevertheless, we have obligations to those who condition and enable our own actions, as they do to us. O'Neill argues, however, that there is an asymmetry in these obligations insofar as some people are rendered more vulnerable to coercion, domination, or deprivation by the institutional relations. While everyone in the system of structural and institutional relations stands in circumstances of justice that give them obligations with respect to all the others, those institutionally and materially situated to be able to do more to affect the conditions of vulnerability have greater obligations.[10]

I interpret both Beitz and O'Neill, along with other theorists of global justice such as Thomas Pogge,[11] as describing transnational social *structures*, and I interpret the injustices they may generate as structural injustices. Allen Buchanan similarly argues that there exists a global basic structure that generates obligations of justice between people across

---

[10] Onora O'Neill, *Faces of Hunger* (London: Allen and Unwin, 1985); Onora O'Neill, *Toward Justice and Virtue* (Cambridge: Cambridge University Press, 1996), chap. 4. Cf. Robert Goodin, *Protecting the Vulnerable* (Chicago: University of Chicago Press, 1985); and Thomas Pogge, *World Poverty and Human Rights* (Cambridge: Polity Press, 2002), esp. chaps. 1, 2, and 4.

[11] See Pogge, *World Poverty and Human Rights*.

national boundaries.[12] Before I conceptualize structural injustice and introduce the concept of responsibility that corresponds to it, however, let me elaborate a particular example of claims about injustice as involving transnational social connection: namely, the anti-sweatshop movement.

III. Example of Global Injustice: Sweatshops

Although I believe that the social connection model of responsibility applies to every case of structural injustice, whether local or global, relationships in the global apparel industry offer a perspicuous example through which I will explain the logic of the social connection model. A vocal and multilayered anti-sweatshop movement, moreover, has in recent years pressed claims on a variety of agents to take responsibility for sweatshop conditions.

Anti-sweatshop activists have made claims on institutions that purchase clothing in bulk, such as city governments,[13] or that market clothing bearing their name or logo, such as universities,[14] to take responsibility for the poor conditions under which these garments are produced, often in factories on the other side of the world. Social movement activists have also passed out leaflets in front of brand-name apparel stores such as the Gap or Nike or Disney, or more generic clothing retailers such as Target and Wal-Mart, explaining that much of the clothing sold in those stores is made under sweatshop conditions, and calling upon consumers to take responsibility for those conditions.

Not a few institutions and individuals find absurd the idea that consumers and retailers bear responsibility for working conditions in faraway factories, often in other countries. Not unreasonably, they say that even if the workers producing the items they buy suffer wrongful exploitation and injustice, we here have nothing to do with it. It is, rather, the owners and managers of the factories who are to blame. Despite the apparent reasonableness of this dissociation, the claims of the anti-sweatshop movement seem to have struck a chord with many individuals and institutions. I think that to understand why this is so, we need a conception of responsibility different from the standard notion of blame or liability.

---

[12] Allen Buchanan, "Rawls's Law of Peoples: Rules for a Vanished Westphalian World," *Ethics* 110, no. 4 (2000): 697–721; Allen Buchanan, *Justice, Legitimacy, and Self-Determination: Moral Foundations for International Law* (Oxford: Oxford University Press, 2004), esp. 83 and 84.

[13] In April 2003, for example, the Milwaukee Common Council voted unanimously for an ordinance requiring the procurement of apparel for city staff from manufacturers that meet several labor-rights conditions; see "Sweatfree Communities Gain Ground," Campaign for Labor Rights, http://www.clrlabor.org.

[14] Lisa Featherstone, *Students against Sweatshops* (London: Verso, 2000); Mischa Gaus, "The Maturing Movement against Sweatshops," *In These Times*, February 16, 2004: 34 and 52.

What, then, are "sweatshops"? Many of the articles of clothing, shoes, and other small consumer items whose production is labor-intensive are produced in relatively small manufacturing centers in less-developed countries, manufacturing centers that operate at the bottom of a chain of specification, distribution, and marketing that often involves hundreds of distinct companies. Research on the global apparel industry has brought to light that sweatshops abound in North America and Europe.[15] The vast majority of sweatshops, however, operate in less-developed countries. Among the merchandise purchased in the United States in 2000, 85 percent of footwear and 50 percent of apparel was imported.[16]

Conditions in such manufacturing facilities vary of course, but the following are typical. The vast majority of workers are female, and often as young as thirteen or fourteen. They are often treated in dominative and abusive ways by bosses, and sexual harassment is common. Typically, they work ten- to sixteen-hour days in peak seasons; if the manufacturer is behind on an order, the workers may be forced to work through the night. They have few bathroom breaks or other opportunities for rest during their long working day. Sick leave or vacation time are generally unavailable; a worker too ill to work is often fired. Violations of the most basic health and safety standards are normal. Factories are often excessively hot with no ventilation, insufficient lighting, excessive noise, little fire-fighting equipment, blocked exits, poor sanitation, unhygienic canteens and bathrooms, and no access to clean drinking water. Typically, workers in these facilities have no freedom to organize unions to bargain collectively with their employers. Workers who complain and try to organize are typically threatened, fired, blacklisted, beaten, and even killed. Local governments often actively or passively support such anti-union activity.[17]

There should be little doubt that conditions such as these violate basic human rights. Many international agreements and conventions prohibit violence and intimidation in the workplace (as elsewhere) and stipulate that workers should not labor under conditions that threaten their basic health and physical safety. The meaning of such rights, moreover, ought to vary little with local culture or level of industrial development. Exhaustion and the need to use the bathroom are cross-cultural experiences. The right to assemble and organize ought to be recognized everywhere, and it is everywhere wrong to intimidate and beat people who try to exercise

[15] See Peter Kwong, "Forbidden Workers and the U.S. Labor Movement," *Critical Asian Studies* 31, no. 1 (2002): 69–88; and Edna Bonacich and Richard P. Appelbaum, *Behind the Label: Inequality in the Los Angeles Apparel Industry* (Berkeley: University of California Press, 2002).

[16] See Kimberly Ann Elliott and Richard B. Freeman, *Can Labor Standards Improve under Globalization?* (Washington, DC: Institute for International Economics, 2004), 55.

[17] For an account of working conditions, see Ellen Israel Rosen, *Making Sweatshops: The Globalization of the U.S. Apparel Industry* (Berkeley: University of California Press, 2002), chap. 2; and Naomi Klein, *No Logo* (New York: Picador, 1999), esp. chap. 9.

this right. To say that these are rights is to say precisely that there is no valid moral argument for trading them off against profits, or policies designed to foster economic growth, or the earnings of the workers. If many workers endure these violations without complaint because they desperately need those earnings, this is a measure of the coercive pressures of their circumstances rather than of their consent.

But what of their earnings? Economists argue that wage levels for the same kind of work appropriately vary with the local cost of living and labor market conditions, and they are right. Those who argue that the standard of living for workers in sweatshops is often higher than in the countryside from which many of them have moved may be correct. The wage levels of workers in the apparel industry are nevertheless often far below the legal minimum wage.[18] Employers too often renege, moreover, in paying even these meager wages.[19] The workers generally have no recourse when employers underpay them, because they often have no formal employment contracts, and the employers keep poor records or no records of the hours employees have worked. It may be true that under normal market conditions a rise in wages for some workers will mean a loss of jobs for others; where the wages of a massive number of workers are below subsistence level, as they often are, this is more an argument against accepting normal market conditions than against paying living wages.

Thus far, I have cited typical conditions for garment workers in factories. A significant portion of the people who put garments together, however, work from their homes. Employers often prefer contracting out to homeworkers because then the employers do not have to pay for facilities and overhead and they are not legally responsible for working conditions. Workers, especially women workers, often prefer home work to factory work even when it pays less, because they can avoid long and potentially harassing travels to work, can stay with their children, and can save face for their husbands, who can pretend that their wives are not working.[20] Homeworkers are often the poorest paid, however, and work the longest self-imposed hours. The children or old people with whom the worker wants to stay home, moreover, are often enlisted to help with the work.[21]

---

[18] Most of the countries in which factories such as those I am describing operate do have minimum wage laws, as well as regulation of other labor conditions. In many cases, these laws could be more comprehensive and stronger, of course. For a comprehensive country-by-country survey of labor regulation, see the Industrial Labor Organization, http://www.ilo.org. The primary problem with labor regulation in much of the world, however, including arguably the United States, is lack of enforcement rather than lack of standards.

[19] See Women Working Worldwide, "Garment Industry Subcontracting and Workers' Rights," http://www.cleanclothes.org.

[20] See Saba Gul Khattak, "Subcontracted Work and Gender Relations: The Case of Pakistan," in Radhika Balakrishnan, ed., The Hidden Assembly Line: Gender Dynamics of Subcontracted Work in a Global Economy (Bloomfield, CT: Kumarian Press, 2002), 35–62.

[21] Andrew Ross, Low Pay, High Profile: The Global Push for Fair Labor (New York: The New Press, 2004), esp. chap. 2.

The subject of this essay is responsibility in relation to injustice. The structure of the global apparel industry diffuses responsibility for sweat-shop conditions. Big-name retailers in North America or Europe rarely themselves own and operate factories in which clothes made to their order are manufactured. Instead, there is a complex chain of production and distribution involving dozens or thousands of contractually distinct entities that bring the clothes manufactured in one place to the stores in which people buy them. In this system, each of the links in the chain believes itself to be operating close to the margin in a highly competitive environment, and usually is under heavy pressure to meet orders at low cost by firms higher up the chain. The firms higher up the chain, however, often have no legal responsibility for the policies and operations of the firms below with which they contract.

Facilities where garments and other items are manufactured are typically small. Their activities are difficult to regulate or monitor because their operations frequently shut down in one place and open up in another. The export processing zone policies of many developing countries encourage investment in such firms and generally turn a blind eye to the extent to which the firms comply with local labor laws.

In their book *Can Labor Standards Improve under Globalization?*, Kimberly Elliott and Richard Freeman describe the structure of one U.S. retailer, J.C. Penney, and its subcontracting relations in one developing country, the Philippines. J.C. Penney purchases finished goods through a U.S. importer, Renzo. Renzo conveys J.C. Penney's specifications to Robillard Resources, a Philippino exporter, which contracts with a Philippino clothing contractor that organizes a production chain that includes numerous subcontracting factories. These subcontractors, in turn, not only organize and supervise factory production of apparel parts, but also organize a system of contracting out to workers in their homes.[22] According to Elliott and Freeman, J.C. Penney alone contracts with over two thousand suppliers in more than eighty countries. Nordstrom has over fifty thousand contractors and subcontractors, and Disney licenses products in over thirty thousand factories around the world.

Another aspect of the structure of this industry that is relevant for issues of assigning responsibility has to do with the way that the positions of employer and employee are often blurred in this system. In some factories, production line leaders act as subcontracting agents for homeworkers, with the permission and assistance of management. Line workers and homeworkers rarely receive written contracts; they are encouraged to think of themselves as "self-employed."[23]

---

[22] Elliott and Freeman, *Can Labor Standards Improve under Globalization?*, 50–54.

[23] Elisabeth Prugl and Irene Tinker, "Microentrepreneurs and Homeworkers: Convergent Categories," *World Development* 25, no. 9 (1997): 1471–82; Women Working Worldwide, "Garment Industry Subcontracting and Workers' Rights."

In this complex system of production and distribution, the workers who make garments are at the bottom of the chain. The wages they earn generally amount to a small portion of the retail price of an item, often under 6 percent.[24] Each layer of subcontracting that runs between the manufacturer and the store in which the consumer buys the finished items adds to the cost of items. Major logo retailers usually make handsome profits from this system; as one moves down the chain of production and distribution, firms operate in more competitive environments. Small subcontractors in developing countries frequently operate right at the edge of solvency.

Anti-sweatshop activists argue that the workers at the bottom of this system suffer injustice in the form of domination, coercion, and need-deprivation within a global system of vast inequalities. Because of the complexity of the system that brings items from production to sale, and the manner in which the system constrains the options of many of the actors within it, this is an example of *structural* injustice.[25] I will now articulate that concept more generally.

IV. Structural Injustice

In *A Theory of Justice*, John Rawls says that the subject of justice is the basic structure of society, which concerns "the way in which the major social institutions distribute fundamental rights and duties and determine the division of advantages from social cooperation."[26] Major institutions, on his view, include the legal system's definition of basic rights and duties, market relations, the system of property in the means of production, and family organization. To these I would add the basic kinds of positions in the social division of labor.

Rawls says little more about what the concept of structure refers to, however. Social theorists use the term in many ways, and I will not review them here.[27] As I understand the concept, structures denote the confluence of institutional rules and interactive routines, mobilization of resources, as well as physical structures such as buildings and roads.

---

[24] See John Miller, "Why Economists Are Wrong about Sweatshops and the Antisweatshop Movement," *Challenge* 46, no. 1 (2003): 93–122; see also Robert Pollin, Justine Burns, and James Heintz, "Global Apparel Production and Sweatshop Labour: Can Raising Retail Prices Finance Living Wages?" *Cambridge Journal of Economics* 28 (2004): 153–71.

[25] In previous work, I have begun developing an account of structural injustice. See Iris Marion Young, "Equality of Whom? Social Groups and Judgments of Injustice," *Journal of Political Philosophy* 9, no. 1 (2001): 1–18; Young, *Inclusion and Democracy* (Oxford: Oxford University Press, 2000), esp. chap. 3; and Young, "Lived Body vs. Gender: Reflections on Social Structure and Subjectivity," *Ratio: An International Journal of Analytic Philosophy* 15, no. 4 (2002): 411–28.

[26] Rawls, *A Theory of Justice*, 7.

[27] For one catalog of uses by English language theorists through the mid-1970s, see Peter M. Blau, "Introduction: Parallels and Contrasts in Structural Inquiries," in Peter M. Blau, ed., *Approaches to the Study of Social Structure* (New York: The Free Press, 1975), 1–20.

These constitute the historical givens in relation to which individuals act, and which are relatively stable over time. Social structures serve as background conditions for individual actions by presenting actors with options; they provide "channels" that both enable action and constrain it.[28]

I will build an account of structure and structural processes using elements derived from several theorists. Sociologist Peter Blau offers the following definition: "A social structure can be defined as a multidimensional space of differentiated social positions among which a population is distributed. The social associations of people provide both the criterion for distinguishing social positions and the connections among them that make them elements of a single social structure."[29] Blau exploits the spatial metaphor implied by the concept of structure. Individual people occupy varying *positions* in the social space, and their positions stand in determinate relations to other positions. Although social theorist Pierre Bourdieu uses very different language and concepts for theorizing social structures, he too begins from a spatial metaphor. He conceives structures as "fields" on which individuals stand in varying positions in relation to one another, offering possibilities for interpretation and action.[30]

The "structure" in social structures consists in the connections among these positions and their relationships, and the way the attributes of positions internally constitute one another through those relationships. Young unskilled workers who migrate from the countryside to the city, or from one country to another, stand in a certain structural class position in relation to the small entrepreneurs who employ them for apparel manufacture. The entrepreneurs, in turn, stand in structural positions in relation to investors in large exporting firms and executives in the multinational corporations whose labels the clothes sport. The workers and potential workers also occupy particular gendered positions in relations to their employers; their positions may also be structured by racial or ethnic differences that render them vulnerable to exclusion or discrimination. These differing structural positions offer differing and unequal opportunities and potential benefits to their occupants, and their relations are such that constrained opportunities and minimal benefits for some often correlate with wider opportunities and greater benefits for others.

It is misleading, however, to reify the metaphor of structure, to think of social structures as entities independent of social actors, lying passively around them and easing or inhibiting their movement. On the contrary, a social structure exists only in the action and interaction of persons; it exists not as a state, but as a process. Anthony Giddens calls this process "structuration." He defines social structures in terms of "rules and

---

[28] Jeffrey Reiman, among others, uses this channel metaphor. See Jeffrey Reiman, *Justice and Modern Moral Philosophy* (New Haven, CT: Yale University Press, 1989), 213.

[29] Peter M. Blau, *Inequality and Heterogeneity* (New York: The Free Press, 1977), 4.

[30] Pierre Bourdieu, *The Logic of Practice* (Stanford, CA: Stanford University Press, 1980), book 1.

resources, recursively implicated in the reproduction of social systems."[31] In the idea of the duality of structure, Giddens theorizes how people act on the basis of their knowledge of preexisting structures and in so acting reproduce those structures. People do so because they act according to rules and expectations and because their relationally constituted positions make or do not make certain resources available to them.

Much about the dynamics of the apparel industry, for example, presupposes practices of fashion. Consumers, especially affluent consumers in the developed world with disposable income, often want to be stylish, and look to friends and media stars to determine what stylish means and whether it is changing. They often "need" new clothes even when those they own are in fine shape. Major retailers both follow the trends of fashion and try to manipulate them. Ideas of what is fashionable, as well as conventions of clothes marketed for different "seasons" during the year, drive much about the size of orders and the speed with which they are expected to be delivered, which constrain manufacturers and lead them to overwork workers. Most of these people act as though fashion is some kind of natural force, when in fact its constraints are produced by the ideas that people have about it and the actions they take presuming those ideas.

Defining structures in terms of the rules and resources brought to actions and interactions, however, makes the emergence of structures sound too much like the product of individual and intentional action. The concept of social structure must also include conditions under which actors act, a collective outcome of action which is often impressed onto the physical environment. Jean-Paul Sartre calls this aspect of social structuration the *practico-inert.*[32] Most of the conditions under which people act are sociohistorical: they are the products of previous actions, usually products of many coordinated and uncoordinated but mutually influencing actions. Those collective actions have left determinate effects on the physical and cultural environment, effects that condition future action in specific ways. The gradual consolidation of land holdings by large firms has left many peasants with poor land or no land from which they can eke out subsistence. Thus, many of them move in search of work, erecting shanty towns at the edges of cities. The export processing zones many governments have established, where some of these migrants find work, are consequences of a history of structural adjustment programs that many indebted governments have been pressured to implement by international financial institutions. The background conditions of the lives of these young workers today are structural consequences of decisions and aggregated economic processes beginning more than three decades ago.

---

[31] Anthony Giddens, *The Constitution of Society* (Berkeley: University of California Press, 1984), 25.

[32] Jean-Paul Sartre, *Critique of Dialectical Reason,* trans. Alan Sheridan-Smith (London: New Left Books, 1976), book 1, chap. 3.

This leads us to a final aspect of the concept of social structure. It is not merely the case that the actions and interactions of differently positioned persons, drawing on the rules and resources the structures offer, take place on the basis of past actions whose collective effects mark the physical conditions of action; these actions and interactions also often have future effects beyond the immediate purposes and intentions of the actors. Structured social action and interaction often have collective results that no one intends, results that may even be counter to the best intentions of the actors. Sartre calls such effects "counter-finalities."[33] When a large number of investors make a speculative run on currencies in anticipation of their devaluation, for example, they often unintentionally but predictably produce a financial crisis that throws some people out of work and ruins the fortunes of others.[34]

Structural injustice exists when social processes put large categories of persons under a systematic threat of domination or deprivation of the means to develop and exercise their capacities, at the same time as these processes enable others to dominate or have a wide range of opportunities for developing and exercising their capacities. Structural injustice is a kind of moral wrong distinct from the wrongful action of an individual agent or the willfully repressive policies of a state. Structural injustice occurs as a consequence of many individuals and institutions acting in pursuit of their particular goals and interests, within given institutional rules and accepted norms. All the persons who participate by their actions in the ongoing schemes of cooperation that constitute these structures are responsible for them, in the sense that they are part of the process that causes them. They are not responsible, however, in the sense of having directed the process or intended its outcomes.

Persons stand in systematically different and unequal social positions due to the way institutions operate together. Rather than being a static condition, these factors that constrain and enable individual possibilities are ongoing processes in which many actors participate. These constraints and enablements occur not only by means of institutional rules and norms enforced by sanctions, but by means of incentive structures that make some courses of action particularly attractive and carry little cost for some people, or make other courses of action particularly costly for others. The injustice does not consist in the bare fact that structures constrain actors, for all social structures constrain as well as enable. Rather, the injustice consists in the *way* they constrain and enable, and how these constraints and enablements expand or contract individuals' opportunities. The institutional rules, resources, and practices through which people act do not constitute, in Rawls's phrase, fair terms of cooperation.

---

[33] Ibid., 277–92.
[34] See Joseph E. Stiglitz, *Globalization and Its Discontents* (New York: W. W. Norton, 2002), chap. 4.

When consumers who take flyers from activists in front of Disney stores react to information about sweatshop working conditions with shock or outrage, they are implicitly making a judgment of injustice. They make the judgment that the workers do not merely suffer misfortune, as though a hurricane had carried away their houses, but that the suffering is socially caused. Somebody, we are inclined to say, ought to do something about this. To make the judgment that poor working conditions are unjust implies that somebody *bears responsibility* for these working conditions and for their improvement. If the injustice has causes rooted in social structures, however, then it would seem that all those who participate in producing and reproducing the structures are implicated in that responsibility. When we say an injustice such as working to exhaustion is structural, we are saying that the workers are not simply victims of mean bosses, although this may be true. Identification of the wrongs that individual actors perpetrate toward them needs to be supplemented with an account of how macro-social processes encourage such wrongs, and why they are widespread and repeated. My question is: How shall we conceptualize responsibility for producing and rectifying structural injustice?

This question presents a puzzle, I suggest, because standard models of responsibility in moral and legal theory do not supply a satisfactory answer. Standard conceptions of legal and moral responsibility appear to require that we trace a direct relationship between the action of an identifiable person or group and a harm. Although structural processes that produce injustice result from the actions of many persons and the policies of many organizations, in most cases it is not possible to trace which specific actions of which specific agents cause which specific parts of the structural processes or their outcomes. In what follows, I offer some steps toward a solution to this puzzle by means of a concept of responsibility in relation to injustice that differs from standard models of moral and legal responsibility. A "social connection model" of responsibility, as I call it, better conceptualizes moral and political issues of responsibility in relation to transnational structural injustice than does what I will call a "liability model" of responsibility.

V. Two Models of Responsibility: Liability and Social Connection

Journalists, religious leaders, social movement activists, and philosophers today sometimes make claims that people in relatively free and affluent countries such as the United States, Canada, or Germany have responsibilities in relation to the harms and deprivations experienced by millions of people in the less-developed world. The claims of the anti-sweatshop movement are one concrete example of such claims and have been relatively successful in getting a hearing and motivating action. To make sense of such claims, I suggest, we need a conception of responsibility different from the most common conception, the liability model. In this section, I offer some elements of a conception of responsibility that, I argue, derives from connection to structural social processes that produce injustice. I explicate this social connection model of responsibility by contrasting it with the liability model.

A. The liability model

The most common model of assigning responsibility derives from legal reasoning employed to establish guilt or fault for a harm. Under this liability model, one assigns responsibility to a particular agent (or agents) whose actions can be shown to be causally connected to the circumstances for which responsibility is sought. This agent can be a collective entity, such as a corporation, but when it is, the analysis treats that entity as a single agent for the purposes of assigning responsibility.[35] The actions found to be causally connected to the circumstances are shown to have been voluntary and performed with adequate knowledge of the situation. If candidates for responsibility can successfully show that their action was not voluntary or that they were excusably ignorant, then their responsibility is usually mitigated if not dissolved. When the actions were voluntary and were undertaken knowingly, however, it is appropriate to blame the agents for the harmful outcomes.[36] A concept of strict liability departs from a fault or blame model in that it holds an agent liable for a harm even if the agent did not intend or was unable to control the outcome, such as when one person's property accidentally causes damage to another person's property.[37] I include such non-blame conceptions of liability together with blame- or fault-based conceptions in a single category of responsibility, because they share the conceptual and functional features I detail below.

In many situations, it is certainly appropriate to apply a liability model of responsibility for human rights violations that occur in apparel factories and in cases where work is subcontracted to homeworkers. When factory owners and managers violate local labor laws, for example, as they often do, they ought to be punished.[38] If states in which factories operate fail to find offenders and punish them, as they often do, they

---

[35] Peter French, *Collective and Corporate Responsibility* (New York: Columbia University Press, 1984).

[36] See George Fletcher, *Basic Concepts of Criminal Law* (Oxford: Oxford University Press, 1999), for a clear statement of this model of responsibility.

[37] See, for example, Tony Honoré, "Responsibility and Luck: The Moral Basis of Strict Liability," in Honoré, *Responsibility and Fault* (Oxford: Oxford University Press, 1999), 14–40.

[38] As I discussed in note 18, in most cases there are labor laws in place, and sweatshop conditions are often violating them. Sometimes this is because the host countries make exceptions to their labor regulation standards in special manufacturing zones. In many other cases, the problem is that factory operators, distributors, retailers, and others are able to ignore labor laws with impunity. See Bonacich and Appelbaum, *Behind the Label*, chaps. 2 and 8.

ought morally to be blamed for this failure, and the international community should perhaps find ways to apply sanctions to them. Bosses that harass and intimidate workers, managers who put productivity above workers' health, and so on, certainly should be held responsible in a liability sense for wrongful harms that these workers suffer.

As I have discussed, however, particular workers in particular facilities in particular places stand within an extensive system of structural social processes that connect the making of garments to those who wear them. Within this system, it is often plausible for the first-line agents of harm to try to mitigate their responsibility by appealing to factors outside their control. They may claim that they have little choice about the wages they pay, and cannot afford to give workers time off or to invest in better ventilation and equipment. They operate in a highly competitive environment, they say, where other operators constantly try to undercut them. They themselves are operating at the edge of solvency and are not exactly making huge profits. They can stay in business only by selling goods at or below the prices of worldwide competitors, and they can do that only by keeping labor costs and other production costs to a minimum.[39] They are under heavy pressure from the exporters who place orders with them to deliver, and the exporters in turn are under heavy pressure from the big-name companies that have placed orders with them. The owners and managers of the factories in which the workers toil are small actors with relatively little power in this global system.

A typical justification for state-enforced labor standards appeals to the need to maintain a level playing field among competitors. If there is a human rights floor below which wages and working conditions should not be allowed to fall, the state is the proper agent to guarantee such a floor through regulation. In this way, those employers who wish to be decent to workers need not fear being undersold by less-scrupulous employers.

Certainly the states in which sweatshops operate must be blamed for allowing them to exist. In these states, many of the agencies charged with enforcing labor regulations are inept and corrupt, and often enough some of their officials directly profit from the system that exploits their poor compatriots. As the anti-sweatshop movement uncovers the existence of factories with sweatshop conditions in the United States and other countries with supposedly high labor standards and good enforcement processes, it should certainly blame these agencies for not doing their jobs.

There is no excuse for national and state governments in the United States not to enforce labor standards in the apparel industry, or any other

---

[39] For an account of the constraints on actors in the global apparel industry, see Rosen, *Making Sweatshops,* chap. 11; see also Bonacich and Appelbaum, *Behind the Label,* chaps. 2 and 5.

industry, and the record here is rather poor.[40] Some governments of less-developed countries, however, can say with some justification that they are under severe constraints that prevent them from improving working conditions. Some of these governments have indirectly encouraged sweat-shop practices by constituting special export processing zones whose factories are exempt from taxation and forms of regulation that apply to other enterprises in the country. They have often been advised to establish such zones by international economic experts. These governments will say that they desperately need investment and jobs, and that to get them they must compete with other poor states to promote a "favorable" investment climate, which includes low taxes and minimal regulation. To avoid or pay down balance-of-trade deficits, they need companies that produce for export. They have never had a strong enough public sector properly to monitor and enforce compliance with the labor regulations they develop, and it is difficult to create one with their low tax base. Public-sector regulating capacity has been reduced further in some cases by policy responses to the actions of international financial institutions such as the International Monetary Fund, which pressures borrowing states to reduce public spending.

A concept of responsibility as blame or liability is indispensable for a legal system and for a sense of moral right that respects agents as individuals and expects them to behave in respectful ways toward others. When applying this concept of responsibility, there must be clear rules of evidence, not only for demonstrating the causal connection between a given agent and a given harm, but also for evaluating the intentions, motives, and consequences of the actions. By proposing a social connection model of responsibility, I do not aim to replace or reject the liability model of responsibility. The foregoing considerations suggest, however, that where there is structural social injustice, a liability model is not sufficient for assigning responsibility. The liability model relies on a fairly direct interaction between the wrongdoer and the wronged party. Where structural social processes constrain and enable many actors in complex relations, however, those with the greatest power in the system, or those who derive benefits from its operations, may well be removed from any interaction with those who are most harmed in it. While it is usually inappropriate to *blame* those agents who are connected to but removed from the harm, it is also inappropriate, I suggest, to allow them (us) to say that they (we) have nothing to do with it. Thus, I suggest that we need a different conception of responsibility to refer to the obligations that agents who participate in structural social processes with unjust outcomes have. I call this a social connection model.

---

[40] See Jill Esbenshade's discussion of sweatshops in the United States and Department of Labor reports concerning these conditions: Jill Esbenshade, *Monitoring Sweatshops: Workers, Consumers, and the Global Apparel Industry* (Philadelphia, PA: Temple University Press, 2004), chap. 1.

B. The social connection model

In ordinary language, we use the term "responsible" in several ways. One of these ways I have already discussed as paradigmatic of the liability model: to be responsible is to be guilty or at fault for having caused a harm and without valid excuses. We also say, however, that people have certain responsibilities by virtue of their social roles or positions, as when we say that a teacher has specific responsibilities, or when we appeal to our responsibilities as citizens. In this meaning, finding an agent responsible does not imply finding the agent at fault or liable for a past wrong, but rather refers to agents' carrying out activities in a morally appropriate way and aiming for certain outcomes.[41] What I propose as a social connection model of responsibility draws more on the latter usage of the term "responsibility" than on the liability usage. It does share with the liability usage, however, a reference to causes of wrongs—here in the form of structural processes that produce injustice.

The social connection model of responsibility says that individuals bear responsibility for structural injustice because they contribute by their actions to the processes that produce unjust outcomes. Our responsibility derives from belonging together with others in a system of interdependent processes of cooperation and competition through which we seek benefits and aim to realize projects. Even though we cannot trace the outcome we may regret to our own particular actions in a direct causal chain, we bear responsibility because we are part of the process. Within this scheme of social cooperation, each of us expects justice toward ourselves, and others can legitimately make claims on us. Responsibility in relation to injustice thus derives not from living under a common constitution, but rather from participation in the diverse institutional processes that produce structural injustice. In today's world, as I suggested above, many of these structural processes extend beyond nation-state boundaries to include globally dispersed persons. The structure and relationships of the global apparel industry illustrate starkly and concretely such transnational social connections. I shall detail five main features of the social connection model of responsibility by contrasting it with the liability model.

1. *Not isolating.* The liability model of responsibility seeks to mark out and isolate those responsible, thereby distinguishing them from others, who by implication are not responsible. Such isolation of the one or ones liable from the others is an important aspect of legal responsibility, both in criminal law and in tort law. Social practices of finding offenders guilty, or finding them to be at fault, or holding them strictly liable, focus on

---

[41] See Henry S. Richardson, "Institutionally Divided Moral Responsibility," *Social Philosophy and Policy* 16, no. 2 (1999): 218–49; see also Robert Goodin, "Apportioning Responsibilities," in Robert Goodin, *Utilitarianism as a Public Philosophy* (Cambridge: Cambridge University Press, 1996), 100–118.

particular agents in order to sanction or demand compensation from them and them alone. A system of moral rules and legal accountability should make clear that agents who violate the rules may face accusation as individual agents.

When harms result from the participation of thousands or millions of people in institutions and practices that produce unjust results, however, such an isolating concept of responsibility is inadequate. Where there is structural injustice, finding some people guilty of perpetrating specific wrongful actions does not absolve others whose actions contribute to the outcomes from bearing responsibility. Hired thugs who beat workers in horribly equipped factories are personally guilty of crimes, as are the factory managers who hire them and target particular workers. Finding them guilty, however, does not absolve the multinational corporations from responsibility for the widespread nature of poor working conditions in the factories producing goods they market. Nor does it absolve those of us who purchase the goods from some kind of responsibility to the workers who make them.

2. Judging background conditions. Under a liability concept of responsibility, what counts as a wrong for which we seek a perpetrator and for which he or she might be required to compensate, is something we generally conceive as a deviation from a baseline. Implicitly, we assume a normal background situation that is morally acceptable, if not ideal. A crime or an actionable harm consists in a morally and often legally unacceptable deviation from this background structure.[42] The liability model considers the process that brought about the harm as a discrete, bounded event that breaks away from the ongoing normal flow. Punishment, redress, or compensation aims to restore normality or to "make whole" in relation to the baseline circumstance.

In contrast, a model of responsibility derived from understanding the mediated connection that agents have to structural injustices does not evaluate harm that deviates from the normal and the acceptable; rather, it often brings into question precisely the background conditions that ascriptions of blame or fault assume as normal. When we judge that structural injustice exists, we mean that at least some of the normal and accepted background conditions of action are not morally acceptable. Most of us contribute to a greater or lesser degree to the production and reproduction of structural injustice precisely because we follow the accepted and expected rules and conventions of the communities and institutions in which we act. Usually we enact these conventions and practices in a habitual way, without explicit reflection and deliberation on what we do, having in the foreground of our consciousness and intention immediate

---

[42] See George Fletcher's discussion of the way that the assignment of criminal liability must distinguish between (1) foregrounded deviations from background conditions assumed as normal, and (2) the background conditions themselves. Fletcher, *Basic Concepts of Criminal Law*, 69–70.

goals we want to achieve and the particular people we need to interact with to achieve them.

We can think of many examples of accepted norms and institutional practices that constitute the background conditions for sweatshops. I have already referred to the fashion system and its seasons as one set of practices that most producers and consumers reinforce to some extent. Executives at major multinational retailers typically devote more attention and money to advertising campaigns to promote the image of the company than to ensuring that the pay and working conditions of the workers who make the clothes they sell are decent. It is normal in this consumer society for companies to devote a large portion of their investment to advertising rather than production. Levels of unemployment in many of the places where sweatshops exist are normally high, and the social processes depriving peasants of the means to make an independent livelihood speedily create more unemployed people. One should expect under these circumstances that each super-exploitive sweatshop job opening will have multiple applicants, and that the workers in these jobs will normally be compliant and urge their coworkers to be so as well. Though today they are largely taken for granted, each of these aspects of the global apparel system can and should come under critical scrutiny, and questions can be asked about the responsibilities those who act on these assumptions have in relation to the injustice to which they serve as background.

3. *More forward-looking than backward-looking.* Assigning responsibility, whether under the liability model or the social connection model, always has both backward-looking and forward-looking aspects. The liability and social connection models of responsibility nevertheless differ in temporal emphasis. On most occasions, application of the liability model is primarily backward-looking. The social connection model, in contrast, emphasizes forward-looking issues.

Under the liability model of responsibility, the harm or circumstance for which we seek to hold agents responsible is usually an isolatable action or event that has reached a terminus. The robbery has taken place, or the oil tanker has spewed its contents on the beach. Usually the purpose of assigning responsibility in terms of blame, fault, or liability, then, is to seek retribution or compensation for this past action. To be sure, such backward-looking condemnation and sanction may have a forward-looking purpose as well; often it aims to deter others from similar action in the future, or to identify weak points in an institutional system that allows or encourages such blameworthy actions, in order to reform institutions. Once we take this latter step, however, we may be leaving the liability model and moving toward the social connection model. The reform project likely involves a responsibility on the part of many people to take actions directed at achieving reform, even though they are not to blame for past problems.

When conceptualizing responsibility in relation to structural injustice, however, we are concerned with an ongoing set of processes that we understand is likely to continue producing harms unless there are interventions in it. The temporality of assigning and taking responsibility, then, is more forward-looking than backward-looking. Because the particular causal relationship of the actions of particular individuals or organizations to structural outcomes is often impossible to trace, there is no point in seeking to exact compensation or redress from only and all those who have contributed to the outcome, and in proportion to their contributions. The injustice produced through structures has not reached a terminus, but rather is ongoing. The point is not to blame, punish, or seek redress from those who did it, but rather to enjoin those who participate by their actions in the process of collective action to change it.[43]

The anti-sweatshop movement illustrates this forward-looking approach. When activists focus on particular factories or on multinationals who contract to manufacture goods under poor factory conditions, they rarely call for shutting down the factory or otherwise simply punishing the operators.[44] The system of incentives and organizational priorities makes it likely that other factories would open in the place of the one closed. Even when particular perpetrators are punished, workers continue to suffer structural injustice.

4. *Shared responsibility.* From the observation that the social connection model differs from the liability model in that it does not isolate those liable (in ways that implicitly absolve others), it follows that all those who contribute by their actions to the structural processes producing injustice share responsibility for such injustice. Philosopher Larry May distinguishes shared responsibility from collective responsibility in that the former is a distributed responsibility whereas the latter is not. A collection of persons, such as a corporation, might be said to be responsible for a state of affairs without any of its individual members being determinately responsible for it. Shared responsibility, in contrast, is a personal responsibility for outcomes, or the risks of harmful outcomes, produced by a group of persons. Each individual is personally responsible for outcomes in a partial way, since he or she alone does not produce the outcomes; the specific part that each person plays in producing the outcome cannot be isolated and identified, however, and thus the responsibility is essentially shared.[45]

---

[43] See Hans Jonas, *The Imperative of Responsibility* (Chicago: University of Chicago Press, 1984), 90–120.

[44] See Elliott and Freeman, *Can Labor Standards Improve under Globalization?*, chap. 3.

[45] Larry May, *Sharing Responsibility* (Chicago: University of Chicago Press, 1993), chap. 2. As formulated in this book, May's theory of shared responsibility remains backward-looking; he is concerned to assign responsibility for harms that have occurred and reached a terminus. Thus, his theory is more continuous with a liability model of responsibility than the theory I am developing here. May also focuses more on subjective states (such as attitudes) as factors that link persons to responsibility for a wrong, and says little about more objective social structures that connect persons to moral wrongs or injustices. See my essay "Responsibility and Global Labor Justice," cited in note 1 above.

5. Discharged only through collective action. A final feature of the social connection model that distinguishes it from a liability model of responsibility is that the forward-looking responsibility can be discharged only by joining with others in collective action. This feature follows from the essentially shared nature of the responsibility. Thousands or even millions of agents contribute by their actions in particular institutional contexts to the processes that produce unjust outcomes. Our forward-looking responsibility consists in changing the institutions and processes so that their outcomes will be less unjust. No one of us can do this on our own. Even if it were possible to do so, a single shopper would not change the working conditions of those toiling in sweatshops by refusing to buy all items she had reason to believe were produced under unjust conditions. The structural processes can be altered only if many actors in diverse social positions work together to intervene in these processes to produce different outcomes.

Responsibility derived from social connection, then, is ultimately *political* responsibility. Taking responsibility in a forward-looking sense under this model involves joining with others to organize collective action to reform unjust structures. Most fundamentally, what I mean by "politics" here is public communicative engagement with others for the sake of organizing our relationships and coordinating our actions most justly. Thus, discharging my responsibility in relation to sweatshop workers might involve trying to persuade others that the treatment of these workers is unacceptable and that we collectively can alter social practices and institutional rules and priorities to prevent such treatment. Our working through state institutions is often an effective means of such collective action to change structural processes, but states are not the only tools of effective collective action.[46] In the next section, I will discuss and evaluate some of the activities of the anti-sweatshop movement.

An important corollary of this feature of political responsibility is that many of those who are properly thought to be victims of harm or injustice may nevertheless share political responsibility in relation to it. On the liability model of responsibility, blaming those who claim to be victims of injustice usually functions to absolve others of responsibility for their plight. On the social connection model, however, those who can properly be argued to be victims of structural injustice can also be said to share responsibility with others who perpetuate the unjust structures, and can be called on to engage in actions directed at transforming those structures.

---

[46] Melanie Beth Oliviero and Adele Simmons recommend using civil society organizations to address issues relating to labor standards; see their essay "Who's Minding the Store? Global Civil Society and Corporate Responsibility," in Marlies Glasius, Mary Kaldor, and Helmut Anheier, eds., *Global Civil Society 2002* (Oxford: Oxford University Press, 2002), 77–107. John Braithwaite and Peter Drahos argue that as transnational social structures impinge on state sovereignty, civil society organizations gain increased ability to influence labor and other business practices; see Braithwaite and Drahos, *Global Business Regulation* (Cambridge: Cambridge University Press, 2000), chaps. 5, 6, and 26.

This point certainly applies in the case of sweatshops. Workers themselves have the strongest interest in combating sweatshop conditions. They also have information and relationships with one another that would be useful in mobilizing to try to alter the structures that perpetuate their exploitation. According to some researchers, employer-sponsored monitoring systems that aim to reform sweatshop conditions but fail to involve workers in a meaningful way are often ineffective or actually harm workers.[47] Even when they do not harm workers, they tend to be implemented as a paternalistic measure, rather than as a means of empowering workers. On the social connection model, workers share responsibility for combating sweatshop conditions and ought to be organized in order to do so. Nevertheless, especially where freedom to organize is not recognized or not enforced, they can discharge their responsibilities only with the support of others, often faraway and relatively privileged others, who make public the workers' grievances, put pressure on the agents that would block their unionization, and give them material aid.

I have been arguing that, when compared to the liability model, the social connection model of responsibility better corresponds to the intuitions expressed in claims about the responsibilities agents have concerning global justice. The social connection model not only has these philosophical advantages, I suggest, but also has rhetorical advantages in public discussion that aims to motivate people to take responsibility for rectifying social injustice. Claims that some persons participate in producing injustice and ought to stop are too often heard under a liability model of responsibility. The actors addressed hear themselves being blamed for harms. More often than not, agents who believe themselves to be targets of blame react defensively: they look for other agents to blame instead of themselves, or find excuses that mitigate their liability in cases where they admit that their actions do causally contribute to the harm. In situations of structural injustice, it is easy to engage in such blame-shifting or excusing discourse, because in fact others are also responsible and there are in fact structural constraints on most of the actors participating in the institutional processes that have unjust outcomes. In many contexts where the issue is how to mobilize collective action for the sake of social change and greater justice, such finger-pointing and blame-shifting lead more to resentment and refusal to take responsibility than to a useful basis of action.[48]

---

[47] See Esbenshade, *Monitoring Sweatshops.*

[48] William Connolly makes a similar distinction between responsibility as blame and a more politically oriented responsibility. For him, the resentment and counter-accusation dialectic that accompanies blame in a discourse of public affairs makes political identity overly rigid and paralyzes action. Thus, he recommends a notion of political responsibility without blame and with a more fluid and ambiguous understanding of the sources of wrong than the implicitly Christian identification of the sinner. See William Connolly, *Identity/Difference* (Ithaca, NY: Cornell University Press, 1993), esp. chap. 4. Melissa Orlie also distinguishes between a sentiment of resentment exhibited in blaming (on the one hand) and holding oneself and others politically responsible (on the other). See Melissa Orlie, *Living Ethically, Acting Politically* (Ithaca, NY: Cornell University Press, 1997), 169–73.

When executives of multinational retailers or consumers who shop at retail outlets hear the claims of anti-sweatshop activists as laying blame on them for the conditions under which goods are produced, they rightly become indignant, or scoff at the absurd extremism of the movement. A social connection model of responsibility that is distinct from (and complementary to) a liability model allows us to call on one another to take responsibility *together* for sweatshop conditions, without blaming anyone in particular for the structures that encourage their proliferation. This does not necessarily mean that all who share responsibility have an *equal* responsibility. The power to influence the processes that produce unjust outcomes is an important factor that distinguishes degrees of responsibility.

VI. Parameters of Reasoning

I have proposed a social connection model of responsibility to correspond to the intuition that those who participate by their actions in the structural processes that produce injustice bear some responsibility for correcting this injustice. In today's world of global interdependence, many of these structural injustices involve people widely dispersed across the globe, and are by no means limited to processes within single nation-states.

So far, I have offered only a way of thinking about responsibility in general. One might well object that the social connection model of responsibility raises as many questions as it answers. For example, the model says that all who participate by their actions in processes that produce injustice share responsibility for its remedy. Does this mean that all participants bear responsibility in the same way and to the same degree? If not, then what are the grounds for differentiating kinds and degrees of responsibility? Most of us participate in many structural processes, moreover, that arguably have disadvantaging, harmful, or unjust consequences for others. It is asking too much to expect most of us to work actively to restructure each and every one of the structural injustices for which we arguably share responsibility. How, then, should we reason about the best ways to use our limited time, resources, and creative energy to respond to structural injustice?

Adequately responding to questions like these would take at least another full essay. Thus, I will only sketch answers here, and illustrate the responses once again through the example of the anti-sweatshop movement.

Some moral theorists argue that responsibility names a form of obligation distinct from duty. Joel Feinberg, for example, distinguishes between an ethic that focuses on obligation or duty and an ethic that focuses on responsibility. On the one hand, a duty specifies a rule of action or delineates the substance of what actions count as performing the duty. A responsibility, on the other hand, while no less obligatory, is more open with regard to what counts as carrying it out.[49] A person with responsibilities is obliged to attend to outcomes that the responsibilities call for, and to orient her actions in ways demonstrably intended to contribute to bringing about those outcomes. Because a person may face many moral demands on her actions, and because changes in circumstances are often unpredictable, just how a person goes about discharging her responsibilities is a matter subject to considerable discretion.[50] Given that a combination of responsibilities may be overly demanding, and given that agents have discretion in how they choose to discharge their responsibilities, it is reasonable to say that it is up to each agent to decide what she can and should do under the circumstances, and how she should order her moral priorities. Others have the right to question and criticize our decisions and actions, however, especially when we depend on one another to perform effective collective action. Part of what it means to be responsible on the social connection model is to be accountable to others with whom one shares responsibility—accountable for what one has decided to do and for which structural injustices one has chosen to address. When an agent is able to give an account of what she has done, and why, in terms of shared responsibilities for structural injustice, then others usually ought to accept her decision and the way she sets priorities for her actions.

These considerations begin to provide an answer to the question I stated above, namely, how should one reason about the best way to use one's limited time and resources to respond to structural injustices? In a world with many and deep structural injustices, most of us, in principle, share more responsibility than we can reasonably be expected to discharge.[51] Thus, we must make choices about where our action can be most useful or which injustices we regard as most urgent. While a social connection model of responsibility will not give us a list of maxims or imperatives, it should offer some parameters for reasoning to guide our decisions and actions. These parameters, in turn, address the other question I raised earlier—the question about kinds and degrees of responsibility. Different agents plausibly have different kinds of responsibilities in relation to particular issues of justice, and some arguably have a greater degree of responsibility than others.

These differences of kind and degree correlate with an agent's *position* within the structural processes. By virtue of this structural positioning, different agents have different opportunities and capacities, can draw on different kinds and amounts of resources, or face different levels of constraint with respect to processes that can contribute to structural change.

---

[49] Joel Feinberg, "Duties, Rights, and Claims," in Joel Feinberg, *Rights, Justice and the Bounds of Liberty* (Princeton, NJ: Princeton University Press, 1980), 135–40. See also Larry May, *The Socially Responsible Self: Social Theory and Professional Ethics* (Chicago: University of Chicago Press, 1996), chap. 5.

[50] See Goodin, "Apportioning Responsibilities," and Richardson, "Institutionally Divided Moral Responsibility."

[51] Liam Murphy develops a useful theory of moral responsibility under conditions of injustice; see his *Moral Demands in Nonideal Theory* (Oxford: Oxford University Press, 2000).

I suggest that persons can reason about their action in relation to structural injustice along parameters of *power, privilege, interest,* and *collective ability.*

A. Power

An agent's position within structural processes usually carries with it a specific degree of potential or actual power or influence over the processes that produce the outcomes. Where individuals and organizations do not have sufficient energy and resources to respond to all structural injustices to which they are connected, they should focus on those where they have a greater capacity to influence structural processes.

Despite the fact that they are often legally separated from the manufacturing facilities whose working conditions and practices violate human rights, large multinational designers and retailers such as Calvin Klein or J.C. Penney have much greater power in global trade processes than do small manufacturers. The anti-sweatshop movement thus rightly concentrates its efforts on pressuring these powerful agents actively to work with manufacturers, host governments, unions, and civic organizations to improve wages and factory conditions for the workers and at the same time protect the workers from being laid off.

Because the agents with the greatest power within social structures often have a vested interest in maintaining them as they are, however, external pressure on the powerful is often necessary to move these agents to action, and to prevent them from taking superficial steps rather than making serious changes. Some of the larger exporters, importers, and retailers in the apparel industry, for example, would appear to be able to change the proportion of the price of a pair of shoes that goes to pay workers and improve working conditions, as compared with the proportion that pays for distribution, marketing, advertising, and decorating stores. Changing those proportions, however, may reduce the companies' own profits to some extent. Nevertheless, public disclosure of a company's connection with poor working conditions is not good for business, and public reporting of a company's support for change seems to be good for its stock price.[52]

B. Privilege

Where there are structural injustices, these usually produce not only victims of injustice, but persons who acquire relative privilege by virtue of the structures. Most who occupy positions of power with respect to unjust structures also have privileges that coincide with this power. In

---

[52] See Michael T. Rock, "Public Disclosure of the Sweatshop Practices of American Multinational Garment/Shoe Makers/Retailers: Impacts on Their Stock Prices," *Competition and Change* 7, no. 1 (March 2003): 23–38.

most situations of structural injustice, however, there are relatively privileged persons who have relatively little power as individuals or in their
institutional positions, at least with respect to the issue of injustice. Middle-
class clothing consumers in the developed world, for example, stand in a
privileged position in the structures of the apparel industry. They benefit
from the large selection and affordable prices that the industry offers
them. Persons who benefit relatively from structural injustices have special moral responsibilities to contribute to organized efforts to correct
them, not because they are to blame, but because they are able to adapt
to changed circumstances without suffering serious deprivation. Lower-
income clothing consumers, whether in the developing or developed
world, may be less able than more affluent consumers to spend more for
clothing in order to ensure that the workers who make it are treated
fairly.[53]

C. Interest

Different people and different organizations usually have divergent
interests in the maintenance or transformation of structures that produce
injustice. Often those with the greatest interest in perpetuating the structures are also those with the greatest power to influence their transformation. Those who are victims of structural injustice often have a greater
interest in structural transformation. Earlier I said that one of the distinctive things about the social connection model of responsibility is that
victims of injustice share responsibility with others for cooperating in
projects to undermine the injustice. Victims of injustice have the greatest
interest in its elimination, and often have unique insights into its social
sources and the probable effects of proposals for change.

This point certainly applies in the case of labor conditions in the apparel
industry. Actual and potential sweatshop workers are the primary victims
of injustice. Analysts of some strategies in the movement to improve
conditions for these workers find that these strategies are sometimes
ineffectual or paternalistic because the workers' point of view and active
participation have not been properly included. Some corporate-sponsored
monitoring systems, for example, conduct inspections of factories without talking to workers, or only talking to workers on the factory site.
Critics argue that workers' experience and complaints must definitely be
a part of monitoring systems, but that workers must be interviewed away
from the factory sites when owners and managers are not present. Coop-

---

[53] See Pollin, Burns, and Heintz, "Global Apparel Production." These authors find that the
amount that retail prices would need to increase to raise workers to a living wage is small,
and is consistent with increases that North American consumers say they would be willing
to pay if they could be assured of "sweat-free" conditions.

eration with local civic organizations whom workers trust is usually necessary to facilitate such interviews.[54]

Other analysts wonder whether the predominance of nongovernmental organizations (NGOs) such as monitoring organizations, education and public accountability organizations, and so on, in the anti-sweatshop movement weakens the ability of workers to organize unions and allows local governments to continue their lax labor-law promulgation and enforcement.[55] Most analysts conclude that NGO activity should work to support unionization and to pressure for greater government protection of workers' rights to form or choose unions.[56] In this case, as in many other cases of structural injustice, victims of injustice have a responsibility to work together to improve their situation, but they are unlikely to succeed without the help and support of other less-vulnerable people who make industry behavior public and who pressure companies to change policies or restructure their business relationships.[57]

D. Collective ability

Sometimes a coincidence of interest, power, and existing organization enables people to act collectively to influence processes more easily regarding one issue of justice than another. That is not always a reason to give priority to that issue, for such ease of organization may be a sign that the action makes little structural change. Nevertheless, given the great number of injustices that need remedy, the relative ease with which people can organize collective action to address an injustice can be a useful decision principle.

The decision by some student groups to focus their anti-sweatshop activism on their colleges and universities illustrates this parameter. The function of universities as large consumers of apparel for their sports teams and as purveyors of apparel through their book stores makes universities obvious targets of activism, because their decisions about

[54] Esbenshade, *Monitoring Sweatshops*. See also Robert J. Liubicic, "Corporate Codes of Conduct and Product Labeling Schemes: The Limits and Possibilities of Promoting International Labor Rights Through Private Initiatives," *Law and Public Policy in International Business* 30, no. 1 (1998): 111–58.

[55] Rainer Braun and Judy Gearhart, "Who Should Code Your Conduct? Trade Union and NGO Differences in the Fight for Workers' Rights," *Development in Practice* 14, nos. 1 and 2 (2004): 183–96; Ronnie D. Lipschutz, "Sweating It Out: NGO Campaigns and Trade Union Empowerment," *Development in Practice* 14, nos. 1 and 2 (2004).

[56] Lance Compa, "Trade Unions, NGOs, and Corporate Codes of Conduct," *Development in Practice* 14, nos. 1 and 2 (2004): 210–15; Dara O'Rourke, "Outsourcing Regulation: Analyzing Nongovernmental Systems of Labor Standards and Monitoring," *The Policy Studies Journal* 31, no. 1 (2003): 1–29.

[57] Ruth Pearson and Gill Seyfang, "New Hope or False Dawn? Voluntary Codes of Conduct, Labour Regulation, and Social Policy in a Globalizing World," *Global Social Policy* 1, no. 1 (2001): 49–78; Archon Fung, "Deliberative Democracy and International Labor Standards," *Governance: An International Journal of Policy, Administration, and Institutions* 16, no. 1 (2003): 51–71.

purchasing and marketing have more impact than those of individual consumers. Campus campaigns politicizing such decisions successfully raise awareness of issues of global labor justice even among students and faculty who do not actively support the campaigns. Universities can relatively easily organize with one another to make an impact on the structural processes of the apparel industry, as they have done by becoming members of the Fair Labor Association and the Workers Rights Consortium.

VII. Conclusion

Obviously each of these parameters for reasoning about the ways that individual persons or institutions might meet their responsibilities under a social connection model—power, privilege, interest, and collective ability—needs further elaboration. This sketch should indicate how an agent's position in the structures that produce injustices might influence the kinds of issues the agent should address and the kinds of actions the agent should take. It also gives more concreteness to the notion that, under a social connection model, agents share responsibility with others who are differently situated, with whom they usually must cooperate in order to effect change. As the example of the anti-sweatshop movement illustrates, however, such need for cooperation does not mean that agents have no conflicts of interest and no need for struggling with one another. Sharing responsibility means, in part, that agents challenge one another and call one another to account for what they are doing or not doing. Global social and economic processes bring individuals and institutions into ongoing structural connection with one another across national jurisdictions. Adopting a conception of responsibility that recognizes this connection is an important element in developing a theory of global justice.

Political Science, University of Chicago

PROCESS VALUES, INTERNATIONAL LAW, AND JUSTICE*

By Paul B. Stephan

I. Introduction

Discussion of international law, as much as of any body of legal rules, invites a distinction between inputs—the processes that convert preferences and beliefs into something recognized as "law"—and outputs—the content of the legal rules generated by lawmaking processes. Most normative accounts of international law consider only the latter. Whether the topic comprises the laws of war or the nature of international human rights, discussion tends to focus on the content of the rule rather than its provenance.

There exists, however, an older tradition that considers the normative value of the international lawmaking process. It reaches back at least to Jeremy Bentham. It maintains that the content of rules cannot be separated from the means of their creation, and that lawmakers are more likely to adopt substantively desirable rules when lawmaking is structured and constrained in a particular way.[1]

A focus on the lawmaking process, I submit, permits us to explore a particular dimension of justice, namely the relationship between law and liberty. Laws that reflect the arbitrary whims of the lawmaker are presumptively unjust, because they constrain liberty for no good reason. A strategy for making the enactment of arbitrary laws less likely involves recognizing checks on the lawmaker's powers and grounding those checks in processes that allow the governed to express their disapproval. The system of checks and balances employed in the U.S. Constitution embodies this strategy, although reasonable people can debate its efficacy. As the economist A. O. Hirschman observed in an influential book, regimes that permit free movement of persons and property similarly restrict the force of arbitrary rules by allowing exit from unwanted restrictions.[2] I want to inquire into the role of checks in international lawmaking.

---

* I am indebted to Ken Abbott, Jean Cohen, Larry Helfer, Robert Hockett, Sean Murphy, Phil Nichols, Ed Swaine, Joel Trachtman, the other contributors to this volume, and participants in a workshop at the University of Virginia School of Law for comments and criticism. Shortcomings are mine alone.
[1] Jeremy Bentham, "Principles of International Law," in John Bowring, ed., *The Works of Jeremy Bentham,* vol. 2 (New York: Russell and Russell, Inc., 1962), 540.
[2] Albert O. Hirschman, *Exit, Voice, and Loyalty: Responses to Decline in Firms, Organizations, and States* (Cambridge, MA: Harvard University Press, 1970).

I recognize that other process values exist—in particular, transparency and participation rights. I have discussed these issues in international lawmaking elsewhere.[3] I choose to focus here on "checking values" to avoid a subtle problem that can enter into any discussion of participation and transparency, namely an implicit assumption about the necessity of lawmaking. Once we decide that a problem requires a collective and coercive response, we want to ensure that the means of constructing that response is both fair and expeditious. Transparency and participation enhance the quality of a lawmaking process that moves inevitably toward some action. A concern for liberty, in contrast, implies a conviction that expedience sometimes must defer to fairness, and moreover that in some cases the optimal outcome is inaction. A focus on checking rests on an assumption that sometimes the interests of liberty require that a coercive authority stay its hand. Most international-law specialists regard any diminution in the scope of international law as a setback and therefore refrain from going down an analytical path that might justify less law. I therefore concentrate on checking to counteract an underlying expansionist bias in international-law scholarship.[4]

Let me deal first with a preliminary, and I believe insubstantial, objection to the way in which I have framed the problem. At first blush, it might appear that the fundamental principle of state consent provides all the checking that international lawmaking needs. This principle holds that a state (and by extension, its subjects) can be bound by a rule of international law only if that state manifests its consent to the rule. As long as states have a real choice, itself subject to internal checks on official decision making, the adoption of the rule should meet basic criteria of procedural justice. Indeed, the correlate of this principle—that each state has a veto over the adoption of international law, at least as applied to the state and its subjects—suggests that international lawmaking poses *less* of a threat to liberty than do conventional municipal lawmaking processes based on majority rule.[5] One might think that, as a result of this principle, no rule will attain the status of international law unless its adoption

---

[3] See Paul B. Stephan, "Accountability and International Lawmaking: Rules, Rents, and Legitimacy," *Northwestern Journal of International Law and Business* 17, no. 2/3 (1996–97): 726–29; and Paul B. Stephan, "The New International Law—Legitimacy, Accountability, Authority, and Freedom in the New Global Order," *University of Colorado Law Review* 70, no. 4 (1999): 1580–82.

[4] Typical is work over the last quarter-century by Professor Louis Henkin, the Reporter of the *Restatement (Third) of the Foreign Relations Law of the United States* and perhaps the most prominent and admired U.S. professor of international law. For a representative example of his expansionist approach to international law, see Louis Henkin, "U.S. Ratification of Human Rights Conventions: The Ghost of Senator Bricker," *American Journal of International Law* 89, no. 2 (1995): 348–50. For an account of the shifts in Henkin's position over the last forty years, see Paul B. Stephan, "Courts, the Constitution, and Customary International Law," *Virginia Journal of International Law* 44, no. 1 (2003): 37–47.

[5] According to the usage of international-law scholars, "municipal" law refers to the domestic law of particular states, whether national or local.

makes some states better off and no state worse off, because no state would embrace a rule that has greater costs than benefits.[6]

One still might argue that state consent is an insufficient safeguard for liberty, because particular states might consent to international obligations that the great majority of their subjects find objectionable. States might sacrifice the welfare of their subjects to obtain benefits for their rulers or for special groups with whom the rulers are allied. Dictatorships provide an obvious case where states may constitute disloyal agents, but even democracies face such problems.[7] I elide this issue here, because even if states were perfect agents, it would not follow that international lawmaking represents a remarkable instance of exclusively Pareto outcomes, that is, a process that benefits at least some participants and makes none worse off.

For an important range of cases, state consent is not a condition for a rule having the force of international law. First, many specialists argue for the existence of *jus cogens* or peremptory norms that apply regardless of state consent.[8] Second, the concept of state consent is artful, and opportunistic decision makers have some freedom to construe consent in ways that circumvent conventional checking processes. Third, political and economic pressure can reduce state consent to an empty formality due to the state's lack of effective options. I discuss each of these points in turn.

For at least the last sixty years, jurists have argued that the international legal system contains some fundamental rules that must exist for inter-

---

[6] By "rule," I mean a command that limits in some way the autonomy that a subject of international law otherwise would enjoy. The rule might reside in a treaty or similar formal instrument, or, more controversially, it might be part of an unwritten body of norms that specialists call "customary international law." For analysis of the analogous problem regarding unanimous voting that arises when creating a constitution, see James M. Buchanan, *The Limits of Liberty: Between Anarchy and Leviathan* (Chicago: University of Chicago Press, 1975); and Dennis C. Mueller, *Constitutional Democracy* (New York: Oxford University Press, 2000), 65–67.

[7] As public choice theory predicts, lawmakers concerned with reelection make laws, including international commitments, that benefit discrete and powerful groups at the expense of the general welfare. I discuss this dynamic and provide examples in Stephan, "Accountability and International Lawmaking."

[8] The *Restatement (Third) of the Foreign Relations Law of the United States* defines *jus cogens* or peremptory norms as follows:

> Some rules of international law are recognized by the international community of states as peremptory, permitting no derogation. These rules prevail over and invalidate international agreements and other rules of international law in conflict with them. Such a peremptory norm is subject to modification only by a subsequent norm of international law having the same character. It is generally accepted that the principles of the United Nations Charter prohibiting the use of force . . . have the character of jus cogens.

American Law Institute, *Restatement (Third) of the Foreign Relations Law of the United States* (Philadelphia: American Law Institute, 1987), sec. 102, comment k. This prestigious but unofficial source about international law is itself controversial, and not all courts regard all its pronouncements as correct. *United States v. Yousef*, 327 F.3d 56, 99–103 (2d Cir. 2003).

national law to be law, and that these rules operate prior to and independent of state consent. The war crimes trials that followed World War II, for example, meted out punishment for violations of rules of fundamental humanity and decency and treated the question of whether Germany or Japan had agreed to respect these rules as irrelevant. In the case of Japan, the deliberate decision of the Imperial Government not to adopt the 1929 Geneva Convention Relating to the Treatment of Prisoners of War made no difference in the judgments, many capital, imposed on the accused. Contemporary commentators argue that a number of rules, such as prohibitions of genocide and torture, operate universally and independently of the various conventions that codify those norms.[9]

Putting *jus cogens* rules aside, what constitutes state consent may depend on the views and authority of the decision maker. At one extreme, parliamentary adoption of a rule of international law mirrors the process of municipal lawmaking, and largely satisfies whatever process values the adopting state observes. At the other extreme, lawmakers with little democratic accountability (for example, judges with life tenure) might embrace the rule in the face of opposition by the political branches. Bentham worried much about the judges, because of what he saw as the obscurantist and secret methods of judicial lawmaking and the unrepresentative nature of the judiciary.

Beside judicial lawmaking, delegation of rulemaking authority to a third party—say, an international body such as the European Commission—also circumvents, in practice if not in form, the principle of sovereign consent. The initial delegation may satisfy municipal process values, but if it encompasses a self-executing authority—as is the case for much of the lawmaking powers of the organs of the European Community (EC)[10]—then rules created pursuant to the delegation may come about without significant checks. Moreover, if independent actors—in particular, domestic courts—possess and exercise the authority to enforce the rules generated by the exercise of delegated authority (again, as is the case for EC law), not much remains of sovereign consent.[11]

---

[9] M. Cherif Bassiouni, "International Crimes: Jus Cogens and Obligatio Erga Omnes," *Law and Contemporary Problems* 59, no. 4 (1996): 63–74.

[10] The European Community (until 1992, the European Economic Community) is the most important, and legally and institutionally the most developed, part of the European Union. It has lawmaking bodies (the Commission, the Council, and the European Parliament) as well as a judiciary (the Court of Justice). See note 21 below.

[11] The 1957 Treaty of Rome, which established the European Economic Community, implies, but does not explicitly state, both that the European Court of Justice (the Luxembourg court) has the authority to deliver authoritative and binding interpretations of Community law, and that the various national courts of the member states have an obligation to apply Community law in favor of national law, even if that means invalidating domestic legislation. Decisions of the Luxembourg court articulated these conclusions, which the courts of the member states in turn accepted and implemented. For further discussion, see Paul B. Stephan, Francesco Parisi, and Ben F. W. Depoorter, *The Law and Economics of the European Union* (Charlottesville, VA: LexisNexis, 2003), 294–325.

Finally, states may have the formal authority to reject a rule of international law but, because of conditions of economic or political dependency, may lack the effective capacity to make a choice. A common example involves the financial and economic policy requirements imposed by the International Monetary Fund (IMF) on debtor states: a sovereign state can refuse to comply with IMF demands, but only if it accepts the loss of access to foreign capital as the price of its independence.[12] Similarly, a member of the World Trade Organization or the European Union theoretically could denounce its obligations under those international regimes, but the costs of extricating a state from the intertwined relationships captured in these arrangements make such a divorce a daunting prospect.[13]

Once state consent ceases to constrain international lawmaking, the question of alternative checks to protect liberty looms. Under what circumstances does the international lawmaking process as currently constituted present a threat of arbitrary force? What kinds of resistance to the results of international lawmaking can process values justify?

I address these questions in three steps. First, I explore whether international law does carry a threat of coercion. If not, concerns about arbitrary restrictions of liberty are misplaced. Second, I discuss the problems arising from delegations of lawmaking authority to international institutions, with specific reference to the 1998 Rome Statute and the body it established, the International Criminal Court. Third, I discuss the process-value issues associated with judicial lawmaking. None of these concerns justifies blanket opposition to international lawmaking. Rather, those interested in making and enforcing international rules need to grapple with these issues and provide another layer of justification for their efforts.

II. INTERNATIONAL LAW AS A POTENTIAL THREAT TO LIBERTY

Legal rules affect liberty in at least two ways. Rules may contribute to the establishment of a reasonably secure political, social, cultural, and economic order that provides a foundation for voluntary interactions and personal flourishing. The concept of "ordered liberty" captures this first function. In addition, rules can restrict the choices made within the framework of ordered liberty. A rule forbidding murder falls into the first category, while one punishing criticism of political authority falls into the second. In normative terms, first-category rules advance the values embedded in liberty, while second-category rules restrict liberty. Categorization depends heavily on context, rather than on a priori principles.

---

[12] Michael N. Barnett and Martha Finnemore, "The Politics, Power, and Pathologies of International Organizations," *International Organization* 53, no. 4 (1999): 699–732.

[13] Not to mention the opinion of some that a right unilaterally to secede from the European Community does not exist. See Joseph H. H. Weiler, "Alternatives to Withdrawal from an International Organization: The Case of the European Economic Community," *Israel Law Review* 20, nos. 2–3 (1985).

For rules to function in either way, however, some mechanism must exist to induce compliance. In municipal law, the state's coercive power (where it exists) supplies the most obvious means of enforcement, either directly or as a background threat. Other pathways to compliance include informal social sanctions. More problematically, some theorists also believe in a process of rule internalization, through which individuals impose psychic costs on themselves for rule transgressions and psychic rewards for rule compliance.[14]

International law as conventionally conceived seems to exclude all means of inducing compliance save informal social sanctions. The international community, as opposed to individual states, supposedly lacks coercive power, and societies *ex definitio* lack interior lives and psychic states.[15] Accordingly, the compliance literature for the most part concentrates on how reputation and retaliation serve to induce states to observe international law.[16]

More recently, however, scholars have identified ways in which international law can have directly coercive effect. International tribunals can issue monetary or punitive judgments that states perceive as having direct effect and therefore uncritically implement. Domestic tribunals can apply international rules in a self-perceived capacity of agent for the international lawmaker.[17] To be sure, these examples rest ultimately on the willingness of national governments and other actors to fulfill their roles in administering coercive sanctions. But this reservation is also true of municipal law, which depends fundamentally on the willingness of individuals to play their part in the execution of the law.

Moreover, most legal academics seem to favor extending the coercive power and reach of international law. To take just one prominent example, the International Criminal Court (ICC) has generated a cottage industry of largely celebratory work, even though it has yet to take on its first case.[18] The ICC, which came into being in 2002, represents a culmination of decades of work, led by the United States, to establish a permanent international body to investigate and prosecute human rights violations arising out of political and social catastrophes. Previously, the United Nations Security Council had established tribunals on an ad hoc basis to

[14] Robert Cooter, "Do Good Laws Make Good Citizens? An Economic Analysis of Internalized Norms," *Virginia Law Review* 86, no. 8 (2000): 1577–1601.

[15] Individual states do have the capacity to impose significant sanctions, including economic punishment and, in extreme cases, use of force. International bodies, as opposed to individual states, may lend their approval to such actions, but they lack the capacity directly to bring them about.

[16] Andrew T. Guzman, "A Compliance-Based Theory of International Law," *California Law Review* 90, no. 8 (2002): 1844–51. For recent work exploring a sociology of state compliance with international law, see Ryan Goodman and Derek Jinks, "How to Influence States: Socialization and International Human Rights Law," *Duke Law Journal* 53, no. 3 (2004).

[17] Robert E. Scott and Paul B. Stephan, "Self-Enforcing International Agreements and the Limits of Coercion," *Wisconsin Law Review* n.v., no. 2 (2004): 599–614.

[18] To be precise, the court itself has yet to take up any case, although the prosecutor has commenced investigations into various atrocities alleged to have occurred in East Africa.

deal with particular disasters. The United States ultimately opposed the final version of the Rome Statute, which created the ICC, because it allows the ICC's prosecutor and judges to decide on their own whether to act, rather than awaiting referral of a case from the Security Council (the practice with the ad hoc tribunals). Professors of international law mostly have deplored the U.S. position. More generally, the U.S. professoriat, by numbers and stature, overwhelmingly favors the exercise of judicial power, both international and domestic, to punish violations of international law; and Commonwealth and European scholars seem largely to envy, on behalf of their national courts, the power that U.S. judges wield. Thus, even if at present the coercive, and potentially liberty-threatening, dimensions of international lawmaking seem marginal, the weight of opinion would wish this lawmaking to acquire great instrumental power.

Accordingly, without exaggerating the practical significance of the issue, we can regard some instances of international lawmaking as coercive and therefore a potential threat to liberty. Individuals have been jailed (and in the case of the post–World War II proceedings, hanged) as a result of the decisions of international criminal courts, and a permanent body to carry out the prosecution and punishment of international crimes now exists. Litigants have used domestic courts to sue individuals and firms for large sums because of purported violations of international law. Business regulation increasingly turns on the decisions of international bodies. The enforceability and interpretation of a widening range of contracts turns on the meaning of international law. Each of these instances contains the potential of arbitrary encroachments on liberty.

By no means do I wish to suggest that all international lawmaking is presumptively a threat to liberty, much less that it does not contribute to the ordering of liberty necessary for human flourishing and freedom. Coercion brought against, for example, persons guilty of torture and murder does not set off many alarm bells. The point, rather, is that whenever enactment of a law creates the possibility of coercion, one legitimately can ask whether the processes involved in its enactment contain at least minimal safeguards to discourage the arbitrary exercise of power.

I also concede that whether given procedures satisfy process values depends on context, and that the contexts of international lawmaking differ in many respects from the context of domestic lawmaking. Because there is no such thing as an international government per se, clear separation of powers, much less elaborate checks and balances, is hard to construct. Because direct election of legislators is virtually absent (the European Parliament providing the only counterexample, and that a qualified one), the problem of lawmaker accountability necessarily involves agency questions.[19] In some instances, the power of national states to

---

[19] By an agency question, I mean the possibility that an agent (here, an international body) has different incentives than does its principal (here, the people for whom the international body acts).   (continued on next page)

reject rules of international law substitutes for separation of powers and checks and balances, but, as I observed above, this mechanism does not always work.

My point, in sum, is that some international rules can be sufficiently coercive to justify an inquiry into the suitability of the lawmaking processes that generated these rules. What constitutes a minimally acceptable lawmaking process is a difficult question, and a simple analogy to domestic lawmaking is an insufficient response. But the growing presence of international rules in contemporary life, and the ambitions of some for an even greater role for these rules, invites an inquiry into the legitimacy of their genesis, interpretation, and application.

III. International Institutions as a Potential Threat to Liberty

Imagine a treaty under which several states agree to establish an international agency invested with the authority to issue binding pronouncements regarding some set of topics. To make the problem more interesting, imagine that the treaty posits that the agency's determinations about its authority to issue particular pronouncements cannot be challenged in national courts. Further imagine that the treaty obligates each signatory to implement the agency's determinations, and in particular to give them "the full force of law."

This lawmaking structure is far from hypothetical. Substitute "Constitution" for "treaty" and "Supreme Court of the United States" for "international agency" and we have the structure of U.S. constitutional law (albeit due to evolved understandings rather than because of the written text of the document).[20] The 1957 Treaty of Rome constitutes the European Court of Justice in similar fashion, and the 1950 European Convention on Human Rights does much the same for the European Court of Human Rights. The 1945 Articles of Agreement of the International Monetary Fund and the International Bank for Reconstruction and Development (better known as the World Bank) arrogate an adjudicatory function for the respective executive bodies of these institutions. The 1998 Rome Statute for the International Criminal Court puts that court in the position

---

As a result of the 1997 Treaty of Amsterdam and the 2001 Treaty of Nice, the European Parliament, which comprises members directly elected by voters in the member states, acquired an expanded role in the creation of the legislation of the European Community. But the Community's other lawmaking organs, the European Commission and the European Council, selected by the members' governments, still dominate the process. For discussion, see Stephan, Parisi, and Depoorter, *The Law and Economics of the European Union*, 247–53.

[20] That is to say, the Supreme Court of the United States acquired the power to render authoritative and binding interpretations of the Constitution as a result of gradual public acceptance of its claim that it possessed this power, rather than because of any express language in the Constitution so providing.

of resolving a number of issues involving the scope and meaning of international criminal law.[21]

Consider in particular what kinds of questions the International Criminal Court must address, how it must address them, and the consequences of its choices. The Rome Statute authorizes punishment of four generic crimes—genocide, crimes against humanity, war crimes, and aggression. The last category is contingent on the later adoption of a definition of that class of crimes, because the authors of the statute concluded that the concept of aggression at present lacks sufficient clarity and acceptance to support prosecutions. The statute's definitions of the three crimes currently proscribed contain many illustrations, but each rests ultimately on stated general principles that invite elaboration and expansion. To take just one of these proscribed acts, a "crime against humanity" entails imprisonment "in violation of the fundamental rules of international law" without further specification, in addition to "persecution" on the basis of, inter alia, politics or ethnic, cultural, or religious differences. But what norm constitutes a "fundamental" rule of international law? What acts amount to "persecution"? How are we to determine the causal links between persecution and difference? These are questions of critical importance that only organs of the ICC can resolve.[22] Much the same goes for other important questions, such as the existence of excuses or justifications for otherwise criminal behavior.[23] Finally, in every particular case, the court must determine either that no state with jurisdiction over an offense is conducting an investigation, or that states that have conducted or are conducting an investigation are unable or unwilling "genuinely" to act.[24]

It is exactly the process by which the prosecutor and the court must make these fundamental substantive choices that is troubling. Under the terms of the Rome Statute, the prosecutor and the court act hermetically. Each must convince itself of the plausibility of its interpretations, and the court may refuse to accept the prosecutor's determinations. But no out-

---

[21] The Treaty of Rome (1957) created the European Economic Community, which the 1992 Maastricht Treaty renamed as the European Community. The European Community is the principal element of the European Union. The Council of Europe, a body of states that antedates the organizations that became the European Union and that always has had more members than those organizations, promulgated the 1950 European Convention on Human Rights, which in turn established the Strasbourg court. At the end of World War II, the victors established the International Monetary Fund (IMF) and the International Bank for Reconstruction and Development (the World Bank) to organize and reform the international financial system. The Soviet Union participated in the negotiations that produced the Articles of Agreement for the IMF and the World Bank, but it and its satellites declined to join those organizations.

[22] See Paul B. Stephan, "International Governance and American Democracy," *Chicago Journal of International Law* 1, no. 2 (2000): 253–56.

[23] See Rosa Ehrenreich Brooks, "Law in the Heart of Darkness: Atrocity and Duress," *Virginia Journal of International Law* 43, no. 3 (2003): 867–69.

[24] See Paul B. Stephan, "U.S. Constitutionalism and International Law: What the Multilateralist Move Leaves Out," *Journal of International Criminal Justice* 2, no. 1 (2004): 13–14.

side body can override these decisions. By the terms of article 16 of the statute, the United Nations Security Council may order a one-year delay of an investigation or prosecution, but such action would require the consent of all five permanent members of the Security Council and in any event would not be conclusive.

In effect, then, the prosecutor and the judges—each subject to no outside review once selected for a nonrenewable nine-year term—have the power to decide whether individual states have "genuinely" pursued an offense, whether particular conduct constitutes an offense, and what constitutes an acceptable excuse or justification for conduct otherwise constituting an offense. They must make these determinations in the face of scanty precedent or historical background, and in contexts that often implicate deep geopolitical antagonisms. They do have access to a burgeoning body of scholarly advice about how they should go about their work, but this, as scholarship typically does, contains as many points of view as there are authors. At bottom, only such internal constraints rooted in the construction of professional identities as these actors might possess (if any) constrain their exercise of significant coercive power.

What the Europeans call the Luxembourg and Strasbourg courts—the EC's European Court of Justice (in Luxembourg) and the Council of Europe's European Court of Human Rights (in Strasbourg)—present similar issues. At the same time, some differences between these bodies, and between them and the ICC, are apparent. Although the Luxembourg court has final say on the interpretation of the Treaty of Rome (the foundational instrument of the European Community), the existence of a separate EC lawmaking process complicates and to some extent confounds the court's freedom of action. Moreover, the court's jurisdiction does not extend beyond the twenty-five members of the EC. Finally, even though the court's decrees are said to have direct effect, they have practical significance only to the extent that national governments comply with them. The Luxembourg court has evinced a fairly high degree of tolerance for foot-dragging and circumvention, suggesting that less coercion attends its edicts than one might assume. Finally, the Luxembourg court has carried on in various forms for fifty years, creating a history that provides an additional layer of constraint.

The Strasbourg court is nested in a different institutional structure. It has functioned in one capacity or another since 1959, but only since 1998 have all persons with human rights claims against the forty-four states bound by the European Convention enjoyed an unqualified right to file suit.[25] Due at least in part to this structural change, the twenty-first cen-

---

[25] Protocol 11, Convention for the Protection of Human Rights and Fundamental Freedoms, *European Treaty Series* no. 155, effective November 1, 1998. Before the amendment, individuals could only direct a request for investigation and prosecution of human rights violations to the European Human Rights Commission, an independent international body created by the European Convention. For a discussion of the pre-1998 practice of European

tury has seen a remarkable increase in the number of the court's controversial decisions, such as those concerning the rights of sexual minorities, the right to die, and the procedures for conducting police investigations.[26] The Strasbourg court faces no counterpart legislative or executive organs, unlike the Luxembourg court. Moreover, the Strasbourg court's ability to enforce its decisions through fines operates fairly automatically, limiting the power of intransigent states to undermine its judgments.[27]

I discuss these bodies because they present the most straightforward instances of delegation of coercive lawmaking power to an international body. Other instances of potentially greater significance exist. Under legal theories that enjoy wide circulation in the academic community and modest support in some domestic courts, various international bureaucracies, such as the United Nations Human Rights Commission and the International Committee of the Red Cross, enjoy a more diffuse power to create "customary international law," which some courts regard as binding. Were this theory to gain widespread credence, many international bodies would take on the role of coercive lawmakers.

For two reasons, however, I defer discussion of these bodies to the next section. First, at present the claims for their lawmaking capacity are outliers rather than mainstream legal doctrine. Second, their actions take on the nature of customary international law only if courts reach this conclusion. The legitimacy of this process thus is part of a broader inquiry about domestic common law methods as means of international lawmaking.

Are the constraints that currently operate on the International Criminal Court, the European Court of Justice, and the European Court of Human Rights sufficient to protect against arbitrary restrictions of liberty? One possible response is that every constitutional court, most particularly the Supreme Court of the United States, functions in this manner, and most people consider the development and empowerment of these institutions a good thing. Why shouldn't these international courts work as well as these national courts do?

---

states in response to rulings of the Strasbourg court, see Tom Barkhuysen, Michiel van Emmerik, and Piet Hein van Kempen, eds., *The Execution of Strasbourg and Geneva Human Rights Decisions in the National Legal Order* (The Hague: Martinus Nijhoff Publishers, 1999).

[26] *Atlan v. United Kingdom,* 34 European Human Rights Reports 33 (2002) (*ex parte* hearings to consider government privilege to withhold evidence in criminal trial); *Pretty v. United Kingdom,* 35 European Human Rights Reports 1 (2002) (right to die); *I. v. United Kingdom,* 36 European Human Rights Reports 53 (2002) (rights of transgendered); *Beck, Copp, and Bazeley v. United Kingdom* (48535/99) [2002] ECHR 679 (October 22, 2002) (right of homosexuals to serve in armed services).

[27] Monetary awards issued by the Strasbourg court become debts that constitute a straightforward obligation of the defendant state. According to the website of the court: "To date States which have been ordered to make payments under Article 50 have consistently done so." Since 1996, the court has added interest charges to judgments not satisfied within three months. http://www.echr.coe.int/Eng/EDocs/EffectsOfJudgments.html (accessed March 16, 2005).

The most obvious rejoinder is that international organs are different
from national courts. To begin with, they draw on agents from different
states with various cultures, historical experiences, and professional identities. They confront a greater range of contested issues than do most
bodies, and they do so without the benefit of an unstated cultural consensus or broad historical memory. Yes, most institutions may go through
a period of foundational angst, during which the absence of a developed
institutional culture or guidance from precedent may complicate choices
about appropriate actions. But the international organs present an aggravated case. The Supreme Court of the United States, for instance, enjoyed
the benefit of its justices' common grounding in British common law, a
frame of reference that they shared with virtually all lawyers of their day.
Nothing similar binds the ICC or the Strasbourg or Luxembourg courts.

The absence of cultural and historical constraints might not matter as
much if these organs largely engaged in technocratic exercises to reach
important but obscure results. One could imagine an international tribunal that, for example, settled disputes over the ownership of particular
locations on the radio spectrum based exclusively on issues of engineering and simple rules of allocational priority. Interestingly, the real-world
analog to this hypothetical organ—the dispute resolution services of the
Internet Corporation for Assigned Names and Numbers (ICANN), which
deals with ownership of internet domain names—does not purport to
bind national legal systems, which remain free to reject ICANN outcomes.[28] An analogous process, the settlement of investment disputes by
international arbitration, has generated heated criticism exactly for its
narrow focus on property rights at the expense of other values.[29] The
mandates of the ICC and the Luxembourg and Strasbourg courts go far
beyond technocratic problems, however. They extend to deep and culturally divisive issues such as the duty to refuse an illegitimate order, the
role of amnesty and reconciliation in the wake of conflict, the balance
between press freedom and protection of individual reputation and group
sensitivities, and the rights, powers, and immunities of members of mar-
ginalized groups.

There is a point of view that maintains that institutions not subject to
conventional democratic constraints ought to resolve emotionally charged
and divisive issues, because democracy breaks down under stress. According to this argument, resolution of fundamental problems requires rea-
soned deliberation, which a society awash in passion cannot sustain. In

---

[28] The Internet Corporation for Assigned Names and Numbers is a nonprofit corporation
established in the Commonwealth of Virginia to administer the domain name assignment
system. All contracts for domain names now contain a clause providing for arbitration of
ownership disputes under ICANN rules. For a fuller description of the legal basis of this
process, see *Barcelona.com, Inc. v. Excelentisimo Ayuntamiento de Barcelona,* United States Court
of Appeals for the Fourth Circuit, 330 F.3d 617 (2003).

[29] See Muthucumaraswamy Sornarajah, *International Law on Foreign Investment,* 2d ed.
(Cambridge: Cambridge University Press, 2004).

lieu of neglecting these problems, a nation can turn to disinterested decision makers operating behind a cloak of moral authority.[30] For proponents of this argument, a different system of checks must apply to such tribunals. Rather than submitting their decisions to formal institutional constraints, the wielders of this power instead must display due regard for the limits of their moral authority. This intangible constraint, in turn, implicates an alliance between the tribunal and its commentators, as the weight of scholarly opinion presumably can bolster or reduce the authority behind a controversial decision.

Even as applied to a well-entrenched and successful institution such as the Supreme Court of the United States, this argument invites considerable skepticism. Whatever the particular endowments of the Supreme Court justices, their collective ability to sense the intangible limits on their authority is impaired by the cloistered lives that their institutional roles impose on them. Institutional checks on an organ's lawmaking powers exist precisely because individual judgment and discretion are not always sufficient to prevent great blunders. The history of the Supreme Court's more ambitious constitutional decision making—the infamous *Dred Scott* decision, only the second occasion on which the Court struck down a federal statute, comes to mind[31]—suggests why something more than intuitive self-restraint may be necessary.[32]

An extension of the democracy-breakdown argument to an international tribunal seems especially implausible. The idea that such institutions from their inception will wield sufficient moral authority to overcome deep conflict strikes me as wishful thinking. The probability that jurists from different nations can build coalitions that withstand local passions and entrenched political opposition veers toward nil. More likely is the rise of perceptions that particular decisions represent national prejudice. The prosecution of Slobodan Milosevic by the UN's special court for the former Yugoslavia (a precursor of the ICC) appears to have united Serbs in a conviction that the rest of Europe hates them, rather than leading them to the realization that their former leader had disgraced their nation with his policies. Conflicts between the British House of Lords and the Strasbourg court give the impression that a controlling majority of the human rights tribunal has thrown its lot in with a Franco-

---

[30] See Cass Sunstein, "Constitutionalism and Seccession," *University of Chicago Law Review* 58, no. 3 (1991): 69–70.

[31] *Dred Scott v. Sandford,* 60 U.S. (19 How.) 393 (1856). This infamous Supreme Court decision invalidated the Missouri Compromise, a congressional enactment intended to limit the spread of slavery to new territories of the United States, on the ground that the legislation infringed constitutionally protected interests of slave owners. The first instance of Supreme Court invalidation of federal legislation was *Marbury v. Madison,* 5 U.S. (1 Cranch) 137 (1803), a decision involving the power of Congress to assign certain cases to the Court's jurisdiction.

[32] See Cass Sunstein, "The Dred Scott Case with Notes on Affirmative Action, the Right to Die, and Same-Sex Marriage," *The Green Bag* 1, no. 1 (1997).

German cabal intent on undermining traditional underpinnings of British liberty in favor of a continental conception of social-democratic *dirigisme*.[33] The point is not that in either case these fears are well founded, but rather that they exist and may become more powerful with the growth and development of international tribunals.

One might sensibly respond that all international organs, the ICC and the Luxembourg and Strasbourg courts included, operate under one basic constraint, namely the process for choosing their members. A selection process that allows for state dissent, combined with limited terms for the persons selected, sets up an *ex ante* check on what an organ can do. States may miscalculate what a judge will do once seated—the United States has some familiarity with this problem—but, with some delay, they can correct for that.

In some instances where discretion is concentrated in a single person, such as the prosecutor of the ICC, the selection power, or more precisely the power not to reappoint, may serve as a check on the actor. In other cases, the selection power may deter extreme deviations from an organ's stated responsibilities. Often, however, the structure of selection of members of these organs militates against discipline. The common practice of international tribunals, including the ICC and the Luxembourg and Strasbourg courts, entails allocating positions to individual states or cohesive blocs of states. As a result, stable coalitions can form to marginalize persons selected by dissident states. In the case of the ICC, for example, a single judge selected by the United States could not defeat a coalition of states hostile to U.S. exercises of power, a scenario that is far from hypothetical.[34]

I do not mean to suggest that any of these tribunals face an insurmountable hurdle. It is not inconceivable that the ICC, for example, might simultaneously avoid taking on any deeply controversial cases while dealing with those obvious outrages that occur. Perhaps, over a decade or more, the leadership of the court might acquire a reputation for balanced action and careful exercise of its powers, thereby accruing moral authority and general respect. But this would take luck as well as prudence. Were a conflict to arise that pitted great powers against each other or

[33] The British courts and the Strasbourg court have differed in several instances, including disagreements over the proper elements of the criminal justice process, *Atlan v. United Kingdom*, 34 European Human Rights Reports 33 (2002) (rejecting rule of *Regina v. Davis*, [1993] 2 All English Reports 643 [C.A.], on obligation of prosecution to disclose statements of confidential informants); over the extent of tort immunity for police officers, *Osman v. United Kingdom*, 29 European Human Rights Reports 245 (2000) (rejecting decision of *Osman v. Ferguson*, [1993] 4 All English Reports 344 [C.A.], on scope of immunity); and over the existence of a privilege under the law of defamation for comment on public figures, *Reynolds v. Times Newspapers*, [2001] Appellate Cases 127 (H.L.) (disregarding Strasbourg court decisions).

[34] For an earlier treatment of this problem that did not consider the possibility of stable coalitions, see Paul B. Stephan, "Courts, Tribunals, and Legal Unification—The Agency Problem," *Chicago Journal of International Law* 3, no. 2 (2002): 336–38.

otherwise seriously divided world opinion, the tribunal would find it exceedingly hard to seem neither partisan nor toothless.

In the case of the ICC, the risks seem especially unnecessary. An obvious model of easily imposed institutional checks existed at the time of the adoption of the Rome Statute. Since the creation of the United Nations, all war crimes tribunals depended on authorization by the Security Council, a body that acts only in the absence of the disapproval of any of the five traditional nuclear powers.[35] In the past, each opportunity for international intervention in the face of domestic inability to redress gross misconduct depended on the existence of the level of consensus that Security Council action entails. Requiring the ICC to await a Security Council resolution before taking jurisdiction over any particular conflict — the position for which the United States continues to hold out, and the reason for its refusal to ratify the 1998 Rome Statute — would have preserved this institutional structure.

In the abstract, one might see a contradiction between the creation of an institution intended to bring the most terrible kinds of crimes to justice and the retention of a great-power veto over its actions. This objection, however, rests on confusion of the two bases of the ICC's jurisdiction. Credible allegations of the commission of an international crime, one should recall, by themselves are insufficient to justify action by the ICC. The ICC also must determine that no state possesses the capacity and desire to engage in a "genuine" effort to prosecute. Its jurisdiction, in other words, depends fundamentally on a determination that state-level action has failed. This latter consideration, unlike the determination of the existence of the elements of a crime, rests on irreducibly political and contestable considerations.

The Security Council is an appropriate body to make judgments about national incapacity to prosecute international crimes. Expecting a freestanding international institution to go after superpowers seems bizarre. In no other area touching on fundamental interests of a great power do we expect the United Nations to impose its will. It is not excessively cynical to believe that the proponents of the ICC who rejected the U.S. position did so largely out of a conviction that the threat to act against great powers would be empty, but that its hollowness would go unnoticed in at least some quarters.

I see nothing objectionable in general about a great-power veto over certain kinds of UN actions. One can embrace the concept of fundamental equality of all people without extending it to states: the United Nations since its inception has embraced the principle that some states are more equal than others. Each great power can prevent the United Nations from

---

[35] The five great powers — the United States, Russia, Great Britain, France, and China — do not have to endorse an action of the Security Council, but for any decision to have effect none must exercise its veto. The establishment of past ad hoc war crimes tribunals involved either the active support or passive acquiescence of all five.

authorizing sanctions against itself or its clients. Allowing great powers also to have a veto over capacity-to-prosecute determinations seems a natural extension of the present structure of the international order.

The Strasbourg court represents a different set of institutional problems. On the one hand, the Council of Europe has no counterpart to the UN's Security Council: there is no club of regional powers that possesses a veto over actions undertaken on behalf of the Council of Europe. Constraining the court's mandate, itself only recently unleashed, thus would involve the construction of a new institution. On the other hand, the court's coercive power, although real enough, is less than that of a comparable common law court. In particular, it lacks the power to nullify laws or practices of which it disapproves or to order nonmonetary punishment for persons who disobey its mandates. Individual states thus can resist its orders at the cost of the payment of fines. Sufficient resistance, in turn, might deter the court from undertaking more challenging projects.

My broader point does not concern the particular value of the ICC, the Strasbourg court, or similar institutions. Rather, I wish to respond to the tendency of many scholars to see these organs as the wave of the future.[36] Judicial bodies no less than other instruments of state power can flourish under conditions of limited power. As more international organs acquire self-executing powers that can operate without substantial state cooperation, greater effort will be required to devise checks other than withdrawal of state consent. The current imbroglio over the refusal of the U.S. to recognize the ICC sheds some light on potential alternatives as well as illustrating the politics of institutional maximalism.

IV. Domestic Enforcement of International Law as a Potential Threat to Liberty

Different checking problems arise when independent national courts create, interpret, and impose international law. The problems are subtle, because the means of judicial lawmaking vary among systems and the uses of international law vary from analogy to direct authority. National courts also may differ in what sources and methods they use to ascertain what constitutes international law. Each of these factors can complicate the question of whether international lawmaking by national courts presents distinctive issues of accountability and constraint.

One important difference between national and international courts is that international institutions have acquired coercive powers relatively recently, and the most interesting and possibly worrisome cases involve proposals for future powers. As a result, institutional-design issues remain

---

[36] See, e.g., Anne-Marie Slaughter, "Judicial Globalization," *Virginia Journal of International Law* 40, no. 4 (2000): 1124; and Jenny S. Martinez, "Toward an International Judicial System," *Stanford Law Review* 56, no. 2 (2003): 432.

central. Domestic courts, by contrast, constitute facts on the ground. The common-law courts in particular have rich as well as lengthy histories. Accordingly, it seems unrealistic to talk about reforming domestic courts as a means of limiting their ability to resort to international law. Rather, more subtle issues of cultural norms and prestige arise.

In the United States, discussion of the role of international law in domestic adjudication often involves one of two categorical claims, each of which I wish to criticize. First, some authorities have suggested that foreign sources of law, including international law, should have no role in the shaping of judicial determinations of domestic law.[37] At the opposite extreme, some scholars have argued that foreign sources should enjoy a privileged status, in the sense that their "otherness" itself strengthens the case for their respectful assimilation.[38] I believe that both these claims display a lack of appreciation of the multiple functions of precedent and authority in the common law process.

A judge might look to outside experiences for various reasons. On occasion, local law itself refers to foreign law, whether due to conventional choice-of-law rules or the application of a doctrine that involves some comparative assessment (such as the *forum non conveniens* doctrine used to dismiss lawsuits that would benefit from being brought in another jurisdiction). Alternatively, judges might seek evidence of the instrumental effects of a particular rule and look at the experience of other jurisdictions as an empirical test. Similarly, judges might look to other sources to expand their conceptual apparatus. Finally, a judge might apply foreign law out of an independent sense of obligation. Unless one wishes to defend judicial ignorance and narrow-mindedness, only the last function raises any difficulties.

On the one hand, those who attack any use of foreign or international law in the common law process are guilty of confusing these different functions and thereby weaken the force of their arguments. On the other hand, those who argue for privileging this category of law have tended to collapse these functions exactly because some seem obviously appealing, thus obscuring the need to defend the more difficult one. In the United States, neither the critics nor the apologists have sufficiently explored the specific issues surrounding the positing of a foreign-source obligation to apply foreign law.

[37] *Thompson v. Oklahoma*, 487 U.S. 815, 868 n. 4 (1988) (Scalia, J., dissenting); *Stanford v. Kentucky*, 492 U.S. 361, 369 n. 1 (1989); *Atkins v. Virginia*, 536 U.S. 304, 347–48 (2002) (Scalia, J., dissenting); *Lawrence v. Texas*, 539 U.S. 558, 598 (2003) (Scalia, J., dissenting).

[38] See Laurence R. Helfer and Anne-Marie Slaughter, "Toward a Theory of Effective Supranational Adjudication," *Yale Law Journal* 107, no. 2 (1997); and Harold Hongju Koh, "International Law as Part of Our Law," *American Journal of International Law* 98, no. 1 (2004): 45–48. These scholars cite with approval the claim of a prominent appellate judge, the former Dean of Yale Law School, that, with respect to the constitutional jurisprudence of countries that have drawn their inspiration from the United States, "Wise parents do not hesitate to learn from their children." *United States v. Then*, 56 F.3d 464, 469 (2d Cir. 1995) (Calabresi, J.).

One argument that I note in order to disregard it is the claim that the privileging of foreign and international authority masks a substantive agenda, namely the importation of *bien-pensant* social-democratic values.[39] It may be true that some advocates of the privileging position fail to explain why the decisions of, for example, the Strasbourg court should count but the law and practices of non-European states do not.[40] Behind this failure may lie undefended normative preferences. However, the more persuasive advocates of using foreign and international law acknowledge the point and mount a general defense of their position.[41] It is this general defense that I wish to address.

The basic argument for giving authoritative effect to international law rests on conformity and safety in numbers. A judicial consensus that crosses national boundaries, so the argument goes, matters more than a split of legal authority. To maximize the deference judges qua judges get from society, they should stick together. Thus, a foreign decision—say, the conclusion by the Strasbourg court that the European Convention on Human Rights contains an implicit ban on the criminalization of sodomy—should influence the Supreme Court of the United States in deciding whether the U.S. fundamental law similarly has an unstated but effective limit on governmental power. Moreover, this influence should rest on grounds other than instrumental observations (civilization as we know it did not come to an end in Europe after the Strasbourg court reached its judgment) or conceptual innovation (the particular arguments used to construct an implicit rule from general language in a fundamental text).[42] Rather, other courts should follow the Strasbourg court because doing so enhances their authority as well as that of the European body.[43]

How does this accretion of authority work? First, the appearance of consensus serves as a secondary source of persuasion. Doubters will be more reluctant to challenge widely held beliefs than those that are openly contested. Second, persons may feel some social pull toward conformity and away from deviance. Cooperation across courts thus builds social pressure.

Accepting that this dynamic exists and can bolster judicial authority, one can still question whether it should proceed unchecked. Judicial authority, one might believe, does not work as an end in itself. We want to empower judges to the extent that they will act in ways that make us

[39] Jeremy Rabkin, "Is EU Policy Eroding the Sovereignty of Non-Member States?" *Chicago Journal of International Law* 1, no. 2 (2000): 273–90.

[40] Roger P. Alford, "Misusing International Sources to Interpret the Constitution," *American Journal of International Law* 98, no. 1 (2004): 64–69.

[41] Helfer and Slaughter, "Toward a Theory of Effective Supranational Adjudication."

[42] For instances of the "civilization did not end" kind of argument, see *Atkins v. Virginia*, 536 U.S. 304, 316 n. 21 (2002); and *Lawrence v. Texas*, 539 U.S. 558, 576–77 (2003).

[43] *Atkins v. Virginia; Lawrence v. Texas;* Slaughter, "Judicial Globalization." For a recent instance of the Supreme Court making this kind of argument, see *Roper v. Simmons*, 543 U.S. (2005).

better off than we would be if they did not act, but not otherwise. For lawyers, of course, this is a hard point to acknowledge, because at least some set of lawyers inevitably will benefit from any accretion of judicial power. Proponents and opponents of any particular move, whether litigators or judges, will grow more powerful from having their controversy gain salience and perhaps will enjoy material rewards as well. Academics will have more to discuss authoritatively. But if we can broaden our horizons to consider the welfare of society, surely we must acknowledge that judges, like other state actors, are capable of arbitrary exercises of power that may threaten liberty.

Checking the lawmaking capacity of judges is tricky, however, because the common law methodology constitutes a style of argument rather than a naked assertion of raw power. Recent proposals in the U.S. Congress to forbid judges from relying on foreign precedent strike me as silly. Judges "rely" on precedent both when they weave it into their arguments and when they act on the basis of their understanding of it, and only the former can be observed. The legislation, in effect, seeks to regulate how judges write opinions, not what they do. The gesture seems empty.

A deeper problem is categorical. Conventional common law methodology simply fills in gaps that legislative enactments can supersede. But constitutional interpretation—in Europe, this means interpretation of the Treaty of Rome and the Convention on Human Rights—operates independently of legislative enactments. Legislatures have no authority to direct courts on how to interpret or apply constitutions.[44] As a result, legislatures cannot override either interpretive strategies or outcomes as to constitutional questions, even where the courts rely on international law. To the extent that courts frame their decisions as constitutional interpretation, Congress in the United States, and national parliaments in Europe, cannot do anything about controversial decisions (involving, for example, the rights and privileges of sexual minorities or the scope of capital punishment) that may incorporate outside sources of authority.

Put aside the problem that, in at least some instances, judges can bring international law into their decisions in ways that displace national legislatures. Are the outcomes based on international law necessarily desirable? The "safety in numbers" argument has a certain appeal. Some regularities in international practice maximize welfare independent of their effect on judicial prestige and power. Justice Antonin Scalia, a leading opponent of the incorporation of international law into constitutional decision making, still argues that the interpretation of international treaties requires judges to take account of the understandings of the treaty parties, including those understandings expressed by courts in other coun-

---

[44] *Dickerson v. United States,* 530 U.S. 428 (2000) (statute intended to determine scope of remedy for violations of constitutional protection against self-incrimination unconstitutionally infringes on judicial prerogatives).

tries.[45] A more formal way of putting the point is that some legal structures have built into them the possibility of network effects, and that efforts of judges to develop these effects can be defended without privileging judicial prerogatives as such.[46]

In sum, two problems face any effort to limit judicial aggrandizement based on the promotion of international solidarity. First, the legislative process cannot plausibly regulate rhetorical moves, as distinguished from discrete outcomes, and also cannot respond to outcomes placed on a constitutional footing. Second, some international solidarity is good, but separating the desirable, network-effects instances from judicial opportunism is hard. No categorical or structural approach seems to work.

Checking of international lawmaking by domestic courts thus requires approaches that operate internally to the domestic legal culture, as opposed to the institutional-design approaches discussed in Section III with respect to international organs. That is to say, the judges must limit their own actions, because limits imposed from outside seem neither reliable nor plausible. Framed in this manner, the problem resembles that involving constitutional development: internalization by judges of certain norms becomes the only effective means of guarding against excesses.

Earlier I questioned whether internalized cultural norms alone can function as checks on international tribunals such as the ICC and the Strasbourg court. The points I raised—lack of cultural solidarity and internalized norms—do not apply to many of the domestic courts that many scholars have asked to contribute to international lawmaking. These bodies, and in particular the federal courts of the United States, operate against a powerful background of tradition and well-developed professional identity. It is not patently inconsistent, then, to expect internalized cultural norms to do some work in checking domestic courts, but to expect less with regard to international tribunals.

The process of internalizing skepticism about the reliance on international authority has several dimensions. Those who select judges—in the United States, the president and a majority of the Senate do this for the most influential members of the judiciary—may try to predict whether a candidate has such skepticism, although *ex ante* predictions of this kind are notoriously unreliable.[47] Leading figures in the judiciary—in the United States, this means first and foremost the members of the Supreme Court— might expound on the reasons for adopting a more skeptical posture. And

[45] *Olympic Airways v. Hussain,* 540 U.S. 644, 659–62 (2004) (Scalia, J., dissenting).

[46] "Network effects" rest on the rediscovery by some economists and legal theorists of activities that entail positive returns to scale, which is to say that increasing the level of the activity increases the average net benefits associated with each unit of that activity. For application of the theory to international relations, see Kal Raustiala, "The Architecture of International Cooperation: Transgovernmental Networks and the Future of International Law," *Virginia Journal of International Law* 43, no. 1 (2002): 63–68.

[47] John C. Jeffries, Jr., "In Memoriam: Lewis F. Powell, Jr.," *Harvard Law Review* 112, no. 3 (1999): 597–600.

those who interact publicly with the judiciary and play a role in shaping judicial reputations, particularly members of the scholarly community, might praise or condemn judges based on whether they display a critical perspective toward claims of foreign authority.

The praise of skepticism runs against a certain grain in the legal academy. Legal scholarship for the most part avoids the scientific method, which means that the expounding of nonfalsifiable claims incurs no costs. Partly for this reason, creativity and shock value count for more than usefulness. A predictable egotism and self-regard leads, if not ineluctably then frequently, to ambitious claims that require the suspension of skepticism. The current popularity for judicial participation in international lawmaking reflects these factors at least to some extent.

Academia contains other forces, however, that may push the debate in another direction. Normal competitive pressures ensure that no conventional wisdom remains unchallenged for long, and an increase in the salience of a position tends to lead to greater critical scrutiny. In the last few years, we have seen in the United States the beginning of a serious debate about the legitimacy and value of the incorporation of international law into domestic common law. Although some of the antagonists have held on to reductive and absolute positions, new scholarship has taken a more nuanced and sophisticated approach to the problem. In particular, the image of international law as a monolithic authority, as well as the portrayal of domestic incorporation as an all-or-nothing proposition, has been superseded by analytically rich accounts that recognize multiple dimensions of the problem.[48]

One consequence of the increasing sophistication of the debate is the subversion of arguments based on the authority, as distinguished from the usefulness, of international law. To be sure, some scholars insist doggedly on the existence of a clear line of practice in which domestic courts consistently over the centuries have used a monolithic body of "international law" to shape municipal norms.[49] But a growing consensus about the complexity of the issue lightens this purported historical burden by demonstrating that earlier judicial practices, far from being canonical evidence of a general pattern, represent discrete responses to distinguishable problems. This necessary first step makes possible a shift in the terms of debate. We now can make normative judgments about the products of

[48] See T. Alexander Aleinikoff, "International Law, Sovereignty, and American Constitutionalism: Reflections on the Customary International Law Debate," *American Journal of International Law* 98, no. 1 (2004); and Ernest A. Young, "Sorting Out the Debate over Customary International Law," *Virginia Journal of International Law* 42, no. 2 (2002). Both these recent works owe a substantial conceptual debt to A. M. Weisburd, "State Courts, Federal Courts, and International Cases," *Yale Journal of International Law* 10, no. 1 (1995).

[49] Koh, "International Law as Part of Our Law"; Gerald L. Neuman, "The Uses of International Law in Constitutional Interpretation," *American Journal of International Law* 98, no. 1 (2004).

the common law process freed from false constraints based on authoritarian claims.[50]

A move away from obligatory reliance on international law in favor of more nuanced and consequentialist discussions may have a salutary effect on the common law process. Judges (much like all people) sometimes seek to avoid the pain associated with difficult decisions by depicting themselves as compelled to reach a result. Arguments based on authority invite the actor to disregard the actor's intuitions about the action's consequences or the extent to which it will displease relevant audiences. Restricting the domain of authority increases the likelihood that the actor will take into account the implications of the action. So cautioned, the actor—in this case, common law judges—may hesitate more often before encroaching on liberty.

V. Conclusion

It may seem odd to think of international law as a potential threat to liberty, and hence to justice. Certainly its proponents see it as a beacon of hope, a means of civilizing the too violent and cruel tendencies of international politics and promoting humane values. I recognize these aspirations, but note that the last century was littered with regimes that attracted adherents by their noble ideals but that too often became instruments of awful crimes.[51] The manifest good faith and eloquence of those who wish to broaden the scope of international law is not itself sufficient to foreclose an inquiry into the possibility of this threat.

The threat I describe is largely potential. Most specialists would argue that the central problem with international law is its inefficacy, not its power. I argue that this rejoinder is backward looking. The trend over the last twenty years involves the accretion of authority by international institutions, and more frequent and more significant invocations of international law by national lawmakers. I do not argue that either development necessarily is a bad thing. I do argue that the time for critical analysis of these trends is now.

Law, University of Virginia

·

---

[50] *Ullonoa Flores v. S. Peru Copper Corp.*, 343 F.3d 140, 170–71 (2d Cir. 2003) (rejecting argument that claims of international law experts constitute an independent source for determining the law of the United States); *United States v. Yousef*, 327 F.3d 56, 74 and n. 35 (2d Cir. 2003) (same).

[51] Stéphane Courtois, Nicolas Werth, Jean-Louis Panné, Andrzej Paczkowski, Karel Bartosek, and Jean-Louis Margolin, *The Black Book of Communism: Crimes, Terror, Repression*, ed. Mark Kramer, trans. Jonathan Murphy and Mark Kramer (Cambridge, MA: Harvard University Press, 1999).

WHAT'S WRONG WITH IMPERIALISM?*

By Christopher W. Morris

I. Introduction

Few people today seem to doubt that imperialism is wrong. All one usually needs to do to condemn an act or policy is to label it as imperialist. There are good reasons for this, as we shall see. For the last two thousand years, many crimes have been associated with empires, and several of the empires of the last century have set new standards for human depravity and cruelty. Still, it is worth asking what exactly is wrong with imperialism. It is often good to raise critical questions about a consensus. And it may be that some features of empire are worthy of our respect.

II. The Wrongs and Horrors of Empire

In our time, the horrors of imperialism are well illustrated by the Japanese conquest of Manchuria or by Leopold II's administration of his Belgian Congo. The extermination of many of the peoples of North and Central America a few centuries ago is another illustration. The history of empire is very much a story of death and destruction. It is also a tale of plunder and exploitation. Spain's early conquests were motivated by the prospect of acquiring precious metals, and older empires always exacted tribute (in goods or gold or slaves). All empires until the nineteenth century were slave-owning. The picture is not attractive.

To the association of empires with death, plunder, and exploitation, we can add *domination*. Empires are systems of the domination of one society or group over another. In a number of ways, this formulation is ambiguous. Empires are typically imposed, established by conquest. In that sense, they are systems of domination. It is not clear how damning a criticism this is, given that most states, if not virtually all, have been imposed or established by conquest. More importantly, perhaps, all systems of governance involve some kind of "domination"—for instance, legislators establish laws and judges and administrators make decisions

* An earlier version of this essay was presented at James Madison University and discussed at a workshop of the Committee for Politics, Philosophy, and Public Policy at the University of Maryland, College Park. I am grateful to members of both audiences for critical questions and comments, in particular to John Brown, Farid Dhanji, Douglas Grob, Peter Levine, Jerry Segal, and Karol Soltan (others are thanked in the notes). Gratitude is also owed to Jose Idler-Acosta, David Lefkowitz, and Ellen Paul for helpful written comments.

153

that must be obeyed. The kind of governance typically associated with empire often excludes what we now (ambiguously) call "self-government." Given that empires typically rule in considerable part indirectly, the absence of "self-government" here may not be very significant; historically, indirect rule often was relatively permissive, at least compared to available alternatives. Until recently, most states were not democratic, so the absence of democratic self-rule is not a damning criticism of older empires. The concern, however, is in the first instance with the absence of political institutions responsive to the interests and concerns of the governed. We can easily say of many, if not most, empires that the imposed institutions were thus unresponsive. Insofar as that is the case, they are systems of domination in an objectionable way.

Another way in which empires are usually objectionable systems of domination lies in the relation of superiority that the conqueror asserts over the conquered. The right of the imperialist is that of the strong to rule the weak and, more importantly, that of the superior to rule the inferior. Many think that imperialism is invariably racist. It is dubious that the empire of Rome or that of the Hapsburgs or the Ottoman invoked a concept of race anything like ours; but racism is a species of asserted superiority, and the latter certainly is important for an appreciation of imperialism. Imperial powers typically claim superiority. They, by virtue of something about them, are superior to the conquered, and this superiority is part of the basis for their rule. Certain forms of this claim are familiar to all students of history; rulers have often based their rule on ancestry or social class. As obnoxious and incredible a claim as it may appear to us, it is hardly novel, merely what most rulers did until a century or so ago.

More credible perhaps is one particular version of this assertion of superiority. Most empires claim a civilizing mission. Rome and most later empires claimed to bring civilization to the conquered. While this claim may at first seem self-serving and false to us, it should be taken seriously and distinguished from other more dubious claims. Most of us believe there are standards of civilization; the question, then, is whether a *mission civilatrice* has anything to say for itself. Today we are skeptical of talk of civilization. Believing that there are standards of civilization commits one to thinking that some social forms may not meet them, though it need not imply that it is possible to rank civilizations that meet minimal standards. Even if it were the case that all civilizations are equal and worthy of respect, it may still be that not all societies are civilized. More will need to be said here, and a distinction between claims to civilization and possession of the one true faith will need to be made. An important question will be whether this civilizing mission is compatible with respect for the subjects in need of instruction and development.

We associate plunder and exploitation with empire, as I indicated above; but it is not always clear that empires are, on net, beneficial to the imperialists. There is a debate among historians and economists as to whether particular empires were in fact beneficial; many of the classical critics of empire stressed the harm to the mother country. Thus, it may be that inefficiency is another fault we may add to the list.

The score card, then, is not favorable: conquest, death, destruction, cruelty, domination, and perhaps wastefulness. It is hard not to condemn imperialism.

III. Preliminary Evaluation

Most modern empires stand condemned by their association with the conditions described above. I am not an expert, and I should expect that good historians will have much to say and much about which to disagree. Nevertheless, I should venture the suggestion that our evaluation of Rome would be mixed and not all unfavorable and that many of the consequences of the British Empire and, to a lesser extent, that of the French were in some respects salutary. Niall Ferguson's recent book *Empire: How Britain Made the Modern World* makes the case for the British Empire, and it is one worth taking seriously. The thought that "empire [may be] a form of international government that can work" is one source of my interest in the topic.[1]

The gross injustices associated with empires may, as I said, lead us to condemn them, but the question will be whether imperialism necessarily is to be rejected. The fact that most empires are established by conquest will also trouble us, but it will be worth noticing that the history of modern states is very bloody and that most, if not virtually all, modern states are founded in conquest. Many of the horrors of empire are familiar to students of the state. If the evils of states are not sufficient to condemn them—and most believe that some states at least are good and worth preserving—then we should ask whether the evils of empires suffice to condemn them.

IV. Features of Empires

We should say more about the characterizing features of empires. I do not hazard a "definition," as I do not believe that complex terms like this one can be characterized precisely in the manner required by a genuine definition. There are, in addition, features of classical empires like that of Rome that distinguish them from modern ones in interesting ways, ways that are hard to capture in short or simple definitions. This is not unusual

---

[1] "In short, what the British Empire proved is that empire is a form of international government that can work—and not just for the benefit of the ruling power. It sought to globalize not just an economic but a legal and ultimately a political system." Niall Ferguson, *Empire: How Britain Made the Modern World* (New York: Basic Books, 2002), 362.

with terms of this kind used in different contexts to designate complex historical phenomena.[2]

Empires are typically *vast*. That is, their territories or domains are large compared to their respective cities (*poleis*) or (modern) states. The imperial possessions, typically acquired by conquest (or by intermarriage or inheritance), lie at some distance from the *metropolis*. Empires are composite entities, formed of previously separate political or social entities.[3] They consequently are typically marked by considerable diversity, to employ a fashionable term. The cultural or, as we now say, the national or ethnic makeup of the subjects of an empire is quite varied, at least compared to that of the metropolis or "center." This diversity, when coupled with unsavory kinds of "domination," may make us suspicious of empire. But this feature of empires is the source of other features that we now admire:

> Because of their size and sheer diversity, most empires have in time become universal, cosmopolitan societies. In order to rule vast and widely separated domains, imperial governments have generally found themselves compelled to be broadly tolerant of diversity of culture and sometimes even of belief, so long as these posed no threat to their authority.[4]

The governance of empires is usually a mixture of direct and indirect rule. Considerations of distance and of technology alone made direct rule an impossibility for virtually all empires, most importantly the classical ones. Subjects were for the most part governed directly by local officials, and the power of the metropolis was mediated by "colonial" governors. This feature of empire is of some interest to students of federalism and of systems such as the European Union.

The core or metropolis of an empire in the ancient world was usually a *polis* or similar political unit.[5] In the modern world, imperialists are almost always states. The existence of a dominant core and a subordinate periphery is an essential feature of an empire. Given the differences between

---

[2] I think the notion of a state is very difficult to capture in a short or precise definition. See Christopher W. Morris, *An Essay on the Modern State* (Cambridge: Cambridge University Press, 1998), chap. 2.

[3] Stephen Howe, *Empire* (Oxford: Oxford University Press, 2002), 15.

[4] Anthony Pagden, *Peoples and Empires: A Short History of European Migration, Exploration, and Conquest, from Greece to the Present* (New York: Modern Library, 2001), xxii.

[5] My potted story is somewhat Eurocentric. This is forgivable given the eminence of the European and Greco-Roman empires. The interesting question of how to classify premodern China—as an empire or a kind of state—is not easy to answer. Also, there are ways in which the nineteenth-century United States may be thought of as an empire. New York State still refers to itself as "the Empire State," and some of the thirteen original American states had "Western Reserves" or territories. See my remarks below about the ways in which empires characteristically view their boundaries.

modern states and premodern forms of governance, there are significant differences in early and later empires. The world of modern states—the "state system"—in which we have lived for several centuries is one where the paradigmatic form of political organization is that of a state (or what many misleadingly dub a "nation-state"). One of the significant aspects of this system of "world" organization is a kind of plurality: necessarily, there are many states. As we see with the case of Rome—and perhaps in a different way with that of premodern China—premodern empires did not presuppose, or acknowledge, such plurality. States, as I have argued elsewhere, have *borders*; when not determined by oceans, state borders are contiguous with those of other states. Rome, by contrast, did not conceive of itself as one empire among many; its "boundaries were not borders, but merely frontiers—the furthermost point reached by conquest."[6] The terms we now use—"empire," "imperialist"—derive from the Latin *imperium*, the power to command or to order (in politics and war), a kind of authority.[7] The distinction we now make between "internal" and "external" sovereignty—the power to govern subjects and a certain independence from other powers—was inconceivable to Rome. The scope of its *imperium* was potentially the *cosmopolis*.[8]

We shall return later to some of the differences between ancient and modern empires. For now, let us think of empires as particular forms of political organization different from classical *poleis* or modern states.[9] They are typically large, composite and diverse, composed of different peoples and previously separate groups or societies, and usually created by conquest. And empires are constituted by a dominant core or center and a subordinate periphery.[10]

V. MUST IMPERIALISM STAND CONDEMNED?

The characterization above, while quite general and imprecise, may be adequate for our purposes. The question before us is whether empires

[6] Morris, *An Essay on the Modern State,* 30–31. In this work I cite, among other writings, the important essay by Friedrich Kratochwil, "Of Systems, Boundaries, and Territoriality: An Inquiry into the Formation of the State System," *World Politics* 39, no. 1 (October 1986): 27–52. He argues that "[t]he Roman Empire conceived of the *limes* not as a boundary, but as a temporary stopping place where the potentially unlimited expansion of the *Pax Romana* had come to a halt" (35–36).

[7] Pagden, *Peoples and Empires,* xxi–xxii.

[8] This feature of Roman imperialism permits it to be the source for what we now think of as cosmopolitan political thought. Given that cosmopolitanism is the most influential contemporary form of anti-statism, it is worth reflecting on its imperial roots.

The fact that empires typically claimed potentially universal jurisdictions is one of the reasons why it is more fitting to think of Vatican City not as a state but as the seat of a former empire. See my *Essay on the Modern State,* 47 n. 85.

[9] In my *Essay on the Modern State,* I characterize the (modern) state as a particular form of political organization and contrast it with a number of alternatives.

[10] This general characterization borrows from Howe, *Empire,* and Pagden, *Peoples and Empires.* See also Michael W. Doyle, *Empires* (Ithaca, NY, and London: Cornell University Press, 1986), chap. 1.

and imperialism (the pursuit of empire) stand condemned by the injustices and evils of most historical empires. I do not want to settle the question by a "definition" which arbitrarily makes the nasty features of empire essential or accidental. Instead, I want to have us think carefully about the central features of empires and of a number of similarities they have with states and other forms of political organization. Empire has a deservedly bad press. But much of it is earned unfairly; nasty empires are (implicitly) compared to reasonably nice states. We would all be anarchists if we were to judge states using similar comparative methods.[11] One of the aims of this essay is to give empires their due.

Let us focus our thoughts by considering a hypothetical empire, a particularly nice one. Suppose there is an empire that is not exploitative or cruel, much less genocidal or homicidal. Its institutions of governance are relatively responsive and relatively efficient—relative to the best alternatives that exist at the time of comparison. It is also relatively just. By this I mean two things: first, it meets most of the fundamental norms of justice and respects most of the fundamental rights of its subjects, and second, it does this, again, as well as the best alternative systems. I assume, implicitly and perhaps contentiously, that people do not have a fundamental right of justice not to be governed by an imperial power (but assuming the contrary would beg the question I wish to consider).

Assume as well that our nice empire is a beneficial venture, that most subjects are better off than in their previous condition. It will be hard to be very precise as well as realistic here. The question of whether *any* complex form of political organization clearly leaves most subjects better off is not a simple one or one that can be answered with precision. Still, this nice empire, like many real ones, builds roads and systems of irrigation, sets up railroad systems, establishes relatively efficient financial institutions and competent civil service institutions, and most of all, protects subjects against foreign invaders and prevents civil or ethnic conflict.[12]

I grant that most empires have not been this nice and that it is not easy to conceive of one that would be. I have intentionally made no mention of the imperial power's assumed sense of superiority or of its civilizing mission. Note that I do not want to exclude the possibility that the empire, even though nice, was founded by conquest. Many nice states have been founded by conquest; a relevant question is whether nice empires could also be.

---

[11] Many contemporary political philosophers are "philosophical anarchists" insofar as they are skeptical of the legitimacy of existing states. See A. John Simmons, "Philosophical Anarchism," reprinted in Simmons, *Justification and Legitimacy: Essays on Rights and Obligations* (Cambridge: Cambridge University Press, 2001), 102–21.

[12] Economists and other social theorists appreciate the public or collective goods provided by institutions. Empires have provided some, and this is the core of Deepak Lal's case for them. See Deepak Lal, *In Defense of Empires* (Washington, DC: American Enterprise Institute, 2004).

My first reaction to this empire is that "it's not so bad."[13] Must nice empires be condemned? Could they not be justified?

I shall argue that empires, when nice, are no harder to justify than states. States that are significantly Pareto-inferior to feasible alternative arrangements are not justified (where an arrangement is Pareto-inferior to another if the move from the first to the second would make at least one person better off and no one worse off). And empires that are as nasty as Leopold's Congo or Japan's Manchuria are not justified either. But perhaps nice empires can be justified.

VI. POLITICAL LEGITIMACY: THE CASE OF EMPIRES

What does it mean to justify empires (or states or other forms of political organization)? We are asking a number of questions about empires, assuming that the case against them is strong. We might try to rebut that case by showing that empires—nice ones, with relatively just liberal institutions—could under certain circumstances be quite good and worthy of our admiration and support. This might be said, in one sense of the term, to *justify* empires or imperialist endeavors that meet certain standards.[14]

To justify a practice or an institution, in some contexts, often involves showing it to satisfy the appropriate standards for things of its kind—for instance, by showing how common criticisms are misconceptions, how things are much better than they appear.[15] Justifying empires in this sense might require showing that they are quite good or beneficial, or it might involve rebutting charges that they are (virtually) always unjust. Such a demonstration would show that the bad reputation of empires is undeserved and mistaken. It would not, however, show that nasty or barbaric empires have any merit. Similarly, justifying states or the institution of marriage would not validate the Soviet Union's legitimacy or the right of men to kill disobedient wives or daughters. More precisely,

---

[13] Woody Allen's character in the film *Love and Death* reacts thus to the prospect of Russia being conquered by the French under Napoleon—or so we surmise from his facial expressions. In a scene that takes place before a major battle, a Russian sergeant harangues his troops. Allen's character expresses skepticism about war, and the sergeant is astonished and outraged: "Imagine your loved ones conquered by Napoleon and forced to live under French rule." (A gasp from the gathered soldiers.) "Do you want them to eat that rich food and those heavy sauces?" ("*No-o-o*," cry the soldiers, except for Allen who seems not in the slightest adverse to French cooking or conquest.) "Do you want to have *soufflé* every meal and *croissant*?" ("*No-o-o*.")

Imagine the prospect of being conquered by an imperial power with British political institutions, French cooking and wine, Japanese rail service, Federal Express running the mail system, etc. This prospect might dampen our anti-imperialism.

[14] In my *Essay on the Modern State,* I in effect consider "nice" states (without calling them that) and argue that they would be justified.

[15] See ibid., 105–12 and 158–61. See also A. John Simmons's important essay "Justification and Legitimacy," reprinted in Simmons, *Justification and Legitimacy,* 122–57.

showing that a practice or institution has a number of good features, perhaps unnoticed or unappreciated, does not usually show that it is legitimate or specifically that it possesses the normative powers it claims (e.g., authority, powers and rights).

States or their partisans do not merely claim that they are justified, in the sense employed above, in existing and in acting as they do. They claim something more: a particular status, namely, *legitimacy*. If a state is legitimate in this sense, it has a right to exist and a right to rule. Minimally, this means that it is permissible for it to exist and to rule (the rights are mere liberties or Hohfeldian privileges). Presumably, however, these are also claim-rights, entailing duties on the part of others. A state's right to exist would thus entail a duty on the part of others not to destroy it or undermine its existence in certain ways. A right to rule would give the state, among other things, the right to establish laws and to adjudicate and enforce them as necessary for the maintenance of order and other ends.

I shall distinguish between weaker and stronger kinds of legitimacy. It turns out that there are a number of different understandings of the right to rule in the literature, and it is important to distinguish at least two. A legitimate state has a right to exist and a right to rule, as I claimed. I shall say that a state is *weakly legitimate* if its second right, the right to rule, entails that subjects are obligated not to undermine it in certain ways. It is *fully* or *strongly legitimate* if subjects or at least citizens have, in addition, an obligation to obey (each valid law).[16] Full or strong legitimacy tracks the notion that seems to dominate most contemporary discussions. Subjects or citizens of states with this status have a general obligation to obey the law, an obligation to comply with every law that applies to them except in circumstances licensed by the law.[17]

Elsewhere I have argued that states that are reasonably just and efficient are weakly legitimate.[18] Something more—perhaps "the consent of the governed"—seems necessary for full legitimacy. However, no state has been able to obtain the *genuine* consent of more than a small propor-

---

[16] The distinction between weaker and stronger kinds of legitimacy is not explicit in my *Essay on the Modern State*. It is developed in my essay "The Modern State," in *The Handbook of Political Theory*, ed. Gerald Gaus and Chandran Kukathas (London: Sage Publications, 2004), 195–209, and in my essay "Natural Rights and Political Legitimacy," *Social Philosophy and Policy* 22, no. 1 (2005): 314–29.

[17] The obligation to obey is typically understood to be stringent or preemptive, as well as content-independent. My understanding of these notions is as follows: An obligation is preemptive in this sense if it is a reason for the performance of an action "which is not to be added to all other relevant reasons when assessing what to do, but should exclude and take the place of some of them." Joseph Raz, *The Morality of Freedom* (Oxford: Clarendon Press, 1986), 46. Preemptive reasons may, of course, be defeasible and need not be absolute. Furthermore: "A reason is content-independent if there is no direct connection between the reason and the action for which it is a reason." Ibid., 35.

[18] See my *Essay on the Modern State*, chaps. 4–6. My argument there is parallel to the case here for the weak legitimacy of nice empires. I argue, in effect, that "nice" states will be weakly legitimate.

tion of its subject population.[19] Let us assume for the moment that I am right, that states are weakly legitimate to the extent that they are just and efficient, and that rarely, if ever, will they be strongly legitimate. Even if some of the details of my account are not accepted, the general position, skeptical of the general obligation to obey, is a familiar one in the literature and may represent an emerging consensus. On this view, it is very difficult to establish the strong legitimacy of states.[20]

It should be equally hard to establish the strong legitimacy of empires, even nice ones. I shall not try.[21] The more interesting question is whether some empires might be weakly legitimate. Such empires would have a right to exist and a right to rule, and others would be obligated not to destroy them or to undermine them in certain ways. Consider our nice empire. It is reasonably just (no slavery, no genocide, little exploitation), its institutions are relatively responsive, and it is beneficial to its subjects.[22] Surely its subjects (and others) have an obligation not to destroy it or undermine it in certain ways. I should think it would have the status ascribed to weakly legitimate states. At the very least, the features that give states weak legitimacy also ground the same legitimacy of empires.

What is missing from our nice, weakly legitimate empire, of course, is "self-government." The subjects of an empire are not permitted "to assume among the powers of the earth the separate and equal station to which the laws of nature and of nature's God entitle them." Thomas Jefferson thought that *peoples*—collectivities of a proto-national kind—had this right, and we may differ with him.[23] We tend to think, however, that groups of people have some claim to govern themselves. The position is formulated vaguely, as there is considerable controversy and much confusion here. But however we differ on the details, we tend to think that groups of humans who were conquered and made part of an empire ought to be allowed, at some point, to govern themselves independently, when they

---

[19] See my *Essay on the Modern State,* 146–47. Note that hypothetical consent is something else, not a kind of genuine consent (see ibid., 126).

[20] For a good selection of the recent literature on obligations to obey—entailed by strong legitimacy—see William A. Edmundson, ed., *The Duty to Obey the Law* (Lanham, MD: Rowman and Littlefield, 1999). See especially the essays by M. B. E. Smith, A. John Simmons, Joseph Raz, and Leslie Green. See also Leslie Green, *The Authority of the State* (Oxford: Clarendon Press, 1988).

[21] Thomas Hobbes thought that conquest and consent were compatible, but his understanding of consent is not ours. The second of the two ways in which a Sovereign may be established is "by acquisition": "A *Common-wealth by Acquisition,* is that, where the Soveraign Power is acquired by Force; And it is acquired by force, when men singly, or many together by plurality of voyces, for fear of death, or bonds, do authorize all the actions of that Man, or Assembly, that hath their lives and liberty in his Power." Thomas Hobbes, *Leviathan* (1651), ed. Richard Tuck (Cambridge: Cambridge University Press, 1991), chap. 20.

[22] An analogue might be British Hong Kong for much of the twentieth century.

[23] The passage is from the opening paragraph of the American Declaration of Independence of 1776, principally written by Thomas Jefferson. For more on Jefferson's view, see my essay "Peoples, Nations, and the Unity of Societies," in *Cultural Identity and the Nation-State,* ed. Carol C. Gould and Pasquale Pasquino (Lanham, MD: Rowman and Littlefield, 2001), 19–29.

so wish. The devil is in the details, of course, and I do not mean to sweep difficult questions under the rug, merely to set them aside for now.

VII. A NEW IMPERIALISM?

The case I have made for the weak legitimacy of our nice empire may not be persuasive; for one thing, I did not offer much of an argument. More importantly, there may be reason to be skeptical of my thought experiment. The notion of a nice empire may turn out to be incoherent.[24] It may be that some of the terms of justice rule out empires, however nice they may be. Our rights to liberty may be very demanding, and it may be that the forms of domination characteristic of empire are unjust. We cannot evaluate this potential challenge without saying much more than we have about justice. Similarly, it may be argued that imperial institutions will rarely be responsive to the interests of subjects. Thus, there may be no nice empires. A defense of the coherence of nice empires against these objections cannot be brief or simple. The worry about the responsiveness of imperial institutions would require an examination of some of the practices, for instance, of British rule in nineteenth-century India. So I merely note these concerns and do not address them here. These and similar challenges may be equally applicable to nice states. Such states may not be just after all,[25] and their responsiveness to their subjects may require that they all be constitutional democracies.

If we grant the possibility of nice and weakly legitimate empires, there are nevertheless two reasons to think that they cannot achieve the same standing as states. The first reason is that empires are necessarily transitional. Our world today is one of states—what is called "a state system." There is a sense in which it is possible to imagine the world remaining such a system forever. It is true that states, in the sense in which I speak of them, are creations of modern times, and it is unlikely that they will continue forever in the form they take at present, without changing in significant ways. But they *could* remain unchanged. There is nothing about the form of modern states that dooms them to extinction or radical transformation.[26] It is different with empires. Most, as we noted, have civilizing missions. With regard to some empires, this may be window-dressing and cynicism, with regard to others it may not be. Or, to put the point differently, the civilizing mission of many empires seems crucial to their justification and to whatever legitimacy they may have. If the subject population were not in need of improvement, some instruction in civili-

[24] I am indebted here to different points pressed against me by Michael Evans, Samuel Kerstein, and Joe Oppenheimer.

[25] See my essay "Natural Rights and Political Legitimacy" for an exploration of the implications of a natural rights conception of justice for the legitimacy of states.

[26] A qualification: In my *Essay on the Modern State,* I argue that states do not live up to their self-image, and this fact may lead us to expect them to change.

zation, then how might being part of an empire make the subject population better off? But that civilizing mission suggests that its success should bring an end to the empire. Speaking of the British Empire in the early twentieth century, Anthony Pagden notes that implicit in its conception of its civilizing mission "was the notion that one day, in however distant a future, the colonized peoples of the world would indeed become 'civilized.' When that happened, they would logically have to be given back control of their own lives."[27] In that respect, it is hard to imagine empires always being with us. Their very self-image (a self-image that implicitly provides part of their justification) is that of a transitional form of political organization.[28]

The second reason to think that empires cannot achieve the same standing as states is that they are anachronistic. In days long gone, it was customary to be governed by one's superiors. The eighteenth-century revolutions were rebellions in part against one form of such rule: rule by those who claimed political power by virtue of their parentage or inheritance. While we may accept the idea that talents are not evenly or equally distributed by nature's God, it is inconceivable to us, as it was to Hobbes, Locke, and Rousseau, to think that any such talents are the ground, independently of convention, of powers to govern—that some are born to rule. The subordinate status of the subject peoples of empires is one that seems incompatible with modern sensibilities. Ours is a world where "self-rule" is thought to be essential to one's standing as a person or as a group. The notion of self-rule or self-government is ambiguous. One kind involves being governed by one's own and not by foreigners.[29] This issue of self-rule raises questions about "the politics of identity" that I do not want to address here. The second kind of self-government is familiar from republican and democratic political thought and movements. It is the idea that a self-governing group is autonomous in the original sense of giving itself its own laws. I call this latter kind "republican" self-rule and the former "post-colonial" or "national liberation" self-rule.[30] It may be that one of the most important features of democratic rule—which we now understand to be surprisingly inefficient in most of its forms[31]—is the fact that democratic citizens may periodically "fire" their rulers; the latter are, in effect, the employees or servants of the former. Autonomy of the republican sort seems important today to our status and conception of our-

---

[27] Pagden, *Peoples and Empires*, 151–52.

[28] Here and elsewhere, Stanley Kurtz's interesting article on democratic imperial ventures is instructive. See his "Democratic Imperialism: A Blueprint," *Policy Review*, no. 118 (2003): 3–20.

[29] For instance, for the British, being governed by the House of Windsor rather than that of Saxe-Coburg-Gotha.

[30] See my *Essay on the Modern State*, 240–42.

[31] I am thinking of the findings of the large literature on "government failures." For a recent survey, see Dennis C. Mueller, *Public Choice III* (Cambridge: Cambridge University Press, 2003).

selves, and the subjects of empires lack such autonomy. In this way, empires are anachronistic.

This second reason for thinking that empires could not achieve the standing available to states suggests that I may have erred in my description of nice empires. It is not that such things are unimaginable; it is that we would not call them empires, and this reveals something of our conceptions. The association of empire with subordination in more archaic senses than mere subjection to law is so deep that we have difficulties using the term for forms of political association that we value or admire. We would call my nice empires "commonwealths" or "federations" or "unions" (as in the European Union).

The labels are not that important as long as clarity is achieved and understanding not thwarted. My thought experiment about nice empires and our reluctance to use the term "empires" to describe them may reveal part of its meaning. The more important questions have to do with how we should organize the world, and here our antipathy to empire may have blinded us to the beneficial influences our imperial pasts have had and continue to have. The mention of the European Union above was not meant in jest. Insofar as the union ceases to be "European" and starts admitting countries that are not normally understood to be European, its borders will resemble imperial frontiers and the scope of its jurisdiction will be potentially unlimited.

It is especially Rome or premodern empires that we might well reflect upon. Rome was an empire in a world without states. I noted earlier the absence of borders; the empire's boundaries were merely frontiers, the farthest points of conquest. The scope of its jurisdiction was, in principle, universal. Unlike modern states, which have borders and which form part of a state system, classical empires are necessarily, at least in self-conception, limitless. It is this feature, as we noted, that permitted Rome to be such an important source for what we call cosmopolitan political thought. The cosmopolis could grow to encompass the world. In one respect—its potentially universal jurisdiction—it is like some of our "international" institutions.

Our world is not only one of states, but also one of nations, the source of additional complications.[32] And the self-conceptions of premodern imperial people are not available to us. But this particular feature of classical empire—the potentially universal scope of its jurisdiction—does suggest something of relevance to us today. Many today, not unreasonably, despair of the state of our world system, wishing for more order and less war; and some counsel strengthening the lawmaking bodies of the international

---

[32] I am thinking of nations in the cultural sense—namely, collections of individuals with common histories, cultures, languages, and the like, members of which recognize other members by virtue of their possession of these attributes. The strength and prevalence of nationalism and associated sentiments only strengthen the desire for republican self-rule—as well as for post-colonial self-rule.

system as the way out of our present disorder. The questions or disagreements here are familiar and quite complex. My interest is in an assumption implicit in this view that bears on our topic, namely, the assumption that the path to greater international order is through international law and the means to the latter is the strengthening of existing "international" bodies (for example, the United Nations). The questions and controversies are too complex to be explored adequately here, but many people, myself included, are skeptical that the UN in particular, unless radically reformed, can offer a promising source of increased order in the world. It is not only that the UN is relatively impotent given the nature of the Security Council (action can be blocked by any of the five permanent members); it is by its nature an organization open to all (and only) states, however unjust or illegitimate.[33] And familiar, even if old-fashioned, worries about "world government" reinforce this skepticism.

Another alternative is suggested by classical empires. Rome spread slowly, mainly by conquest. Its spread established the rule of law, such as it could be, in many places where it never existed. Niall Ferguson argues that the British Empire did the same. The suggestion is that systems of law may come to be by a number of different means and that empire may prove to be a better mechanism than, say, the UN. If one thinks that strengthening existing international organizations may risk greater global disorder, then one must think of alternatives. Empire is an obvious possibility. It may be argued that empire is a more promising means, in our world, for securing greater global order and establishing the rule of law. The anachronistic nature of empires, as well as various nasty associations, may require the use of another term. I am suggesting, however, that the "imperial" imposition of order by the great powers—in particular, the United States or the European Union, or possibly India—may be a more effective road to global order than the available alternatives.[34]

VIII. CONCLUSION

The empires of the past—the Roman, Austro-Hungarian, Ottoman, and British empires—continue to influence the present. Yet our interest in empire is not only to discern the shadow of the past; there is much to be said for empire. Nice empires are "not so bad," and empires are not harder to justify or legitimate than states. Lastly, empires may be better

---

[33] An organization of businesses which did not exclude illegal or unjust enterprises (e.g., the Mafia) could not be expected, say, to reduce corporate crime.

[34] I do not mean this brief discussion to suggest that the main route to greater world order must be imperial. For an important discussion of the multiple ways that order is being created by the development of multiple and multifaceted "government networks," formal and informal, see Anne-Marie Slaughter, *A New World Order* (Princeton, NJ: Princeton University Press, 2004). Philosophers who simply assume—in my view, naively—that world government is the best prescription for global order should read Slaughter's book.

suited to securing global order today than the apparent alternatives. There is something good to be said about empire, and our automatic condemnations, although understandable, should not let us lose sight of this. Just as "philosophical anarchists" and other skeptics of the state can admire and support decent states, so anti-imperialists may after all be able to give one cheer for empire.

Philosophy, University of Maryland

THE JUST WAR IDEA: THE STATE OF THE QUESTION

By James Turner Johnson

I. Setting the Context

One of the most striking and most important developments in American moral discourse on uses of military force over the past forty-odd years has been the recovery and practical use of the idea of just war to guide moral analysis and judgment. As a result, various forms of just war discourse can be found today in religious, philosophical, military, political, and legal contexts, and while there is an important common substratum uniting these, there are also notable differences and even tensions. What should be said about this? How should these contemporary forms of just war reasoning be tested against historical just war reasoning (which has also taken diverse forms), or indeed, should it be tested in this way at all? In particular, what is to be said about new themes that have appeared in recent just war discourse and have in some versions of the contemporary just war idea become the principal moral criteria for whether a resort to force is justified or not? In short, what should be the parameters within which contemporary just war reasoning develops?

This essay examines the idea of just war in two ways. Section I is historical and thematic, identifying major benchmarks in the recent recovery of just war thinking, exploring characteristic elements in each, and setting them against the deeper just war tradition which first came together in the Middle Ages and has continued to develop in the modern period. Section II identifies and analyzes several major themes that have been put forward in contemporary just war discourse, judging them by reference to the deeper tradition of just war. Throughout the essay, I argue for a contemporary conception of just war that is solidly grounded in this deeper moral tradition. This leads me to be critical of certain elements in the recent recovery and restatement of just war thinking. My aim, in short, is to answer not only the question of what the contemporary just war idea is, but also what it ideally should try to be.

In the United States, before the contemporary recovery of just war thinking began, moral discourse on war was largely polarized between various forms of pacifist rejection of all war as inherently evil and an embrace of total war, expressed sometimes in terms of political realism and at other times in the language of crusade, as the necessary means of combating and wiping out evil when thrust upon us. Indeed, these two poles tended to converge in practical terms, since the pacifist's rejection of war in any form, for whatever reason, as inherently evil left nothing to say about possible moral limits to war once it had begun, while the idea of total war ruled out such limits in principle. Thus, the carnage in the trenches of World War I, the destruction of entire cities by strategic bombing in World War II, and even the introduction of atomic weapons could be looked at, from the pacifist's perspective, as evidence of the inherently evil nature of war, while from the opposite end of the spectrum they could be justified as what was necessary to defeat the aggressors who had started the war. What was missing in these two extreme approaches to moral discourse about war was a conception of the use of force that accepted it as a sometimes necessary tool of good statecraft, but at the same time set strict yet meaningful moral restraints on the resort to force and the practical application of such force.

A. The shaping of the classical just war tradition

There was, of course, an old and deeply embedded tradition in Western culture that understood war in a very different way from either of the polar opposites I have mentioned. This was the just war tradition. On the terms of this tradition, the use of armed force might serve good or evil depending on whether it was undertaken on the authority of a sovereign, that is, a person or persons responsible for the common good of his/her/ their political community, whether it was undertaken to protect that common good, or the broader fabric of relations on which all political communities depended, against injury or the threat of injury, and whether it was undertaken out of a right intention—not to do an injustice to another but to seek to preserve or establish peace. The deepest roots of this tradition reach back into the history of biblical Israel and into the thought and practice of classical Greece and Rome. A specifically Christian version of it traces at least to Augustine in the fourth and early fifth centuries. A coherent and systematic form of this tradition came together in the Middle Ages, over roughly the three centuries from the canonist Gratian's magisterial collection, the *Decretum*, in the mid-twelfth century to the end of the Hundred Years War in the mid-fifteenth century. At the beginning of the modern period, seminal thinkers from Francisco de Vitoria (1492-1546) to Hugo Grotius (1583-1645) assumed the terms of this tradition and applied them to the political conditions of their own times.

The tradition these thinkers inherited had taken shape as a broad cultural consensus, one whose content had been shaped by inputs from a wide variety of sectors of medieval culture: church law and theology; secular law, including the recovery of the Roman legal concepts of *jus gentium* and *jus naturale;* the code of knighthood (the chivalric code); works of political theory, especially the literary tradition defining the responsibilities of the good ruler; and the practical experience of government and of warfare.

In its classic form as it had come together by the end of the Middle Ages, the just war idea consisted of two parts: one defining when resort to armed force is justified (later called the *jus ad bellum*), the other defining right conduct in the use of armed force (the *jus in bello*). The *jus ad bellum* included three requirements: that only someone in sovereign authority, and thus responsible for the common good of the political community, could justly authorize resort to armed force; that there must be a just cause, specifically defense of the common good against serious injury, recovery of something wrongly taken, or punishment of wrongdoing; and that resort to armed force must manifest right intention—not aggression, domination, implacable enmity, just plain cruelty or the like, but the intention to protect, restore, or establish peace. These three requirements corresponded directly with the three ends of good politics in the Augustinian tradition of political thought: order, justice, and peace. Thus defined, the justified use of armed force was understood to be a tool for aiding the achievement of these ends and protecting them when established. All other uses of force were by definition unjust, notably including all uses of armed force by private persons on their own authority and all uses of force manifesting tyrannical intent. The *jus in bello* included two major elements: a listing of classes of persons who normally, by reason of their personal characteristics (age, gender, degree of mental or physical competence) or social function, were to be regarded as noncombatants and not to be directly, intentionally attacked during a just war; and some rather moribund efforts to define certain means of war as impermissible because of their inherently indiscriminate or disproportionate effects.

B. Development of the just war idea in the modern period

Beginning in the sixteenth and early seventeenth centuries, this unified common tradition broke apart and subsequently developed in separate streams of thought and practice. Grotius effectively began one of these separate streams in his *De Jure Belli ac Pacis* (1625), where he took the inherited tradition of just war, reinterpreted it in terms of natural law and the common practices of nations, and refashioned it into a theory of the law of nations or international law. Another distinct stream developed within the military sphere, with such writers as Pierino Belli (1502–75) focusing on that portion of the just war tradition having to do with conduct in war and, at the same time, with the emergence of codes of military discipline that remade just war ideas from a system of morality into a set of rules for disciplined conduct under arms. A third stream led into the realm of secular philosophy, eventuating in the "perpetual peace" movement of the Enlightenment era and effectively losing contact with the just war idea as reflecting perennial necessities of statecraft. In the religious sphere, Protestant theology gradually lost conscious sight of just war tradition, while Catholic thought maintained it as a doctrine but generally paid no attention to it.

With the rise of the absolutist state beginning in the seventeenth century, the just war *jus ad bellum* decayed into the idea of a *liberum jus ad bellum*, the right of the absolute sovereign to initiate war for reasons of state. At the same time, the requirement of a public declaration of war came to be stressed, so that others could judge the decision to go to war and react as they might. The moral restraints of the just war *jus ad bellum* thus effectively disappeared, being replaced by calculations of interests and the relative likelihood that other states might respond to a declaration of war by making war against the initiator. At the same time, and perhaps in some sort of compensation for the greater freedom to initiate war implied by the *liberum jus ad bellum*, greater attention was given to the elements of the *jus in bello*: protection of noncombatants and limits on the means of war, including both weapons and tactics. The practice of limited war (or "sovereigns' war," as it has sometimes been called) during the eighteenth century illustrates both these developments. The emergence of both the theory and practice of total war in the early nineteenth century temporarily eclipsed this emphasis on limiting the conduct of war, but by the time of the American Civil War it was once again possible for writers on international law to speak of "the laws and customs of war," by which they meant effectively the content of the just war *jus in bello*: avoidance of harm to noncombatants and a sense that the means of war should not be unlimited. The political theorist Francis Lieber's *Guerilla Parties* (1862) and *Code* (1863), as well as the U.S. Army's *General Orders No. 100 (1863)*, based on Lieber's *Code*, put all this into the form of military law and rules of engagement. At about the same time, the first Geneva Convention (1864) put one kind of noncombatant protection—amelioration of the condition of the wounded in armies fighting each other in the field—into the form of an international agreement. The subsequent development of a positive law of armed conflict in international law reflects both Lieber and the first Geneva Convention. In the United States military, *General Orders No. 100 (1863)* initiated a way of thinking about the government of military forces in combat that has eventuated in the present-day Code of Military Discipline, specific codes of conduct in all the service branches, and increasingly detailed rules of engagement for specific military contexts.

As this illustrates, the military and legal spheres have continued to develop their distinctive approaches to regulating the conduct of war; yet this history also illustrates a substantive dialogue between these two spheres. It also shows the significant continuing presence of just war tradition in both. James Brown Scott in the 1930s, and more broadly the Carnegie Institution's series *Classics of International Law*, demonstrated the historical linkage between just war tradition and international law at the beginning of the modern period.[1] For anyone who knows just war tradition, however, the thematic and structural content of the positive law of armed conflicts demonstrates the connection in its own way: in both just war tradition and the law of armed conflicts, there are lists of classes of persons defined as noncombatants, together with prohibitions on harming them directly and intentionally; in both, there are limits on the means of war, including bans on weapons and restrictions on how acceptable weapons are to be used. The same linkage is also visible in the military code and in the rules of engagement for recent conflicts involving United States forces.

As regards the resort to war, the picture is somewhat different. Here the convergence has been between international law and the philosophically based version of just war thought that produced the "perpetual peace" literature of the Enlightenment era. That literature sought to limit resort to force by individual states through creating a new super-state structure for international relations, so that only under the authority of the super-state institutions could armed force be rightly used. At the same time, the "perpetual peace" tradition aimed toward abolishing war, seeking instead to settle all international disputes through arbitration. It was but a small step conceptually to the League of Nations (1920), the Kellogg-Briand Pact (1928), and the United Nations (1945). What is lost here is the just war tradition's realistic focus on the possibility of genuine order, justice, and peace only in the context of particular political communities and the tradition's effort to define the use of armed force in terms of the responsibility of the sovereign to protect the common good. The line of development in both this philosophical tradition and in positive international law has responded to the excesses of the absolutist state, which rests on assumptions about sovereignty and international order that can be traced to the Peace of Westphalia in 1648.[2] These assumptions are inherently problematical from the standpoint of just war tradition. But together they establish a context in which just war discourse about the resort to armed force is difficult, because it goes against the assumptions about the state

[1] See particularly James Brown Scott, *The Spanish Origin of International Law* (Oxford: Clarendon Press; London: Humphrey Milford, 1934). Scott (1866–1943), one of the most prominent international lawyers of his generation, was a professor of law at Columbia University, George Washington University, and the University of Chicago, a United States delegate to the second Hague Conference (1907), and a trustee and secretary of the Carnegie Endowment for International Peace (1910–40), where he oversaw the creation of the series *Classics of International Law*.

[2] The Peace of Westphalia ended the Thirty Years' War, the last, longest, and most destructive of the wars of religion following the Protestant Reformation. It is generally regarded as establishing the pattern for international relations in the modern period, based on formally equal territorial states, with difference of religion repudiated as a just cause for war. Its conception of sovereignty, defined by recognized rule over a particular territory and the people living in it, provides the basis for the international system centered on the United Nations.

and international order that are embodied in the effort to abolish war and to create an international institution superior to individual states.

To return more explicitly to the matter of why just war discourse disappeared from moral reflection on war and armed force during the modern period, the developments I have just sketched show how philosophical thought on these matters moved in the direction of an internationalist pacifism. At the same time, there was also a movement in exactly the opposite direction, toward justifying the absolutist state and its totalistic quest for power by whatever means, a movement that produced both Nazism and Stalinism. Taken along with the development of internationalist pacifism, this shows exactly the kind of polarization I identified earlier, between rejection of war as such as inherently evil and an embrace of total war. In the United States, internationalist pacifism became an important element in the pacifistic rejection of all war, while the reaction to Nazi and Stalinist totalitarianism fueled the idea that war against such enemies—and by extension, all war—should be prosecuted without limits.

Religious moral thought, as I indicated earlier, effectively forgot its just war heritage over the course of the period from the seventeenth century through the middle of the twentieth, following along the same lines as sketched out above for internationalist philosophy and international law. At the same time, other forms of pacifism unique to the religious context also grew. Christianity has a long tradition of sectarian, or world-rejecting, pacifism. In not entirely self-consistent but psychologically persuasive ways, sectarianism's critique of the state could recognize common cause with the critique of the state in internationalist utopianism. British historian Martin Ceadel has studied this closely for Christian pacifism in England in the context of the two World Wars; what he found was convergence of very unlike forms of pacifism prior to the wars, followed by a falling apart of the convergence during the wars themselves, and then a coming together again after the wars ended.[3] The American pattern seems to have been the same.

C. The contemporary recovery of the just war idea

It is possible to identify three important benchmarks in the contemporary recovery of the just war idea. The first is the work of Paul Ramsey in the 1960s. In two books, *War and the Christian Conscience*[4] and *The Just*

---

[3] Martin Ceadel, "Christian Pacifism in the Era of Two World Wars," in W. J. Sheils, ed., *The Church and War* (Oxford: Basil Blackwell for the Ecclesiastical History Society, 1983), 391–408.

[4] Paul Ramsey, *War and the Christian Conscience: How Shall Modern War Be Conducted Justly?* (Durham, NC: Duke University Press, 1961). The context into which this book appeared was the debate over nuclear weapons, deterrence strategy, and the possibility of use of nuclear weapons in war.

War: Force and Political Responsibility,[5] Ramsey developed and used a version of just war thinking to challenge both liberal Christian pacifism and the political realism of the policy community in the context of the debates over nuclear weapons and, to a much lesser degree, the war in Vietnam.[6] He based his reconstruction of just war theory fundamentally on the theology of Augustine. To the liberal Christian pacifists, he made an argument based on the obligations of Christian love, as he read this through Augustine and through the New Testament story of the good Samaritan. Love of neighbor, Ramsey argued, does not imply that Christians should stand aside when others are being threatened or harmed. Rather, such love implies what Ramsey called a "twin-born" attitude toward the use of force: first, permission to use force to protect the innocent neighbor from such harm; second, limitation on the force used, because the assailant is also a neighbor whom Christians are commanded to love. The concept of love as permitting, and even requiring, the use of force to protect the neighbor set the use of armed force once again on the table of moral possibilities for Christian ethics; fundamentally, it was the basis for a *jus ad bellum.* Similarly, the theme of limitation served as the basis for Ramsey's *jus in bello,* which he developed in terms of two moral principles, discrimination and proportionality. Discrimination, or not directly and intentionally harming noncombatants, he defined as an exceptionless moral rule deriving directly from the obligation of love. Proportionality, by contrast, required the operation of moral prudence, since it implied a calculation of the likely effects of a particular use of force.

In entering the secular policy debate, Ramsey shifted his language somewhat. There he argued that both the permission to use force and the limitation on such force follow from the nature of politics itself: as he put it, force "is inseparable from politics' *proper* act of being politics, inseparable from the well-being of politics, inseparable from the human pursuit of the national or the international common good by political means."[7] The principles of discrimination and proportionality equally follow from consideration of the orientation of good politics toward the common good. Now, these two arguments seem quite different, but for Ramsey

---

[5] Paul Ramsey, *The Just War: Force and Political Responsibility* (New York: Charles Scribner's Sons, 1968). This book ranged more widely than its predecessor, still treating the questions of nuclear deterrence and possible use of nuclear weapons in war, but also including sections on political ethics, on the implications of the Second Vatican Council's treatment of war, and on insurgency warfare and the war in Vietnam. All in all, it is a fuller presentation of Ramsey's thought on war in the frame of Christian theology and political ethics than Ramsey's 1961 book.

[6] Ramsey (1924–94), one of the leading Christian ethicists of the twentieth century and longtime professor of religion at Princeton University, over a career that began in the 1940s and ended five decades later, did seminal work on a variety of topics, including the central place of love in Christian ethics, the relationship of love and justice in human communities, and the ethics of medical care, as well as the ethics of the political use of force, the frame within which he developed his conception of just war.

[7] Ramsey, *The Just War,* 5.

they were connected: though the latter argument does not explicitly recognize the moral demands of love, he understood love as embedded in
the order of things after the manner of Augustine's argument in *The City
of God*, so that the goals of good politics are the same as those of an
individual ethic of love of neighbor.

Ramsey only relatively infrequently drew out elements of his *jus ad
bellum* and never developed it systematically, arguing that the choice to
resort to force is a matter for good statecraft, not for a moral theoretician.
Yet he had no inhibition about developing at length the implications of
his *jus in bello*, which he regarded as bearing not only on the policy sphere
but also on the sphere of personal morality. The result was a somewhat
one-sided just war theory that spoke powerfully and directly about the
obligation not to harm noncombatants and to limit overall destruction but
only treated the question of moral resort to force in general terms.

Ramsey also did not seek to engage the historical just war tradition in
his effort to recover the just war idea. He wrote as a theologian interpreting a fundamental Christian theological ideal and as a political philosopher interpreting classical understandings of politics. This is evident, I
suggest, in his definition of the limits to be observed in using force by
means of two moral principles, whereas the classical tradition had defined
its limits in terms of concrete listings of categories of persons not normally to be targeted in war and concrete efforts to ban or restrict specific
means of war. Military and legal usage, as I have shown above, held on
to the language and method of the classical just war tradition on the *jus
in bello*, but Ramsey, reaching back over the historical tradition to the
theology of Augustine, produced a more generalized and simultaneously
more abstract conception of the *jus in bello*.

While Ramsey's work initiated the recovery of just war thinking in
American moral discourse on war, the particular form and focus of his
work also left a legacy of problems for that discourse as it has subsequently developed. Two problems in particular should be noted. The
first follows from Ramsey's reliance on the idea of moral principles rather
than the concrete restrictions found in the historical tradition. While the
principle of discrimination translates fairly directly into identifying classes
of noncombatants who should never be directly, intentionally targeted, its
lack of specificity left the door open for arguments that in modern war
there are no noncombatants. The difficulty for the principle of proportionality has been that the concept is harder to keep focused. As a result,
in subsequent usage the concept of proportionality has been made to
mean essentially whatever one might want it to mean in a given argument. The second problem follows from Ramsey's emphasis on the *jus in
bello* and relative lack of focus on the *jus ad bellum*. This has opened the
door to a widespread phenomenon in recent just war discourse, making
the *jus in bello* categories do *jus ad bellum* duty. Specifically, some have
argued, if discrimination and proportionality are moral obligations in the

use of force, then if they are not observed or cannot be expected to be observed, there can be no just resort to force. Ramsey himself opposed this line of argument, calling it a *bellum contra bellum justum,* that is, a "war against just war." Nonetheless, it has provided a powerful tool in the hands of opponents of nuclear weapons and of all modern war as inherently indiscriminate and disproportionate, and thus never able to be just.

The second major benchmark in the recovery of just war thinking for American moral discourse on war is Michael Walzer's 1977 book *Just and Unjust Wars.*[8] In the preface, Walzer explicitly embraces the goal of such a recovery: "I want to recapture the just war for political and moral theory."[9] Like Ramsey, Walzer's analysis did not engage historical just war tradition. Unlike Ramsey, however, Walzer was not interested in making connections with either the requirements of love of neighbor or with classical political theory as the basis of his analysis. Rather, he proceeded through a series of close looks at specific historical cases, first to establish war as a moral reality, then to treat in order the questions of justified resort to war, conduct in war, and individual responsibility in war. The result was a conception of just war that treated the justification of force as a response to an unambiguously recognizable evil (aggression, harm to the innocent) and the limits on force as avoidance of evils similarly easily recognized (rape, war against civilians, torture, terrorism). Walzer's book placed discussion of the just war idea squarely in the frame of philosophical and political-theoretical debate. Its effort to ground just war in universally recognizable moral reactions gave it broad appeal, and the sensitivity with which Walzer drew out the implications of specific historical cases brought readers into his argument at a very basic level. That *Just and Unjust Wars* is now in its third edition and has been for some years a central text used at the United States Military Academy testifies to its importance and its continuing influence.

The publication in 1983 of the United States Catholic bishops' pastoral letter *The Challenge of Peace* provides the third major benchmark in the recovery of just war thinking in American moral discourse about the use of armed force.[10] Unlike the case of Ramsey and Walzer, this document explicitly engaged historical just war tradition, though it did so somewhat spottily, and its overall position was also significantly shaped by nuclear pacifism and by the broader sectarian pacifism associated historically with the monastic movement within Catholicism. Like the historical

---

[8] Michael Walzer, *Just and Unjust Wars: A Moral Argument with Historical Illustrations* (New York: Basic Books, 1977). Walzer (1935–), who formerly taught at Princeton University and at Harvard University, is a professor at the Institute for Advanced Study. A prominent and widely cited political philosopher, he has written on a wide variety of topics, including political obligation, nationalism, ethnicity, and economic justice, as well as just war.

[9] Ibid., xiv.

[10] National Conference of Catholic Bishops, *The Challenge of Peace: God's Promise and Our Response* (Washington, DC: United States Catholic Conference, 1983).

just war tradition, *The Challenge of Peace* defined a distinct *jus ad bellum* and *jus in bello*, describing each by a listing of concrete criteria for moral deliberation. But its reading of contemporary war reflected two factors that loomed large in the historical context out of which this document came: concern over the destructive potential of nuclear weapons and, more broadly, of modern warfare as such, as well as an increasingly influential argument that what was beginning to be called "the Catholic peace tradition" defined pacifism as an ideal for all Catholics, not only those in the life of the religious orders. The result was an understanding of just war that significantly diverged from that found in the classical tradition.

The bishops began with what has become a trademark idea for them: that Catholic teaching "establishes a strong presumption against war." [11] On this formulation, the just war criteria exist only to provide the possibility for exceptions, in particular cases, to this general rule. This understanding differs significantly from how the use of force is regarded in the classical just war tradition, where it is morally neutral in itself but may be good or evil depending on circumstances. When used by someone in a position of sovereign authority to protect the common good by restoring or establishing justice with the end of creating peace, armed force was understood as an instrument of positive good; when it was understood as evil, it was because one or more of these necessary factors was lacking. The idea that just war tradition begins with a "presumption against war" first appeared in *The Challenge of Peace*. Where did it come from? Briefly, I regard it as expressing three different influences, two of which I have already mentioned: first, concern over the destructive potential of nuclear weapons and, more generally, of modern warfare as such; second, the growing influence of faith-based pacifism. The first of these tapped into a century-old effort to reject modern war as inherently too destructive to serve any value, a position generically known as "modern-war pacifism," of which nuclear pacifism was a particular expression. The second depended on an idea coming out of the Second Vatican Council (1962–65), that all Catholics should seek to realize in their own lives elements of the spirituality of those in the religious life, including their rejection of participation in war. The drafting committee that produced *The Challenge of Peace* included persons who wanted the entire document to reject war for both these reasons; and as a result, treating the just war criteria as having to do with individual exceptions to a general "presumption against war" was in fact a compromise position between this Catholic and modern-war pacifist position and the inherited doctrine on just war as found in earlier tradition. The third influence that led to this formulation had to do specifically with the language and structure of thought expressing it. This influence was a 1978 article, "Just War Theories," published in the influ-

---

[11] Ibid., 22 and elsewhere.

ential Jesuit journal *Theological Studies.*[12] The author of this article, James F. Childress, was an academic ethicist of Quaker background; though published in a Catholic journal, this was in no way an attempt to analyze Catholic thinking on the just war criteria but rather undertook to understand the idea of just war in terms of philosopher W. D. Ross's concept of an ethic of prima facie duties. Childress argued that war is fundamentally morally problematic, as the killing and other harm that takes place in war goes against the prima facie duty of nonmaleficence: "Because it is prima facie wrong to injure or kill others, such acts demand justification."[13] In just war theory, he went on, the function of the various criteria is to provide this justification or, as he also put it, to "overrule" the prima facie obligation. *The Challenge of Peace,* though without reference to Childress's article or to the logic of an ethic of prima facie duties, replicates the structure of this argument exactly: just war theory begins with a presumption against war, and the just war criteria function to override this presumption (or to show that it should not be overridden) in particular cases.

The specific list of *jus ad bellum* criteria provided in *The Challenge of Peace* differs in important ways from the traditional listing. As I have noted, the classical *jus ad bellum* included three requirements: sovereign authority, just cause, and right intention (the end of promoting peace), a formulation already settled by the time of Aquinas. These three requirements correlated directly with the ends of good politics as conceived in Augustinian political theory: order, justice, and peace. It was important for classical just war tradition to put the *jus ad bellum* requirements in this order, because doing so expressed a priority: only one in sovereign authority could justly employ force, and he could do so only in pursuit of justice and for the end of peace. *The Challenge of Peace,* by contrast, lists the *jus ad bellum* criteria as follows: just cause, competent authority, comparative justice, right intention, last resort, probability of success, and proportionality.[14] These last three had been explicitly named also by Childress. While they are arguably prudential concerns that ought to be taken into account in the decisions of statecraft, they never appeared as distinct, formal requirements of the just war idea before this. Their use, both in *The Challenge of Peace* and subsequently, has largely been to reinforce the "presumption against war," that is, to deny the possibility of a just war today. Placing just cause before what the bishops called "competent authority" makes the determination of just cause for the use of force something

---

[12] James F. Childress, "Just War Theories: The Bases, Interrelations, Priorities, and Functions of Their Criteria," *Theological Studies* 39 (September 1978): 427–45; the citation below is from the version of this paper that appeared as "Just War Criteria," chapter 3 in James F. Childress, *Moral Responsibility in Conflicts: Essays on Nonviolence, War, and Conscience* (Baton Rouge and London: Louisiana State University Press, 1982), 63–94.

[13] Ibid. ("Just War Criteria"), 71.

[14] National Conference of Catholic Bishops, *The Challenge of Peace,* 28–31.

that takes place prior to the exercise of that authority, suggesting that people other than those in such authority make the call as to whether there is just cause for the use of force. The addition of the category of comparative justice, described as "designed to relativize absolute claims" in a dispute, is also described as "designed to emphasize the presumption against war."[15] Its historical context was arguments in the public sector that placed the American democratic system morally higher than the "evil empire" of Soviet Communism: the requirement of comparative justice denied that such claims provided a justification for resort to armed force.

As for the bishops' treatment of the *jus in bello*, I have already discussed how, in the classical just war tradition, the matter of moral limitation on conduct in war was approached in two ways: by defining specific classes of people normally to be regarded as noncombatants because of personal characteristics or social function, and thus not made the object of direct, intended harm in war; and by setting restrictions on the means of war. As I have also already noted, international law and military tradition have taken shape around the same two approaches. *The Challenge of Peace*, however, adopted the language of Ramsey, defining its *jus in bello* through two principles, which it listed in reverse order from Ramsey's: proportionality and discrimination. The context of the discussion makes clear why the bishops placed proportionality first: "the destructive capability of modern technological warfare" and the expectation that any war, "however initially limited in intention and in the destructive power of weapons employed," would escalate to "the use of weapons of horrendous destructive potential." As a result, the bishops judged, "today it becomes increasingly difficult to make a decision to use any kind of armed force."[16] On this reasoning, then, the bishops' *jus in bello* in effect took on a *jus ad bellum* role: having given up on the possibility that uses of armed force might remain limited once begun, the bishops used their *jus in bello* principles to question the possibility of a just resort to armed force in the first place.

Whereas Ramsey's and Walzer's influence had up to this point been largely limited to relatively narrow religious, intellectual, and policy circles, *The Challenge of Peace* had a far broader impact. The drafting committee held public hearings and heard testimony from a wide variety of types of people, including representatives of the Reagan administration. The second draft of the pastoral letter made the front pages of both the *Washington Post* and the *New York Times*, where its text was printed in its entirety. Numerous colleges and universities held conferences and hosted talks relating to the developing pastoral letter and the larger topic it dealt with. The U.S. Army's annual conference of its major command chaplains—

---

[15] Ibid., 29.
[16] Ibid., 31.

the colonel-level chaplains assigned to the Army's various major command regions throughout the world—included a focus on this developing statement and what its implications might be for a military whose membership was very heavily Catholic. After the final version of *The Challenge of Peace* was adopted, the United States Military Academy included presentations and a discussion of the letter in its annual Senior Conference, whose audience is senior military and civilian defense officials. *The Challenge of Peace* has also had a longer-term effect in that its way of presenting the idea of just war has been adopted by others, both Catholic and non-Catholic, as what this idea means.

In any case, by the time *The Challenge of Peace* was published, the recovery of the idea of just war as a focus and resource for moral reflection and debate on the use of armed force was an accomplished fact. The just war idea is now part of the curriculum at all the United States service academies and at the war colleges; in the civilian academic world, it not only has entered the curriculum in such diverse fields as philosophy, political science, and religion but has continued to be treated in academic conferences and in campus lectures; and it has been an element in public debate over the use of armed force in every conflict since the 1980s.

My own place in this recovery of the just war idea has been dual: to seek to identify and recover the historical tradition in its setting and fundamental purpose, and to apply an understanding of just war based in knowledge of that tradition to contemporary issues. These dual aims have produced two different kinds of books: three historical studies, *Ideology, Reason, and the Limitation of War*,[17] *Just War Tradition and the Restraint of War*,[18] and *The Quest for Peace: Three Moral Traditions in Western Cultural History*;[19] and two books of moral analysis and argument focused on contemporary issues in armed force and its use, *Can Modern War Be Just?*[20] and *Morality and Contemporary Warfare*.[21] Over the last decade or so, I have also engaged in comparative historical and thematic study of the tradition of *jihad* in Islamic religion and culture, expressed in two jointly edited books, *Cross, Crescent, and Sword*[22] and *Just War and Jihad*,[23]

---

[17] James Turner Johnson, *Ideology, Reason, and the Limitation of War: Religious and Secular Concepts, 1200–1740* (Princeton, NJ, and London: Princeton University Press, 1975).

[18] James Turner Johnson, *Just War Tradition and the Restraint of War: A Moral and Historical Inquiry* (Princeton, NJ, and Guildford, Surrey: Princeton University Press, 1981).

[19] James Turner Johnson, *The Quest for Peace: Three Moral Traditions in Western Cultural History* (Princeton, NJ, and Guildford, Surrey: Princeton University Press, 1987).

[20] James Turner Johnson, *Can Modern War Be Just?* (New Haven, CT, and London: Yale University Press, 1984).

[21] James Turner Johnson, *Morality and Contemporary Warfare* (New Haven, CT, and London: Yale University Press, 1999).

[22] James Turner Johnson and John Kelsay, eds., *Cross, Crescent, and Sword: The Justification and Limitation of War in Western and Islamic Tradition* (New York, Westport, CT, and London: Greenwood Press, 1990).

[23] John Kelsay and James Turner Johnson, eds., *Just War and Jihad: Historical and Theoretical Perspectives on War and Peace in Western and Islamic Traditions* (New York, Westport, CT, and London: Greenwood Press, 1991).

and in my own *The Holy War Idea in Western and Islamic Traditions*.[24] I understand just war tradition as expressing fundamental values in Western culture, expressed in different ways in different cultural and historical contexts. Just war is not a theory but a tradition, in which a variety of theories can be found; it is not simply a product of religion or theological reflection but a way of thinking about statecraft and the use of force within the context of statecraft that has implications for law, international order, military affairs, and other aspects of individual and common life. One of my goals has been to restore, at least in part, the dialogue across now-distinct disciplines and social sectors that shaped just war tradition in its classical form. More substantively, however, I am convinced that it is necessary to attend to both the form and the content of the classical just war tradition and to the underlying values it expresses. I agree with the classical just war tradition, as well as with Ramsey and Walzer, that the use of power, including the use of armed force, is a necessary element in the good exercise of statecraft. I also agree with these contemporary theorists that it remains possible to make moral distinctions today, as ever in the past, about when it is justified to have recourse to armed force, that it is possible to formulate policies and make decisions based on those judgments, and that it is possible to act in morally informed and discriminating ways to carry out those policies and decisions. In short, I believe the absolute pacifists are utterly wrong about the shape of human communal life in history, and I believe the modern-war and nuclear pacifists are fundamentally mistaken in arguing that the advance of weapons technology (and also, perhaps, the nature of the contemporary state) makes war immoral as such. This conditions both my contribution to recent debates on matters having to do with armed force and its use and my reaction to the arguments put forward by some others in these debates, including certain theorists who profess to lay out what the idea of just war requires. Let me now turn to some specific ideas that have been prominent in recent just war discourse, examining them from my own perspective tutored by the just war tradition in its classical form.

II. Important Themes in Current Just War Discourse

A. Is there a presumption against war or against the use of military force?

That there is such a presumption is, as we have seen, the position taken by the U.S. Catholic bishops in *The Challenge of Peace*. There it was framed as a "presumption against war" to be found in Catholic teaching but held to be universally binding. In the bishops' 1993 statement *The Harvest of Justice Is Sown in Peace*, the phrasing was slightly different: "The just-war

---

[24] James Turner Johnson, *The Holy War Idea in Western and Islamic Traditions* (University Park: Pennsylvania State University Press, 1997).

tradition begins with a strong presumption against the use of force."[25] A
third phrasing appeared in the bishops' November 2003 "Statement on
Iraq": "the strong presumption against the use of military force."[26] These
changes, I think, were adopted to fit better the context of uses of military
force short of formal war between states, and I do not read in them any
important change in meaning. The critical question, however, is whether
such a presumption actually is to be found in the tradition. My answer is
no. I have argued this in other connections, including my 1999 book
Morality and Contemporary Warfare.[27] Briefly stated, my argument against
the claim that just war tradition begins with a "presumption against war"
is that such a presumption is nowhere to be found in the classical tradition as it took shape in the Middle Ages and developed through much of
the modern period. What one finds there is a "presumption against injustice," as in the standard medieval formulation that a resort to force is just
if it seeks to repel an injury, to restore something wrongly taken, or to
punish evil. Augustine's emphasis, as Ramsey saw clearly, was to defend
the neighbor against unjust attack; the emphasis of Aquinas and scholas-
tic just war thinking after him was, as the French scholar Alfred Vanderpol
put it, "vindicative justice," that is, an action to reestablish justice by
vindicating those who had received injustice.[28] Similarly, in the transition
to the modern period, the increasing emphasis on self-defense followed
from the concern that force should be used to maintain or reestablish
justice in international relations. On my reading, the beginnings of the
idea of a "presumption against war" are to be found in moral outrage
against the destructiveness of modern war, specifically as read through
the examples of the Franco-Prussian War and World Wars I and II. The
idea's near relation is modern-war pacifism and its particular expression,
nuclear pacifism.

Now, who is right about the place of this "presumption against war" in
relation to just war thinking? Fr. Bryan Hehir, who was the principal
drafter of the 1983 pastoral letter of the U.S. bishops, writes in a review of
my *Morality and Contemporary Warfare*:

> Johnson has often stated his view that such a construct [that of the
> presumption against war] is detrimental to the use of just war tra-
> dition and cannot be found in the classical authors. I think all would
> concede the last point and contest the first.... [T]he substantive
> reason for placing a presumptive restraint on war as an instrument of
> politics is, in my view, entirely necessary. Both the instruments of

---

[25] National Conference of Catholic Bishops, *The Harvest of Justice Is Sown in Peace* (Washington, DC: United States Catholic Conference, 1993), 454.

[26] United States Conference of Catholic Bishops, "Statement on Iraq," available online at:
http://www.usccb.org/bishops/iraq/htm (accessed February 9, 2004).

[27] See note 21 above.

[28] Alfred Vanderpol, *La doctrine scholastique du droit de guerre* (Paris: A. Pedone, 1919), 250.

modern war and the devastation of civilian society which has accompanied most contemporary conflicts provide good reasons to pause (analytically) before legitimating force as an instrument of justice.[29]

I am happy that Hehir has conceded my point about the primacy of justice, and the absence of a presumption against war, in the authors who classically defined the idea of just war and thus gave a coherent shape to the tradition. For them it was not force as such that was wrong; for force, they believed, could be an instrument of good as well as of evil, depending on how it was used. Hehir's challenge is now directed to this last point, the idea that force can be anything other than an instrument of evil, and his argument is that "the instruments of modern war and the devastation . . . which has accompanied most contemporary conflicts" provide the reasons for maintaining a presumption against war. That is, war today is inherently too horrible to be a neutral instrument of good or evil. I note that this is the modern-war pacifist argument in a nutshell. It is, however, problematic in several fundamental ways. First, it tars all uses of force with one brush. I do not see the equivalence between the devastation caused by Iraq's 1990 invasion of Kuwait—including its destruction of much of Kuwait City and its intentional setting on fire of Kuwait's oil fields when its forces were forced out—and the destruction caused by the allied forces against Iraq in response to this aggression, up to and including the air strikes against structures in Baghdad and dual-use targets such as communications nodes and the power grid. Nor do I see the equivalence between the ethnic cleansing of Bosnia (and more recently, Kosovo) and the air strikes used with the aim of bringing such warfare against noncombatants to an end. Moreover, the doctrine, training, technology, and actual employment of force by the United States military in both Afghanistan in 2002 and Iraq in 2003 provide a strong indication that the weapons of contemporary warfare are not all inherently grossly destructive, as Hehir wrongly assumes, and that they do not lead necessarily to "the devastation of civilian society." His description of "the instruments of modern war and the devastation . . . which has accompanied most contemporary conflicts" fits the model of World War II very well, and it also reflects the concerns about the level of destruction that would arise from superpower nuclear war, the focus of the 1983 pastoral letter. However, it has little to do with the actual face of contemporary war, whether the low-technology warfare of Somalia or Rwanda (or of contemporary terrorism) or the high-technology warfare the United States military now practices. Nor does Hehir's argument make any distinction as to how, by whom, and to what ends armed force is used. Contrary to Hehir's argument and the idea of the "presumption against war," for just war tradition as a whole the mere existence of military power does not itself stand as an

---

[29] J. Bryan Hehir, "In Defense of Justice," *Commonweal* 127, no. 5 (March 10, 2000): 32–33.

evil, for it remains within the compass of moral decision whether and how to use the power available. That is where the focus of just war thinking traditionally has been, and in my view it is where it should properly remain.

I confess to some puzzlement as to what the "presumption against war" means in practical terms when, as in much recent religiously based language, it stands alongside a vigorous argument in favor of armed intervention in defense of human rights when these are being egregiously violated. To take an example, the U.S. Catholic bishops' 1993 statement *The Harvest of Justice Is Sown in Peace* includes a citation from Pope John Paul II that "humanitarian intervention [is] obligatory where the survival of populations and entire ethnic groups is seriously compromised" and follows it with the judgment that "military intervention may ... be justified to ensure that starving children can be fed or that whole populations will not be slaughtered."[30] If intervention in such circumstances is an "obligation," and if the obligation may include military means when they are all that will suffice, then where is the presumption against such means? Further, what does it add to the moral analysis to include such a presumption, when the analysis itself already takes account of concerns of last resort, reasonable hope of success, and the requirement that the means used not cause more harm than good? May not, in some circumstances, a preference for a nonmilitary response to egregious violations of human rights lead to a worse disaster than the quick use of military force? (I think of the case of Rwanda in 1994. Many who observed the beginnings of that massacre, including the Canadian general commanding the United Nations peacekeeping force, believed that a limited use of professionally trained and equipped military force early on against the marauding Hutu gangs could have prevented the genocidal killing of Tutsis that ensued.)

B. What constitutes "last resort" in the use of military force?

Disagreement over the meaning of the just war criterion of "last resort" is closely related to the idea of the "presumption against war." Let me take as an example the debate during 1990–91 on whether to use force against Iraq to expel it from Kuwait and punish its aggression. At that time, much religious opinion, Catholic and mainline Protestant alike, opposed the use of force against Iraq for a variety of reasons, arguing instead for other measures, including economic and diplomatic sanctions, to compel Iraq to withdraw and to set things right. Use of military force against Iraq, it was argued, should not be undertaken until it was clear that all these other measures, including economic and diplomatic sanctions, had had time to work. Opposition to the use of force, accordingly,

---

[30] National Conference of Catholic Bishops, *The Harvest of Justice Is Sown in Peace,* 15.

was put (in part) in terms of the just war requirement that resort to force be a *last* resort, understood by those opposing the use of force to require that all other measures conceivably available be used and found to fail first. A decade later, by contrast, one no longer heard about how the sanctions should have been given time to work; rather, moral concerns were being loudly voiced over the effects of the existing sanctions on the civilian population of Iraq. If this was a problem a decade later, it was surely a problem in 1991.

In the debate of 2002–03 over whether to use armed force to remove the Saddam Hussein regime, the U.S. Catholic bishops did not appeal to the "last resort" criterion in their formal statement arguing against the use of such force. Others, however, did so, interpreting this criterion as meaning that every other alternative should first have been tried and proven ineffective. A prominent example of such reasoning was that of former president Jimmy Carter in a *New York Times* op-ed piece that appeared on March 9, 2003.[31] Carter here explicitly appealed to the idea of just war, placing the criterion of last resort first among the just war principles as he listed them (last resort, discrimination, violence "proportional to the injury we have suffered," legitimate authority, and establishing a peace that is "a clear improvement over what exists"). Last resort, he argued, means that "all nonviolent options [must be] exhausted."

But the just war criterion of last resort does not mean that everything except military force must first be tried and have failed. Rather, this criterion, like the resort to force itself, has to be interpreted via a judgment as to the proportionality of proposed nonmilitary means—whether they will cause more good than harm—and as to whether they have any reasonable hope of success. That is, last resort is a criterion to be used in analyzing whether force is the most reasonable and proportionate choice, among all the choices available, to bring about the justified end. It is wrong to use the criterion of last resort as a means of postponing indefinitely *any* resort to military force.

C. What should we say about sovereign authority today?

At the beginning of his question "On War" (*Summa Theologica* II-II, q. 40, a. 1), Thomas Aquinas (1225–74) lays down that for a war to be just, three things are necessary: sovereign authority, just cause, and a right intention, which for him included both the aim of peace and avoidance of wrong intention, such as the desire to dominate, "implacable animosity," or lust for personal gain or power. (He drew all of these requisites from Augustine, whom he cited in explaining them. They had been introduced into the canon law tradition in the twelfth century via Gratian, who also drew them from Augustine.) It is very interesting and important that

---

[31] Jimmy Carter, "Just War—or a Just War?" *New York Times*, March 9, 2003, section 4, 13.

Aquinas began by requiring sovereign authority, and it is especially notable since nearly all present-day accounts of the *jus ad bellum* begin with
the requirement of just cause. There are two fundamental reasons why
Aquinas began here. First, for him as for Augustine and Gratian before
him (and the whole thrust of classical just war tradition after him), only
the person in sovereign authority, and not any private person, has the
right to resort to force. Thus, the sovereign has the ultimate responsibility
to weigh whether a just cause exists and decide whether to use force to
correct any violation of justice that may appear. Second, the sovereign is
responsible for the common weal—immediately, the good of the society
over which he is sovereign, and less immediately, the good of the larger
order of societies. (Aquinas developed more fully the sovereign's responsibilities in his treatise *On Princely Government*, and to understand more
broadly what sovereignty was understood to entail in medieval and early
modern thought, one should consult the body of literature on the good
ruler right down through Erasmus.) So authority to resort to armed force,
for Aquinas, had to be sovereign authority, because of the sovereign's
particular responsibility for the common weal of his society and the order
of nations as a whole. This is what lay behind Aquinas's use in this
connection of Romans 13:4, a biblical passage much cited in medieval just
war discourse: "For rulers are not a terror to good conduct, but to bad. . . .
[The ruler] does not bear the sword in vain; he is the servant of God to
execute his wrath on the wrongdoer." What might this imply today?

The first thing to ask is where "sovereign authority" to use force, one
of the principal requirements of the just war tradition, lies today. There
are three contenders: the United Nations, and in particular the Security
Council; regional security alliances; and individual states. In positive international law, individual states, and by extension alliances of states, have
the right and authority to resort to force in defense against an armed
attack, whether credibly threatened or in progress. Most armed interventions historically have fitted under this rule; this was the international-
law justification for the armed response to Iraq after its takeover of Kuwait.
Beyond uses of armed force in defense, the United Nations Charter gives
the Security Council the responsibility to authorize such force to deal
with threats to international peace and security. This allows for Security
Council–authorized military actions, including armed interventions, when
the Council has determined that a threat to international peace and security exists.[32]

---

[32] Though my discussion here is not directed to the problem of nonstate actors who use
armed force, there is no doubt that over most of the historical development of just war
tradition, the requirement of sovereign authority was understood to forbid anyone not in a
position of sovereign responsibility from having resort to armed force. An example encap-
sulating this attitude is Martin Luther's position on the German peasants' rebellion of 1525.
Though he sympathized with the peasants' grievances, he admonished them to seek peaceful redress. When they instead took up arms, he called on the German princes to put down

Positive international law derives from the Westphalian system of international order, in which the bedrock assumption is the right of territorial sovereignty. On this assumption the ruling authorities of any state were long held to have the right to do whatever they might wish in dealing with their own population, whatever its shape or consequences. It was only in the wake of World War II and the Holocaust that this conception began to be modified and limited by the growth of a new body of positive international law defining human rights and establishing protections based on them. This new level of recognition and protection of human rights provides much of the impetus for humanitarian intervention in the contemporary context. What is not settled either in positive or in customary international law is exactly what authorities have the right to undertake armed interventions for protection of human rights. Is this to be understood by extension of the right of individual states and alliances of states to use force in defense of themselves or of others who ask for help? Or is it to be understood by extension of the Security Council's right to authorize force in cases of threats to international peace and security? Recent history provides examples of all three sorts of actors and both kinds of rationales for humanitarian interventions.

In traditional just war terms, the state is inherently most capable of meeting the moral requirements of the idea of sovereign authority. The United Nations lacks several important attributes of such authority: it is not in fact sovereign, taking its power from the agreement of its constituent states; it is not responsible or accountable to the people of the world, but only to these states; and it lacks command and control mechanisms, so that it cannot direct the use of force responsibly. Regional security alliances such as NATO have a level of authority, in just war terms, somewhere between that of sovereign states and the United Nations. Concern to maintain the moral meaning of authority to use force leads me to caution internationalists that there remains an important place for individual action by properly governed and rightly motivated states. I am dubious of efforts to restrict the authorization of humanitarian interventions or other uses of force to the United Nations alone. Besides the problems with understanding the United Nations as possessing sover-

---

their rebellion by force, calling it a duty to do so. See Robert C. Schultz, ed., *Luther's Works*, vol. 46 (Philadelphia: Fortress Press, 1967), 3–56. As for contemporary just war thinkers, Ramsey treated the issue only in the context of a discussion of intervention, parrying the Communist claim that "national liberation" movements have a right to use armed force by responding that in fact such movements are proxy wars supported from abroad, not indigenous rebellions. See Ramsey, *The Just War*, 23–24. Walzer, at various places in *Just and Unjust Wars* (see chapters 6, 11, and 18), seems to require that movements which take arms in rebellion against the established authorities must have the purpose of serving the general good of their people. Such was explicitly the position taken by Richard John Neuhaus in Peter L. Berger and Richard John Neuhaus, *Movement and Revolution* (Garden City, NY: Doubleday and Company, 1970); Neuhaus in fact laid down the more stringent requirement that a revolutionary resort to arms is justified only if it meets all the just war requirements. This is my own position as well.

eign authority in the just war sense, it is a sad fact that the United Nations (and in particular the Security Council, which according to the Charter is the body that may authorize the use of armed force in response to threats to international peace) is often prevented from taking action by internal politics. Recent examples include the cases of Rwanda and Kosovo, not to mention Iraq in 2002–03. As for uses of armed force by regional alliances, such as the NATO intervention over the conflict in Kosovo (undertaken in the absence of a Security Council mandate, though the Council's approval was given after the action), I think we should regard these essentially as the consensual joining together of individual states in support of a purpose widely recognized in international humanitarian law. Indeed, such consensus is important as a check on the motivation of any such intervention; on this I agree with Bryan Hehir and others.[33] The more robust the consensus the better; yet I would insist that the just war understanding of authority means that individual states may also act alone in cases of pressing need.

The moral understanding of the concept of sovereign authority is also what gives states, groups of states, and the Security Council the right to override territorially defined sovereignty when the latter is being abused. When do the rights and protections of sovereignty disappear, on this moral analysis? Under either of two conditions: first, when the governing authorities violate the basic human rights of some or all of their people (since the sovereign's authority to rule follows from service to the common weal, sovereignty is lost, in the moral sense, when state power is used to oppress some or all of the people who live under its rule); and second, in the case of rogue states, states that employ their power to menace others (this, I take it, is the moral meaning of the international-law concept of threats to international peace and security). On this understanding, humanitarian intervention and other uses of force against a state or government that has engaged in massive human rights abuses or that threatens other states or the international order as a whole do not violate the sovereign rights of the state or government that is the object of the intervention, because it has already forfeited those rights by its wrongdoing.

Thus far, I have been discussing issues in the current debate that have to do with the justified resort to force: that is, issues relating to the question of the *jus ad bellum.* Now let me turn briefly to the current state of thinking related to the question of *jus in bello,* right conduct in employing justified force.

D. The question of discrimination

First, what is the current thinking about what discrimination requires? The baseline of most recent just war thought on this subject has been the

---

[33] J. Bryan Hehir, "Intervention: From Theories to Cases," *Ethics and International Affairs* 9 (1995), 1–13.

formulation of Paul Ramsey: discrimination requires that there be no direct, intentional attacks upon noncombatants, though the rule of double effect allows indirect, unintentional collateral harm to noncombatants from attacks against combatant targets. Michael Walzer, in *Just and Unjust Wars,* added a further qualification to the meaning of the double effect rule: that the attacker, "aware of the evil [collateral harm], . . . seeks to minimize it, accepting costs to himself."[34] With this background, there are two fundamental questions having to do with what discrimination requires in the current debate. The first is a perennial one: Exactly what is the distinction between a combatant and a noncombatant in contemporary armed conflicts? The second comes from the difference between Ramsey's and Walzer's interpretations of what double effect requires.

As to the first of these questions, recent debate has reintroduced the idea that in contemporary war the combatant-noncombatant distinction collapses. I have never found this argument convincing, and I do not think we need to go beyond Ramsey's and Walzer's response to it: that the argument is overblown, and that there are in every conflict some people who would be noncombatants by any reasonable reckoning. There is good historical reason to hold that the problem with modern warfare is not that the combatant-noncombatant distinction blurs or disappears, but that such warfare has often involved the conscious decision to target noncombatants. An example from World War I is provided by the German Navy's deliberate choice to bombard undefended English channel towns in violation of Hague Convention IX of 1907.[35] Between the two World Wars, the theory of strategic bombardment developed as an explicit rationale for attacking noncombatants as a way of undermining the enemy's civilian morale and hurting its ability to wage war. During the Cold War, though the rule of double effect was often invoked (beginning with Ramsey) as a way by which at least some use of nuclear weapons might be morally justified, the fact remains that the destructiveness of an actual nuclear attack would cause extraordinarily high levels of harm to noncombatants— whether they were directly, intentionally, targeted or not.

It helps the cause of the combatant-noncombatant distinction that one of the most evil features of many contemporary armed conflicts, as of contemporary terrorism, is that this distinction has in fact been turned on its head, so that it is not just ignored, but noncombatants have been preferentially targeted as a way of prosecuting war. (Think of the Rwanda genocide, the ethnic cleansing in former Yugoslavia, the terrorism in Northern Ireland, Israel, and Sri Lanka, the amputations of limbs of noncombatants in the conflict in Sierra Leone, the deliberate targeting of the World Trade Center towers in the 9/11 attacks, the deliberate endanger-

---

[34] Walzer, *Just and Unjust Wars,* 155.

[35] For a description of this decision and its context, see Robert K. Massie, *Castles of Steel: Britain, Germany, and the Winning of the Great War at Sea* (New York: Random House, 2003), 319–27.

ing of noncombatants as a tactic used by the Fedayeen Saddam in Iraq in 2003, and the similar targeting of civilians by the Iraqi insurgents today.) But it does not help the idea of this distinction that the air war against Serbia over Kosovo trended in its final days toward something increasingly like strategic bombing, which by definition is bombing aimed at the civilian noncombatant society of the enemy, not at his armed forces or his government. The drift toward justifying such targeting is insidious when it occurs, and it needs to be headed off by planners and target selectors before it develops. At the same time, I think it needs to be said clearly that from the perspective of just war tradition (and, indeed, from both Ramsey and Walzer) there is a real moral difference between (1) hitting a legitimate target with collateral noncombatant harm and (2) directly, intentionally hitting the noncombatants. The mere fact that noncombatants suffer from a bombardment, for example, does not mean that the bombardment was unjust, though it may become unjust if disproportionate. Appreciation for this distinction was not always present in the moral debate over nuclear weapons, and it is not always present now.

The second question, though, is how far the attacker must go, morally speaking, in seeking to avoid collateral harm to noncombatants. What degree of risk or cost should the attacker shoulder? Walzer's argument, or something like it, seems to me to lie behind the moral disquiet some critics expressed over the way the Kosovo intervention was carried out: by planes flying high above the range of Serb air defenses, so that the pilots bore essentially no risk. A similar argument might be made regarding the air war over Afghanistan in 2002 or Iraq in 2003, where in both cases the defense against such attack was minimal. What can one say about this argument? I am sympathetic with the thrust of Walzer's argument, but I think it is wrongly used when it is applied in such cases as these. There is no moral responsibility to take risks and incur costs to oneself when it makes no difference in the outcome, or when the difference made would be negative. Whether a contemporary precision-guided missile (PGM) hits the intended target is not affected by how high the pilot is flying, so long as he remains within the required range. Indeed, for some PGMs (for example, JDAM-equipped bombs) it is necessary for the pilot to fly high so that the aiming device has time to acquire the necessary satellite signal. A further, and different, kind of consideration is that bombing with PGMs may be more accurate when there is no threat from air defense, since such damage-limiting factors as time of day, angle of attack, and choice of weapons-delivery platform then become more important. Indeed, in some cases, higher collateral damage may result from a low-flying plane than from a high-flying one. Walzer makes an important moral point, but it must be applied intelligently, taking into account the realities of the kind of warfare in question. The important moral questions, in any case, are the selection of the target and the means used to attack it.

The principle of discrimination imposes a moral requirement to develop and employ weapons capable of close accuracy and thus able to be less destructive in their effect. Contemporary precision-guided munitions are thus a morally important development, since they are inherently more capable of being used discriminately (and their lower yields make them more proportionate in their effects as well). Some critics have charged that the nature of these weapons—their ability to discriminately hit a given target and cause little or no damage beyond it—may lead to their being used more frequently, perhaps capriciously. Certainly in the recent context, where there have been many pressures for humanitarian intervention and for action against rogue states, the availability of cruise missiles, laser-guided bombs, and other precision-guided munitions may suggest a relatively cost-free line of action that circumvents the moral consideration that should be undertaken before any use of force. If this is the case, then the problem is a possible misuse of the *jus ad bellum* decision, not of the *jus in bello* discriminateness and proportionality of these weapons themselves.

The weapons themselves, of course, are only part of the story: also needed is the will to use them discriminately and the embodiment of this will in the training given to those who use them, the development of strategies and tactics for their use focused on avoiding harm to noncombatants, and the monitoring of targeting decisions by a team including experts in the application of the requirements of the law and morality regarding noncombatant immunity. In all these respects, the United States military is currently far out front in development of the capacity to fight so as to minimize harm to noncombatants. The role of the moralist in regard to the conduct of war should be to hold that conduct to the standards that these capabilities have made possible.

E. What constitutes disproportionate force?

I have already referred, in the *jus ad bellum* discussion above, to the argument of modern-war pacifists, also called just-war pacifists, that modern war is inherently disproportionate in the destruction it causes. I have never found this argument convincing. One problem is: disproportionate to what? It is clear that modern warfare as exemplified by the two World Wars was very destructive; but that modern warfare is inherently so remains to be proven. In any case, the only way to measure moral proportionality in the use of force is to compare the destruction caused with the good produced (which also includes the evil averted). In the *jus in bello* sense, some just war thinkers have in the past interpreted the requirement of proportionality as meaning opposing force with similar force and no more. This seems to have been one reason for moral criticism of the massive force deployed against the Iraqis in Operation Desert Storm and, in the Kosovo intervention, criticism of the air campaign. But opposing force with similar force can lead to more destruction, not less, as each force is bloodied similarly by the other, additional forces are drawn in on both sides, and the conflict drags on and escalates. There is a proportionality argument for the use of overwhelming force, though this is seldom admitted by persons who regard force itself as the central problem. Again, the proper measure of proportionality in just war terms is harm done against good done; calculation of whether a given amount of force is proportionate or disproportionate follows from that.

But this calculation of proportionality also requires us to ask whether a particular means is the best way to a desired end. The air campaign against Serbia did nothing directly to protect the ethnic Albanian Kosovars, and it may, as some have argued, have triggered worse violence against them by the Serb troops and paramilitaries in Kosovo. Admittedly, the air strikes were expected to cause the Serb forces to cease their violence against the Kosovars, and it was bad calculation that this did not happen. It is also the case that ground-force options were very limited. Yet this discrepancy between ends sought and means employed is the sort of thing one should look at when thinking in terms of the just war requirement of proportionality during an armed conflict, rather than the matter of how much destruction, in raw terms, has been created.

The particular problem of attacks against dual-use targets (those which have both civilian and military uses) raises questions of both discrimination and proportionality. Discrimination does not mean that such targets cannot be morally attacked; rather, the rule of double effect implies just the opposite. Nevertheless, considerations of proportionality may limit such targeting or argue against it entirely. Dual-use targets include power grids, communications nodes, critical highways, railroads, bridges, and the like. These can be legitimate military targets in terms of the criterion of discrimination as defined via the rule of double effect. But military forces typically have a range of backups for all these that noncombatant society lacks. Thus, the collateral damage to noncombatants from an attack on a dual-use target may be disproportionately greater than the damage to the combatants. Again, proportionality requires measuring the damage caused against the justified end. Attacks on dual-use targets may sometimes satisfy this calculation, but sometimes they may not. The decision to attack such targets is thus not just a matter of whether discrimination is satisfied; proportionality must be satisfied as well. For whatever reason, the decision was made in Operation Iraqi Freedom, before the use of armed force began, not to target dual-use facilities. I regard this decision as morally very significant. This was a general rule that might be (and was) overruled in specific, limited instances, when the military value of a facility was judged to be sufficient to warrant its destruction. This illustrates the right way, in my judgment, to approach the targeting of dual-use facilities: saying no to such targeting in general, but with the possibility of overriding this general rule if considerations of military value warrant it and if the requirements of discrimination and proportionality can be satisfied.

F. What about the end of peace?

I find it deeply ironic that the U.S. Catholic bishops' 1983 pastoral *The Challenge of Peace* did not include the end of peace in its listing of the just war criteria. It is the more tragic that most recent just war debate has paid little attention to this, and that, as events have shown, planning for Operation Iraqi Freedom included disproportionately little on the peaceful rebuilding of Iraqi society, compared to the attention given to the military campaign itself. Nor did the U.S. Catholic bishops address this issue in their "Statement on Iraq"—a fact not excused by the context of their being opposed to the use of force in the first place.

Surely the just war tradition regards the purpose of achieving a genuine peace as a necessary element in the decision on whether the resort to force is justified or not. But having such a purpose implies having the will to achieve it and taking the necessary steps, including planning and commitment of resources, to achieve it. Moreover, the just war tradition includes significant resources for helping to understand what such peace means in fact. In the first place, this peace is the result of creating a justly constituted social and political order. Second, the responsibility of establishing such an order and providing for its continuation and protection is among the obligations of sovereign authority—the same sovereign authority that must make the decision to use force in the first place. The rightness or wrongness of the decision to use force is not simply about the use of force itself, so long as it lasts, but a commitment to the purpose of peace at which the use of force should aim. It is an immoral choice simply to declare military victory and depart.

I suggest that we have, in practical terms, learned a great deal about what is needed for the actual establishment of the conditions for social and political peace in societies ravaged by war (and by previous egregious abuses of human rights) through the experiences of Bosnia and Kosovo. These show both how difficult it is, and how long it is likely to take, to create the conditions for genuine peace. Fundamental institutions have to be rebuilt, often from scratch; the infrastructure of civilian life needs to be repaired or rebuilt; and not least the people who have good reason to mistrust one another must be brought to learn how to live cooperatively with one another. It may well be that doing all this is beyond the physical resources of any single nation—even one as wealthy and powerful as the United States—and the cases of Bosnia and Kosovo argue that, in any case, there is much to be said for a genuinely international participation in the effort to rebuild. Diversity in participation in such an effort may lead to a certain level of inefficiency and even chaos, but it also provides a richness that goes beyond what any one nation may be able to provide. Moreover, the cooperation of diverse nations around the achievement of common goals, motivated by common values, provides a powerful model for societies whose populations have been divided by war. Such cooperation also reduces the likelihood that efforts to establish a just social and political order—and therefore a society at peace within itself and with others—will be regarded as "victor's justice."

What is notably lacking in recent just war debate is a serious commitment to explore what the end of peace may require, both negatively—that is, in terms of the effort to oppose a regime that systematically violates the core meaning of peace, a just social and political order for its people—and positively—that is, in terms of the commitment implied by the decision to use force to correct the first kind of evil.

Let me conclude this discussion of the end of peace with a few remarks on a special topic, that of war crimes. The commission of war crimes is directly a war-conduct (or *jus in bello*) issue; but the question of war crimes investigations, prosecutions, and punishment has to do with the end of peace, one of the premier *jus ad bellum* concerns. For a society to punish its own citizens who are guilty of war crimes is an important ideal, an indication of that society's commitment to a just order. Yet in cases in which such national action is unlikely or impossible, international judicial processes offer an alternative. Almost forty years passed between the Nuremberg and Tokyo trials and the present, ongoing war crimes tribunals for Rwanda and former Yugoslavia, but a standing international war crimes court (the International Criminal Court) now exists and the question of war crimes is much in discussion in various contexts today. It has taken a while for this discussion to develop, and it is still developing. For a time, many in the conflict-resolution debate looked approvingly on the Chilean solution for dealing with atrocities during conflict: "lustration," or identification of the atrocities and perhaps the perpetrators, but the extension of amnesty toward them. The South African Truth and Reconciliation Commission leaned heavily on this model, but the commission's work was paralleled by more traditional legal investigations, prosecutions, and punishment of those who did not participate in the lustration process and receive amnesty. The atrocities of Rwanda and the former Yugoslavia were so severe and widespread that the international community united around the creation of war crimes tribunals to deal with the perpetrators. This may have implicitly dealt a death blow to the idea of lustration, as the effort to bring former Chilean head of state Augusto Pinochet to trial suggests. One argument against war crimes prosecutions, favored by some in the diplomatic and conflict-resolution communities, was that the most important thing in armed conflicts is to achieve a cease-fire, and the threat of war crimes prosecutions tended to prevent this. Think, for example, of the very different treatment given to Yugoslav head of state Slobodan Milosevic at the time of the Dayton

Accords[36] and now, in the wake of the Kosovo atrocities. My own judgment is, as I have suggested before, that the aim of a just war is not simply to end the fighting, for peace without justice is no real peace at all. Rather, just war tradition requires a peace with justice, a peace in which the rule of law is established or restored, one in which civil society does not need to cope with the ongoing fear of powerful figures who perpetrated evil acts during the conflict and remain free to engage in similar acts again. The end of peace, thoroughly understood, requires a commitment to achieving such a society, so that the moral work is not done when the decision to resort to force is taken, or when the force is itself being used, but only when a real peace is established in the end. Exactly what this implies, together with how to provide the resources necessary for it, needs to become a much more central part of moral debate on the justified use of armed force.

III. CONCLUSION

Exactly what to make of the just war idea in the contemporary context has been the subject of this essay. While there has been a robust growth and establishment of just war thinking in American moral discourse on the use of armed force over the last four decades, this has sprung from somewhat different conceptions of just war (as illustrated by the three benchmarks I discussed in Section I), has either not engaged the deeper historical just war tradition at all or has done so only spottily, and in some cases has introduced new moral assumptions and criteria which, both in principle and in practice, have reshaped the thrust of just war argument in a way that is at odds with its historical purpose. At the same time, new concerns, such as the meaning of the requirement of sovereign authority in the era of the United Nations and the problem of how to understand the requirement of discrimination in contemporary warfare, have opened the door to a variety of arguments and a corresponding diversity of conclusions.

It is certainly clear that if it is to be a meaningful source for moral wisdom regarding the use of armed force in any historical context, the just war idea must be relevant to that context. The internal development of the just war tradition is in fact a story of its interpretation and adaptation to changing contexts over history, and the contemporary use of just war reasoning should correspondingly be expected to engage the world as it is. But this does not mean attempting to invent the idea of just war anew, treating its categories as shells without content to be filled with contemporary meanings, or modifying it in ways that are at odds with its

---

[36] The Dayton Peace Accords, initialed at Wright-Patterson Air Force Base, Dayton, Ohio, on November 21, 1995, and signed in Paris on December 14, 1995, established the framework for peace in Bosnia-Herzegovina, ending its war for independence.

historical content and intention. Accordingly I have argued that contemporary just war discourse needs to be tested and disciplined by reference to historical just war tradition, especially by reference to the normative content and purpose of that tradition in its classical form as reached by the end of the Middle Ages and the beginning of the modern period. In the previous section of this essay, I have shown how I think such testing ought to be done, using the classical form of just war tradition as a critical tool for dealing with several prominent themes in recent just war discourse. It is simply not the case, I think, that "the making of the moral world" can be divorced from "its present character," as Michael Walzer suggests in *Just and Unjust Wars*;[37] rather, the moral world as it was made in the past continues to be with us in the present, and responsible moral discourse must have a significant dialogue with that past and the processes which made it. A recovered conception of just war thus holds promise on several fronts. Not only does it provide a way of thinking morally about the resort to force, and right conduct in the use of force, as an element in seeking the goods that political community can offer. It also puts us in touch with the moral theory of politics in which the idea of just war took root and out of which it developed. And if we seek to understand, interpret, and apply the idea of just war in the way I have argued for, by engaging the developing just war tradition of the past, then undertaking to think about war in the idiom of just war discourse opens a window into understanding and appreciating the history that has made us who we are, thus informing and deepening how we think about the moral values relating to political community and the use of armed force in the service of such community.

Religion, Rutgers University

---

[37] Walzer, *Just and Unjust Wars*, xiv.

HUMANITARIAN MILITARY INTERVENTION: WARS FOR THE END OF HISTORY?

By Clifford Orwin

I. Introduction

For a year and a half prior to September 11, 2001, I roamed the academic world delivering a paper on humanitarian military intervention. It was a living. But on that day the world changed, and my paper has had to change with it.

With the publication of *The Responsibility to Protect: The Report of the International Commission on Intervention and State Sovereignty*, two eras crossed in the mail. The *Report* was the work of a blue ribbon international commission and was published by the Canadian government with the blessing of UN Secretary General Kofi Annan. "Largely completed before the appalling crimes of September 11, 2001," the *Report* appeared just three months after them.[1] An artifact of a past so recent and yet so remote, does it remain relevant to the present and the future?

The *Report* makes a strong case for humanitarian military intervention, where necessary, not just as a right but as an obligation (the "responsibility to protect") of whoever is capable of undertaking it. The *Report* thus represents a further stage in what is, on paper, the triumphant rise of humanitarian concerns to the forefront of the world's agenda. It is the latest expression of a new moral awareness of the responsibility of each for the "human security" of all, and of all for the "human security" of each. In this, it echoes numerous statements of Kofi Annan, the 1997 Carnegie Commission Report *Preventing Deadly Conflict*, and the writings of Michael Ignatieff (himself a member of the International Commission on Intervention and State Sovereignty).[2]

Yet *The Responsibility to Protect* also raises the question of just what this supposed responsibility is likely to yield in practice. The authors begin by admitting that humanitarian intervention "has been controversial both when it happens, and when it has failed to happen," and they immedi-

[1] The authors do address "the kind of challenge posed by [the appalling attacks] of September 11, 2001," but only "in passing." *The Responsibility to Protect: The Report of the International Commission on Intervention and State Sovereignty* (Ottawa: International Development Research Centre, 2001), preface, viii–ix; 1.29.

[2] See ibid., 2.16–2.33, on the emerging new consensus in favor of "human security" and thus in favor of its correlative, the "right to protect."

ately concede that the most grievous of these failures, that of Rwanda in 1994, has cast doubt on the credibility of intervention as such.[3] This is an issue only exacerbated by 9/11 and its aftermath.

II. PRELUDE: 1945–1992

Humanitarian intervention was not entirely unknown before the 1990s. If you open Michael Walzer's *Just and Unjust Wars*, one of the most important books of 1977, you will find that he not only mentions the topic but analyzes two instances in detail. (These were the interventions of the United States in Cuba in 1898, and of India in East Bengal in 1972.) Still, at the time of Walzer's writing the issue was not a lively one. His own attention fell primarily on the Vietnamese conflict and mutually assured destruction and other dilemmas of the Cold War.[4] The armed and ideological were everywhere in those days; the armed and humane still awaited their day in the sun.[5]

In this respect as in many others, the Cold War had immobilized the West. To see this, we need look no further than Cambodia in the late 1970s. Despite the stunning carnage there and the relative weakness of the Khmer Rouge, neither global nor local configurations of power permitted an armed intervention. Only George McGovern, quixotic as ever, proposed that the international community undertake one. (Despite his suggestion that this enterprise occur under the banner of the United Nations, his initiative was not well received by his recent allies in the antiwar movement.)[6] The honor of deposing the Khmer Rouge fell instead to their former allies the Vietnamese Communists, whose motives were less humanitarian than imperial (and who were acting as a proxy

---

[3] Ibid., 1.1.

[4] Michael Walzer, *Just and Unjust Wars* (New York: Basic Books, 1977), 101–8. The preface to the third edition of 2000 contains an expanded treatment of humanitarian intervention. Walzer was my teacher, and I owe much of my interest in these matters to his example.

[5] This is the case unless we take the view that the golden age of Western imperialism was also a golden age of humanitarian intervention, in the form of the white man's burden or the *mission civilisatrice*. On this, see David Rieff, *A Bed for the Night: Humanitarianism in Crisis* (New York: Simon and Schuster, 2002), 57–70. Rieff's argument has the advantage of calling attention both to the genuinely philanthropic aspects of imperialism and to the neo-imperialistic possibilities latent in current humanitarianism. Yet what we mean by humanitarian intervention strictly precludes imperialism in principle and is subject to strict limitations wholly foreign to it. Theodore Roosevelt spoke with justice of the "savage wars of peace": yet it is central to our notion of humanitarian intervention that it eschew all savagery. On the strict limitations incumbent upon intervenors, see *The Responsibility to Protect*, "The Operational Dimension," 7.1–31. To grasp how different were "the savage wars of peace," one might consult Max Boot's book of that title (New York: Basic Books, 2002), which deals with the American cases, or, for two vivid narratives drawn from personal experience, the young Winston Churchill's first books, *The Story of the Malakand Field Force* and *The River War.*

[6] See William Shawcross, *The Quality of Mercy: Cambodia, Holocaust, and Modern Conscience* (New York: Simon and Schuster, 1985), 68–69; and Samantha Power, *"A Problem from Hell": America and the Age of Genocide* (New York: Basic Books, 2002), 132–36 (which notes that McGovern's unlikely ally in this quixotic effort was William F. Buckley).

for the Soviet Union against China). The sequel brought continued war and faction, floods of refugees with all the hardships to which those are subject, and finally fears of famine in the shattered country. A conventional humanitarian operation under the auspices of the UN accomplished some limited good. Through it all, Cambodia remained wholly hostage to the relations among the great powers and between these and their local clients.

None of this was at all surprising. Throughout the Cold War, humanitarian considerations had yielded to exigent political ones. The decoupling of the two was a luxury that even the best intentioned could not afford. By 1990, however, the long struggle was over. Of the two contending alliance systems, only one remained on the board, its vast military power still intact. America and its allies thus enjoyed surplus military capacity. If they chose to turn it to humanitarian ends, the way seemed clear for them.

This was another respect in which the moment was ripe for military humanitarianism. Western sensibilities were growing more humane by the hour. They were also growing ever less warlike. The liberal democracies were busy reducing the size of their armies—the United States was no exception—and everywhere the ethos of military service was in decline. The cell-phone-toting unisex cosmopolitan citizen of the European Community (and soon of the World Wide Web) affected the least warlike way of life ever known to man—or should we say to persons? Traces of belligerence lingered, but the evolving moral consensus relegated them to racquetball. History offered no precedent of countries at once so powerful and so unwarlike.

While this trend boded ill for armed undertakings generally, it was less prejudicial to humanitarian ones than to others. For such interventions were no ordinary wars. Compare them with their predecessors. Consider the old order of things, which prevailed from the Stone Age until roughly 1990. In those days, belligerents, the powerful and the weak alike, had gone to war to advance their interests. Sometimes these interests were legitimate in the view of their neighbors, sometimes not. Sometimes they coincided with the interests of other parties, sometimes not. Sometimes, then, the interest underlying a conflict could be openly avowed, sometimes not. But for war to rest on an interest of some kind was not only permissible but obligatory. In making the case for a given war, you had to show that the interest at stake was vital—not that it was less of an interest than it might have been but that it was more of one. Take "repelling aggression," that blanket justification of armed action which invoked the failure of appeasement in the 1930s and resounded through the Cold War years. It expressed not altruism but an appeal to the common interest of nations confronting a common threat.

Of course, "interest," while dear to hard-nosed social scientists, captures only one aspect of political life. There are also "grievances," and the two do not always coincide.[7] Here too, however, the rule has been for nations to declaim on behalf of the grievances of others while resorting to war only to redress their own.

The end of the Cold War had reduced the prospect of war between the liberal democracies of the West and outsiders. It seemed to many to portend a world free of irreconcilable clashes whether of interest or ideology. True, Saddam Hussein's seizure of Kuwait in 1990 intervened to remind the world that the new situation needn't prove more peaceful than the old. Forty-five years after the founding of the United Nations, an international regime of collective security was still a work in progress. Still, we could hope that the establishment of a "New World Order" lay just around the corner. The very unanimity of the response to Saddam's aggression prefigured a future of global concord.

III. A Decade of Fitful Interventionism

In retrospect, the decade of the 1990s will likely appear the golden age of humanitarian military intervention. In politics all things are relative, of course—even golden ages. Still, this was the epoch in which humanitarian intervention, whether or not it succeeded and even whether or not it was attempted, loomed largest on the public agenda. Croatia, Somalia, Bosnia, Rwanda, Haiti, Kosovo, Macedonia, the Congo, Sierra Leone, Liberia: it was a long list. In the American presidential election debates of 2000, humanitarian intervention ranked first among the topics of foreign policy discussed.[8]

This epoch came to a fiery end on September 11, 2001. No one would mistake the wars the United States and its allies waged after that date for humanitarian interventions. No apology is required for having deposed two regimes that governed with such murderous disregard for the fundamental rights of their citizens. Still, one cannot pretend that the primary motive in either case was to benefit the afflicted people. Just as warfare inflicts so-called collateral damage on the civilian population, so the liberation of the Afghan and Iraqi peoples represented collateral benefit.[9]

---

[7] See David Welch, *Justice and the Genesis of War* (Cambridge and New York: Cambridge University Press, 1993).

[8] Reportedly at the insistence of moderator Jim Lehrer, one half of one televised debate was devoted to questions of foreign policy. (I am grateful to William Kristol for this information.) On this occasion, both George W. Bush and Al Gore agreed that they would not have intervened in Rwanda in 1994. By contrast, Bill Clinton apologized in 1998 for his inaction on that occasion, and in 2004 told interviewer Larry King that not having intervened was his greatest regret as president.

[9] On the humanitarian aspects of the Afghan campaign as ancillary to the military aspect, see Fiona Terry, *Condemned to Repeat? The Paradox of Humanitarian Action* (Ithaca, NY: Cornell University Press, 2002), 81–82.

Consider, by way of contrast, American motives in opposing the Greater
Serbia policies of Radovan Karadzic and Slobodan Milosevic. Here you
will find nothing obviously personal. There was no flag to plant in Sarajevo
or Pristina emblazoned with the names of murdered Americans. There
was no supposed presidential grudge arising from a plot by the enemy to
assassinate his father and predecessor. There was no fear of weapons of
mass destruction or of Serbian support of terrorism against the United
States. America's Balkan interventions were, if not wholly disinterested,
as reasonable a facsimile as you could hope to encounter in the international arena—which was just why humorist P. J. O'Rourke took it upon
himself to skewer them:

> Conservatives were flummoxed by Clinton's interventions in Haiti,
> Bosnia, Kosovo and elsewhere. But Clinton had found a way to
> conduct "peace by other means." He was purposely using military
> force solely as an instrument of pointless moralizing, on missions
> that neither defended American security nor extended American geo-
> political power. Clinton thereby was able to harness warmongering's
> political power and prestige without losing the support of smug lefty
> pacifists. He is Franklin Delano Gandhi.[10]

Note how O'Rourke blends so-called realism with a pinch of just war
theory. The only thing that can vindicate a war is a pressing interest of
one's own. Because humanitarian intervention fails this test, it stands
exposed as "warmongering." O'Rourke doesn't just claim that war is too
important to be left to the disinterested. His cynicism goes further. Scratch
a preacher of humanity, he implies, and you will find a conniving pol.
Compared with Clinton, even the Mongols were paragons of rectitude.
They rode about "extending their geopolitical power"; he disgraced himself posturing on the stage of domestic politics.

O'Rourke is right at least to this extent: humanitarian intervention
enjoyed the prestige that it did despite or because of the fact that it was
so anomalous. It was somehow military without being military, political
without being political, partisan without being partisan. It was all these
things precisely insofar as it was humanitarian, a category—*the* category—
that by transcending warfare, politics, and partisanship, transformed them
into something new and shining.

This is not the place to attempt a history of the humanitarian outlook.
I will merely sketch its current incarnation. Today's humanitarianism
begins from a preoccupation with the overwhelming evils of the twentieth century. First among these was genocide. In the decades since 1945,
what has come to be known as "the Holocaust" has emerged as the

---

[10] *National Post* (Toronto), March 20, 2000; from *The Spectator* (London).

negative moral reference point in human affairs.[11] It has become for us what the state of nature was for Hobbes or what despotism was for Montesquieu, a negative political standard that overshadows all positive ones.[12] (And as the reality of genocide, like that of Stalin's Gulag, was unimaginably worse than the most dire imaginings of Hobbes and Montesquieu, so its moral grip on us is deeper and more pervasive.) The ethics of the Holocaust fixes not on what we must do but on what we must never again permit to be done. Morality becomes an exercise in remembrance designed to preempt repetition. Humanitarians have undertaken to serve as the world's conscience on this score. They often attest to the force of this concern in shaping their commitment to their profession.[13]

A second factor shaping the humanitarian outlook, particularly among intellectuals, is the decline of the traditional Left. Throughout the West, educated people have abandoned any hope (and even any thirst) for the fundamental transformation of their comfortable welfarist societies. Certainly in North America today, your typical youthful idealist does not aim to ignite a proletarian revolution or even to unionize Wal-Mart. Between her BA and her MBA, she plans to spend a year in some wretched venue working for an NGO. In this she resembles her counterpart in Berlin or Barcelona.

The evolution is nowhere more visible than in *Médecins sans Frontières* (Doctors without Borders) and its schismatic offshoot *Médecins du Monde* (Doctors of the World), the agencies at the cutting edge of the new humanitarianism. Their leading figures, Rony Brauman and Bernard Kouchner,[14] are alumni of the militant Left in France. Like many of their comrades in the movement, they began life steeped in Marxism but eventually

[11] For some reflections on the application of this term to the Nazi genocide against the Jews, see Shawcross, *The Quality of Mercy*, 419–24. For a brief account of how the Holocaust was "transformed from an assemblage of searing family memories to a totemic event," see Robert Kaplan, *Warrior Politics: Why Leadership Demands a Pagan Ethos* (New York: Vintage Books, 2003), 96–101; and for a full length study, Peter Novick, *The Holocaust in American Life* (Boston: Houghton Mifflin, 1999). For a theoretical discussion of genocide, see Alain Finkielkraut, *L'avenir d'une négation: Réflexion sur la question du génocide* (Paris: Editions du Seuil, 1982); for a practical discussion of the issue as it has figured in the era of humanitarian intervention, see Power, *"A Problem from Hell"*.

[12] Cf. Michael Ignatieff, *The Warrior's Honor* (New York: Viking, 1998), 19: "Modern moral universalism is built upon the experience of a new kind of crime: the crime against humanity." Cf. ibid., 3–5.

[13] For moving personal testimonials, see Shawcross, *The Quality of Mercy*, esp. 15–18, and Bernard Kouchner, *Ce que je crois* (Paris: Editions Grasset, 1995), 16–17. Note also the remarks of Stephen Solarz (D-NY), one of the American congressmen who most ardently supported intervention in Bosnia, quoted in Power, *"A Problem from Hell,"* 128.

[14] Kouchner has stated his credo in *Ce que je crois*. For his critique of the old Left and his defense of humanitarianism as the new one, see pp. 11–22, 53–56, and 139–55. I have not been able to obtain Rony Brauman's *L'humanitaire: Le dilemme* (Paris: Les Editions Textuel, 1996). Other important French contributions to this debate are Bernard Hours, *L'idéologie humanitaire, ou, Le spectacle de l'altérité perdue* (Paris: Harmattan, 1998); and Alain Finkielkraut, *L'humanité perdue: Essai sur le XXe siècle* (Paris: Editions du Seuil, 1996), which offers a critique of humanitarianism.

renounced it root and branch. They now devote themselves to an activity that they understand as anti-ideological. Pol Pot collaborated with Aleksandr Solzhenitsyn to light this passage for them.[15]

In a sense, this transition from Marxism to humanitarianism signals a moderation of the Left. Humanitarians have renounced vast goals of social transformation in favor of the finite and practical one of relieving suffering in those regions of the world where it is worst. They have repudiated Marxism not only as impractical but as dangerous, recognizing that in the Third World as elsewhere it has swelled the sum of suffering in the world rather than reducing it. At the same time, humanitarianism has preserved the moral fervor of the Left. It thus combines the zeal typical of modern ideology with that rejection of "totalizing" systems (including the various modern ideologies) which defines postmodernism.[16]

With a roll of drums, a few more words about postmodernism. This new outlook on the world consolidated its intellectual hegemony in the West during the 1980s and 1990s, just as humanitarianism was also gathering steam. Its ascendancy likewise reflects the collapse of the intellectual authority of Marxism. Through the efforts of throngs of (mostly French) intermediaries, Nietzsche and Heidegger have superseded Marx, but Nietzsche and Heidegger as housebroken to the needs of the Left—including humanitarianism.

Postmodernism went further than the relativism of the 1950s and 1960s in subverting the notion of an authoritative way of life or an affirmative code of morality. While the liberals of those earlier decades had held that moral relativism supported liberalism, the postmodernists drove home the point that this just wasn't so. Even if we could still bring ourselves to cherish our Western heritage as positive, we had to acknowledge its contingency or arbitrariness. As Richard Rorty has put it, the postmodern liberal "does not think that her vocabulary is closer to reality than others."[17] True, Rorty also reassures us that since all ways of life are equally arbitrary no one could blame us for sticking with our own. It would also seem to follow, however, that neither could anyone blame us for breaking with it. "Our way, no better or worse than any other way"—that's not much of a battle cry.

Yet precisely by its weakness in this respect, postmodernism has promoted the appeal of humanitarianism. Compared to those robust princi-

---

[15] A similar fate has befallen the academics and activists in the Anglo-Saxon world who promoted socialism as a means of development in the Third World. While prosperity has indeed taken root in such countries as Singapore, Taiwan, and South Korea, the socialist model of development has fizzled. For at least a decade, the question of which schemes will foster development in Sub-Saharan Africa has been upstaged by that of intervention to cope with the disastrous effects of their failure to develop. On this, see Rieff, *A Bed for the Night*, 100–105.

[16] Rieff, *A Bed for the Night*, 91–108, seems to argue both that humanitarianism is "utopian" and that it is not, but it isn't clear just what Rieff means by this term.

[17] Richard Rorty, *Irony, Contingency, and Solidarity* (Cambridge: Cambridge University Press, 1989), 73–74.

ples of liberty, democracy, and tolerance that were at issue in the Second World War and subsequently in the Cold War, humanitarianism represents a greatly diluted version of "Western values." It marks one of the points at which the Western ethos passes over into the post-Western one.[18]

True, humanitarianism is a distinctly Western development. Even the Buddhists who preach it learned it first from the West.[19] With rare exceptions, humanitarian intervention is an encounter between Western or Westernized nations and non-Western ones, between lands where liberal democracy and technology have triumphed and lands where they have not. It is a cardinal instance of what political scientist Pierre Hassner calls the dialectic between "the bourgeois and the barbarian": "an encounter between two kinds of societies" of which the one characteristically shrinks from violence while the other takes its dominion for granted.[20] To a West that has become morbidly sensitive to the charge of imposing its values, humanitarianism commends itself as impartial or neutral not least between the Western way of life and others. It is the white man's burden purged of its inconvenient whiteness. Precisely because it passes for nonpolitical, the relief of suffering affords a uniquely noncontroversial ground of political action.[21]

As moralities go, then, humanitarianism is a minimalist one, but in the current mood of the West this only enhances its appeal. "What is man?"

---

[18] Consider the following remarkable assertion by Jean Baudrillard: "There is a difference between humanitarianism and humanism. The latter was a system of strong values, related to the concept of humankind, with its philosophy and its morals, and characteristic of a history in the making. Humanitarianism, on the other hand, is a system of weak values, linked to salvaging a threatened human species, and characteristic of an unraveling history." Baudrillard, "When the West Stands in for the Dead," *Libération*, July 17, 1995, translated by James Petterson, in Thomas Cushman and Stjepan G. Meštrovic, eds., *This Time We Knew: Western Responses to Genocide in Bosnia* (New York: New York University Press, 1996), 89. Michael Blake has noted (in comments on the present paper) that even a more robust version of liberalism—such as Baudrillard may have in mind by "humanism"—would hesitate to intervene militarily in the affairs of a sovereign state, whether on humanitarian or any other grounds, and this for a wide variety of reasons. I agree; my comments speak only to the unique allure of humanitarianism as a ground for intervention in an age shaped by postmodernism.

[19] Buddhism may be widely touted as the world's most compassionate religion, but prior to Buddhism's exposure to the West this compassion had never assumed the form of humanitarianism.

[20] Pierre Hassner, "Par-delà le national et l'international: La dérision et l'espoir," in Hassner, *La violence et la paix: De la bombe atomique au nettoyage ethnique* (Paris: Éditions Esprit, 1995), 343–44. The irony is that, in this case, it is the society committed to peace that applies force to the one inured to violence in order to curb the latter's entrenched endemic violence.

[21] Cushman and Meštrovic have argued (in their introduction to *This Time We Knew*) that postmodernist relativism has tended to make Western intellectuals more tolerant of everything, including genocide, which "is explained away by recourse to a lazy relativism . . ." (12). Such is also the view of one of their contributors: Daniele Conversi, "Moral Relativism and Equidistance in British Attitudes to the War in the Former Yugoslavia," ibid., 244–81. I do not think that these writers make a persuasive case. The examples of moral equivocation that they offer do not seem to rest on relativism; there are other sources of moral weakness. Nor were most Western postmodernist intellectuals neutral as between the Serbs and the Bosnians, even if their sympathy for the latter was slow to translate itself into effective action by their governments.

asks Rony Brauman, cofounder and theoretician of *Médecins sans Frontières:* "Man is a creature who is not meant to suffer."[22] Brauman preaches a negative teleology. We cannot say what nature means us to do, but we can say what she doesn't mean us to stomach. On this, at least, we can take our stand, wager our lives, and bear to look at ourselves in the mirror each morning as the sun rises pitilessly above Kigali—or merely as we glimpse the horrors there unfolding on television.

This is the truth in O'Rourke's claim that progressive intellectuals would prefer only wars certifiable as "peace by other means." Not that they would rule out a military response to an actual attack on their homelands. From the end of the Cold War until September 11, however, they followed almost everyone else in regarding such an attack as improbable. The question was how strong, prosperous nations like their own were to deal with poor, weak, unstable ones. It was here that so many were so squeamish about the claims of national interest as actually to prefer that a given intervention *not* be defensible in these terms. Humanitarian intervention caters to this longing for a genuinely high-minded war.

It is not my purpose to eulogize Bill Clinton. As Machiavelli taught us, however, few men know how to be all good or all bad. I see no evidence that Clinton was one of them. An ambition to do good has haunted him throughout his career. Nor can I concur in O'Rourke's dismissal of the motives of the citizens who supported intervention. Those on the right were not simply truculent, nor were those on the left simply fatuous. And even if they were, we would still have to account for all those in the middle—ordinary citizens who defy classification in terms of left and right. In America as among her Western European allies, the policy of military intervention enjoyed broad public support. It appealed to a healthy satisfaction in the assertion of national power in a just cause, as well as to a generous concern with relieving the suffering of distant, hardly known peoples. It appealed not to what was worst in democratic citizens but to their best intentions. As the French statesman Talleyrand once cautioned, "we must beware of our first inclinations, gentlemen; they are almost always good." And so they are. They are also almost always weak—easily diverted, diluted, or mislaid.

Fortunately, the presence of lofty intentions does not preclude the participation of lower ones. These last are commonly the leaven without which the cake could not rise. Certainly the record suggests that humanitarian motives rarely shine forth in indubitable purity. If O'Rourke goes too far (as is the humorist's task), he does so in two opposing respects. On the one hand, he minimizes the unselfish element in humanitarian intervention; on the other, he trivializes the real interests at stake in the cases confronting Clinton.

---

[22] Brauman, *L'humanitaire*, quoted in Rieff, *A Bed for the Night*, 93. Cf. Kouchner, *Ce que je crois*, 93–110, on the "pessimism" of humanitarianism.

In intervention as in politics generally, in politics as in life generally, the motives behind any policy are almost always mixed. If they weren't, they wouldn't carry the day against the mixture of opposing motives. This is especially true in the case of humanitarian intervention, where the opposing considerations are so entrenched, powerful, and various. The classic example of a military intervention in which humanitarian considerations eclipsed all others remains that in Rwanda in 1994. It was the classic example of such an intervention not least in that it didn't happen. In fact, it didn't come close to happening, or come close to coming close to happening: we could prolong this regress infinitely. If Clinton truly wanted to play Franklin Delano Gandhi, here was his opportunity. Its knock went unanswered.

IV. If Only . . .

In the face of such massive evils as the genocides in Bosnia and Rwanda, we cannot but feel that much more could have been done. If only the will to act had been stronger, if only it had swept all before it to vindicate not in word but in deed the obligation to intervene to thwart this most terrible of all crimes against humanity. . . .

If only. In writing on this subject, it is *de rigueur* to deny either that you are a cynic or that you countenance complacency in others. I do hereby so deny. Still, we must raise the question of whether this chronic weakness of humanitarianism is not somehow a structural one. The public premise of a humanitarian intervention is that it is disinterested. The project evokes not our attachment to our own welfare but our attachment to that of the beneficiaries. It defines a situation in which we go to war without the usual incentives to warfare. In return we are spared the usual moral qualms attending it. The question is where this leaves us in terms of the depth of our commitment.

Professors today preach "ethical cosmopolitanism" and deprecate patriotism.[23] To hear them tell it, morality strictly forbids any partiality toward one's own or those who otherwise resemble oneself. David Rieff also subscribes to this view, although he is a journalist rather than a professor. He denounces not only all who were slow to recognize the need for action in Bosnia, but himself who so insistently promoted it. Why? Because despite rallying to the Bosnians, he failed to muster equal urgency in

---

[23] For an egregious example, see Martha C. Nussbaum, *For Love of Country?* (Boston: Beacon Press, 2002). One might also cite Peter Singer's famous article "Famine, Affluence, and Morality" (1972), reprinted in Singer, *Writings on an Ethical Life* (New York: Ecco Press, 2000); and Peter K. Unger, "Living High and Letting Die," reprinted in Unger, *Living High and Letting Die* (New York: Oxford University Press, 1996). There are many other such examples. For a powerful contrary argument, see Walter F. Berns, *Making Patriots* (Chicago: University of Chicago Press, 2001). For a compelling rejoinder to Singer and Unger in particular, see Neera K. Badhwar's essay "International Aid: When Giving Becomes a Vice" (elsewhere in this volume).

behalf of other victimized peoples. His sin was to respond to the besieged of Sarajevo not as human beings simply but as Westerners much like himself.[24]

This fashionable view abstracts from the *political* aspect of morality, which always implies a distinction between one's own and outsiders. The French sociologist Luc Boltanski divides responses to the suffering of others into two categories: the humanitarian and the communal (*communautaire*).[25] A response is communal wherever there exists a prior bond between observer and victim arising from a shared particular identity. In the absence of any such previous connection, the spectator's response to the sufferer is humanitarian, and it is this response alone that forges the link between them. Inevitably, a humanitarian crisis evokes from the vast majority of spectators a humanitarian response, grounded in nothing save a sense of common humanity. Unfortunately, this is commonly the weaker of the two responses.

We naturally sympathize more intensely with those with whom we identify not just in their bare humanity but as our own. From a cosmopolitan perspective, the murder of ten Belgian peacekeepers (in 1994) may seem but a trifle in comparison with the genocide of 800,000 Rwandan Tutsi that it accompanied. All politics is local, however, and one aspect of locality is point of view. The world never looks quite the same from one vantage point as from another. So the people of Belgium followed the rest of the world in being stunned by the genocide, while exercising their right to be uniquely enraged at the murder of their fellow citizens. Professors to the contrary, Belgium wouldn't be much of a country, or the Belgians much of a people, if they didn't care more for their own peacekeepers than for the strangers among whom they perished trying to keep the peace. And the Belgian government would not be much of a government if it did not recognize its obligations to its own people as primary, and as defining the lens through which it views its alleged responsibilities to all others.

Governments and peoples, unlike certain elites (including the authors of *The Responsibility to Protect*), are unlikely to accept the notion that they in particular are morally required to risk their treasure and the blood of their citizens to rescue other peoples in need. A people may well favor such an effort, where the price does not seem unreasonably high, and will pride itself on having undertaken it. It will view such undertakings as all the nobler for not being, strictly speaking, required. But as it will recoil from the prospect of unreasonable losses incurred to this end, so it will balk at submitting to any international arrangement that will take the decision as to whether it will participate in such projects out of the hands of its own government.

[24] Rieff, *A Bed for the Night*, 127–29.
[25] Luc Boltanski, *La souffrance à distance: Morale humanitaire, médias, et politique* (Paris: Métaillié, 1993), 24–29.

There is thus an inevitable tension between humanitarian intentions and communal attachments, and it is only sober to expect the latter to undermine the former. Bare unfortified compassion will provide a broad constituency in favor of humanitarian intervention, but not a very deep, determined, or persistent one. Such compassion will not go so far as to support the notion of an enforceable "responsibility to protect." "Someone really should help those people" stops several paces short of "We in particular are obliged to risk the lives of our young people to help them."

Accepting this last premise will spare us a lengthy discussion of the failings of the mass media. Learned critics will dispute whether streams of images of suffering ultimately tend to quicken our sympathy or to dull it. You can argue it both ways, and probably be right both times.[26] Yet in assuming that the problem is in our media rather than in ourselves, discussion of this sort puts the cart before the horse.

No one denies that in the absence of media coverage humanitarian crises would be trees falling in forests where no one could hear them. Once the televised crash has broken upon their ears, by contrast, audiences cluck and grow agitated. They soon press their respective governments to do something, anything, to stop the bleeding. (This is the much-discussed "CNN factor.") For the purpose of evoking an immediate response, an image may be worth a thousand words. A steady stream of them leaves the viewer with nowhere to hide.

At the same time, it is true that such images of hardship reach a point of diminishing returns. There is so much suffering in the world, no matter what anybody does; why go to the trouble of trying to alleviate it? When one crisis cools, the media will just serve up another. Awareness of many such emergencies distracts us from paying effective attention to any one of them. Yet concentrated media focus on one threatens to glut and overwhelm us.

The logical consequence of critiques of this kind, as the novelist and critic Susan Sontag suggested, would be to vex television with censorship of Platonic rigor, assuring that it provides us with neither too few nor too many images of a given instance of suffering, but just the right number of images of just the right kind. Sontag intends this as a *reductio ad absurdum*.[27]

---

[26] See Susan Sontag, *On Photography* (New York: Farrar, Straus, and Giroux, 1977), 3–24, 105–11, 167; Sontag, *Regarding the Pain of Others* (New York: Farrar, Straus, and Giroux/Picador, 2003); Clifford Orwin, "Distant Compassion: CNN and Borrioboola-Gha," *The National Interest,* Spring 1996, 46–54, and *Books in Canada* 25, no. 3 (April 1996), 21–24; Michael Ignatieff, "Is Nothing Sacred? The Ethics of Television," in Ignatieff, *The Warrior's Honor,* 9–33; Ignatieff, *Virtual War: Kosovo and Beyond* (New York: Viking, 2000), 191–96; Susan D. Moeller, *Compassion Fatigue: How the Media Sell Disease, Famine, War, and Death* (New York: Routledge, 1999); Kaplan, *Warrior Politics,* 124–29; and Rieff, *A Bed for the Night,* 31–56. Boltanski's book (cited in note 25) is also indispensable for this whole subject. For an accessible presentation of Baudrillard's views on this subject, see the newspaper columns translated in Cushman and Meštrovic, eds., *This Time We Knew,* 80–89.

[27] Sontag, *Regarding the Pain of Others,* 104–8.

Declaimers speak of "compassion fatigue" as if it were a pathology to be blamed on journalists. The unstated premise is that compassion is a commodity in abundant natural supply, any shortfall in which must be due to defective methods of extraction. In fact, sympathy is always scarce relative to the demand for it. In E. M. Forster's novel *A Passage to India*, two characters react to the death of a third, whom the reader has come to know and cherish but whom they have not:

> The other smiled, and looked at his watch. They both regretted the death, but they were middle-aged men who had invested their emotions elsewhere, and outbursts of grief could not be expected of them. . . . If for a moment the sense of communion in sorrow came to them, it passed. How, indeed, is it possible for one human being to be sorry for all the sadness that meets him on the face of the earth, for the pain that is endured not only by men, but by animals and plants, and perhaps by the stones? The soul is tired in a moment, and in fear of losing the little she does understand, she retreats to the permanent lines which habit or chance have dictated, and suffers there.[28]

Middle-aged or not, we have all "invested our emotions elsewhere," that is, somewhere other than in the day's televised calamity. We are busy people, not in that we are too busy for sympathy, but in that our sympathy too is already busy. We may reasonably be expected to suffer along with those we know and love, or with those with whom we identify more intensely than most through some perception of affinity. To expect us to exude compassion on demand, however, is unreasonable and indeed inhuman. God may know compassion for all created beings—animal, vegetable, and (following Forster) mineral—but in vain do we emulate Him.

If humanitarian military intervention tends to half measures, that is because so does humanitarianism as such. Just as many Americans of my generation shrank from dying in a war in Vietnam that they saw as unnecessary, unjust, and unsuccessful, so few today are eager to risk their own lives or those of their fellow citizens in a war they hold to be both necessary and just—but only on humanitarian grounds.

Let me stress once more that my point is not that Western citizens today lack genuine humanity. Rather, it is that genuine humanity is weak. Saints may rise above this rule, but they are few—that's what makes them saints. Committed humanitarians may rise above it, and they are more numerous than saints. They don't enlist in armies, however. There is no French Humanitarian Legion.[29]

---

[28] E. M. Forster, *A Passage to India* (Harmondsworth: Penguin Modern Classics, 1966), 240.
[29] Although Kouchner does recommend the creation of a permanent *Armée des droits de l'homme* (*Ce que je crois*, 126–28).

This, then, is the basic flaw in the fabric of humanitarian intervention: the weakness of compassion as a motive for the fortitude required in war. Footage of the Darfur crisis in Sudan, however stark, can do no more than foster a humanitarian bond between the nomad of the Sahel and the ordinary Joe watching the news in Cleveland. This bond will be genuine as far as it goes, but will remain peripheral, inconstant, and weak. Take the couch potato and make a soldier of him, and you may find him willing to risk his life for his comrades, his country, and mankind (in that order).[30] Leave him on his sofa, and you will likely see him disposed toward rescue in Darfur but reluctant to risk his or many other American lives to that end. You may also find him easily distracted by the next gripping news item, by the late movie following the news, and by the need to replenish his bowl of salsa. (Let this last need stand in for all his others.)

True, appeals to compassion (and its associated indignation) have played some part in all those great conflicts of our age that evoked the most intense commitment on the part of the belligerents. We need only harken back to "the rape of Belgium." Yet America would not have entered the First World War solely because of that blatant violation of the neutrality of a third party, or even because of the harshness of the German occupation, however exaggerated by Allied propaganda. In the event, America plunged into the fray only after the Germans had declared unrestricted submarine warfare—thus violating American neutrality and murdering American citizens. Once engaged in war in defense of one's own, it spurs dedication to the common task to hold that the fate of humanity also rides on the outcome. Americans have often inclined to this view—and not entirely without reason. At the core of their warlike resolve, however, since September 11 as in 1942, 1918, and 1898 ("Remember the *Maine*"), lies something other than humanitarianism.[31]

Good citizens indignant in their own country's behalf thirst to chastise the enemy. While welcoming foreign allies, they would not delegate all retribution to them. When President Bush stood at Ground Zero on September 14, 2001, it was to announce that the assailants would soon be hearing from "all of us"—"all of *us*," not America's Pakistani allies and not the United Nations.

---

[30] To put this in Rousseauian terms, as human beings we naturally will the good of all human beings: this is the most general of wills, embracing all human beings as such. Yet as the most general of wills, it is also the weakest, the intensity of any will being inversely correlated with its generality.

[31] Rieff (*A Bed for the Night*, 74–75) rightly distinguishes (1) the charity that Abraham Lincoln called those on the Union side to show to their Confederate brethren once defeated from (2) the zeal that had been required to defeat them. Cf. my discussion of this same passage of Lincoln's Second Inaugural in Orwin, "Princess Diana and Mother Teresa: Compassion versus Christian Charity," in Amy L. Kass, ed., *The Perfect Gift: The Philanthropic Imagination* (Bloomington: Indiana University Press, 2002), 188–211.

Such martial ardor rarely swells at the prospect of humanitarian intervention. Even those who favor strong action typically care more that something be done than that their country be the one to do it. They would not object very strenuously to someone else bearing the risk and trouble.

This natural tendency to pass the buck of intervention is aggravated by two further considerations. The first is the legalism that blankets humanitarian issues. It, like all legalism, is rich in respectable excuses for inaction. The second consideration is the cover afforded for dereliction by the mantle of that multilateralism so favored by all who undertake intervention. The differences among the parties, masked by their agreement to take common action, reemerge to bedevil the decision as to what action to take. These centrifugal forces may easily prove stronger than the uncertain forward thrust supplied by humanitarianism.

The Balkan quagmire of the 1990s clearly displayed the strengths and weaknesses of the politics of humanitarianism. The strengths were mostly verbal, the weaknesses only too actual. Through five years of successive crises, the powers relied heavily on the United Nations. UNPROFOR, however (the United Nations Protective Force for Bosnia), wanted no part of protecting Bosnian Muslims. Like the character Rick in *Casablanca* before he rediscovers his better self, it wouldn't stick out its neck for anybody. To be fair to it, UNPROFOR was undermanned, under-armed, and in no way a match for the forces of the Bosnian Serbs.

To be fairer still to the force, its mandate was not only restricted but contradictory. That was because there was no agreement among the major players as to what to do in Bosnia beyond trying to keep the lid on there. Everyone involved in the debacle—from the NATO countries and the permanent members of the UN Security Council to the United Nations Secretariat and its flock of agencies, on down to the International Committee of the Red Cross and the throng of other nongovernmental organizations (NGOs)—had interests of their own which told against effective intervention.[32]

Obviously such an outcome frustrates the humanitarian impulses in response to which the various governments have acted. Yet it also faithfully mirrors the vagueness and wavering of those impulses. Humanitarianism may not want to take no for an answer, but it tends to be satisfied with a very weak yes. It will be especially timid when poised on the brink of war.

O'Rourke to the contrary, even the most avid partisans of humanitarianism will tremble at resorting to force in its name. While this may be the kind of military action most acceptable to them, they are still far from comfortable with it. They will always be inclined to give peace (yet another) chance. In any situation in which armed intervention looms, other initia-

---

[32] David Rieff, *Slaughterhouse: Bosnia and the Failure of the West* (New York: Simon and Schuster/Touchstone, 1996).

tives will be underway. Much will be invested in such initiatives, and each will boast a vocal constituency.[33] These constituencies may include governments for whom humanitarianism is the perfect cover for military inaction.[34]

The prospect of military intervention thus inevitably finds humanitarianism divided against itself. This will blunt the thrust of popular pressure on governments to act. Leaders may respond as well by delaying hostilities as by resorting to them, all the while urging the earnestness of their humanitarian concern. Eventually, the necessity of armed intervention may become clear to just about everyone—but usually only because it has failed to take place soon enough.

V. WARS OF HALF MEASURES

This natural lukewarmness of humanitarianism constrains not only the choice of occasions for intervention but the manner in which such campaigns are fought. The purpose of humanitarian warfare is to end suffering among the victimized people, not to submit to it ourselves. This is illustrated by, among many other examples, the willingness of the NATO leaders to intervene in behalf of Kosovo in 1999 by means of an air campaign against Serbia, but their aversion to committing ground troops to that campaign.[35] One of the ironies of intervention is that our righteous David never sallies forth unless he enjoys the military superiority of Goliath. On second thought, make that the superiority of David, whose sling enabled him to strike his foe from a safe distance.

Yet this expectation that a humanitarian intervention be waged so as to avoid mortal peril to the intervenors clashes with another expectation: namely, that as a humanitarian intervention it be waged as cleanly as possible. The same policy cannot combine doing as much as possible to avoid risk to one's own soldiers and to avoid risk to enemy noncombatants—or even to those victims in whose behalf the intervention was mounted—hence the report of Human Rights Watch accusing the NATO forces of "violations of the international humanitarian law of war" in Kosovo.[36] The report presents as unconfirmed the relationship between

---

[33] To say nothing of the fact that those humanitarians performing these other missions would be imperiled by the outbreak of hostilities. They and their sponsors may therefore stop at nothing to prevent such an outbreak. Rieff has chronicled this process in *Slaughterhouse*, his account of the war in Bosnia.

[34] Such is Rieff's persuasive analysis of what was going on in Bosnia; see Rieff, *Slaughterhouse*; and Rieff, *A Bed for the Night*, 131–54.

[35] Cf. Ignatieff, *Virtual War*, 161–91; and Power, *"A Problem from Hell,"* 434–38. One should not overemphasize this point; it is not as if the Western publics demand that such campaigns be entirely free of casualties. Still, politicians understandably prefer to err on the side of caution in this matter.

[36] Human Rights Watch, "Civilian Deaths in the NATO Air Campaign," http://www.hrw.org/reports/2000/nato/Natbm200.htm.

the standoffish bombing policy and the numerous cases of civilian death due to mistaken identity. (Many of the civilian victims were Kosovar refugees in flight from the conflict who were mistaken for Serbian forces.) It would be perverse, however, not to suppose there was some connection. And as the tendency toward such violations is inherent in the political constraints incumbent on the conduct of an intervention, so too is a lack of zeal such as NATO displayed for investigating allegations of such violations.

Similar reflections apply to the seemingly gratuitous destruction of the civilian infrastructure of Serbia—bridges, television station, and such— also indicted by Human Rights Watch. Where the potential for escalation is as limited as it is in cases of humanitarian warfare, blurring the always fuzzy distinction between military and civilian targets offers the attackers some leeway. While they are forbidden from mounting overt attacks on civilians, they will still wish to apply pressure to them. It stands to reason, then, that so high-minded a war will be waged somewhat underhandedly, especially if (as in Kosovo) the war stretches on and the attackers become exasperated.

In their own discrete and distinctive way, then, humanitarian interventions may take their place among what Teddy Roosevelt called the "savage wars of peace." This is not an argument for eschewing them where necessary to prevent savagery of a much worse sort. Keeping it in mind may serve, however, to moderate our self-righteousness as intervenors.

The humanitarianism of an intervention will also constrain it on the political side. Other kinds of wars, where successful, settle many things (while unsettling many others). A humanitarian intervention, however, is by definition a stopgap. It seeks not to impose the solution most satisfactory to the conquerors—the intervenors are not conquerors—but to compel or persuade the parties on the ground to resolve their differences. If it denies victory to the perpetrator of the humanitarian outrage, it stops short of conferring victory on his victim. Intervention hopes to ease the transition from war to "conflict resolution."

The question that mattered and continues to matter for both Serbs and Kosovars (as for any other groups engaged in a struggle to determine their respective futures) is that of sovereignty. This is a political question, not a humanitarian one; the intervenors cannot make the issue of the combatants their own. Ultimately, the sympathy each side craves is just what humanitarianism must deny it: solidarity with its burning resentment of the other.

Thus, humanitarianism, while it may afford a politically convenient basis for intervention, can offer no basis for a settlement. Here it is dogged once again by its fundamentally negative character. A humanitarian intervention seeks to avert the worst; only when the worst appears imminent will nations finally undertake such an intervention. The project enjoys no popular mandate beyond this, and once it has been accomplished, the business tends to drop from public sight. What follows for the intervenors/victors/"peacebuilders" is a long and painful hangover.[37]

The initial success of an intervention introduces a new status quo which itself becomes the object of persistent contention. It does not help that the new situation is always nominally provisional, or that it falls short of an occupation. Crisis management will settle into tension management. Having balked at deciding the struggle of the parties, the intervenors must stay on to umpire it. This task is thankless. Nor is it likely that the intervenors will be as resolute at it as the strongest party among the locals will be to foil them. So it is that since the Kosovars have been de facto masters of their own house, it has been open season on the Serbian minority there.[38] That is not the only unflattering thing that can be said about what Kosovo has become under the stewardship of NATO. And recently the allegation has surfaced that what is left of Bosnia has become a bubbling cauldron of Islamic terrorism.[39]

None of this implies an argument against the practice of intervention. Averting terrible evil is an admirable accomplishment whether or not we agree with the humanitarians that it is the worthiest thing going these days. Much of its nobility lies, however, precisely in the fact that it promises no happy ending beyond averting the evil in question. It seems that there is no humanitarian intervention the outcome of which is satisfactory— unless one considers the alternative.

VI. Farewell to Intervention?

Has the era of humanitarian intervention (such as it was) now passed? True, humanitarian commitments have expanded on paper—the progress charted by Michael Ignatieff[40]—and conceivably could expand even further through the adoption of a "responsibility to protect." But will the nations that matter honor such commitments in practice? Revolutions in moral sensibility are fuzzy, while military intervention requires boots on the ground. Today those boots are grounded elsewhere, in Afghanistan and Iraq.

[37] Chapter 5 of *The Responsibility to Protect* states and articulates "the responsibility to rebuild." It offers a detailed catalogue of the frustrations and quandaries that accompany this stage of intervention. The reader will not emerge from this chapter with much confidence that the intervening states will muster the resources and determination sufficient to build stable states and good neighbors where there were none before—assuming, of course, that this is even a task within the capacity of intervenors.

[38] See the Human Rights Watch report "Failure to Protect: Anti-Minority Violence in Kosovo, March 2004," http://www.hrw.org/reports/2004/kosovo0704, which includes a summary of events from the beginning of the NATO occupation.

[39] "U.S. Hunts Islamic Militants in Bosnia," *The Telegraph* (London), July 26, 2004, http://www.telegraph.co.uk/news/main.jhtml?xml=/news/2004/07/26/wbos26.xml&sSheet=/news/2004/07/26/ixworld.html.

[40] See Ignatieff, *The Warrior's Honor;* and Ignatieff, *Human Rights as Politics and Idolatry,* ed. Amy Gutmann (Princeton, NJ: Princeton University Press, 2001).

For this reason among others, the authors of *The Responsibility to Protect* might have paid more attention than they did to the "appalling events" of 9/11. Unfortunately for those in need of rescue, the Axis of Evil will always upstage that of Misery. Like any benefaction, humanitarian intervention is only for those who can afford it. While the 1990s seemed to make few demands on Western nations in seeing to their own security, the semblance proved delusory. Islamism was on the rise and indeed already on the offensive; we have since reaped the harvest of our insouciance. Then too, those years were ones of economic expansion, whereas these last have been ones of retrenchment. If the mood of the prosperous countries was (relatively) expansive then, it is cautious and vigilant now. This is true whether they have supported the American engagement in Iraq or have distanced themselves from it.

Inasmuch as Western publics are preoccupied with other foreign policy concerns, humanitarian crises have predictably receded from view. In North America, certainly, the plight of Darfur has received much less coverage than past dilemmas of comparable gravity. No journalist who mentions it omits to speak of its direness, yet neither is it front-page or first-item news. It has been upstaged, the victim of a vicious circle. The less concerned the public, the less the journalistic exposure, and the less the exposure, the less concerned the public. By the same token, statesmen feel less pressure from their constituents to intervene. Fear of terrorism, like that of hanging, wonderfully concentrates the mind, and like all fear also hardens the heart. As political theorist Harvey C. Mansfield has put the teaching of Machiavelli, "a man or a country may be able to afford generosity today but what of tomorrow?" [41] Yesterday was the West's today, and today is its tomorrow. The threat of global terrorism has left us with less to spare—in our wallets, our arsenals, and our hearts. Americans in particular find themselves overstretched in more than just their troop deployments.

Here a personal anecdote may serve. In August 2001, I encountered a young Army major named John Nagl. Clearly a rising star, he had proceeded from West Point to Oxford University on a Rhodes Scholarship, had returned to command an armored detachment in the Gulf War, and since had split his career between armor assignments and staff positions. He loved armor but doubted that the tank would prove the weapon of tomorrow. The future, he thought, held more humanitarian interventions, and he hoped for the creation of a corps within the Army dedicated to that activity, in which he himself aspired to serve. (In this, it seemed to me, ambition of advancement mingled with genuine idealism.) Two years later, I noticed his picture on the cover of the *New York Times Magazine*,

---

[41] Harvey C. Mansfield, "Machiavelli's Virtue," in Mansfield, *Machiavelli's Virtue and Other Studies* (Chicago: University of Chicago Press, 1996), 8.

which profiled him as the Army's leading young tactician of counter-insurgency. Not surprisingly, the interviewer had found him in Iraq.

In the present situation of global tension, the further legalization of intervention, whether by a declarative resolution of the General Assembly of the United Nations or some other means,[42] is unlikely to accomplish very much. If the United Nations is presumed to remain the intervenor of first resort, the problems that have dogged its previous such ventures will hamper new ventures under this new rubric. One can hardly exaggerate how badly the United Nations has acquitted itself in this role in the past, or offer plausible grounds for supposing that it will do better in the future. Of course, one can always entertain one's readers with proposals for reform of the organization. (Or change the subject by noting how necessary it is to the world in other respects.) One doesn't even have to despise the United Nations to recognize that waging war is just not its *métier*.

At most, then, the United Nations can authorize a humanitarian intervention, but anything beyond that presupposes the willingness of a major power and its allies to shoulder the burden. Suppose they held an intervention and nobody came? Even if the nations of the world should accept the "responsibility to protect" on paper, it is hard to imagine them leaping to perform it. As they have dragged their feet in the absence of such a convention, so they would likely drag their feet to evade it. As they have hemmed and hawed in spite (and because) of the Genocide Convention of 1948, so they would in spite (and because) of a Convention to Protect. Like the bean in the old shell game, this difficulty can be shuffled about, but darned if you won't always find it lurking under the final shell.

Heap up international covenants as you will, there can be no effectual coalitions except of the willing. There can be no (enforceable) responsibility to assume the responsibility to protect. If everyone accepts it nominally while seeking to fob it off on others, face will be saved, and little accomplished, just as in Darfur to this point. The duty of intervention will become a hot potato. All respectable nations will want to touch it, but only to hand it off to others. The United Nations will remain the most popular vehicle for achieving this transfer.

The pattern is clear from the recent cases of the Congo, Liberia, Sierra Leone, and now Darfur. All parties will pay lip-service to the humanitarian principle, and those wealthy nations remote from the suffering will farm out the duty of intervention to countries in the affected region. Wealthy nations will restrict their own participation to passing resolutions and offering logistical assistance. Think of this as a kind of outsourcing, wholly benign from the perspective of the more developed nation since the job is one that no one at home wants to fill.

---

[42] See *The Responsibility to Protect*, 8.28. Cf. Kouchner, *Ce que je crois*, 127–28.

216

CLIFFORD ORWIN

To be sure, the countries thus enlisted have more pressing interests in the local outcome than we Westerners do. In this sense, they are more appropriate intervenors. The problem, of course, is that these interests are more pressing than ours precisely because they are not humanitarian. Nor, of course, may these local forces display the honesty and competence required to protect the imperiled population. Still, as we have seen, the basic imperative of humanitarian public opinion is that something be done, anything, but preferably something not too risky to one's fellow citizens. However wanting in other respects, the strategy of devolution fills that bill. It does not preclude a major power stepping in briefly, as the British did in Sierra Leone and the Americans did in Liberia, if the situation proves obviously beyond the capacity of the local intervenors. Yet, as I have already noted, the more overstretched the major powers, the slighter the prospect of their intervention, and the less effective the threat of it as a deterrent.

We Westerners no longer aspire to rule other peoples and have lost most of our optimism that we can teach them to rule themselves. We trade with them, which profits us and may also be deemed to benefit them. In the realm of politics, we leave it to international organizations to patrol the interface between ourselves and the barbarians. Increasingly, those in the front lines of this effort will themselves be drawn from barbarian ranks. By continuing to address only extreme cases of the consequences of misgovernment rather than the misgovernment itself—which is what it means to remain on the plane of humanitarianism rather than politics—the "international community" will both salve its conscience and limit its exposure to risk.[43]

Humanitarianism (and the humanity underlying it) will always be with us. At the same time, few of us will be willing to suffer much ourselves in order to redeem others from suffering. At most, Western leaders will sometimes confront a strong consensus in favor of weak action. Claiming credit for having acted on our best intentions, they will pray for results murky enough for them to declare humanitarian victory. This is a modest prayer, and as such likely to be granted. Oh what a tangled web we weave, when first we practice to relieve.

When I delivered an earlier version of this paper to an audience of Canadian foreign policy professionals, one of them observed that I should have called it "Wars for the End of History." On reflection I decided that he was right. On September 11, however, the end of history ended.

VII. CONCLUSION

Did this paper have to end there? Evidently not, as here it is slowly creeping a little further. The authors of *The Responsibility to Protect* claim that the past decades have seen a great broadening of the moral conventions governing global politics. They contend that this rising tide of moral-

---

[43] On the necessity that intervention stop short of regime change, see *The Responsibility to Protect*, 4.33.

ity has swept away the barriers that formerly divided humanity into sovereign states that enjoyed effective immunity to persecute their own citizens while conversely acknowledging no obligation to the welfare of citizens of other states.

There is truth to this argument, as far as it goes. The problem, as I have argued, is that it does not go far enough to sustain the firmness required in wartime. Except among professors (who don't flock to enlist), communal concerns will continue to trump humanitarian ones. Governments, accordingly, will scruple to risk the lives of their citizens to rescue those of other peoples, and humanitarian military interventions will remain safe, legal, and rare.

Yet writers like Ignatieff, Rieff, and the authors of *The Responsibility to Protect* (to say nothing of Kofi Annan in his public appeals) also offer a different and a more "realistic" case for humanitarian intervention. Earlier in this paper, I spoke of "collective security" and "repelling aggression," two typical doctrines of the Cold War era, neither one of which was an appeal to altruism. There exists a parallel argument in behalf of intervention: in a world as interconnected as ours has become, a major disruption anywhere threatens to export major difficulties everywhere.

This claim is not always persuasive; it convinced no one in the case of Rwanda. Still, such as it is, this argument gains force from the recent upsurge of Islamic terrorism. Terrorism too is a great dissolver of boundaries. The attacks of 9/11 offered a brutal demonstration that we do live in a global village. They taught Americans that what happens in obscure and distant places is relevant to their security. Thanks to these attacks, Americans again see the world in terms of "us" and "them," just as they did during the Cold War. This perspective is far more supportive of decisive military action than the purely humanitarian one. It counsels helping friends as well as harming enemies, and it justifies acting to win friends or prevent neutrals from becoming enemies. America in particular must not just think but act globally. It is striking that the ranks of those inside and outside the Bush Administration who support the war in Iraq include many who earlier distinguished themselves as "humanitarian hawks."

Naturally, we cannot intervene militarily in all or even many cases of flagrant persecution and injustice. For as long as the United States is tied down in Iraq, the massive investment of manpower there will hobble its efforts elsewhere. Still, it could make some contribution to a multilateral intervention. The same impulse (at once both generous and self-interested) that underlies the project of establishing a democracy in Iraq can underwrite other novel ventures. Will the Bush Doctrine prove to embrace preemptive humanitarian interventions? Stranger things have happened. Judging from the case of Darfur, however, this one has not happened yet.

Political Science, University of Toronto

COLLATERAL BENEFIT*

By Michael Blake

I. Introduction

Political philosophers often imagine themselves as advisors to political leaders. Much of what such philosophers do consists in offering principles by which the decisions of political leaders might be guided, criticized, and assessed. We offer, as it were, moral standards by which the actions of governments might be evaluated; the more ambitious of us hope that such governments might, indeed, be guided by our words.

This is a perfectly legitimate goal for political philosophers. It need not be, however, the only focus of philosophical inquiry in political life. In what follows, I want to begin an exploration into a different area of political ethics. We need, to be sure, ethical principles applicable to the decisions of those agents directly controlling the decisions and policies of governmental power. We would also, I believe, benefit from an examination of ethical principles applicable to the behavior of those agents whose relationship to governmental power is less direct. There are, after all, a multitude of agents with roles to play in the political process: citizens, unions, ethnic associations, political parties—all these, and more, have roles to play in the wider process of governance. The specific task of some of these agents, however, consists primarily in the response to governmental policy, rather than in the direct exercise of governmental power. I refer to such agents as "second-order political agents" when their primary mode of agency involves the critical response to governmental action, rather than the exercise of state power. The decisions faced by such agents, that is, often involve deciding what to do in the face of state policy, rather than in the direct formulation of such policy.

If such a distinction is possible, then there seems to be a need for ethical principles directly applicable to such agents. These principles, I think, will not be reducible to those applicable to the more standard questions of political justice. Second-order agents, I suggest, have a distinctive role to play in the process of political governance; the specific nature of the decisions they face makes it appropriate for us to examine what ethical principles might be employed to evaluate their actions. It is, I think,

* Previous versions of this paper were presented at Brown University, the Edmond J. Safra Center for Ethics at Harvard University, and the Carr Center for Human Rights Policy at Harvard University. I am grateful to all participants for their questions and comments. Thanks in particular go to the editors of this volume, whose help with this paper has been especially valuable. Responsibility for errors, of course, remains my own.

possible that the roles such agents play provide them with distinctive sets of ethical permissions and responsibilities. Second-order agents, on this analysis, must look directly at the ethical principles appropriate for their political role, rather than at the ethical principles appropriate for the decision making of statesmen and governmental officials.

Or so, at any rate, I will attempt to argue. In what follows, I will examine this thesis with regard to one particular form of second-order agent, and in the context of one particular form of political question. The question I want to examine is the ethical justifiability of humanitarian military intervention; the type of second-order agent I want to focus on is the human rights nongovernmental organization (NGO). A wide variety of such agents have arisen in recent years, in an attempt to place the moral importance of human rights on the political agenda.[1] These agents have a wide variety of specific competences; many of them specialize in the reporting and documentation of human rights abuses. They also, however, have the ability to enter the public debates surrounding policy issues more generally, by marshalling their considerable moral authority to condemn or praise specific acts of government.[2] The question we must therefore ask is: What ethical principles ought to guide human rights NGOs in their decisions on how to respond to governmental military actions?

One simple answer, of course, is to rely upon moral canons developed for the justification of military actions overall. On this analysis, the primary question to be asked by such humanitarian organizations is whether or not a given military action is justifiable as a humanitarian intervention. This methodology has recently been employed by the human rights NGO Human Rights Watch (HRW) in its analysis of the recent military action in Iraq.[3] The methodology reflects, I believe, the default position of many human rights organizations—namely, that a military action ought not be defended by a human rights NGO unless the intervention is itself a morally justified action for a governmental agent to undertake. There is, on this analysis, a single moral question to be asked by both governmental agents and NGOs: Does the proposed military action constitute a humanitarian intervention, on our best moral reading of this term?

This simple answer, I suggest, might be inadequate. NGOs concerned with the preservation and protection of human rights might, I think, have a legitimate role-based permission to defend and promote military inter-

[1] A good survey of such organizations can be found at http://www1.umn.edu/humanrts/links/ngolinks.html.

[2] It is possible, indeed, that such condemnation and praise is difficult to avoid; human rights NGOs deciding whether or not to accept government conditions such as embedding within the military context are aware that their decisions will be interpreted as supporting or condemning the military decisions themselves. I am grateful to Daniel Wikler for discussion of this topic.

[3] See Ken Roth, "War in Iraq: Not a Humanitarian Intervention," the keynote essay of the 2004 HRW Report on Human Rights. Document available at www.hrw.org.

vention abroad in a wider set of cases. These organizations play a specific role within the overall process of political argumentation; this role, I believe, may provide them with a distinct set of moral principles, on which it might be permissible to defend and promote even some forms of warfare not legitimately defensible as humanitarian interventions. Just as a defense attorney has a role-based permission to look specifically to the interests of her client, rather than the overall justice of the court's disposition of the case, so might human rights NGOs have a role-based permission to defend military interventions benefiting human rights—even when such interventions would not rise to meet the moral tests applicable to the decision making of state officials. The acceptance of such role-based moral principles, I believe, might ultimately do a better job of protecting human rights abroad than the simple moral answer described above.

In what follows, I will try to establish this conclusion. My argument will have three parts. I will begin by examining the moral relevance of intention. On this analysis, even if right intention is a legitimate criterion for an intervention's moral status as humanitarian, human rights NGOs have no need to demand right intention as a precondition for the moral approval of military intervention. Military interventions undertaken even for selfish or narrowly political reasons might have sufficiently beneficial consequences for human rights to justify an NGO's approving of such interventions; the notion of "collateral benefit," I believe, might provide the starting point for this analysis.[4] The second part of my argument will examine the possibility of morally supporting an intervention when its consequences for human rights are significant and beneficial, but not sufficient to justify the intervention overall. In this context, I will argue, human rights organizations may legitimately rely upon a role-based permission to defend the intervention, even when the moral canons of evaluation might condemn the governmental agents undertaking the intervention. The final portion of my argument will address two potential objections to my position, and offer some tentative conclusions.

II. Intention, Intervention, and Permissibility

The motive of the intervenor is frequently held to be morally relevant to the legitimacy of the intervention. A humanitarian motive, in particular, is frequently taken as a prerequisite for moral approval as a legitimate humanitarian military intervention. There is no agreement, of course, on the degree of purity required to justify humanitarian action; more realistic theorists admit that state actions frequently have multiple rationales. Condemning interventions taken partly out of state interest, on this account,

---

[4] I use the term "collateral benefit" as the inverse of the term "collateral damage." Collateral benefit, that is, represents beneficial results of a military action, where such benefits do not form any part of the justification or motivation for undertaking that action.

runs the risk of making all intervention illegitimate; all that is required for moral approval is a dominant or primary humanitarian motive.

There are, of course, a variety of ways of criticizing even this more relaxed position. We might, after all, derive an account of humanitarian military intervention in which moral approval is not conditioned even slightly upon the nature of the intervenor's motive. For the moment, however, let us assume that the legitimacy of an act of intervention depends in part upon the motive of the agent. What must be the case for such an analysis to hold true? Any plausible account of such a moral view, I believe, will be amenable to a distinction between the ethics applicable to the decisions of a governmental agent and the ethics applicable to the decisions of a second-order political agent such as a human rights NGO. To make this case, we may note that there are two ways in which motive might matter to the moral permissibility of an intervention. It might matter intrinsically, in that the proper intention is itself a prerequisite to the very possibility of legitimate intervention; or it might, in contrast, matter derivatively, in that only interventions undertaken for the proper reasons are likely to be pursued with a proper concern for human rights. We will consider these in turn.

What, then, would it mean for intention to matter intrinsically in this context? The most promising version, I think, would make a humanitarian motive a conceptual prerequisite for legitimate humanitarian military intervention. To act *as* a humanitarian intervenor, that is, simply is to act for the right reasons; the limited moral exception carved out from state sovereignty requires right motive as well as right circumstance, so that motive is conceptually necessary for legitimate humanitarian intervention.

Some version of this analysis might be sufficient as a basis for the decision making of governmental agents. It seems, however, that no such analysis could apply to the decision making of agents such as human rights NGOs. When reasoning about another's actions, after all, we may legitimately distinguish between judgments of the permissibility of the action and judgments regarding the character of the agent.[5] To see this, imagine a third party evaluating the action of an agent who acts for another's benefit, but from selfish or unworthy motives: say, a man who saves another from drowning, but only in the hope of thereby gaining fame and public acclaim. The best analysis of this situation, I think, would distinguish between the moral permissibility of the action, and the character of the one who acts. We may legitimately endorse the action of saving another from drowning, while condemning the unpleasant character of one who performs this action only for selfish motives. Sufficient moral reasons exist to mandate saving another from drowning; an agent of good character will find these motivating, but the mere fact that such

[5] This analysis draws on T. M. Scanlon's analysis. See T. M. Scanlon, *What We Owe to One Another* (Cambridge, MA: Harvard University Press, 1998).

reasons exist is sufficient for us to think that the action of saving a drowning swimmer is morally permitted. If this is true, then what matters most for the permissibility of a given act of intervention is not whether the agent acts for the right reasons, but whether the intervention is itself a morally justifiable act. To put this another way, it is not whether a humanitarian reason motivated the intervention, but whether sufficient reason exists to justify such intervention, that ought to be our concern when we judge whether the act of intervening ought to be performed.

To hold the reverse, I think, borders on the precious. Imagine what might be said to the potential beneficiary of a morally justifiable intervention—one for which sufficient reason to intervene exists—if we condemn the intervention out of a concern with motivation. It would be good if you were helped, we might say, but you can only be legitimately helped by an agent concerned primarily with your welfare. Any other intervenor is morally blocked from providing such aid. The response of such a potential beneficiary, I think, would most likely be bewilderment or anger. If an intervention has sufficient reason to be undertaken, then observers may legitimately applaud the act of intervening—even if the intervenor's motives show a deficiency of moral character. The purity of the intervenor's heart is unlikely to be of primary importance to those whose dignity the intervention will end up protecting.[6]

The more plausible version of the relevance of intention, I think, is the second possibility discussed above: the possibility that motive might matter derivatively. This version rests not upon the inherent moral relevance of humanitarian motives, but upon the likely causal consequences of intervening without a humanitarian motive. On this analysis, humanitarian military intervention requires a humanitarian motive for predictive and probabilistic reasons; the intervenor makes a wide variety of decisions during the course of the intervention, and only a humanitarian intention ensures that the proper moral concerns will be the basis of such decision making.

This version of the story seems to be the foundation of HRW's insistence that intention is relevant for the evaluation of the legitimacy of intervention.[7] While this analysis seems more persuasive, I think there is still reason here to question whether or not a second-order agent such as HRW ought to limit its support to interventions undertaken for the right reasons. There are, in this context, two specific factors I wish to analyze:

---

[6] I use the notion of dignity in its Kantian sense here, as a moral concept potentially capable of grounding the more specific human rights referred to in international law. If this notion of dignity is rejected, no damage seems to follow to my present thesis—the more specific rights can be used instead of the grounding moral concept.

[7] "[A] dominant humanitarian motive is important because it affects numerous decisions made in the course of an intervention and its aftermath that can determine its success in saving people from harm." Roth, "War in Iraq: Not a Humanitarian Intervention." For a similar analysis, see Samantha Power, "Humanitarian Intervention: A Forum," *The Nation*, July 14, 2003; available at http://www.thenation.com/doc.mhtml?i=20030714&c=4&s=forum.

the framing of the relevant policy alternatives, and the possible prudential benefits of mixed motivation.

First, how we understand the relevant alternatives may make a difference to our moral analysis of the situation. The analysis employed by
HRW and others seems to imagine a choice between two alternatives: a
humanitarian military intervention undertaken for the right reasons, and
one undertaken for selfish or malign reasons. This is, perhaps, an appropriate frame of reference for how military and governmental agents ought
to analyze their own proposed policies. They may have good reason to
articulate a humanitarian motive, so that their own decisions—and, as
importantly, the decisions of those charged with the implementation of
the intervention—are consistently aimed at the preservation and protection of human rights. This is not, however, the only frame of reference we
might imagine. We might also imagine a choice between the suboptimal,
selfishly motivated intervention, and no intervention at all. This latter
frame of reference, I believe, might be a better vision of how second-order
political agents ought to understand the specific decisions they face in
deciding how to critically respond to governmental policy.

To make this more concrete, note that HRW's analysis condemns the
intervention in Iraq by means of a comparison with a hypothetical intervention undertaken with humanitarian motivation. This is, perhaps, an
appropriate comparison set for governmental agents, who have responsibility for designing and implementing a policy from the ground up. It
is not clear that it is an appropriate comparison for second-order agents
such as HRW, who are charged not with the design but with the evaluation of political policy. They face governmental action, that is, in a much
more restrictive context—as, in part, consumers, rather than producers. If
this is so, then they have good moral reason to consider the policy proposed in comparison with its absence, rather than with some imagined
superior alternative. To do otherwise seems morally perverse; it seems, in
short, to let the perfect be the enemy of the merely beneficial. If the
proposed policy falls short of a hypothetical ideal policy, but is nonetheless more justifiable than mere inaction, then it seems quite unjustified to
condemn such a policy because it is not what it might have been. NGOs
such as HRW have good moral reason to support even ethically imperfect
interventions; so long as the proposed intervention is justifiable in terms
of its likely effects, it is morally perverse to condemn such an intervention
with reference to an intervention it might conceivably have been.

All this, of course, depends upon the consequences of the intervention
being sufficiently positive and sufficiently predictable to justify intervention. This is the second factor I wish to analyze under the general heading
of the extrinsic moral relevance of intention. HRW's policy argues that a
humanitarian military intervention must be undertaken for humanitarian
motives, or else the consequences for human rights are likely to be malign.
This is, of course, a probabilistic response; we cannot with any certainty

know what the full consequences of any intervention will be. It is crucial, in response, to note that there are important reasons to think that selfishly motivated interventions may sometimes be more likely, rather than less, to produce good effects for human rights. On occasion, that is, there may be sufficient collateral benefit to justify the intervention—and the NGO's support for such an intervention.

To see this, note that intervention requires not simply the willingness to intervene, but the willingness to maintain intervention in the face of potential violence and loss of life. Such political will, in turn, seems to be more easily provided when the intervention is justified not simply through reasons of morality, but through reasons of state as well.[8] The experience of the American intervention in Somalia provides a bitter example of how easily altruistic motivations can vanish in the face of significant violence.[9] In the face of images of mutilated American bodies, the United States quickly began to scale back the scope of its intervention; given the purely humanitarian nature of the conflict in Somalia, the political will evaporated in the face of such violence. Where more selfish reasons exist to motivate intervention, there may be found more willingness to bear the costs—both material and human—of such intervention.

Nothing in this, of course, mandates the conclusion that humanitarian motives will be—all things considered—less effective than selfish motives at achieving aims of human rights. All I hope to have established at present is that this question is, ultimately, an empirical one. Organizations such as HRW have introduced reasons to think that an intervention not grounded in humanitarian motivations will not effectively defend human rights. If what I have said here is correct, then such organizations have a duty to pay attention to both sides of the issue. There are factors favoring both selfish and altruistic interventions; which is more likely to produce effective protection for human rights awaits a more complete analysis. Humanitarian NGOs have good moral reason to be careful before dismissing interventions based upon non-humanitarian motivations. Inasmuch as they are charged with the effective protection of human rights, they have good moral reason to approve of those policies which are likely to offer such protection. It is a mistake to look at only one part of the probabilistic equation and condemn governmental policy without a wider examination of the potential benefits of even thoroughly selfish intervention. Such organizations, in sum, have good moral reason to examine the

---

[8] This is also noticed by the Danish Institute of International Affairs. See *Humanitarian Intervention: Legal and Political Aspects,* submitted to the Minister of Foreign Affairs, Denmark, December 7, 1999.

[9] The United States attempted a humanitarian intervention in Somalia in 1993; it quickly withdrew its troops following televised images of mutilated American soldiers dragged through the streets of Mogadishu. See Simon Tisdall, "Mogadishu Outrage Puts Clinton in Firing Line," *The Guardian,* October 5, 1993, 10. Similar images of mutilated Americans in Iraq did not cause the same demand for withdrawal. See Gwynn Dyer, "Footage Could've Brought a Mogadishu Moment," *Minnesota Star-Tribune,* April 4, 2002, 1AA.

beneficial effects of imperfect interventions rather than waiting for ethical perfection in governmental policy.

I do not, of course, claim that the current action in Iraq necessarily falls under this heading. That, on my analysis, ultimately awaits the answer to a host of empirical questions. I will not attempt to answer these questions here. Nor will I address several other questions which might be legitimately raised in this section—such as questions about the risks of American hegemony, and the moral status of international law.[10] What I hope to have shown is that NGOs need to develop a distinct ethic appropriate to their role, rather than simply asking questions about the legitimacy of humanitarian intervention. I hope also to have shown that even if governmental agents have good reason to act for humanitarian motives in intervening, NGOs may have good reason to support intervention even when such motives are absent. I turn now to some more partial and tentative conclusions in an even more complex area of inquiry: May such NGOs offer their support even to interventions where sufficient moral reasons to intervene are not to be found?

III. Impermissible Interventions, Permissible Support

The foregoing section has concerned itself with one way in which NGOs may be permitted to support ethically imperfect interventions. Such interventions are those where the motive of the intervenor is not humanitarian, but the humanitarian consequences are sufficient to justify the intervention. That is, although reasons of humanitarianism did not motivate the political agent, these considerations are present in such cases to such a degree that they might have formed a legitimate rationale for the intervention. In such cases, I have suggested, NGOs such as HRW have good reason to support the intervention, even though such interventions might fail to accord with moral principles designed to guide political leaders.

What I now want to consider is a more difficult situation: that of interventions which could not be justified in terms of human rights—where, that is, no sufficient justifying reason exists which might be employed to legitimate the intervention. In particular, I want to ask about interventions that are likely to cause a significant improvement in human rights— but where that improvement is not enough to justify the intervention itself. Many such cases can be imagined. Interventions may be undertaken into states whose antecedent human rights record is not sufficiently horrifying to justify intervention. Alternatively, we may imagine an intervention that is likely to cause a significant increase in respect for human

---

[10] These questions, I suggest, might ultimately be placed under the heading of consequential considerations to be weighed in the probabilistic balance. I do not try to prove this in the present context, however.

rights—but at a cost that is out of proportion to the benefit to be attained. As I have discussed elsewhere, there is almost universal support for the thesis that governments ought to limit their interventions to those cases in which the abuses of human rights are most egregious.[11] Are human rights NGOs permitted to support interventions that go beyond these limitations?

The first question we might ask, of course, is why an NGO would even want to do so. If an intervention ought not be undertaken in the first place, what reason would an NGO have to offer its moral authority in support of such an intervention? There are, I think, several possibilities here. It may be politically advantageous for an NGO to offer its support to a government, thereby ensuring a greater voice for considerations of human rights in foreign policy. It may also be the case that such support is sufficient to keep considerations of human rights at the forefront of popular debates about the intervention in question. NGOs with specific areas of expertise—such as Physicians for Human Rights—may be more able to bring that expertise to bear if they become partial allies in the intervention at issue. Most generally, I suggest, it is possible that by such selective defenses in the public sphere, human rights NGOs may be able to provide some normative pressure upon governmental policy; in the long term, such public endorsement may make it easier for governments to justify interventions when significant human rights benefits result from such interventions, and comparatively less easy to justify less beneficial military actions. In this way, human rights NGOs may be able to act to increase practical support for human rights. By selectively endorsing proposed military actions in this way, NGOs might act as an additional point of normative pressure, making it easier to justify such military actions when they are likely to provide substantial benefits for human rights. Whatever the reason, we may imagine that an NGO wants to offer its support for an intervention which is not justifiable, but which is likely to lead to an increase in respect for human rights. Is this action morally permissible?

The answer to this question, I think, is not to be found in the simple fact of the moral impermissibility of the intervention itself. Whether one must act to stop an act of injustice—or, more controversially, whether one may act to enable another to commit injustice—is a separate area of moral inquiry. If one agent attacks another agent, for instance, an observing third party does not necessarily have a duty to stop the attack; there may be good reasons—in this case, reasons stemming from self-preservation and the imposition of risk—to permit the third party to refrain from intervening. Our focus here will be on whether there are good reasons to permit a third party to offer support and encouragement to an agent

[11] Michael Blake, "Reciprocity, Stability, and Intervention: The Ethics of Disequilibrium," in Don Scheid and Deen Chatterjee, eds., *Ethics and Foreign Intervention* (Cambridge: Cambridge University Press, 2003).

committing an injustice—but, as above, an injustice likely to produce beneficial effects for human rights.

Such reasons, I think, do exist; and they may be found in considerations surrounding the role of human rights NGOs within the systems of international and domestic politics. Within these systems, agents do not act simply as persons; they act from a particular standpoint, with a particular responsibility to defend and foster concern for a particular issue. Actions of second-order agents such as NGOs are, I think, therefore best evaluated in terms of role-based moral permissions. In domestic role-differentiated contexts, there are limited permissions offered to parties inhabiting certain roles to aim not at the overall good, but at the partial good of some person or point of view.[12] The most prominent example here is the practice of law within adversarial legal systems. The lawyer acts not with a concern for overall justice, but for his or her client; the lawyer has a permission, moreover, to engage in badgering, rudeness, verbal chicanery, and a wide variety of ethically unsavory techniques in defense of that client. The permission to act in favor of a partial point of view is defensible, in this context, by the presumption that such an adversarial system produces justice overall. Individual agents need not act in the interests of justice, so long as the system within which they act is able to do so.[13]

Is something similar available to the human rights NGO? I think it is, at the very least, plausible to answer yes. As I have said, second-order agents in political life are understood not as mere collections of natural persons, but as representatives and advocates of particular interests and points of view. Focusing on such NGOs, rather than simply on political leaders and an undifferentiated citizenry, may lead us to think that an adversarial process undergirds much of political as well as legal life. If this is so, then human rights NGOs such as HRW may have a permission to encourage and defend even unjust interventions, so long as those interventions tend to increase respect for human rights. There are many powerful constituencies that have representatives in adversarial politics; the human rights community represents those who are least powerful of all—those who face major abuses of basic human rights. The voices of such people, understandably, tend not to be heard. If a human rights NGO decides to support those interventions which tend to increase respect for human rights, it is at least possible that such support might increase the degree to which human rights are made effective in the actual world

[12] Arthur Applbaum, *Ethics for Adversaries: The Morality of Roles in Public and Professional Life* (Princeton, NJ: Princeton University Press, 1999).

[13] It is an open question for me as to how this latter idea is to be fleshed out. Applbaum suggests that the system as a whole must be justified for such permission to exist; my own view is that such a permission might exist when the presence of one's role within the system increases the justifiability of the system—even when the system as a whole receives no moral justification. This latter notion, of course, would provide more defense for the human rights NGO role I describe—as well as for the defense lawyer in her practice of adversarial lawyering. On this, see Applbaum, *Ethics for Adversaries*, 45–75.

of politics. If this is true, then the fact that such interventions are unjust does not seem sufficient to condemn the actions of such NGOs. If an increase in respect for human rights is a morally significant goal—and it seems hard to deny that it is—then surely those who advocate for human rights within an adversarial system may aim at that goal, rather than focusing on the justification of particular cases of intervention. They may, in other words, stress the collateral benefit of some cases of military intervention—so that the moral relevance of human rights gets an adequate hearing in the wider process of political discussion.[14]

This conclusion, naturally, is in need of amplification; there are undoubtedly cases where this adversarial permission would fail. I will not explore the precise strength of this permission here. I will limit myself to one final question: If NGOs participate in and support unjust forms of intervention, do they thereby share in the injustice? Are they, that is, worthy of being condemned for their support just as they are also worthy of commendation? The answer, I think, is likely yes; the notion of dirty hands seems now to apply as much to second-order political agents as to political leaders. Just as political leaders must sometimes perform blameworthy actions in order to achieve praiseworthy goals, so must second-order political agents engage in morally problematic actions in the pursuit of political justice.[15] The reason for this, ultimately, is that political action depends upon action within a given political role. Our political roles are set up so that pursuing justice effectively may require us to engage in morally questionable actions along the way. There is no place, within a political system resting upon conflict and cooperation between adversaries, for ethical puritanism.

This conclusion applies, however, with as much force to those who respond to political decisions as to those who make them. Whether or not the phenomenon of dirty hands is a real ethical phenomenon, I cannot here say. I will note only that if there are true cases of dirty hands, they are as likely to apply to second-order political agents as to political leaders. Human rights NGOs may have to get their hands dirty, then, in order to work for the dignity of all.

IV. CONCLUSION

I want to conclude by replying to two potential objections to what I have said here. The first concerns the legal notion of humanitarian mili-

---

[14] Arthur Applbaum has suggested to me that one means by which this might be accomplished is the politically minded use of intentionality. As I have argued above, human rights NGOs have no reason to regard selfish motivation as always sufficient to discredit military action. But they might argue as if they did, for those interventions without adequate collateral benefit, and remain silent on the matter of intention when the intervention would prove beneficial. This partial mode of arguing, I think, would be justifiable as an analogue to the defense lawyer's partial decision of what to emphasize in the defense of a client.

[15] The notion of dirty hands is, of course, morally controversial. The canonical discussion of the idea in current philosophical literature is found in Michael Walzer, "Political Action: The Problem of Dirty Hands," *Philosophy and Public Affairs* 2, no. 2 (Winter 1973): 160–80.

tary intervention itself and asks whether the willingness to consider collateral benefit rather than humanitarian intervention might weaken the moral "currency" of humanitarian intervention. The second concerns the moral authority of humanitarian NGOs and asks whether such authority might be undermined by the more pragmatic role I have suggested for such organizations. I will answer these objections in turn.

The first objection, I think, can be met by considering the purposes of maintaining the concept of humanitarian intervention as part of our conceptual vocabulary. Such a concept is valuable insofar as it provides moral (and, more controversially, legal) justification for military intervention; such intervention, in turn, is valuable to the extent that it provides concrete assistance in the process of defending human rights. It is possible, I think, that the concept itself may have only limited value in this latter context. If it is possible that human rights would be more effectively protected by humanitarian organizations focusing upon collateral benefit, rather than upon the concept of humanitarian intervention, then the argument in favor of maintaining such a concept might not be persuasive. It is possible, of course, that the concept's moral importance might be established if it could be shown that beneficial military interventions would be reduced in number and scope in the absence of this concept. This latter question, of course, is largely empirical in nature; I am, however, extremely skeptical that such evidence would ever be forthcoming. The relatively small number of military interventions meeting the canonical tests for humanitarian interventions suggests that effective protection of human rights norms might be best achieved by the more role-dependent methodology I have here described.

The nature of this role-dependent morality, however, gives rise to our second objection. The moral authority of the human rights NGO, it might be suggested, is established primarily from its position as moral exemplar—concerned only with the defense of human rights, neutral in the face of political conflict, and not beholden to any particular government or political program. This authority, it seems, might be undermined if a human rights NGO began to make arguments of the form described above. In asserting the desirability of even an unjustifiable intervention, would such an NGO not lose much of its moral authority?[16]

---

[16] Michael Ignatieff has suggested to me that the organizers of many human rights NGOs believe that their organizations ought to stand for the absence of compromise, in part to counter the persistent need for compromise in the world of political agency. Whereas most political agents must be willing to compromise and seek the lesser evil, those who run organizations devoted to the moral relevance of human rights frequently take themselves to have duties both to defend the moral relevance of principle and to embody such principles in their own behavior. If what I have said here is correct, however, then such organizations may have a duty to deviate from principle in behavior—to be willing, that is, to engage in more ordinary forms of political compromise—if they are to be able to effectively defend such principles in the wider political context. Defending the moral rights of others, on this analysis, may require those who work for this goal to be more open to political compromise than they conventionally believe.

This objection, I believe, has a great deal of merit; it represents, in my view, the most powerful objection to the argument I have made above. I do not think, however, that the argument is dispositive. Human rights NGOs have reason to value moral authority only to the extent that they can use that authority to defend human rights as a political value. Even if the argument I have made might implicate NGOs in what might be derided as petty gamesmanship, the resulting loss of moral authority might be more than justified by the increased protection offered to human rights. This is, of course, only an empirical contention; human rights NGOs would have reason to be very careful to maintain their moral status, so as to preserve the possibility of their playing a useful role within the political process over the long term. Moral authority is useless without concrete effects, but such effects might not be forthcoming without some continuing source of moral authority. In the end, I suggest, a balance must be struck by human rights NGOs: they must carefully preserve their moral authority for the long term, while ensuring that such moral authority is used effectively in the present. I would suggest, in this context, only that it is not clear to me that such moral authority requires a refusal to play the political role I have described here. It would require, to be sure, playing the role carefully—avoiding, for instance, significant destruction of moral capital for limited benefit. But it would not require, I think, a complete withdrawal from the engagement with collateral benefit. If this makes the job of a human rights NGO considerably more difficult than it is presently understood to be, I would reply only that it seems that the role of such NGOs may indeed be more demanding than we often believe.

I will conclude by emphasizing the tentative and partial nature of what I hope to have established here. I have not tried to establish any particular conclusions about the present conflict in Iraq; still less have I tried to articulate a complete ethical framework for second-order political agents. I will be happy if I have given some reason to think that such a framework is required, and that it is likely to be distinct from the framework applicable to political leaders. Contrary to the position of HRW, human rights NGOs have good reason to support even interventions not motivated by humanitarian concerns. Such NGOs may, indeed, have permission to support interventions which political leaders could not justly undertake. All of this, I hope, is sufficient to demonstrate the desirability of a distinct role-based ethic appropriate for such agents. We have good reason to examine more carefully the role of second-order political agents in our explorations of political morality.

Public Policy and Philosophy, Kennedy School of Government,
Harvard University

THE UNEVEN RESULTS OF INSTITUTIONAL CHANGES IN CENTRAL AND EASTERN EUROPE: THE ROLE OF CULTURE*

By Svetozar Pejovich

I. Introduction

Social activity involves human interactions on two levels. The first level concerns the development, modification, and specifications of institutions. Institutions define the basic framework within which people interact with one another; we can refer to them as the rules of the game. The second level of social activity concerns human interactions within the prevailing institutional arrangements; we can refer to this level of activity as the game itself. The two levels of social activity are interrelated. By constraining the scope and contents of human interactions, the rules help interacting individuals to predict each other's behavior, or, to put it another way, the rules lower the transaction costs of playing the game. Of course, lower transaction costs mean a higher level of economic activity. By implication, a change in the rules changes both the way the game is played and the level of economic activity.

The institutional framework consists of formal and informal rules, all of which create their own behavioral incentives. Formal rules are constitutions, statutes, common law, and other governmental regulations. They are enacted, enforced, and changed by governmental authorities. Informal rules include traditions, customs, religious beliefs, and all other norms of behavior that have passed the test of time and that bind the generations. The enforcement of informal rules takes place by means of sanctions such as ostracism by friends and neighbors, loss of reputation, or alienation (expulsion) from the community.

After the collapse of their Communist governments in 1989, Central and Eastern European countries (hereafter C&EE) started the process of institutional restructuring. The intention of the new leaders was to trans-

* My colleague and friend Fred Fransen made two major contributions to this essay: he helped me identify numerous inconsistencies in the essay, and he changed a number of my perceptions on the relationship between culture and economic performance. James Buchanan, Ljubo Madzar, Henry Manne, Milic Milovanovic, and Katarina Ott gave me useful suggestions and comments on earlier drafts. I am grateful to Victor Vanberg and Ulrich Witt for the opportunity to discuss this essay with their colleagues and students at the University of Freiburg and Max Planck Institute in Jena, Germany.

231

form C&EE countries into free-market, private-property economies.[1] Their choice of capitalism seemed quite rational. After decades of oppressive socialism[2] and economic deprivations, people in C&EE were hoping for more freedom and better economic conditions of life.

Numerous academic studies have shown that the relationship between capitalism and economic prosperity arises from the fact that the institutions of capitalism create economic freedoms and protect individual rights.[3] The *Index of Economic Freedom* (published annually by the D.C.-based Heritage Foundation and the *Wall Street Journal*) and the *Economic Freedom of the World Index* (published annually by the Fraser Institute, located in Vancouver, British Columbia) confirm those results. James Gwartney, one of the founders of the *Economic Freedom of the World Index,* has written: "The maintenance over a lengthy period of time of institutions and policies consistent with economic freedom is a major determinant of cross-country differences in per capita GDP. . . . [C]ross-country differences in the mean rating [a measure of a country's level of freedom] during 1980–2000 explain 63.2 percent of the cross-country variations in 2000 per capita GDP."[4] And Ana Isabel Eiras, a contributor to the *Index of Economic Freedom,* has said: "As Frederick von Hayek foresaw more than 60 years ago, economic freedom . . . with a strong rule of law will foster a culture

---

[1] The end of socialism in Central and Eastern Europe in the late 1980s opened the region to an influx of new ideas and opportunities. Indeed, everybody wanted a piece of the action. Overnight, former dissidents became political leaders and social innovators. The old ruling elite quickly forgot "the laws of history" and has been trying to find ways to retain power and influence. Western politicians saw an opportunity to extend the political and economic influence of their countries. Western businesses eyed new markets. Western scholars realized that social changes in C&EE were likely to create enormous opportunities for research grants, promotions, and publications in academic journals. In an about-face, many academics from the West who used to preach socialism, economic planning, and all sorts of industrial democracy schemes joined their free-market colleagues in supporting the process of transition to capitalism. In order to "strengthen" their grant proposals and submissions to academic journals, Western scholars needed cooperation from their colleagues in C&EE, and they had no problem getting that support. In exchange for funding, travel, and possible visiting appointments in the West, many scholars from C&EE were eager to join their Western colleagues on projects they privately considered irrelevant.

[2] The twentieth century experienced two major applications of socialism: National Socialism, and Marxism-Leninism or communism. Those two brands of socialism were equally unrelenting in their oppression of inferior races and the bourgeoisie, respectively. It is perfectly legitimate to refer to C&EE countries as either former socialist or former communist countries.

[3] See, for example, Jacob de Haan and Jan Sturm, "On the Relationship between Economic Freedom and Economic Growth," *European Journal of Political Economy* 16 (2000): 215–41; Johan Torstensson, "Property Rights and Economic Growth," *Kyklos* 47, (1994): 231–47; Douglass North, and Barry Weingast, "Constitution and Commitment: The Evolution of Institutions Governing Public Choice in Seventeenth-Century England," *Journal of Economic History* 49 (1989): 803–32; and Svetozar Pejovich, ed., *The Economics of Property Rights* (Cheltenham: Edward Elgar, 2001), vol. 2, part IV.

[4] James Gwartney, "What Have We Learned from the Measurement of Economic Freedom?" paper presented at a conference titled "The Legacy of Milton and Rose Friedman's *Free to Choose*: Economic Liberalism at the Turn of Twenty-First Century," Federal Reserve Bank of Dallas, 2003, p. 3.

of investment, job creation, and institutional respect—all essential factors in massively improving the living standards of ordinary people."[5]

It is predictable, then, that to measure economic freedom, both indexes use the factors that also define capitalism. The Fraser *Index* uses the following categories: size of government, economic structure and use of markets, monetary policy and inflation, freedom to use alternative currencies, credibility and stability of property rights, free trade, and freedom of exchange in capital markets. The Heritage *Index* covers the following categories: trade policy, fiscal burden of government, government intervention in the economy, monetary policy, capital flows and foreign investments, banking and finance, wages and prices, property rights, regulation, and the extent of the black market. A differentiating feature of the Heritage *Index* is the classification of each country as either *free, mostly free, mostly unfree,* or *repressed.* I will use the same classifications in my analysis.

Neoclassical economics provided the general framework for the debate in the early 1990s over how best to conduct the transition to capitalism. According to the tenets of neoclassical economics, the transition to capitalism required macro-stabilization (i.e., stable rates of interest, low inflation, low unemployment, etc.), privatization, and market prices. Given the neoclassical assumption of zero transaction costs, Central and Eastern Europeans were expected to quickly perceive new opportunities, evaluate their consequences, and make the utility-maximizing choices. Privatized assets, regardless of their initial ownership, would quickly end up in the hands of the highest-valued users. In this scenario, it seemed appropriate to encourage new leaders in C&EE to use the strong hand of the state to build capitalism. The road to capitalism was seen as merely a technical problem.

Many property-rights and public-choice scholars regarded neoclassical economics as ill suited for carrying out the process of transition in C&EE. Major reasons for their doubts were the failure of neoclassical economics to appreciate that structural change from above must be consistent with people's mental models and its failure to acknowledge the importance of transaction costs.[6] Long before the end of socialism in C&EE, Ronald Coase suggested that if neoclassical proposals were carried out, the allocation of resources would indeed be optimal—but he dismissed such policies as "the stuff dreams are made of" and as impossible to carry out. "In my youth," Coase wrote, "it was said that what was too silly to be said may be sung. In modern economics it may be put into mathematics." He added: "The reason why economists went wrong was that their theoretical system did not take into account a factor that is essential if one

[5] Ana Isabel Eiras, *Ethics, Corruption, and Economic Freedom,* The Heritage Foundation Lecture no. 813 (Washington, DC: The Heritage Foundation, 2003), 1.

[6] Of course, neoclassical economics was mainstream economics in the 1990s (and still is); it is supported by the majority of economists as well as major organizations such as the World Bank. Perhaps the most prominent figure was Jeffrey Sachs.

wishes to analyze the effect of a change in the law on the allocation of resources. This missing factor is the existence of transaction costs."[7]

Indeed, economic policies based on neoclassical economics have produced a host of unintended political and social consequences, culminating in the rising strength of pro-socialist parties in the region.[8] Fifteen years after the process of transition began in C&EE, the Heritage Foundation's *Index of Economic Freedom* lists only one country in the region (Estonia) as a free-market country, seven countries (Lithuania, Latvia, Czech Republic, Slovakia, Hungary, Slovenia, and Poland) as mostly free, nine countries (Croatia, Bulgaria, Moldova, Albania, Russia, Ukraine, Romania, Bosnia, and Macedonia) as mostly unfree, and two as repressive (Serbia and Montenegro, and Belarus).[9] The road to capitalism turned out to be quite bumpy.

The main purpose of this essay is to show that culture plays an important role in the process of institutional restructuring. To accomplish this objective, I seek to demonstrate, in Section II, that cultural differences in C&EE create transaction costs specific to the process of transition, and that those transaction costs, in turn, explain the uneven results of institutional restructuring from the early 1990s until 2004. In Section III, I address an important issue: Are changes in informal rules or culture possible, and if so, could those changes in entrenched cultural values reenergize the process of institutional restructuring in C&EE, and at what cost?

The following pairs of terms are used interchangeably throughout the essay: "informal rules" and "culture"; "rules" and "norms of behavior"; "capitalism" and "the free-market, private-property economy"; and "formal institutions" and "law."

II. The Costs of Transition: It's the Culture, Stupid!

A. Culture and economic performance

As early as 1976, James Buchanan wrote that mathematical techniques and econometrics were taking the discipline of economics in the wrong direction. "The principle that exposure to economics should convey," he wrote, "is that of spontaneous coordination, which the market achieves. The central principle of economics is not the maximization of objective functions subject to constraints. Once we become methodologically trapped

---

[7] Ronald Coase, *The Firm, the Market, and the Law* (Chicago: University of Chicago Press, 1988), 175 and 179.

[8] Svetozar Pejovich, "After Socialism: Where Hope for Individual Liberty Lies," *Journal des Economistes et des Etudes Humaines* 11 (2001): 23–27.

[9] The Federation of Serbia and Montenegro was ranked as repressive in the 2003 Heritage *Index of Economic Freedom* and was dropped from the index in 2004 for lack of information.

in the maximization paradigm, economics becomes applied mathematics or engineering."[10]

Twenty-five years later, Enrico Colombatto argued that the process of institutional restructuring in C&EE is a cultural problem rather than merely a technical one.[11] This implies that culture affects economic life. The question is: why and how?

There is no generally accepted definition of culture.[12] I follow the lead of scholars who see culture or informal rules—I use the two terms interchangeably—as the synthesis of a community's traditions, customs, moral values, religious beliefs, and all other informal norms of behavior that have passed the test of time and that bind the generations.[13] Culture is, in effect, the repository of the community's values. Of course, no community is culturally homogeneous. There are always some individuals and/or groups whose behavior is below the accepted margin, and there are others whose behavior is exemplary. Yet all communities have their mainstream informal rules of the game, which are the results of selective evolution. I will use the term "prevailing culture" to refer to these mainstream informal rules. And the more entrenched the prevailing culture is, the more costly it is to change informal rules by government fiat.

Thus, the process of institutional restructuring is about the enactment of new formal rules. A new formal rule creates new choices for human interactions or modifies old ones. In either case, it changes the opportunity set within which the game is played. The effect of this new rule on economic performance must then depend on how individuals perceive and subjectively evaluate new trade-offs. And how individuals perceive new opportunities depends on the prevailing culture in the community. The prevailing culture thus plays a major role in determining the costs of integrating the new rule into the prevailing institutional structure. The relationship between new formal rules and the prevailing informal rules can be summarized in terms of what I will call *the interaction thesis*:

> When members of the community perceive the consequences of new formal rules to be in conflict with their prevailing culture, the transaction costs of integrating those rules into the institutional frame-

---

[10] James Buchanan, "General Implications of Subjectivism in Economics," paper presented at a conference titled "Subjectivism in Economics," University of Dallas, 1976, p. 2.

[11] Enrico Colombatto, "The Concept of Transition," *Journal of Markets and Morality* 4 (2001): 269–88.

[12] For different definitions of culture, see Vernon Ruttan, "Cultural Endowments and Economic Development: What Can We Learn from Anthropology?" *Economic Development and Cultural Change* 36 (1988): 247–71.

[13] Douglass North, *Institutions, Institutional Change, and Economic Performance* (Cambridge: Cambridge University Press, 1990), 37. Ernest Gellner defined culture as "a distinct way of doing things which characterizes a given community." See Gellner, *Plough, Book, and Sword* (London: Collins Harvill, 1988), 14.

work will be high, will consume more resources, and will reduce the production of wealth. And when members of the community perceive the consequences of new formal rules to be in harmony with their prevailing culture, the transaction costs of integrating those rules into the institutional framework will be low, will consume fewer resources, and will increase the production of wealth.

Of course, rules do not interact, people do. However, rules create incentives, which in conjunction with individuals' subjective perceptions of reality produce economic results.

B. Culture and transition in Central and Eastern Europe

Once we recognize that culture matters, the analysis of its effects on the transition to capitalism has to address two issues: (1) What are the most important formal institutions of capitalism, and what incentives do they generate? And (2) what kind of culture supports those incentives?

1. Basic formal institutions of capitalism. The institutions of capitalism are many. However, following the works of Bruno Leoni, Friedrich von Hayek, James Buchanan, and many other scholars, I take it that the basic formal institutions setting capitalism apart from other systems are private property rights, the law of contract, an independent judiciary, and a constitution that *de facto* protects individual rights.[14] These formal institutions create their own behavioral incentives, which enhance individual rights and promote economic efficiency. For example, by encouraging individuals to interact with people they do not know, an independent judiciary promotes trade.[15] A constitution protects individuals (and individuals' wealth) from majority rule. That is why Buchanan has often said that the constitution or the rule of law should come before democracy. Robert Barro has written: "Madeleine Albright once [said that] democracy was a prerequisite for economic growth. This response sounds pleasant but is simply false. . . . For a country that starts with . . . little democracy and little law, an increase in democracy is less important than an expansion of the rule of law as a stimulus for economic growth."[16]

---

[14] I refer to a constitution that is credible (i.e., protects individual rights *de facto*) and stable (i.e., difficult to change). Many constitutions (e.g., Soviet constitutions) are not worth the paper on which they are written.

[15] Two major requirements for an independent judiciary are that judges expect their decisions to be carried out and that their jobs do not depend on legislators and/or bureaucrats. An independent judiciary should not be confused with a good judiciary. It all depends on the people who become judges.

[16] Robert Barro, "Rule of Law, Democracy, and Economic Performance," in *2000 Index of Economic Freedom* (Washington, DC: The Heritage Foundation and the Wall Street Journal, 2000), 47. In the West, the rule of law and democracy go together. However, Fareed Zakaria argues that a number of countries that have multiparty elections are, in effect, illiberal democracies; they do better on political liberties than on civil and economic ones. See Fareed Zakaria, "The Rise of Illiberal Democracy," *Foreign Affairs* 76 (1997): 22–43.

Private property rights provide strong incentives for those who own resources to seek the highest-value uses for their assets. The law of contract reduces the transaction costs of identifying the value of resources in alternative uses; hence, it promotes trade. Buchanan alludes to the fact that private property rights and the law of contact create incentives for interacting individuals to equalize private and social costs of using scarce goods: "Economic performance can only be conceived in values, but how are those values determined? By prices, and prices emerge only in competitive markets. They have no meaning in a non-market context, where the choice-influenced opportunity costs are ignored."[17]

2. A culture supportive of capitalism. The incentive effects of the basic institutions of capitalism require a culture that encourages individuals to pursue their private ends—that is, the culture of individualism. Cambridge University anthropologist Alan Macfarlane has traced the origin of the culture of individualism to thirteenth-century England. He defines it as "the view that society is constituted of autonomous, equal units, namely separate individuals, and that such individuals are more important, ultimately, than any larger constituent group. It is reflected in the concept of individual property, in the political and legal liberty of the individual, in the idea of the individual's direct communication with God."[18]

By holding that the individual is superior to any group, the culture of individualism encourages behavior based on the principles of *self-interest*, *self-responsibility*, and *self-determination*. These principles of behavior, in turn, encourage the community to reward competitive performance, to promote risk-taking, and to view income inequalities as desirable results of entrepreneurship and free trade. We can say that the culture of individualism sees the community as a voluntary association of individuals who, in the pursuit of their private ends, join and leave the community by free choice.

The free-market, private-property economy and the culture of individualism are Western phenomena. They developed spontaneously in response to events in the West over a period of several centuries. In the sixth century, Pope Gregory I initiated the process that eventually replaced the extended family with the nuclear family. He did it by overturning four traditional and legal practices: marriage to close kin, marriage to the widows of close kin, the transfer of children by adoption, and concubinage.[19] Pope Gregory VII's institutional reforms in the eleventh century provided cultural unity as well as the enforcement of property rights and contracts in a politically decentralized Europe. The rise of individualism in thirteenth-century England has already been noted. The emergence of major trading centers such as Florence, Genoa, and Venice led to

---

[17] Buchanan, "General Implications of Subjectivism in Economics," 8.
[18] Alan Macfarlane, *The Origins of English Individualism* (London: Blackwell, 1979), 196.
[19] See Deepak Lal, *Unintended Consequences* (Cambridge, MA: MIT Press, 1998), 83.

the legal protection of property rights and contracts. The alienation of philosophy from theology in the fourteenth, fifteenth, and sixteenth centuries initiated the revival of the inquisitive spirit of the ancient Greeks. The adoption in England and the United States of common law, which is rooted in customs and traditions, reduced the conflict between the formal institutions of capitalism and cultural values. The Protestant Reformation in the sixteenth century encouraged individualism and the work ethic. It also opened the market for salvation by offering an alternative to the Roman Church's interpretation of guidance to the attainment of redemption.

C. *The prevailing culture in Central and Eastern Europe and the costs of transition*

The prevailing culture in Central and Eastern Europe has a bias toward collectivism, egalitarianism, and shared values that predates communism. The community in C&EE tends to be seen as an organic whole in which individuals are expected to subordinate their private ends to the pursuit of common values (however defined). Predictably, the extended family has always played an important role in most C&EE countries.[20]

The behavioral consequences of the nuclear family and the extended family illustrate major differences between the culture of individualism in the West and the culture of collectivism in C&EE. By encouraging the concept of a polity consisting of natural equals, the nuclear family in the West creates incentives for bonding among individuals across family lines. By emphasizing egalitarianism and collectivism, the extended family in C&EE raises the transaction costs of interactions between individuals belonging to different groups.

Professor Avner Greif of Stanford University provides an excellent comparison of the collectivist culture of the Maghribi community (a community of Arab traders) and the individualistic culture in Genoa from the eleventh to the thirteenth centuries.[21] He explains the behavioral incentives of the rules of the game in the Maghribi community (which are similar to those we observe today in both developing countries and those undergoing a transition to capitalism) and the incentives and rules in Genoa (which resemble those we observe in the West). Greif summarizes his results as follows: "Collectivist cultural beliefs led to a societal organization based on the group's ability to use economic, social, and, most

---

[20] I thank James Buchanan for his comments on the extended family.

[21] In a letter to the author of this essay, Professor Avner Greif wrote: "'Maghrib' means 'West' in Arabic. During the medieval period and long after, the term was used to refer to the Muslim World's west: North Africa, Spain, and Sicily. The Maghribi traders migrated from Iraq in the tenth century to the Maghrib and hence they were called 'the Maghribi traders.' The documents that I have used reflect the correspondence of the Maghribi community in Fustat (known today as Old Cairo)."

likely, moral sanctions against deviants. In contrast, individualist cultural beliefs weakened the dependence of each individual on any specific group [and] led to a societal organization based on legal, political, and economic organizations for enforcement and coordination."[22]

While egalitarianism and collectivism are important common traits in C&EE, the prevailing culture in the region is not homogeneous. The culture of collectivism and egalitarianism gets stronger the farther east and southeast one travels. For example, this is how a Bulgarian scholar, Antonina Zhelyazkova, describes the structure of contemporary families in Albania: "Family community [is] composed of three or four generations, with a high level of internal solidarity. Within the [family] there is a strict, clear-cut age hierarchy, where the father's ... word is law. ... [T]his is due to the age-old internal ethno-cultural mechanism, which ... contributes to the preservation of their tradition."[23]

We can attribute the heterogeneity of informal rules in C&EE to the influence of three empires (Austro-Hungarian, Russian, and Ottoman), three religions (Roman Catholic, Orthodox, and Islam), and to the internal strength of ethnicity and/or nationalism. I turn now to a few examples that capture the essence of those influences.

The following quote from historian Perry Anderson suggests why the transaction costs of accepting the right of ownership have been relatively lower in C&EE countries that belonged to the Austro-Hungarian empire or had strong relations with the West: "The age in which 'absolutist' public authority was imposed was also simultaneously the age in which 'absolute' private property was progressively consolidated. It was this momentous social difference which separated the Bourbon, Habsburg, Tudor or Vasa monarchies from any Sultanate, or [the Russian Empire]."[24]

Writing about informal rules in Russia and their implications, Silke Stahl, at the time a researcher at Max Planck Institute in Jena, argued that such rules are not supportive of the principles of behavior based on self-interest, self-responsibility, and self-determination. Especially important are Stahl's references to the sources of egalitarianism and collectivism in Russia: "In Russia [informal] institutions found their expression in egalitarianism and collectivism. Egalitarianism is the psychological disposition of a group of people who consider material equality as the essential base of social interaction. Collectivism ... refers to a societal organizational pattern, which centers on the group and not the individual

---

[22] Avner Greif, "Cultural Beliefs and the Organization of Society: A Historical and Theoretical Reflection on Collectivist and Individualist Societies," *Journal of Political Economy* 102 (1994): 942.

[23] Antonina Zhelyazkova, *Albanian Prospects* (Sofia: International Center for Minority Studies, 2003), 140–41. Young Albanians who go abroad work hard and save their money. Most of them continue to live in their own cultural ghettos. Those who return to their homeland bring along the money they have saved but not necessarily Western values.

[24] Perry Anderson, *Lineages of the Absolutist State* (London: Verso, 1974), 429.

as the basic unit in society. . . . The reasons for egalitarianism and collectivism [in Russia] can be found in religious beliefs."[25]

The idea of the immorality of charging interest on loans and the absence of the concept of legal personality—still prevalent in many Islamic countries—have influenced the development of both formal and informal rules in the areas of C&EE that used to be controlled by the Ottoman empire.[26] The absence of the concept of legal personality has been especially costly. By ruling out the law of limited liability, and hence the anonymous alienability of shares, the absence of legal personality arrested the development of institutions that encourage small savers voluntarily to pull together large amounts of capital for long-lived ventures.[27]

Historically, communities in C&EE have responded to outside influences by creating strong informal rules developed along ethnic lines and/or around national myths (for example, the Kosovo myth in Serbia and the thousand-year dream of national independence in Croatia). As repositories of old unsettled scores, as well as of various national myths, informal rules strengthen mutual understanding within each ethnic group while simultaneously (and predictably) treating other groups as alien. The result is relatively higher transaction costs for social contacts across ethnic lines. In addition, religious differences among C&EE countries reinforce the alienation of one ethnic group from another. The Serbs in Croatia, the Albanians in Macedonia, the Turks in Bulgaria, the Hungarians in Slovakia (like the Basques in Spain and the Arabs in France) are just a few examples of alienated ethnic groups.

Analysis suggests that in the early 1990s, the prevailing culture in C&EE was not in tune with the behavioral incentives required for the successful functioning of the basic formal institutions of capitalism. This means that the conflict between the behavioral incentives of the institutions of capitalism and the prevailing culture in C&EE creates transaction costs *specific to the process of transition*. Transaction costs specific to transition can be categorized as *subjective* or *objective*. Giving up the predictability of other people's behavior, accepting the risks of nonroutine behaviors, and estrangement from friends and neighbors who are slower in abandoning old rules are examples of subjective costs arising from the conflict between the formal institutions of capitalism and the prevailing informal rules. Objective costs include sunk investments in the development of the prevailing informal rules, and the strength of the groups and coalitions that stand to gain from preserving the status quo (such as officials of the former Communist governments in C&EE).

---

[25] Silke Stahl, "Transition Problems in the Russian Agriculture Sector: A Historical-Institutional Perspective," in Pejovich, ed., *The Economics of Property Rights*, 157.

[26] Timur Kuran, "Why the Middle East Is Economically Underdeveloped: Historical Mechanism of Institutional Stagnation," unpublished manuscript.

[27] The law of limited liability was known in Europe as early as the eleventh century. See Lal, *Unintended Consequences*, 81–82.

A common response by most countries in C&EE to the conflict between their prevailing cultures and the institutions of capitalism was to enact "clarifying" laws and regulations. These included the reintroduction of price controls over some goods, restrictions on the flow of capital, and rules concerning laying off workers. The stated intent of these laws and regulations was to reduce the conflict arising between new formal institutions and the prevailing culture; however, the consequences of these laws, whether those consequences were intended or unintended, have been a slow return to the old system of *dirigisme* from above. Eventually, people ended up with a government-engineered compromise between capitalism and the old system, with the costs of transition being borne by all citizens regardless of whether they wanted institutional reforms, opposed them, or didn't care one way or the other. The legal theorist Cass Sunstein has noted the costs of these laws and regulations in C&EE. "Without strong constitutional provisions on behalf of property rights, civil society, and markets, there will probably be a substantial temptation to intrude on all these institutions, and, by so doing, recreate the very problems that such institutions are supposed to solve."[28]

D. Culture and the results of transition

Given that the prevailing culture in C&EE is not homogeneous, the transaction costs of transition differ from one country to another, and these differences in transaction costs translate into different transition results. Since the culture of individualism is a Western phenomenon, this analysis suggests that the results of institutional restructuring should correlate with the extent of Western influence in the various countries of C&EE. To test this hypothesis, we can divide C&EE countries into two groups: those that have had more cultural and political interactions with the West, and those that have had less or none.

The Czech Republic, Croatia, Hungary, Slovakia, and Slovenia used to be part of the Austro-Hungarian empire. The empire, which lasted several centuries and came to an end in 1918, was short on democracy but strong on the rule of law and the enforcement of property rights. It is reasonable to expect that the prevailing informal rules in those countries have retained memories of the rule of law and individual rights. Western culture entered Poland via the Catholic Church. In addition to playing a major role in the development of informal rules in that country, the Church also helped the Poles to preserve their customs and traditions during several periods of Russian aggression (including the post–World War II years). For centuries, the Baltic states maintained strong contacts with merchants from Germany, Sweden, and Finland. Christianity arrived in the Baltic states from the West. Estonia and Latvia have become predominantly Lutheran,

---

[28] Cass Sunstein, "On Property and Constitutionalism," *Cardozo Law Review* 14 (1993): 935.

while Lithuania is Roman Catholic. Through religious contacts and trade, Western culture contributed to customs and traditions in the Baltic states.

In the process of transition, the Baltic states, and especially Estonia and Latvia (which have Russian minorities amounting to about 30 percent of total population), had an important starting advantage over other C&EE countries. Since de-Communization did not happen in C&EE, Communists and fellow travelers, with their well-established "old boy" network, joined the new ruling elite and provided strong support to the forces that preferred to maintain collectivist values. However, most important political positions in the Baltic states under Communist rule were held or controlled by Russians. In the early 1990s, leading Russian Communists either fled back to Russia or lost jobs and influence because of their ethnic origin. Hence, the culture of collectivism in the Baltic states lost a major source of support.[29]

After a brief rule (1682–1725) by Peter the Great, who appreciated the importance of Western culture, the Romanovs chose to isolate the middle and lower classes in Russia from the West. The Russian Orthodox Church played a major role in helping the ruling elite to preserve this cultural isolation of Russia (and the countries dominated by Russia, such as Belarus, Moldavia, and Ukraine) from the West. To say that Eastern Orthodox churches, including the Russian church, have historically shunned the culture of individualism is merely a factual observation, which does not imply a judgment about the worthiness of their religious beliefs and dogmas. As recently as the late 1990s, the Russian church lobbied the state to prohibit or at least restrict the spread of Western influence via Protestant and Catholic churches.

The Ottoman empire influenced the development of informal rules in the parts of the Balkans it controlled during most of the period from the fourteenth through the nineteenth centuries (Greece, Serbia, Bulgaria, Romania, Albania, Bosnia, and Montenegro). However, two factors limited Turkish influence on local cultures. First, the Turks did not interfere in civil disputes between Christians, which helped to preserve local customs. Second, Christians were obliged to wear distinctive clothing, which, while marking them as second-class citizens, reinforced their ethnic loyalties.

Contrary to many local myths, the Ottomans did not repress Christian religious services. In fact, until the second half of eighteenth century, Ottoman rule was quite tolerant. Professor Andre Gerolymatos, director of Hellenic Studies at Simon Fraser University, offers this description of Ottoman rule in the Balkans: "The Ottoman era in Southeastern Europe was marked by periods of not only great upheaval and hardship, but also benevolent administration and prosperity that enhanced the living stan-

---

[29] I thank Professor Andreas Freytag from Friedrich-Schiller University in Jena, Germany, for this point.

dards of all Ottoman subjects. . . . [The fact that] the Ottomans did not embark on wholesale forcible conversions enabled the Balkan people to maintain their identities into the nineteenth century."[30]

While maritime trading helped the Greeks (and the small percentage of Montenegrins living along the Adriatic coast) to become aware of other cultures, Serbia, Macedonia, Romania, Bulgaria, Bosnia, and Montenegro had no permanent access to Western culture until the early nineteenth century. The Renaissance and the Reformation, new scientific discoveries, classical liberalism, and Adam Smith all had their effects long before those countries opened their borders to the West. Interactions with Serbs living in the Austro-Hungarian empire helped the people of Serbia, for example, to open their first important window to the West only in the late eighteenth century.

Table 1 divides C&EE countries into those that experienced greater and lesser influence from the West. The table then provides data from the Heritage *Index of Economic Freedom* in order to measure the results of institutional restructuring. Since institutional restructuring is a process rather than an event, the table shows the results of transition in two different years, 1996 and 2004.[31] The Heritage *Index* scales of economic freedom run from 1 (the best) to 5 (the worst) and separate all countries into four broad categories: *free* (1.95 or less), *mostly free* (2.00–2.95), *mostly unfree* (3.00–3.95), and *repressed* (4.00 or higher).

Table 1 provides striking evidence in support of the interaction thesis, which states that the conflict between the incentive effects of the formal rules of capitalism and the prevailing culture of a given country creates transaction costs specific to the process of transition in that country. In 1996, the Heritage *Index* ranked only Estonia and Czech Republic as *mostly free* countries. All other countries were ranked as *mostly unfree.* The mean rating of the countries influenced by the West was 3.1, already close to the *mostly free* ranking. The mean rating of the countries not influenced by the West was 3.5.

In 2004, the Heritage *Index* ranked all countries influenced by the West, except Croatia, as *free* or *mostly free,* and all those not influenced by Western culture as *mostly unfree* or *repressed.*[32] From 1996 to 2004, the mean rating of countries influenced by the West improved from 3.1 to 2.5. The reason for this improvement, I would suggest, is that the memories of Western culture and the rule of law were strong enough to overcome resistance to institutional changes. During the same period, the mean rating of the second group of countries remained about the same.

---

[30] Andre Gerolymatos, *The Balkan Wars* (New York: Basic Books, 2002), 73–77.
[31] See *1996 and 2004 Index of Economic Freedom* published jointly by the Heritage Foundation and the *Wall Street Journal.*
[32] It is important to repeat that the ranking of countries in the Heritage *Index* is in terms of economic freedoms only.

TABLE 1. Economic freedom in Central and Eastern Europe
and the effects of prior Western influence

COUNTRY	ECONOMIC FREEDOM	
Greater Western Influence	**2004**	**1996**
Estonia	1.8	2.4
Lithuania	2.2	3.5
Latvia	2.4	3.2
Czech Republic	2.4	2.3
Slovakia	2.4	3.2
Hungary	2.6	3.0
Slovenia	2.7	3.7
Poland	2.8	3.2
Croatia	3.1	3.5
Average	*2.5*	*3.1*
Lesser Western Influence	**2004**	**1996**
Bulgaria	3.1	3.5
Moldova	3.1	3.5
Albania	3.1	3.6
Russia	3.5	3.6
Ukraine	3.5	3.7
Romania	3.7	3.4
Belarus	4.1	3.4
Macedonia	3.0	not rated
Bosnia	3.3	not rated
Serbia and Montenegro	4.2 (2003)	not rated
Average	*3.5*	*3.5*

Values are from the Heritage *Index of Economic Freedom* scale of 1 to 5, with 1 representing the greatest economic freedom.

The evidence in support of the interaction thesis has an important implication. By assuming that the road to capitalism is a technical problem, economic reforms based on neoclassical economics ignored the fact that capitalism is much more than an alternative method for the allocation of resources. It is *a way of life*. The effort to impose the transition to capitalism via the strong hand of the state had the effect of forcing upon ordinary people institutional changes that were alien to the fabric of community life in C&EE. This became more true the farther east and southeast one traveled. All that ordinary people got was the switch of one set of institutions for another set, neither of which they chose for themselves.

This failure of neoclassical economics to recognize the importance of cultural values has been observed by the economist Douglass North: "Many Latin American countries adopted the U.S. Constitution (with some modifications) in the nineteenth century, and many of the property rights laws of successful Western countries have been adopted by Third World countries. The results, however, are not similar to those in either the United States or other successful Western countries. Although the rules are the same, the enforcement mechanism, the way enforcement occurs, the norms of behavior, and the subjective models of the actors are not [the same]."[33]

III. CAPITALISM BY CHOICE: THE ROAD TO LIBERTY

A. Framework for analysis

An alternative method of transition is to identify and enact formal rules that would encourage *voluntary changes* of informal institutions in Central and Eastern Europe. The three critical factors that would encourage the process of spontaneous changes in informal rules and reenergize the process of transition from within the system are the market for institutions, the carriers of institutional restructuring, and the margin of acceptable behavior. I will discuss each of these in turn.

1. The market for institutions. A well-functioning market has two major functions: to create incentives for institutional innovation and to reduce the costs of adaptive behavior. The former provides individuals with freedom to seek changes in the rules of the game. The latter gives the community as a whole freedom to accept or reject those changes voluntarily. Not infrequently, new informal rules eventually become formal rules. Gary Libecap, professor of economics at the University of Arizona, has demonstrated the development of informal property-rights arrangements in the American West and their eventual enactment into formal rules. As "the mining industry boomed, spurred by huge ore discoveries," he writes, ". . . pressure on existing legal institutions forced new ownership structures to emerge. This resulted in the observed progression in mineral rights law from general, *unwritten rules* in the 1850s to highly specified statutes and court verdicts by the end of the century."[34]

To develop the market for institutions, C&EE countries would have to enact, admittedly from above, the basic institutions of capitalism, namely: private property rights (the enactment of private property rights is not to be confused with the abolition of other types of existing property rights; the important requirement is that the legal system treat all types of property rights equally), the law of contract, the constitution, and an indepen-

---

[33] North, *Institutions, Institutional Change, and Economic Performance,* 101.
[34] Gary Libecap, "Economic Variables and the Development of the Law: The Case of Western Mineral Rights," in L. Alston, T. Eggertsson, and D. North, eds., *Empirical Studies in Institutional Change* (Cambridge: Cambridge University Press, 1996), 57 (emphasis added).

dent judiciary. As I have noted (in Section IIB), these rules create incentives for individuals to accept the risk and uncertainty associated with innovation, and they lower the transaction costs of the integration (or rejection) of a novelty into the prevailing institutional framework.

The basic institutions of capitalism enforce individuals' claims of non-interference against the rest of the world, provide protection against all levels of government, and make these claims enforceable in the courts. Hence, the basic institutions of capitalism in effect protect negative rights.[35] And it is negative rights that give individual members of the community both the freedom and the incentive to pursue innovation *without* using the strong hand of the state to enforce such innovation upon the community as a whole.

Referring to the importance of negative rights for the process of institutional restructuring in C&EE, Cass Sunstein has written: "The case for a firm negative constitution, and for creation and protection of [stable and credible] property rights and free markets, is very strong in Eastern Europe."[36] Sunstein's reference to the protection of negative rights is critical (for an example, see the appendix at the end of this essay). The enactment of negative rights does not necessarily guarantee the protection of individual rights and efficient markets. To have the desired consequences, negative rights must be stable and credible. For rights to be credible, people must believe that their rights are protected by the constitution and enforced by an independent judiciary. For rights to be stable, government must not arbitrarily change the rules of the game; stable rules lower the costs of making decisions that have long-run consequences. We can refer to a country where the legal system is credible and stable as a "rule of law" country. In an extensive cross-country study, researcher Bernhard Heitger of the Kiel Institute for World Economy found that "a doubling in the index of property rights more than doubles living standards."[37]

While many new leaders in C&EE countries may have sincerely rejected socialism, they have matured professionally in collectivist cultures under socialist political traditions. At the same time, they are faced with the task of establishing institutions that would protect individual rights. Thus, the development of the market for institutions in C&EE is a difficult public choice problem.

2. The carriers of institutional restructuring. Decisions that are said to be made by governments, parliaments, corporations, and other organizations are actually decisions made by individuals. That is, the individual is the carrier of economic activities, including institutional innovations. As

---

[35] In contrast, positive rights, such as a right to free public education, call for interference by the state.

[36] Sunstein, "On Property and Constitutionalism," 918 and 935.

[37] Bernhard Heitger, "Property Rights and the Wealth of Nations: A Cross-Country Study," *Cato Journal* 23 (2004): 400.

economists Armen Alchian and William Allen have written: "Groups, organizations, communities, nations, and societies are institutions whose operations can best be understood when we focus attention on the action and choices of constituent members. When we speak of the goals and actions of the United States, we are really referring to the goals and actions of the individuals in the United States."[38]

The community's voluntary acceptance of innovation means that the carrier of change (hereafter the "pathfinder") has made the community better off; otherwise, the innovation would have been rejected. Thus, successful institutional innovation enhances economic development. Since it is the consequence of a pathfinder's vision and of incentives to accept risk, innovation can be neither planned for nor predicted in advance. To maximize the flow of potential innovations, then, all members of the community must be free to innovate and must have incentives to do so. That is, the freedom to innovate requires the absence of arbitrary power on the part of the ruling group, and the subjection of all citizens to the same laws.

3. *The margin of acceptable behavior.* The essence of a culture lies in the values it embraces. Being entrenched in the social fabric of society, those values determine the margin of acceptable behavior. The term "margin of acceptable behavior" separates informal rules that fall within the margin from unacceptable norms of behavior that fall outside it. Every culture (and subculture) has its own margin of acceptable behavior. However, these margins of acceptable behavior are not written in stone. A lowering of the margin of acceptable behavior means the addition of a previously submarginal norm to the set of acceptable rules.[39] The market for institutions and the freedom to innovate create incentives to change the margin of acceptable behavior.

B. Changes in informal rules and transition

A spontaneous change in the prevailing culture means a change in the margin of acceptable behavior. And to change the margin of acceptable behavior requires an individual willing and able to take the risk of overcoming the objective and subjective costs of carrying out a submarginal activity. Human history is full of successful and unsuccessful attempts by pathfinders to change the margin of acceptable behavior. Successful cultural changes at the margin range from the social acceptance of interracial marriages, single motherhood, and cohabitation arrangements in the West, to allowing young people to choose their own partners in marriage in

[38] Armen Alchian and William Allen, *University Economics* (Belmont, CA: Wadsworth Publishing, 1964), 12.

[39] In this essay, I use the terms "lowering" and "changing" the margin of acceptable behavior interchangeably.

many developing countries, to truly major changes like the birth of Christianity. However, the basic mechanism of change is pretty much the same.[40]

Suppose that a new idea or opportunity for human interactions were to become available to a community from without or be discovered from within. In either case, the agent of change would be the pathfinder who perceives prospects for personal gain from exploiting such new opportunities. If the new opportunities for human interactions were not in tune with the prevailing culture in the community, a conflict would arise between the pathfinder trying to exploit those opportunities and the community at large. That is, the behavior of the pathfinder would be below the margin of acceptable behavior. In practice, such conflicts have surfaced in many different forms in Central and Eastern Europe. People have said that individuals seeking new contractual arrangements are foreigners "who want to take our money abroad," or women "who should be staying at home," or enterprising men "who want to profit at other people's expense," or Baptist missionaries "who want to destroy our Orthodox faith."

While the costs of changes in formal rules imposed from above are borne by taxpayers, including those who either oppose or do not care about reforms, the pathfinder bears the costs of innovation.[41] If pursuing submarginal contractual activities provides the pathfinder with a differential return, the success creates incentives for others to engage in the same or similar activities. And if the returns from those activities continue to be sustainable, an ever-increasing number of individuals will find it in their self-interest to join in. Eventually, spontaneous pressures will arise from within the system to embrace the novelty. If (and only if) such pressure turns out to be strong enough to overcome the subjective and objective costs of the community's commitment to prevailing cultural values, the margin of acceptable behavior will change.

If my analysis is correct, then spontaneous changes in informal rules have four important social consequences:

(1) The cost of pursuing a submarginal activity is borne by those who expect that *their benefits* will exceed *their costs* of violating the margin of acceptable behavior.
(2) The market for institutions and the freedom to innovate lower the transaction costs of carrying out a submarginal activity.
(3) A spontaneous change in informal rules means that changes in the margin of acceptable behavior are sustainable at low transaction costs.

---

[40] As far as I know, an article by Goetz Briefs is the earliest attempt to interpret the consequences of the relationship between formal and informal rules via changes at the margin. See Goetz Briefs, "The Ethos Problem in the Present Pluralistic Society," *Review of Social Economy* 15 (1957): 47–75.

[41] In addition to financial losses, those costs could range from losing friends to losing jobs and alienation from the community.

(4) The pathfinder's freedom to engage in a submarginal activity does not prejudice the direction of institutional changes. For example, the Amish people in the United States have, at a cost borne by themselves, maintained their prevailing culture.

James Buchanan has contrasted this method of institutional restructuring with alternatives that rely on the strong hand of the state:

> An activist state [is] ever ready to intervene when existing rights to property are challenged, ever willing to grasp the nettle and define rights anew, which once defined, immediately become vulnerable to still further challenges. [In a passive state,] there is an explicit prejudice in favor of previously existing rights, not because this structure possesses some intrinsic ethical attributes, and not because change itself is undesirable, but for the much more elementary reason that only such a prejudice offers incentives for the emergence of voluntary negotiated settlements among the [individual members of the community].[42]

Detailed analysis of the factors through which the free market for institutions affects the prevailing informal rules in C&EE, and the circumstances upon which those factors depend, is beyond the scope of this essay. However, it might be useful to point out briefly the effects of two important factors, entrepreneurship and the corporate firm, on cultural change.

1. Entrepreneurship. Privatization of state-owned firms has not done much to change the prevailing culture in C&EE. Those firms have out-of-date assets. Their employees are accustomed to a paternalistic environment.[43] Their managers are members of the old ruling elite or fellow travelers. Moreover, business managers and the employees of state-owned firms have frequently negotiated with the legislators and bureaucrats mutually favorable methods of privatization. Indeed, many C&EE countries have adopted privatization schemes that can easily be characterized as stealing.[44]

An alternative for the new leaders in C&EE is to invest time and effort in encouraging the development of never-privatized, owner-managed firms. The laws of contract and property create incentives for entrepreneurs to form new business enterprises. The efficiency of owner-managed firms arises from the marriage between the owners' right to capture the

---

[42] James Buchanan, "Politics, Property, and the Law," *Journal of Law and Economics* 15 (1972): 451–52.

[43] For an example of this, see the appendix.

[44] Milic Milovanovic, "Endogenous Corruption in Privatized Companies," unpublished manuscript.

benefits of their decisions and the fact that they bear the costs of those decisions.

However, improving economic performance is not the most critical role that entrepreneurs play in the transition process. The essential contribution they make to the transition process lies in bringing closer the culture of capitalism and the prevailing culture in C&EE. That is because the owner-managed enterprise is the breeding ground for a work ethic, a capitalist exchange culture, and a way of life that rewards performance, promotes individual liberties, and places high value on self-responsibility and self-determination. To maximize incentives for entrepreneurship, new leaders must keep the costs of entry into business low, avoid piling up business regulations, and eliminate the disincentive effects of taxation.[45]

The argument that subsidies or low-interest loans are viable alternative methods of enhancing entrepreneurship is invalid. Whatever the facade of words, the allocation of subsidies is a political decision. This means that subsidies raise the transaction costs of allocating resources to the highest-valued users. The assumptions that the government is capable of identifying the most productive users at a lower cost (compared to resource allocation in competitive markets) and that the government would use this information if it had it, require a staggeringly large leap of faith. Most important, entrepreneurs who fail are not going to repay loans; therefore, the costs of their failures will be borne by foreigners, international financial institutions, local taxpayers, or all of these. Subsidies and low-interest loans do not deliver a lesson in the culture of individualism.

2. The corporate firm. The corporate firm is the most effective method of voluntarily gathering large amounts of capital for long-lived ventures. This advantage of the corporate firm over other types of business enterprises derives from the anonymous alienability of shares, which the law of limited liability made possible. The anonymous alienability of shares enables individual owners (shareholders) to buy and sell shares without requiring the approval of other owners of the firm or even caring who they are.

The ability of the corporate firm to attract a large number of investors to buy its shares is not a free good. It depends on the strong protection of investors. Protection of investors refers to ways of ensuring that the firm pursues the objectives established by the initial investors in the charter of incorporation and that shareholders' wealth is protected from redistribution in political markets.[46] The protection of investors presupposes the freedom of contract and credible property rights, and those two factors create strong incentives for large and small investors (savers) to become

---

[45] See Simeon Djankov et al., *The Regulation of Entry* (New York: National Bureau of Economic Research, Working Paper 7892, 2000).

[46] Subsequent investors (shareholders) are buying into those initial contracts made by original investors. In transparent financial markets, share prices incorporate the expected effects of initial contractual terms.

shareholders. The dispersion of shareholding, then, is a predictable consequence of the ability of the corporate firm to gather large amounts of capital voluntarily, which, in turn, depends on the strong protection of investors.

Leaving aside its economic benefits, the dispersion of shareholding could be a major channel for the transmission of the culture of individualism in Central and Eastern Europe.[47] The potential effects of the dispersion of shareholding on the prevailing informal rules are the following:

(1) The dispersion of shareholding means that investors can diversify their portfolios and avoid firm-specific risk. An implication of this is that potential pathfinders have incentives to invest in risky ventures due to the ability to mitigate those risks through diversification.[48] The dispersion of shareholding then encourages innovation, risk-taking, and bearing the consequences of one's decisions.

(2) The dispersion of ownership contributes to the development of a middle class whose members have significant and diversifiable stakes in the free-market economy.

(3) A corporation is not a democracy. Leaving aside the tiny fraction of corporate activists, all that shareholders want is the highest possible value for their shares. By selling or threatening to sell their shares, shareholders lower the transaction costs of replacing management. Hence, corporate managers have strong incentives to pursue shareholders' interests.

The dispersion of shareholding is not a worldwide phenomenon. Numerous studies have shown that common law gives shareholders better protection compared to the protection provided by statutory laws. Not surprisingly, the dispersion of shareholding is much greater in the United States than in Western Europe, where large families, a few large shareholders, and financial institutions like banks own shares.[49] Consequently, we observe that the culture of individualism and the flow of innovation

---

[47] Research and evidence have totally undermined Adolf Berle and Gardiner Means's analysis of the costs of the dispersion of shareholding (Berle and Means, *The Modern Corporation and Private Property* [New York: Macmillan, 1935]). To paraphrase Armen Alchian, the "separation of ownership from control" hypothesis is an empty piece of poetry. Of course, if corporate managers could and did transfer shareholders' wealth to themselves, how do we explain that literally millions of large and small savers are purchasing shares? There is no law that says that they have to do so. And in the United States, people have many other alternatives for investing their funds.

[48] See Jonathan Macey, *Gli Stati Uniti: Un Paese Senze Legge* (Turin: International Centre for Economic Research, Working Paper no. 2, 1998).

[49] See, for example, Katharina Pistor, *Patterns of Legal Change: Shareholder and Creditor Rights in Transition Economies* (Basel, Switzerland: European Bank for Reconstruction and Development, Working Paper no. 49, 2000); and Rafael La Porta et al., "Corporate Ownership Around the World," *Journal of Finance* 54 (1999): 471–513.

are stronger in the United States than in Europe. For example, economists Alberto Alesina and George-Marios Angeletos have demonstrated the difference in the way Americans and Europeans react to income inequalities. While 71 percent of Americans maintain that the poor could pull themselves up by their bootstraps, only 40 percent of Europeans think so. Hence, we observe that the alleviation of poverty in the United States emphasizes work effort, while European governments prefer redistributive policies from above.[50]

New leaders in C&EE have failed to appreciate the importance of the dispersion of shareholding. Otherwise they would have paid more attention to the freedom of contract and the protection of shareholders' property rights. Under the combined influence of their prevailing informal rules, the socialist heritage, and the impact of European Union bureaucracy, C&EE countries (with a few exceptions, such as Estonia) consider the corporate firm a vehicle for promoting the subjective preferences of the ruling elite, rent-seeking coalitions, and the so-called stakeholders. Those preferences include the protection of jobs, the promotion of public interests (as defined by the ruling elite), provision of welfare benefits, and support for various industrial democracy schemes—everything but the protection of shareholders' wealth.

IV. CONCLUSION

The analysis in this essay suggests three conclusions regarding the effects of culture on institutional restructuring in Central and Eastern Europe. First, the incentive effects of the formal institutions of capitalism and the prevailing culture in C&EE create transaction costs specific to the process of institutional reforms. Differences between those transaction costs, on a country-by-country basis, explain both the uneven results of using the strong hand of the state to impose capitalism from the early 1990s through 2004 as well as the rising strength of pro-collectivist political parties.

Second, the promotion of economic liberty could reenergize the transition to capitalism in C&EE. The enactment of credible and stable property rights and free trade would provide incentives for risk-takers in the community to engage in activities that, while fully legal, are not in tune with the prevailing culture. And the success of capitalism in protecting individual rights and producing sustainable economic growth would create incentives for pathfinders to move the prevailing cultural values in C&EE closer to a culture supportive of capitalism. In a nutshell, liberty supports capitalism.

---

[50] Alberto Alesina and George-Marios Angeletos, *Fairness and Redistribution: U.S. vs. Europe* (New York: National Bureau for Economic Research, Working Paper 9502, 2002).

Third, common law would have been more effective than statutory laws in promoting and protecting entrepreneurship and corporate firms in C&EE. This is true because common law is more flexible in adjusting the entrenched cultural values to the changing requirements of real life. The legal scholar Henry Manne said it well: "A common law system does seem peculiarly well suited to the need in any legal system to respond appropriately to new circumstances. In its origin . . . common law was primarily local, tribal, or customary law, and, probably for this reason, common law judges have always had a predilection to subsume local customs into decision rules." [51] Central and Eastern European countries are not likely to institute their own common laws subsuming local customs and traditions. However, if they did, an opportunity would be created for the spontaneous changes in informal rules that I discussed in the second section of this essay.

Appendix

As I noted in Section II, the expected economic effects of negative rights depend on both their credibility and their stability. The following account illustrates this point.

Niksicka Pivara (Niksich Brewery) in Montenegro was known all over Europe for its excellent beer.[52] The firm won numerous prizes in tough European competitions. While the firm sold beer all over the former Yugoslavia and many European countries, its main profit came from summer sales in cities and towns along the coast of Montenegro.

The end of socialism in the early 1990s led to the privatization of many enterprises, including the Niksich Brewery. A foreign investor bought a 70 percent interest in the brewery. The buyer paid 16 million German marks (this happened before the advent of the euro) in cash and promised to invest another 25 million marks in the firm. The employees and local citizens kept a 30 percent interest in the brewery. In addition, the foreign investor promised that the average real salary paid to the employees would not fall below the average real salary in the brewery at the time it was purchased. The average salary in real terms was 200 marks (about $100) per month. In those uncertain political and economic times in the Balkans, the German mark served as the currency of choice.

The owners kept their contractual promise and invested more than 25 million marks in the brewery. Yet, after decades of socialism, private ownership was out of tune with the prevailing culture in Montenegro. The employees discovered that shirking, tardiness, and long coffee breaks

---

[51] Henry Manne, "The Judiciary and Free Markets," *Harvard Journal of Law and Public Policy* 21 (1997): 21.

[52] The material in this appendix is adapted from Svetozar Pejovich, "Understanding the Transaction Costs of Transition: It's the Culture, Stupid," *Review of Austrian Economics* 16 (2003): 355–56.

were out, while disciplined work was in. Former managers and some employees lost a number of pecuniary and nonpecuniary benefits characteristic of property rights in socialism, such as using company trucks for private business, frequent trips abroad, cheap credit, and subsidized housing. Local officials lost gifts and patronage.

The first strike occurred over the salary issue. The local union asked the firm to raise the average salary to 600 German marks. Management said no. From then until 2002, strikes, threats of strikes, and labor disputes continued to plague the brewery. In May 2002, just as the tourist season was to begin, the employees demanded, through their local union, a salary increase of 35 percent. At that time, the average wage in the brewery was 100 percent above the average monthly pay in Montenegro.

In addition to higher pay, the employees also wanted the firm to buy a car for the union office, to give a share of its profit to the union, to put a representative of the employees on the board of directors, to provide opportunities for the employees to travel abroad at company expense, and to earmark a large amount of the firm's revenue to build subsidized apartments for workers. By the fall of 2002, the owners had had enough. They decided to move the brewery out of Montenegro. The response from the striking employees and local politicians was quick and reflected their "understanding" of the right of ownership. They said the new owners had not built the factory and, therefore, had no right to close it down.

The message of the story is that the enactment of private property rights in many Central and Eastern European countries means little. To have the desired effects on economic life, private property rights have to be both stable and credible.

Economics, Texas A&M University and the International Centre for Economic Research, Turin, Italy

EQUALITY, HIERARCHY, AND GLOBAL JUSTICE

By James M. Buchanan

I. Introduction

In any ordered society, two contrasting attitudes may describe the positions that persons take, one toward another, in evaluating and organizing their relationships, whether these be personal, social, or political. A person may consider and treat others as "natural equals," as potential players in the cooperative-competitive game who are capable of reciprocating behavior and hence deserving of respect. Or, by contrast, a person may consider and treat others as determined by classification of their positions in a "natural hierarchy," as superiors or inferiors and hence deserving of either deference or domination—a stance that may or may not be informed by ethical standards. The attitude toward others taken by any individual will embody some mix of these two contrasting positions, and, by extension, so will the social interaction structure for any particular society.

My thesis is that differences along this attitudinal dimension may make it difficult to extend precepts of justice across political boundaries because the basic meaning of justice becomes different in the two positions. A society that is primarily described by institutional structures derived from precepts for "justice among natural equals" may seem to fail when measured against criteria that apply to treatment among classified unequals. My subordinate thesis is that the societies of the United States, on the one hand, and Western European welfare states, on the other, are sufficiently distinct along the dimension emphasized to offer at least a partial explanation for differing public support for particular institutional practices, for example, the practice of capital punishment. In summary, even if put dramatically, Europe must shed remaining vestiges of medieval hierarchism before precepts for global justice can command cross-national minimal consensus.

In Section II, I discuss in more detail the attitudes noted, and I personalize the argument by relating it to familiar figures in philosophical discourse. Further, I relate the discussion both to developments in intellectual history and to the implications for institutional structures. In Section III, I examine the equivocal ethics of modern welfare states. Section IV is likely to prove controversial, since I suggest that the differing American and European attitudes toward capital punishment may find their origins in the differing public understandings of human interactions. In Section V, I discuss the more general implications of the two foundational perspectives.

255

The severe limits of the inquiry here should be emphasized. My concern is with problems that may arise as precepts of justice are extended beyond political boundaries *within* the nexus of "liberal" or "decent" polities[1] that institutionally embody the existence and value of individual autonomy. More difficult issues that may emerge as globalization prompts expansion to include nonliberal peoples are simply left out of the account here.

II. Plato and Adam Smith

My concern is with how persons think about other persons in their social order—persons who are outside the genetically defined limits of tribal groupings. I limit attention to attitudes that embody recognition that other persons are units of consciousness capable of independent behavioral response. I shall not discuss the stance of the genuine moral anarchist who simply takes the presence of other persons to be a part of the state of nature—an element of empirical reality. The distinction I am concerned with is the one between equality and inequality along relevant dimensions. Are others, generally, encountered as moral equals, or are they classified, pre-behaviorally, as moral unequals?

The discussion may be personalized with reference to familiar names in moral philosophy—that of Plato, on the one hand, and Adam Smith, on the other. In the Platonic vision of social reality, the vision that has been important in political philosophy through the centuries, persons may be hierarchically classified along a spectrum of inferiority-superiority. Persons may fall anywhere along the extended spectrum, but are always hierarchically defined relative to one another in an ordered ranking, superior to inferior. In Orwellian language, some are always more equal than others.

Along almost any and all particularized dimensions, the Platonic vision, empirically, would seem to carry the day. Ordinary observation suggests that persons differ from one another in a multitude of characteristics (gender, age, race, religion, cultural heritage, physical appearance, genetic makeup, and many others that may be made possible by developments in biotechnology). Further, a scalar of sorts may be established for each dimension that allows for classification. Any identified person is older or younger than another identified person. Any person is male or female. Such differences are not at issue. The question is whether or not there exists, or should exist, a general criterion of superiority, in some relevant moral meaning, that allows for a preliminary classification of persons. Are some persons simply "better" than others? And, if so, how is the criterion of "betterness" to be defined?

[1] John Rawls, *The Law of Peoples* (Cambridge, MA: Harvard University Press, 1999), chap. 1, pp. 11–23.

It is at this point that the issue is joined. The empirically observed facts of human differences along any and all dimensions may be acknowledged alongside a denial that persons are unequal in any sense that is relevant for the organization of society. For Adam Smith, along with other philosophers in the Scottish Enlightenment, the starting point is one of natural equality. Smith's familiar reference is to the basic equality between the philosopher and the common street porter, each of whom, by inference, is fully capable of being accorded the same standing in any consideration of organizational structures.[2] For Adam Smith, and for Thomas Jefferson, who aligned himself with Smith in placing the words "created equal" in America's Declaration of Independence, there may have been a more positive assessment of the human prospect than in our more skeptical epoch. Such an assessment was perhaps reinforced by ideas that emerged from the eighteenth-century discovery of basic uniformities in human nature, which made possible the emergence of sciences of behavior, notably classical economic theory.

As an aside, it is perhaps worth noting that the classical economists were among the most vocal critics of slavery in the early nineteenth century, as opposed to the dominant literati, led by Thomas Carlyle, who based their support of slavery on the presumption of Platonic hierarchy.[3]

Despite its possible positive underpinnings, however, for Smith, and for classical liberals then and now, the primary thrust of the argument here is normative. There is no agreed-upon general criterion of moral superiority among persons, and any attempt to force a hierarchical classification scheme into the political construction of society is to be rejected out of hand. Persons are to be treated as if they are equals, regardless of the empirical reality observed, and, as equals, they are to be accorded equal standing. This message was central to the whole Enlightenment project, and it found dramatic expression in the rhetoric of the American Revolution.

Much more importantly, the basic institutions of Western political-legal order embody the presupposition of equality among all citizens/subjects. There is no hierarchical classification scheme that defines one law for one set of persons and another law for another. The bedrock principle of the rule of law is equal and universal applicability. Similarly, the universality and equality of the franchise has (over time) come to be accepted as the defining attribute of democracy. The separately defined rights that characterize the constitutional order of Western polities are themselves general rather than particular. Persons are accorded equal liberties to speak, write,

---

[2] "The difference between . . . a philosopher and a common street porter . . . seems to arise not so much from nature, as from habit, custom, and education." Adam Smith, *The Wealth of Nations,* Harvard Classics, vol. 10 (New York: Collier, 1909), book 1, chapter 2, pp. 21–22.

[3] For an interesting account of the debates and the role of the economists, see David M. Levy, *How the Dismal Science Got Its Name: Classical Economics and the Ur-Text of Racial Politics* (Ann Arbor: University of Michigan Press, 2001), and Sandra J. Peart and David M. Levy, *The "Vanity of the Philosopher": From Equality to Hierarchy in Post-Classical Economics* (Ann Arbor: University of Michigan Press, 2005).

assemble, exercise religion, and engage in voluntary exchanges. The presupposition of equality among all citizens/subjects is so much a part of the
political-constitutional-legal fabric that it is scarcely discussed explicitly.

In a practical sense, Adam Smith seems to have won the day over Plato.
Philosophically, however, the academy has never fully embraced the
Enlightenment dream. The Platonic ideal of the philosopher-kings who
are chosen from a hierarchical classification that separates the rulers from
the ruled remained for centuries the dominating normative ideal in political theory. The obvious inconsistency between this ideal and the precepts
of democracy has been widely overlooked, as modern political scientists
continue to model politics as a search for "truth," often referred to as the
"public good" or the "public interest," which presumably exists "out
there," waiting to be discovered. At least by implication if not directly, a
designated subset of the citizenry is presumed more capable of discovering political truth than outsiders who are to be subjected to its revelation in practice.

III. The Equivocal Ethics of the Welfare State

Contemporary Western democratic welfare states embody an institutionalized admixture of the two contrasting attitudes—natural equality
and natural hierarchy. As noted, the basic legal and political structures
presume the absence of any grounds for differentiation among persons.
At the same time, however, the politically sanctioned massive transfer
programs necessarily involve discriminatory treatment, or so it would
seem. The operation of such programs separates persons into classes of
net gainers and net losers, with readily computable differentiation among
subgroups within each of these two inclusive sets. Some mitigation of the
apparent ethical contradiction inherent in the institutional underpinnings
of the modern welfare state is achieved by introducing the temporal and
stochastic dimensions that inform programs for collectively imposed transfers. The presupposition of natural equality among persons is not violated so long as criteria for eligibility, both for potential tax costs and
transfer benefits, are defined inclusively or generally rather than discriminatorily. For example, a program that imposes taxes on current income
earners to finance transfers to pensioners or retirees does not in itself
involve hierarchical classification, provided that all persons become eligible for transfer benefits due to age criteria alone. Similarly, transfers to
persons who become disabled may satisfy criteria of generality so long as
eligibility is not arbitrarily restricted.[4]

----

[4] For extended treatment of the generality norm, see James M. Buchanan and Roger D.
Congleton, *Politics by Principle, Not Interest: Toward Nondiscriminatory Democracy* (New York
and Cambridge: Cambridge University Press, 1998).

Many of the transfer programs of contemporary welfare states cannot, however, readily be justified based on criteria of generality. Many programs are explicitly discriminatory in the sense that persons and groups are targeted for differential treatment on either the tax or the transfer side of the fiscal account. And it is with these programs that the foundational ethical understandings may come into conflict. How can a program that is described by tax-financed transfers to designated groups—say, the able-bodied homeless in a city—be morally justified?

The immediate response to such a question invokes reference to an extension of Christian charity, involving compassion and kindness for those who are unfortunate. Such a response, in itself, seems to establish, at least implicitly, the legitimacy of the hierarchical classification, based on criteria that allow for easy separation between those who are potential recipients and those who are not. Such tax-transfer programs, as they are morally justified, as they are interpreted, and as they are administered, almost necessarily imply violation of any foundational presupposition of natural equality. And, so interpreted, these programs seem to counter the presuppositions that Western societies embody. How can transfers to the homeless, or to people with AIDS, be justified on the basis of compassion while, at the same time, these people are accorded equal standing, through democratic processes, in the determination of the extent and scope of the transfer itself?

The continuing uneasy mixture of the two ethical starting points in the modern welfare state seems unlikely to be clarified. The whole enterprise undertaken by John Rawls may be understood as a valiant effort to bring philosophical order into the discussion.[5] Rawls sought to derive basic principles of justice for a society of natural equals despite the observed facts of inequality among persons along many dimensions. The veil of ignorance became the device that shifted the discourse from the discussion of justice among unequals to that of justice among natural equals. With this construction, Rawls was able to derive a justificatory logic for redistributive transfers, exemplified in the difference principle.[6] (Unfortunately, he failed to note that this particular principle was only one among many that might emerge from agreement among the natural equals situated behind the veil of ignorance.)

The point to be emphasized is that this Rawlsian ethical construction does not, in any variant, invoke considerations of charity or compassion for those who are potential recipients of transfers on the part of those who are the critical decision makers for the collectivity. It is as if, almost literally, the contractors behind the Rawlsian veil are choosing for them-

---

[5] John Rawls, *A Theory of Justice* (Cambridge, MA: Harvard University Press, 1971); Rawls, *Political Liberalism* (New York: Columbia University Press, 1993); and Rawls, *The Law of Peoples.*

[6] On the veil of ignorance, see Rawls, *A Theory of Justice,* sec. 24. On the difference principle, see ibid., sec. 13.

selves the basic redistributive scheme to be put into place.[7] In this way, the bridge over the otherwise impassable gulf between individualized self-interest and something that might be called the general interest is crossed. Any necessity of introducing utility interdependence as a motivation for altruism in the sense of benevolence is thereby avoided.

In rather dramatic contrast at this point, the norms for the differential treatment of unequals in tax-transfer policy, as well as the institutional implementation of these norms, must rely, in some ultimate motivational sense, on the presence of utility interdependence. To exhibit charity and compassion toward those deemed eligible for differential treatment requires an acknowledgment by the individual decision maker that the well-being of others matters. In economists' jargon, the utilities of others must enter into the utility function for the individual, whereas in the Rawlsian-Kantian construction there need be no such direct interpersonal interdependence. The whole Rawlsian enterprise becomes absurd to those who approach problems of social interaction from the hierarchical perspective. How can it be meaningful to place oneself behind a veil of ignorance when prior identification is presumed? A person who thinks of himself as naturally superior or naturally inferior to others cannot reduce himself to the level of evaluation, even in some stylized exercise, that removes individualized and group differentiation. To any such person, questions of justice involve the treatment of (and by) human beings, who are acknowledged to be members of the same species but who are classified by their locations in the imagined scalar of obligation or merit.

It is evident that the Rawlsian construction, to the extent that it comes to inform the attitudes of those who are deriving principles of justice, opens up prospects for general agreement on such principles, whereas agreement becomes almost impossible in the alternative (hierarchical) construction. Those who classify themselves as superior beings in the social hierarchy may accept some obligation to give succor to those who are classified as inferior, but those who make up the claimant group will scarcely be acquiescent in any imposed scheme. Conflict almost necessarily emerges, not only in any practical implementation but also at the level of philosophical argument. What behavior on the part of anyone is required to meet the demand that he be "his brother's keeper"?

IV. America, Europe, and the Death Penalty

My provisional hypothesis is that the United States and the nations of Western Europe (for this purpose, including Canada) differ substantially

---

[7] The Rawlsian construction closely parallels that of James M. Buchanan and Gordon Tullock, *The Calculus of Consent: Logical Foundations of Constitutional Democracy* (Ann Arbor: University of Michigan Press, 1962), although for a quite different analytical purpose. In the Buchanan-Tullock construction, observed institutions of redistribution in post-constitutional politics emerge from consensus at the constitutional level derived basically from insurance motives.

in the mix between the ethical foundations I have been discussing—one based on equality, the other on hierarchy. All of these countries qualify as welfare democracies, and all are described by large collectively financed transfer sectors, thereby extending the scope of political activity well beyond the financing and provision of productive state services. These transfer sectors are proportionately larger in Europe than in America, but not sufficiently so to warrant categorical distinction.

Differences in the mix between the two contrasting ethical presuppositions need exert little influence on the continuing political debates concerning the size of transfer sectors in the separate national economies. Argument may be joined related to the extension or contraction of these sectors and may proceed from either one of the two ethical positions. The advocates of welfare-state expansion may call on a Rawlsian evaluation to criticize the limits of collective redistribution, invoking the presumption of natural equality of persons behind the veil of ignorance. Other advocates may base their criticism of observed margins on more direct claims to the effect that those who are privileged in the natural hierarchy are obligated, on grounds of charity and benevolence, to support extended collective aid to those who are naturally inferior. And, of course, a similar comparison applies to the other side of the continuing political debate. Supporters of contraction in the size of the transfer sector (or opponents of further extension) may base their arguments on either one of the two ethical positions: the position that postulates natural equality or the one that postulates, explicitly or implicitly, natural hierarchy.

Things may become quite different, perhaps dramatically so, when we shift our attention to discussions and evaluations of collectively imposed punishments for violations of the law. Whereas the differing implications of the two ethical presuppositions seem rather innocuous in discussions about changes in the size of the welfare state, these implications may become major barriers to mutual understanding in treatments of punishment. In the setting of interaction among persons as imagined by Smith, Kant, and Rawls (the world of natural equality), the principles upon which the institutions of punishment are established emerge either from a disembodied impartial spectator or from a stylized contractual dialogue. No person is identifiable in advance as a potential transgressor, but each also recognizes that some persons (possibly including himself) may become such transgressors. These principles, this "constitution," is chosen and put in place *before the fact*, before any violation of law occurs. In this conceptualization, neither the disutility (or utility) of those who impose the punishment nor the disutility of those who are punished, *after the fact* of law violation, enters into the calculus. Indeed, those who are punishing and those who are being punished are by definition indistinguishable at the previolation stage when the institutions are put in place.

As noted previously, this idealized construction provides a bridge that allows individual self-interest to be reconciled with something like a general interest. Punishment institutions emerge from a setting in which persons are not asked to or required to evaluate other people. Postviolation utilitarian considerations, whether involving some aggregation in the classical sense, or evaluations restricted to the level of individual participants in the process, have no place in the logical structure. A person who violates a law suffers the previously agreed penalty; he has no recourse in pleas to the benevolence or compassion of others who abide by the law.

Criteria for evaluating the observed institutions of punishment are strictly procedural. Did these institutions emerge from a constitutional consensus? Or, failing this, could they have emerged from the judgments of a genuinely impartial spectator or from some idealized contractual agreement among natural equals? Put in this way, it seems evident that any observed set of institutions is one among many that might qualify under these procedural norms. There is no unique solution that emerges.[8] Nevertheless, the criteria remain sufficiently robust to rule out punishment that is differently applied to differing groups of law violators, regardless of utilitarian measurements.

In contrast, consider now the theory of punishment that is grounded on the presupposition of natural hierarchy rather than that of natural equality. On its face, the whole conception of equality before the law, the rule of law itself, does not sit well with those who view the human spectrum in hierarchical terms. If, indeed, persons can be classified on some scalar of inherent superiority-inferiority, the legal treatment accorded different persons and groups would be different, on almost any criterion of acceptability. And such differentiation in treatment would, of course, extend to participation in collective decision making. There is no logical basis for universal and equal franchise under the Platonic vision of human society.

At best, therefore, there is an uneasy accommodation between the stance of those who adopt the hierarchical starting point and the established institutions of Western democracies, all of which embody the rule of law in its varying manifestations. The ethical disjuncture here comes to the foreground of discussion when the institutions come into operation, and notably when these institutions imply that law violators should be subjected to punishment, after the fact of law violation itself. The very act of breaking the law allows for a classification between the lawbreakers and "others," and the more or less natural reaction is to treat the first group differentially and to determine levels of punishment that seem to be dictated by considerations of post-act utility, that of the law-abiders and the lawbreakers as aggregated in some fashion. Levels of punishment that might have been agreed upon in the stylized "constitutional" setting, in which persons behind the veil of ignorance consider themselves or are considered equal as potential lawbreakers, may lose effective force if the

---

[8] See James M. Buchanan, *The Limits of Liberty: Between Anarchy and Leviathan* (Chicago: University of Chicago Press, 1975), for extended discussion of the argument in this section.

dialogue is opened up for post-act judgments, whether privately assessed or collectively determined. Compassion and charity for those who have come to be personally identified as criminals must enter into such judgments; the anonymity made possible by the construction of the veil can no longer be fully effective.

The two contrasting ethical positions may generate predictably differing attitudes toward punishment in particular cases, with the subsidiary hypothesis that, in the twenty-first-century moral environment of Western democracies, lawbreakers are likely to suffer less onerous punishment when the ethical mix tends toward the Platonic as opposed to the Smithian-Kantian-Rawlsian position. Compassion toward those classified as "inferior" may be dominant in modern ideas and practices, perhaps reversing attitudes that may have described earlier epochs.

The argument may be exemplified in contemporary attitudes toward capital punishment, where European and American positions seem to differ substantially. Surface examination of the public as well as academic discourse would seem to suggest that Europeans, generally, condemn the institutions of capital punishment, which they consider to be the heritage of the quasi-anarchistic, pre-civil environment of the frontier society that was America. By contrast, in the United States, there is no general consensus on the appropriateness of the death penalty, either at the level of open discussion or in legal practice (some of the American states allow for capital punishment; others do not).

Americans might argue, in contraposition, that European attitudes and practices embody residues of the medieval heritage, which did involve classification of persons and groups into classes, movement among which, occupationally and geographically, remains relatively difficult. Any overt effort to derive principles from a world-of-equals perspective would seem to violate basic understandings of the human interaction process. That is to say, the attempt to impose the natural-equality presupposition on human reality would be more "jarring," and hence less effective, than in the American setting.

Absent such a perspective, however, how could the basic principles that guide punishment be derived? Clearly, what is left here is some Benthamite utilitarianism that must take into account a calculus of utilities, positive and negative—a calculus that recognizes that persons differ from one another in their prospects for law violation, in their compassion both for those who are victims and for those who themselves break the law, and in their post-act utility reactions on observation of punishment itself. Persons will, of course, differ along each of these, and other, dimensions, but it is not surprising that, for many, capital punishment, even for the most heinous crimes, would not secure approval in this mind-set. What seems surprising, to Americans, is the consensus that Europe appears to have attained on what seems, at best, to be a stance upon which reasonable persons may disagree.

I should emphasize that the death penalty, even if restricted to the most heinous crimes, need not describe the stylized outcome of the contractual process conducted by reflective persons situated behind a veil of ignorance, or even the judgment of Smith's impartial spectator. Such a penalty may or may not emerge, as current American discourse and practice suggest. The point of emphasis is, rather, that the death penalty cannot, *ex nihilo*, be ruled out as being inconsistent with principles of justice derived from the presupposition of natural equality.[9] To Americans, the extent to which the death penalty, as such, is emplaced in the institutions of punishment becomes a matter for continuing political dialogue, which proceeds within the presupposition that, by their very existence, the institutions in place imply at least tacit consent. There is nothing that seems to warrant the apparent consensus that describes modern European attitudes in this respect.

V. Conclusion: Implications for Global Justice

Unless it is derailed by the still unresolved and wholly unexpected emergence of terrorism, globalization, in a meaningfully descriptive sense, will proceed apace, as driven by technology as well as efficiency. Increasingly, persons and groups will find it advantageous to interact, economically and socially—to "trade"—with other persons, groups, and organizations beyond the confines of historically defined political units. The movement toward integration of the world economy seems inexorable.

This movement toward inclusiveness of the whole economic nexus will necessarily be accompanied by an increase in relevant "border crossings," in which the legal structures of separate political units come into conflict. Contractual arrangements which are valid under some systems will be invalid under others. Persons who would be deemed to be law violators in one country may not be so judged in another. Citizens in one jurisdiction may seek asylum in others. Damage claims against value produced in one country may be challenged, if such claims are mounted from outside the national limits.

These and many other institutional frictions must bring with them increased demands for more widespread agreement on some set of international conventions. Attention must increasingly be paid to problems of formulating principles for "global justice." Conflicts will be exacerbated

---

[9] Many will recall the TV miniseries *Lonesome Dove* based on the novel by Larry McMurtry, *Lonesome Dove* (New York: Simon and Schuster, 1985). In the narrative, Gus and Woodrow, former Texas Rangers, are driving a herd northward across the Great Plains to Montana. Along the way, they capture a gang of horse thieves, among whom, to their surprise, they find their former Ranger colleague, Jake Spoon. They proceed to hang Spoon, along with the other horse thieves, because such thievery is a capital crime. They show no compassion for their friend and treat him no differently from his partners in crime. Nor does Spoon himself expect to be treated differently; instead, he acquiesces in his fate. He has broken the law; he accepts the consequences.

and agreement on enforceable conventions will be made more difficult to the extent that the mix between the two ethical foundations for interpreting social interaction varies from one country to another. Institutional practices or the lack thereof which seem to violate precepts of justice derived largely from the hierarchical perspective may be broadly acceptable from the procedurally derived base of presumed natural equality.

Conflicts seem especially likely to arise as the economies of developing countries come to be more fully integrated into the world nexus. Practices that cannot be condemned by the generality norms inherent in the natural-equality framework of evaluation may fail to pass muster when evaluated by the more substantive criteria invoking treatment of identified unfortunates. For example, labor standards, or the absence thereof, which are applied without discrimination may yet be deemed "unjust" by those who cannot share, even conceptually, in the veil-of-ignorance experiment as it might be carried out within the developing country itself. This putative extension of the European welfare-state norms for "justice" is, of course, reinforced by the protectionist coalitions who rely on such arguments for domestic political purposes.

For any level of discourse, it remains always difficult to reconcile considerations for justice among equals with considerations for justice among unequals. Such difficulties surface more or less necessarily in any treatments of "global justice." The argument of this essay may be summarized in the claim that potential conflict across national political boundaries will be lessened only to the extent that the Enlightenment presupposition of man's natural equality, applied among the citizens of each separate nation-state, comes to dominate, and ultimately to sublimate, the Platonic vision of natural hierarchy.

Economics, Center for Study of Public Choice, George Mason University

FEUDING WITH THE PAST, FEARING THE FUTURE: GLOBALIZATION AS CULTURAL METAPHOR FOR THE STRUGGLE BETWEEN NATION-STATE AND WORLD-ECONOMY

By Irving Louis Horowitz

I. Introduction

No sooner has the issue of globalism been elevated into a general proposition of paradigmatic dimensions, than its death has been declared. In *Harper's*, the journalist John Ralston Saul states simply enough that not only is there a "collapse of globalism," but also a "rebirth of nationalism." He is only the most recent to post an obituary.[1] My own sense of the situation is that the language of "tendencies," "strains," and "forces" better represents reality than the heated rhetoric of "birth" and "death." The international economy is not reduced to rubble by ideological missives, nor has the national state been dissolved by the recognition that the world is whole, round, and virtually boundless.

Globalization has been perceived either as the latest and most pernicious form of imperialism or as the latest form of modernization. Whatever position one takes on globalization—whether one is in mute support or unabated opposition—it is clear that globalization has become not just a thing unto itself, but a metaphor of fundamental values of peoples and systems alike. My purpose here is to examine how this term has become part of the polarization of the American culture. The controversy over globalization has become a struggle over the shaping of the world's economy, but it is also a political and cultural struggle. In this process, old battles between political systems and economic structures have acquired new dimensions. But the struggle remains recognizable to past and present generations alike. In order to keep from converting a brief examination into a metaphorical exegesis, I will limit my illustrations to specific technological developments in fields such as electronics, transportation, and communications. In this way, the cultural meanings of globalization can be better understood by such references to quotidian affairs as are required for practical purposes.

---

[1] John Ralston Saul, "The Collapse of Globalism: And the Rebirth of Nationalism," *Harper's* 308, no. 1846 (March 2004): 33–44.

II. Views of Globalization

Perhaps the most prominent theorizing on this subject is an approach that sees in globalization an extension—one hundred years later—of the Hobson-Lenin theory of imperialism.[2] Taking up the alarms of the Leninist persuasion in particular is the political scientist William I. Robinson, who in a new book offers a theory that global integration is the epitome of a new capitalist class and a new type of social formation that moves beyond immediate profit-making and beyond national boundaries. In this vision, global capital mobility has allowed capital to reorganize production worldwide in accordance with a wide range of considerations that allow for maximizing profit-making activities.[3] This decentralization and fragmentation of the production process has taken place alongside the centralization of command and control of the global economy in transnational capital. In turn, this economic reorganization finds a political counterpart in the rise of the transnational state.

In direct contrast to this hegemonic-colonial hypothesis, the economist Philippe Legrain in a new work claims that the theory of globalization has been entirely misrepresented. It does not eliminate local affairs or make governments irrelevant. On the contrary, the return to protest groups and street politics only complicates the need to address globalization as a serious element in the international economy. In this view, globalization is a positive good for modernization, a mechanism whereby all major factors in the economic equation—workers, companies, governments, national economics, industry and agriculture, patents and profits, money and finance—are free to choose a future course of action that maximizes benefits for all on a world stage. There is the broad assumption among economists that post-national capitalism, or economic globalization, encourages everything from healthy competition to regional alignments and shared standards.[4]

The polarization of opinion on globalization has inclined many outstanding economists and social scientists to "navigate a position between the polar alternatives" of a dark vision at one end and an upbeat world at the other. The fine economist and policy advisor Murray Weidenbaum

---

[2] John A. Hobson was the author of a work entitled *The Evolution of Modern Capitalism,* which initially appeared in 1894. It was a critique of new forms of capitalist expansion (imperialism) predicated on banking and commercial fusions across national lines. It was widely used by Vladimir I. Lenin in his own work on imperialism. Lenin acknowledged the primacy and importance of Hobson, but sharply criticized Hobson's attachment to John Stuart Mill and reformist tendencies in British economic doctrine at the close of the nineteenth century. See V. I. Lenin's review of Hobson's work, published in 1899 in the magazine *Nachalo* (Whole Number 5), reproduced in *Lenin: Collected Works* (Moscow: Progress Publishers, 1964), vol. 4, pp. 100–104.

[3] William I. Robinson, *A Theory of Global Capitalism: Production, Class, and State in a Transnational World* (Baltimore, MD: The Johns Hopkins University Press, 2004).

[4] Philippe Legrain, *Open World: The Truth about Globalization* (Chicago: Ivan R. Dee, Publisher, 2004).

exemplifies this middle ground. While arguing the virtues of globalization, especially the rise of a competitive environment, Weidenbaum recognizes the problems that have been created as well: unfair competition from low-cost sweatshops, increased pollution of the environment caused by transportation of goods over long distances, and the starvation of entire populations in the midst of the opulence that exists in the relatively few advanced societies. His solutions tend toward the standard set offered by economists in the policy field: reform of the World Trade Organization (WTO), the creation of new jobs for those put to pasture as a consequence of technological unemployment, and the strengthening of the International Labor Organization (ILO) as a means for establishing worldwide standards on labor laws and regulations. At a more informal level, globalization makes possible giving ordinary people a greater voice in decision making through the Internet. Citizens can expect more information from authorities, and there is a growing independence of the communications system from reliance on government.[5] This is clearly a vision stimulated by the American experience, although policy developments in former totalitarian regimes support this view of what might be called globalization from below—a mechanism to link globalism with democracy.

The problem with these sorts of palliatives, and with Weidenbaum's final recommendation—that the number of conflicts around the world could be diminished by holding global summits—is that these recommendations are simply national policies writ large, on a global scale. They presuppose a common framework of legal and moral relations that people throughout the world hold in common. Of course, it is precisely the issue of what people hold in common, whether there is an acceptance or rejection of globalization, that requires careful review. In a universe of terror bombings, suicide attacks, and indiscriminate hostility to Western values, one is hard put to prove the case for modest policy measures that might have trouble working even within the confines of a Midwest U.S. community. In short, while Weidenbaum and other economists are correct to note that the anti-imperial and pro-rational arguments are not particularly new, neither is the middle-way option especially persuasive or compelling.

Extremists and centrists alike are looking through a crystal ball into an indeterminate future and seeing either what they dislike or what they like. My own thinking leads me to believe that globalization as a political-economic force is an ongoing process that aims to create common world standards in the electronics and communications industries. To a large extent, this process is well underway, with the United States, Germany, and Japan taking the lead, and other nations such as the United Kingdom,

[5] Murray Weidenbaum, "Globalization: Wonderland or Wasteland?" *Society* 39, no. 5 (July–August 2002): 36–40. See also Murray Weidenbaum, *One-Armed Economist: On the Intersection of Business and Government* (New Brunswick, NJ, and London: Transaction Publishers, 2004).

India, China, and South Korea functioning as active participants. Even such thinking has become something of a platitude, however. Differences that arrive at the level of economic rationalization reflect attitudes toward the marketplace as such, and reflect little dispute as to the actual nature of the changes involved.

However, globalization as a political culture is a realm unto itself. To see globalization as an imperfect equilibrium (or for that matter, as an unsteady equation) between the international economy and the national state systems, is to miss the central point of the process well underway—and that point is the radical transformation in the cultural climate ushered in with the new century. This is best illustrated by a globalization of terrorism, its fusion of well-trained insurgents with manifestly criminal elements. This political culture puts on display a vivid fusion of well-financed organizations, well-trained operatives, cross-national groups that are united in language and theology rather than nationalism and ideology, and groups trained in the use of weapons of mass destruction. Globalization provides for a political culture with an extralegal set of rules and regulations.

Nor should this new political culture be seen as necessarily or uniformly violent or in opposition to the economic system. Even the most placid variety of new tendencies can be described by the cultural and social phenomenon of globalization: a new classicism in music, with "world-class styles" at its core; simplified modes of personal dress that stress private comfort over status identification; automobile styling that again reflects an international standard of everything from owning a factory to driving a vehicle; currency reforms that pose transnational options to older nation-grounded currencies; and above all, standards of performance identified with specific corporate responsibilities—responsibilities for providing service, repair, and innovation in one fell swoop. In some curious ways, members of the younger generation that attacks globalization as an ideology of imperialism are the ones who have most strongly embraced its benefits: cellular telephones, high-speed messaging and traveling, and a fierce move to overcome ethical, legal, and national obstacles to the assertion of personal desires. The political culture is one in which claims of rights are unfettered while statements of obligations are often muted and barely heard above a whisper.

The emergence of globalization changes political equations, since traditional extreme Left and Right both rely heavily upon cultural styles based on folklorist (*volkish*) lifestyles. With the rise of world-class systems comes the emergence of world-class cultures, and that signifies the early collapse of inherited modalities based on the folk song or the jazz tune. Traditional cultural formations are easily absorbed and taken up and incorporated into the new music. Similar patterns are underway in painting, dance, and architecture. With regard to architectural projects, competitions for new designs are now increasingly international, entered into by individuals who may have roots far removed from the country where the project will be built. Not only are designs becoming universal, so too are reviewing committees with professional competence to judge submitted designs. In short, the struggle between civilizations, and within societies, involves an acceptance of globalization as a fact and of modernization as a consequence. The choice between the acceptance and the rejection of globalism and modernity has become the alpha and omega of the present cultural struggles between Western secular societies and Middle Eastern religious cultures.

III. Rationalization

There are two distinct ways of understanding the concept of rationalization and what it means with respect to globalization. A system may be rationalized when some rule of reason is imposed on the system as a whole: for example, through the establishment of a bureaucratic or administrative apparatus. This is a top-down imposition of order. Alternatively, one can understand the free market as a rational process in that it makes possible efficient resource allocation, and conveys information rapidly and accurately. This might be viewed as a bottom-up characterization. While it might be desirable for both meanings to be tightly wrapped, the fact is that many varieties of political systems and economic arrangements are compatible with rationalization in the first sense. Global interchanges require common standards in everything from electrical grids to automotive emissions; as a consequence, the rationalization process is a requirement for all nations wishing to partake in and derive advantages from the international economy.

Because so much writing on globalization comes from the pens of social scientists and economists, these actual technological trends on the ground are neglected or sorely reduced in importance. The path of globalization seems to be rooted more in past struggles between the free market and the controlled market environments of post–World War II Europe than in a realization of just how radically transformed the new integration of communication, culture, and economy has actually become. The issue of globalization is not resolved by policy mandates issued by the WTO or the ILO, or even constraints on international trade, but by the wide recognition that changes in culture already indicate and presage what is in store. To study culture as a local or national trait, and then ignore the same factors in examining the world at large, is a dangerous form of intellectual myopia—one to be avoided at the policy level. This brings me to the essential core of my own position on globalization as the expression of a fusion of culture and economy.

The automobile industry may offer the best illustration of this near inexorable tendency toward technological rationalization. The automobile is arguably the most singular pragmatic and aesthetic product that involves members of every social and economic class. Despite tremendous nationalist pressures in the United States to "buy American" after the attacks of September 11, 2001, the very concept itself dissipated in the face of global realities. Treaties such as the North American Free Trade Agreement (NAFTA) and the General Agreement on Tariffs and Trade (GATT) just about mandate that transnational companies may design and develop a car in one country, set up assembly lines in another country, and then build the car from components sourced from yet other countries. A company's sales efforts may be directed toward the market of yet another country, while multinational banks finance the company's loans. In addition, ownership arrangements have become part of a world system. Daimler-Benz owns Chrysler; Nissan of Japan is controlled by Renault of France; Rolls-Royce, the former symbol of British upper-class good living, is built by BMW. The Swedish Saab is a subsidiary of General Motors.[6]

Specific automobiles are themselves globalizing. Dodge Caravans carry Mitsubishi motors; Saab upscale cars carry Volkswagen downscale parts; and components from air-conditioning to radio packages are exported from Mexico to Japan. While national differences are revealed in everything from emission standards to actual exterior designs, these differences have been steadily reduced over the years. Auto manufacturers have been forced to merge and to forge alliances to limit overlapping costs and to share technology. The same desire to reduce costs and rationalize products has permitted Honda, Toyota, Mazda, Subaru, and Isuzu to set up shop in Ohio. German and Korean automakers are now profitably ensconced in Alabama. The impact on American auto manufacturers has been to sharply improve production and product to match the level of quality of imported automobiles in every detail. The J. D. Powers Quality Survey now ranks Buick, Cadillac, and Mercury at the same level as Lexus, Infiniti, and Acura. In addition, an industry that in an earlier era was dominated by American cars has now had to allow for nonunion workers in its midst. The estimates are for one in four automobile workers to be outside the fold of the United Automobile Workers, with many of these nonunion personnel employed in newly created positions.[7]

---

[6] Dana Frank, *Buy American: The Untold Story of Economic Nationalism* (Boston: Beacon Press, 1999). For his examination of Japanese and American auto manufacturers, see pp. 160–86. A recent and skillful update of global patterns in this industry is contained in Peter Bohr, "American Made?" *AAA World,* January–February 2004, 38–45.

[7] If one includes foreign auto manufacturers with branch plants in the United States, one in four autoworkers are already outside the UAW fold. Beyond that, while employment in Michigan increased from 3.8 million to 4.2 million (from 1992 to 2002), union membership declined 10 percent during the same period. UAW trends are not exempt from this trend; indeed, the data indicate that with a decline in domestic auto firms, the overall decline in union membership is slightly higher than an already high norm. See the annual report of the Mackinac Center for Public Policy (Midland, Michigan), Report number 5368, issued in 2003.

Preferences in automobiles are thought to reveal national differences: for example, Americans generally are thought to prefer larger cars with greater horsepower, and Japanese smaller cars with lesser horsepower. Yet even this is rapidly changing. Asian and European automobiles are clearly appealing to an American audience, and the desire of Asians and Europeans for bigger cars seems to be growing. Nearly every major auto manufacturer provides a full range of autos to maximize audience appeal with respect to size, styling, comfort, and electronic accessories to assist drivers. Indeed, the technological demands for uniformity of standards often lead to sociological demands for greater stylistic differentiation. And while globalization severely limits nationalism, it also may serve as a stimulant to design uniqueness as a selling tool. Once all of these elements are taken into account, it becomes evident, or at least it should, that globalization is to imperialism what music is to martial tunes—a distant cousin. When Nissan becomes the local car of choice in Mississippi, it is hard to sustain hoary arguments predicated on an American octopus. Beyond that, in old and new industries alike, one witnesses a cross-fertilization of firms that requires us to distinguish globalization from Americanization. For example, in publishing, of the ten largest firms in dollar volume in the United States, nine are owned by European conglomerates (especially conglomerates based in Germany, The Netherlands, and the United Kingdom). If the twentieth century was defined as the American Century, it might well be that the twenty-first century will become the Asian and/or European Century. One might say that we have a case of old wine in new bottles, but it is no less a case of new wine in old bottles. Behemoth exists, but in terms that easily and readily move beyond the old nation-state.[8]

IV. MODERNIZATION

Why, then, should globalization have become the centerpiece of bitter contention? My own response, and one that I believe is verified by the evidence, is that globalization represents modernization as such. There is a fear of the new—the rejection of a highly secularized environment, one in which both religious fanaticisms and political ideologies have very little compelling power—that sustains the social movements that now abound. Indeed, the attractiveness of products that range from automobiles to computers to high-definition television both competes with and limits the potency of traditional political environments. It serves to remind the mullahs of all sorts that globalization carries with it secularization.

[8] Irving Louis Horowitz, *Behemoth: Main Currents in the History and Theory of Political Sociology* (New Brunswick, NJ, and London: Transaction Publishers, 1999); see esp. the concluding chapter, "Between Politics and Economics: Welfare State versus Global Economy," 449–66.

Some nations, such as Saudi Arabia and the United Arab Emirates, face a series of quandaries that make them vulnerable on all sides. Their leaders derive oil revenues from the sale of commodities, but also lend their support to religious fundamentalism as a way of life. So many new products and technological innovations appeal to the individual and the family, without requiring support or approval from theological and/or political leaders. Such demands for personal satisfaction do not easily square with collective celebrations or pilgrimages. And the Middle East in particular is faced with globalization as an ideology and not just a series of new products and innovations.

Modernization is less a system than a process. It has a near-infinite variety of formations. Taken as a whole, however, it opens up prospects for change that cannot easily be bottled or contained. The ferocity with which the enemies of modernization have responded to these processes is well exemplified in the Middle East. By the same token, the enthusiasm with which these same modernizing tendencies have been embraced by many Asian nations—even those with ostensibly anticapitalist political regimes—indicates that nations that wish to compete (or at least participate) in the modern world system find themselves virtually compelled to accept modernization as a fact on the ground if not a theorem in the realm of theological and ideological disputation.

V. STANDARDIZATION

The problem of modernization is an old one, involving the difficulty of reconciling contemporary and traditional lifestyles and social values. But globalization also entails a search for common or universal standards in a cacophony of national differences. In certain areas, such as the provision of electricity, a modus vivendi has been reached, where three or four different outlets and two types of currents are widely if not universally utilized. However, once we move beyond the engineering of goods into the conveyance of services, the problem of globalization becomes thorny.

One admittedly small, but nonetheless significant, illustration of this problem is the controversy over governmental regulation of mental-health professionals in France. It is a problem that exists in nearly every advanced society and relates to the impact of regulation on the cost and quality of services. In this particular case, the French government wants to institute regulations for professional conduct in the treatment of patients and wants to root out what it considers to be unlicensed charlatans. The psychoanalysts—some twenty thousand strong—hold that such a move is an assault on private practice and that it amounts to regulation of what shall be considered proper treatment. It is the French version of the struggle between chemical treatment and couch treatment of those in need of mental-health services. Within a single nation this is a difficult issue, but at least manageable. When it becomes a matter of globalization, then the issue of culture itself becomes implicated in settling both economic and ethical claims.

As those who have studied the social regulation of professional practice have pointed out, if the European Union now mandates uniform standards for the licensing of physicians so as to insure portability across national boundaries, this mandate may have a range of unexpected consequences. For example, it may require that Italy "create" an independent profession of dentistry (whereas previously dentistry was carried out by licensed physicians). Similarly, what implications does the French proposal to regulate mental-health professionals carry for the development of a licensed profession of psychoanalysis in, say, Germany or Ireland? One can multiply such hypothetical situations to near infinity: from modes of dress in public places, to the languages to be used in conducting official transactions. If globalization can be seen as a set of universals, a form of rational imposition across borders, the same view can hardly be advanced for the cultural realm—a terrain in which distinctions of language, folk traditions, religions, and ethnicity continue to loom large.

VI. Old Cultural Wine in New Ideological Bottles

The close of the Cold War, or more positively, the triumph of the free market (with or without a corresponding move to democratic rule), brings with it its own compelling reasons for a desire on the part of peoples everywhere to become part of a new power equation. The emergence of the United States as the unique superpower, paralleled by the growth of the European Union, also compels a reluctant acceptance of globalization, even on the part of those smaller nations that have few such ambitions. Backwardness may be a fine situation for a society that sees its future bound up with inherited religious and cultural traditions. But in an epoch of aggressive development—economic as well as political—the attack on globalization carries huge risks to the internal stability of societies. Young people in particular—the very individuals most likely to protest globalization—are the ones most caught up in the process of embracing styles from Milan, cellular phones from Helsinki, airbuses from Paris, sneakers from Jakarta, jeans from San Francisco, electric shavers from Munich, and so on over a huge range of products that define a culture. Moreover, this process occurs with little notice paid to repetition or even quality control, much less to the source of the goods being absorbed.

The dissolution of the bipolar world of the United States and the USSR, and the imagined emergence of a unipolar world in which the United States emerges culturally dominant, intensifies uniform standards and, even more, a sharing of the product innovations that flow from market developments. Over the past half-century, in one part of the world after another, U.S. influence has moved into the vacuum left by the Soviets and other departing powers. The drive to share in new systems of communication and transportation overwhelms even the most profound faith in traditional mores. Often with reluctance (as in the Middle East), not always with success (as in Vietnam), but in any case as the preeminent option among several alternatives (as in South Korea, Singapore, and Kuwait), smaller nations and economies link their future with globalization as a process rather than linking their future with any larger nationalist aspirations.

What America shares with earlier empires is an insufferable sense of mission. What distinguishes it is the total conviction that it is a force for good in world affairs. Any force for change, good or bad, presents a challenge to an existing order, and brings resentment with it. That would be enough to raise hackles. But America represents a special type of challenge to the world. That challenge has been recognized, feared, resented, and finally hated by those less favored in world affairs. From a frontier era, when it appeared to be an ungovernable land with an inhospitable climate; to the nineteenth-century European conceit that America was a failed society, racked by vices obsolete in Europe (like slavery); to the triumph of American economic expansion and military power, the success of what is now the world's sole superpower has caused anti-American resentment to become a frontal assault against globalization. The actual reduction in American power that results from globalization is disguised by the visible signs of that power—from fast-food franchises to electronic systems.

America as a new society, pioneered by the huddled masses of other nations' teeming shores, aggregating the energies of its mixed population and outperforming all others in virtually every branch of modern human endeavor, is less acceptable than a new imperium. America's early critics thought its people would grow malnourished and weak. Later critics thought its racial divide would be its undoing. Others doubted its capacity for concerted action, viewing it as a nation to be despised rather than feared. Add to this a popular culture—replete with junk food and a surfeit of popular movie fare that leaches like a solvent at aristocratic, landed cultures—and the discontented in many lands will see a mortal threat to their way of life.

That some multinational goods and services may be marked "made in the USA" might be an irritant to some purists, but for the most part, children wearing sweatshirts that say *Dallas Cowboys* in a language unknown to the wearer, see such garb as liberating—as an identification with the idea of personal freedom rather than with a political system. Seen in this way, as an offshoot of the dominant cultural representations, globalization's friends best view it as a fusion of culture and economy in an era of advancement in the technologies of production, distribution, and communication. At the same time, it is viewed by its enemies as a fusion of industry and culture in an era of latter-day imperialism.

It is significant to point out that the forces of the traditional culture, the values of family and community, and the practice of identifying the political system with religious fervor, will not dissolve easily. It is not simply that theocratic systems of backward nations will move to rally about the state as a source of resistance to globalization; in less overt ways, so too will democratic systems of advanced nations see the state as a mechanism to preserve adhesion to the sacred values of the political community that give the idea of nationhood its compelling force. Indeed, in such advanced states, places where appeals to religion and to national, regional, and parochial values are becoming increasingly ineffective mechanisms of social solidarity, the state will become the focal point of the struggle against globalization—that is, against the new economy coming into being worldwide, with little regard to national boundaries or organic solidarities.

The essential contradiction of the new millennium is shaping up as a struggle to control the culture as such. For without such control, economic forces in search of development are likely to flounder and falter. By the same token, the political forces that tend toward the preservation of continuity are also likely to be swept aside if they mindlessly embrace globalization. The dilemma is clear enough: the power of the state derives from the strength of the economy, from the revenues it provides to make war and finance welfare programs (and hence maintain loyalty). The state cannot simply stand in opposition to globalization. What it can do is establish a system of controls (not unlike those proposed by the economic centrists mentioned earlier) to contain, to bridle, the most rapacious features of change—without applying a stranglehold. At the same time, the forces of the global economy can and will continue to develop mechanisms that make the state seem irrelevant, such as worldwide networks of communication that sweep away national boundaries and cultural constraints.

What we are left with is old wine in a new bottle. We have returned to well-trodden areas of controversy over what really matters: community or civilization, personal choice or public necessity, and yes, the bureaucratic state or the freewheeling economy in search of becoming a law unto itself. Whether those young people carrying placards denouncing globalization realize that they are the representatives of convention and tradition, the carriers of the ancient traditions of law and order, is itself a type of high irony. That the demands of "radicals" should lead down the primrose path of conservative values of law, order, and folk traditions is not quite as strange as it may first appear. After all, the twentieth-century totalitarian political movements, such as Nazism, Fascism, Communism, and the like, revealed the capacity of the state to mobilize its forces, and even modernize them, in an effort to hold back destabilizing tendencies toward unbridled behavior and unsanctioned belief.

This is now well appreciated. Less well understood is how the state assumes a monopoly over the legal process as well as the political process—and how, in that capacity, the state can, when necessary, use this power to bite the bourgeois hand that feeds its own insatiable appetite for control over economic growth. The state must regulate not only competing economic forces, but also distinct sectional groups and ethnic rivalries. But the prize in this struggle of modern titans is nothing less than the culture itself. In that sense, the pathetic protests and parades against globalization may well be the last hurrah of those for whom the culture is a free-floating entity in its own right. While the outcome of these multifaceted struggles remains hard to predict, one thing is certain: there are new permutations and combinations of allies and enemies being forged in this struggle to define and delimit the nature of globalization.

VII. A Post-Marxian Postscript

It is interesting to return to the works of Marx and Lenin, since my thesis on the fundamental schism between the state and the bourgeoisie was both anticipated and rejected in the writings of the communist sages. For his part, Marx (in *The German Ideology*) well understood that "[t]he bourgeoisie itself, with its conditions, develops only gradually, splits according to the division of labor into various fractions, and finally absorbs all propertied classes it finds in existence." Marx makes the point that such schisms cease "only insofar as they [i.e., members of the bourgeoisie] have to carry on a common battle against another class; otherwise they are on hostile terms with each other as competitors." The instrument by which internal divisions yield to the larger struggle against the revolutionary classes as such is nothing other than the state: "The State is the form in which the individuals of a ruling class assert their common interests, and in which the whole civil society of an epoch is epitomized."[9]

The forces of what Marx liked to call "real" (as opposed to "abstract") history have not been kind to the old master of communism. Divisions of mental and physical labor have dissolved under the impact of new technologies; the great divide of rural and urban life has all but disappeared in post-industrial society; and the legal scaffold of the state has served more to level differences than to accentuate them. The pessimistic predictions of the diminishing relevance of labor have also fallen by the wayside. It is precisely the capacity of the state to serve civil society as a whole that has enabled it to bridle the bourgeoisie. The opponents engaged in the struggle may be evenly matched, but it is by no means a struggle that dissolves in the presence of revolutionary factions. Indeed, these factions themselves take refuge on either side of the cultural divide: as the mass base of a state seeking to preserve classical values or as the elite vanguard of the global economy. In short, the state, the very mechanism

---

[9] Karl Marx and Frederick Engels, *The German Ideology* (1845–46), in *The Marx-Engels Reader*, 2d ed., ed. Robert C. Tucker (New York and London: W. W. Norton and Co., 1972–1978), 146–200.

that Marx saw as the balance wheel of civil society, is itself in a full-fledged struggle for its centrality in a globalized economy.

Lenin, for his part, valiantly sought to defend Marx from the charge of obsolescence. In *Imperialism: The Highest Stage of Capitalism,* Lenin sets forth the thesis that differences between capitalist countries "only give rise to insignificant variations in the form of monopolies or in the moment of their appearance." Lenin held that the start of the twentieth century corresponded with the shift from industrial capitalism to international banking, a time when "[c]ompetition [became] transformed into monopoly." It was a shift from "the domination of capital in general to the domination of finance capital." Lenin spoke at considerable length of monopoly capitalist associations, cartels, syndicates, and trusts—elements of what is now referred to as globalization. He also appreciated the degree to which new developments, such as electrification, brought about new forms of cooperation between major nations, or simply new levels of "the economic division of the world." In short, "imperialism is the monopoly stage of capitalism." Lenin refined and embellished this definition to include ample space for "the formation of international monopolist capitalist associations which share the world among themselves." [10]

Oddly enough, Lenin breaks off the analysis at this point and does not explain how the state mediates these various international bourgeois claims. Only in his polemical essay *The State and Revolution* does he offer even a rudimentary coming to terms with the state "as an instrument for the exploitation of the oppressed class." As a consequence, Lenin deals with the relation between the two mighty forces of economic class and political power only in the most abstract terms. Puzzling out the nature of this relation became a task for post-Marxians such as Georges Sorel, Robert Michels, Gaetano Mosca, Ferdinand Toennies, and, above all, Max Weber. Once Lenin denied the state a role as an agent of reconciliation, and reaffirmed only its antagonistic social characteristics, the problem remained how the global capitalism envisioned in *Imperialism* was to be arranged or by whom. The effort to study the state became clumsy the more the polemics of repression substituted for analysis of the economic system as such. The study of the state became a matter of the "practical politics" of arranging the dictatorship of the proletariat for the revolutionary process. The issue of the modern economy, however, was lost in this political shuffle by Lenin.

The problem lies in locating the contemporary discourse within a Marxist framework—determining how an instrument such as the state, which

---

[10] Vladimir I. Lenin, *Imperialism: The Highest Stage of Capitalism* (1917), in *The Lenin Anthology,* ed. Robert C. Tucker (New York and London: W. W. Norton and Co., 1975), 204–74. The same anthology contains Lenin's 1916 polemic *The State and Revolution,* 311–98. Since the two works were written only one year apart, differences in style and substance, and above all, the near utter failure to see the connections between state and economy, can hardly be overlooked.

drives inexorably toward absolute national control, can accommodate the international economy. The latter, too, drives toward absolute control. This essay is not intended as an exercise in general socialist theory, but rather to show how the ideological tradition that harbored such theorizing failed precisely to explain the relationship of the forces that it took as its starting point. One is left with two giant forces (the state and the economy) that coexist in separate realms, with presumably similar aims (the oppression of the working people), and yet with little evidence of interaction. I submit that the reason for this is that to have developed such a model of state-economy competition would have reduced the theory of proletarian revolution to sheer ash; the system of stratification would have led to class alignments within the economy (proletariat) and also within the nation-state (bureaucracy) that would have highlighted the struggle between the public and the private sectors. To have done this would have brought Marxism closer to reality but would have left it farther removed from its goal: world revolution.

This remains the problem with those who advocate a mindless end to globalization. Apart from the emptiness of the slogan, there is the vacuity of the attempt to install a social contract that could scarcely move beyond old-fashioned anarchist doctrine—a world without state or administrative power. This approach ignores the fact that, as the social philosopher Steven Grosby reminds us, globalization in the form of empires is a long-standing tradition.[11] I have offered this postscript, not to belabor problems in the theory and practice of communist doctrine, but to indicate the more serious and practical problem for those who—in the name of general theory or world revolution—would carry out a frontal assault against the rationalization and standardization embodied in globalization. In a world where the locomotive was the highest expression of technology (Marx), or one in which electricity was its highest expression (Lenin), one could still compartmentalize categories and avoid dealing with cross-national networking. In a world in which electronic communication and international air travel are routine, such compartmentalization is simply not feasible—at least not without revising the political process as a whole.[12]

VIII. CONCLUSION

The relationship of economic systems to political orders must be dealt with seriously, and not treated as an opportunity for polemics among

---

[11] Steven Grosby, "The Fate of Nationality," *Society* 42, no. 2 (January–February 2005): 15–20.

[12] See Russell D. Howard and Reid L. Sawyer, eds., *Terrorism and Counterterrorism: Understanding the New Security Environment* (Guilford, CT: McGraw-Hill/Dushkin, 2004). This collection is distinguished by an emphasis on the globalization of terror. The essays by Bruce Hoffman and the editors are of exceptional worth; see pp. 2–85 and 243–308.

ideological enemies. My remarks in this essay are an attempt at such an effort at macro integration. The references to Marx and Lenin are simply intended to move beyond where the discourse within socialist circles on the connection of state and economy broke off a century ago—only to be amplified and enriched (but hardly resolved) within capitalist circles as exemplified by the various branches of the Austrian school of economics, from Joseph Schumpeter to Ludwig von Mises. The various responses to globalization can perhaps best be viewed as the latest installments in the nearly two hundred years of struggle in advanced European societies (now joined by American and Asian nations) in their love-hate relationship with state power (at one end) and their search for economic development (at the other). One is entitled to presume that those whose strongest passions are rooted in past political and economic arrangements will not resolve the big issues of the new stage in international political economy. My own, admittedly biased view, influenced by the late and great social philosopher Lewis S. Feuer, is that political culture, with its emphasis on nationalism, religiosity, and ethnicity, trumps inherited theories of political economy as an autonomous activity.[13] In addition, the analysis of world systems by pure theorists of the subject has proceeded in disregard of the relatively autonomous developments in science and technology. However, in a postmodern environment, it is precisely the emergence of such new formations and structures that has shaped economies.

In conclusion, we are each entitled to view critically the long history of exploitation and arrogance that is linked to forces that extend beyond local or national boundaries. The ambitions of modern economic and political forces are hardly unqualified examples of rationalization. To view this history critically, however, requires that we look with equal frankness at the no less onerous history of exploitation and domination linked to parochial institutions and so-called nongovernmental agencies aimed at human betterment. The liquidation of human beings in the name of global justice or its quasi-juridical equivalent does not entitle advocates of nationalism to a special place of honor. Quite the contrary: a democratic vision burdens both ideologies, nationalism and globalism, with the task of locating mechanisms for avoiding past mistakes.

There is no geographic or economic monopoly on heavy-handed extreme ideologies that preach democracy but deliver sophisticated varieties of dictatorship. I am myself inclined to the view of the Catholic theologian George Weigel: "History is driven, over the long haul, by culture—by what men and women honor, cherish, and worship; by what societies deem to be true and good, and by expressions they give to those convic-

---

[13] Lewis S. Feuer, *Ideology and the Ideologists* (Oxford: Basil Blackwell, 1975); see esp. "The Re-Anthropomorphism of the World," 17–20.

tions in language, literature, and the arts; by what individuals and societies are willing to stake their lives on."[14] A flinty vision of modern history is one that needs to be learned and observed by internationalists and nationalists alike. The tough-minded and the tenderhearted alike should cling to the belief that victory belongs to what ordinary people crave, not to what grandiose ideologies claim.

Sociology and Political Science, Rutgers University

---

[14] George Weigel, "Europe's Problem—and Ours," *First Things* 140 (February 2004): 18–25.

TOWARD GLOBAL REPUBLICAN CITIZENSHIP?

By Waldemar Hanasz

I. Introduction: The Republican Renaissance

The growing popularity of civic (or classical) republicanism can hardly be unnoticed. Numerous studies attempt to demonstrate not only that republican ideas were extremely influential in the past—in republican Rome, Renaissance Florence, or Revolutionary America—but also that they offer us an inspiring perspective on how to perceive political thinking today. In particular, republicanism is often seen as a leading alternative to both liberalism and communitarianism. Some scholars have gone as far as to speak of a historical "paradigm shift," a "republican revival," or a "republican turn" in political thought.[1]

Inspired by Hannah Arendt, two historians of ideas, J. G. A. Pocock and Quentin Skinner,[2] initiated the revival of civic republican theory, and soon many others followed. Philip Pettit, John Braithwaite, Maurizio Viroli, Nicholas G. Onuf, Cass Sunstein, John Maynor, Iseult Honohan, Michael Sandel, and Adrian Oldfield, to name a few, have developed the ideas of republicanism in a variety of areas.[3] They have established a contemporary version of the classical theory and have emphasized the extra-

---

[1] See Philip Pettit, *Republicanism: A Theory of Freedom and Government* (Oxford: Oxford University Press, 1997), 4; Cass R. Sunstein, "Beyond the Republican Revival," *The Yale Law Journal* 97, no. 8 (1988): 1541; and G. E. White, "Reflections on the Republican Revival: Interdisciplinary Scholarship in the Legal Academy," *Yale Journal of Law and Humanities* 6 (1994): 1. With respect to the relative merits of republicanism and liberalism, some authors make very strong claims. According to Maurizio Viroli, for instance, "liberalism can be considered an impoverished or incoherent version of republicanism, but not an alternative to republicanism." See Maurizio Viroli, *Republicanism*, trans. Antony Shugaar (New York: Hill and Wang, 2002), 61.

[2] J. G. A. Pocock, *The Machiavellian Moment: Florentine Political Thought and the Atlantic Republican Tradition* (Princeton, NJ: Princeton University Press, 1975); Quentin Skinner, *The Foundations of Modern Political Thought*, 2 vols. (Cambridge: Cambridge University Press, 1978); Quentin Skinner, "The Paradoxes of Political Liberty," in Sterling M. McMurrin, ed., *The Tanner Lectures on Human Values* (Salt Lake City: University of Utah Press, 1986).

[3] Pettit, *Republicanism*; John Braithwaite and Philip Pettit, *Not Just Deserts: A Republican Theory of Criminal Justice* (Oxford: Oxford University Press, 1990); Viroli, *Republicanism*; Nicholas G. Onuf, *The Republican Legacy in International Thought* (Cambridge: Cambridge University Press, 1998); John W. Maynor, *Republicanism in the Modern World* (Cambridge, MA: Polity Press, 2003); Adrian Oldfield, *Citizenship and Community: Civic Republicanism and the Modern World* (London and New York: Routledge, 1990); Sunstein, "Beyond the Republican Revival"; Iseult Honohan, *Civic Republicanism* (London: Routledge, 2002); Michael Sandel, *Democracy's Discontent: America in Search of a Public Philosophy* (Cambridge: Cambridge University Press, 1996).

ordinary importance of its historical roots. New republicans treat very seriously the wisdom of the old masters and attempt to show its vitality. They constantly refer to Cicero, Montesquieu, James Harrington, Jean-Jacques Rousseau, Alexis de Tocqueville, and Alexander Hamilton, among others. Niccolò Machiavelli, however, remains the towering authority and the main source of inspiration. The publication of Pocock's *The Machiavellian Moment: Florentine Political Thought and the Atlantic Republican Tradition* (1975) brought with it a renewed interest in Machiavelli's political thought. In the view of Skinner, Machiavelli's ideas remain "by far the most compelling presentation of the [civic republican] case,"[4] and many writers admire Machiavelli's *Discourses on Livy* as the magnum opus of classical republicanism.

The civic republican tradition offers a conception of citizenship that is based on the ancient Roman ideas of the *res publica*, *virtus*, and *civitas*.[5] According to that tradition, the good life is possible only in a commonwealth, the *res publica*, where individuals live together, free from external aggression as well as internal tyranny. Only in such a state can citizens enjoy their lives in liberty and mutual respect. The rule of law is the main tool of protection. A variety of republican institutions—a constitutional framework, a system of representation, a mixed government, and checks and balances—make the whole system stable and secure.

However, these formal political institutions could not function effectively without a deeper moral background. In order to sustain the free community and to make it secure, citizens must conscientiously exercise their duties and responsibilities. Citizens must be politically active, voice their views in public forums, and perform public service. Civic *virtus*, a commitment to the *res publica*, provides citizens with the moral energy to participate in political activity. To participate, citizens have to be loyal, righteous, and courageous; their emotional commitment to the commonwealth is crucial. Values and virtues must be deeply rooted in the hearts and habits of the citizens.

The civic community, the *civitas*, is a union of the political institutions of the *res publica* and individual civic engagement, the *virtus*. In order to build such a union, the republic must actively strive to shape its citizens in a politically effective way, through some form of civic education. Compulsory public education is one such form, and most classical republicans also view religion as an effective tool of civic education and as a source of political morality.

---

[4] Quentin Skinner, "On Justice, the Common Good, and the Priority of Liberty," in Chantal Mouffe, ed., *Dimensions of Radical Democracy: Pluralism, Citizenship, Community* (London: Verso, 1992), 216; cf. Philip Pettit, "Negative Liberty, Liberal and Republican," *European Journal of Philosophy* 1, no. 1 (1993): 31.

[5] Thus, in a recent book, *Liberty before Liberalism* (Cambridge: Cambridge University Press, 1998), Quentin Skinner characterizes the republican tradition as "neo-Roman."

If, as some argue, globalization is "the defining feature of human society at the start of the twenty-first century,"[6] then the status of civic republicanism in the modern world demands scrutiny. In particular, the notion of citizenship deserves special attention. Citizenship is the centerpiece of the republican tradition, and it remains the focus of recent theoretical discussions proposing a new concept of global citizenship.[7] Contemporary republican theorists claim that their traditional theoretical framework can be readily adapted to the new reality of the global world, and my intention in this essay is to explore the viability of this claim. I argue that a number of serious limitations make the republican conception of citizenship unable to satisfy the requirements of a world of globalization. The traditional ideas of civic republicanism—the stress on strong patriotic identity and high demands of public service, the rhetorical approach to individual rights and political participation, the multiple functions of the republican state, among others—are hardly ever adjustable to the global reality. Attempts to incorporate concepts of contemporary political theory into republican thought— for instance, the models of deliberative and contestatory democracy—are usually inconsistent with the old tradition.

In what follows, I attempt to examine the role of civic republican theory in a global world. I organize my discussion around several components associated with the notion of citizenship:[8] (1) The members of a political entity share some common identity. (2) They share a set of specific rights and liberties. (3) They share goals that require certain responsibilities. (4) Active involvement and political participation are necessary to realize these goals. (5) The ultimate goal of political activity is to build a community, a civic body. In the following five sections, I explore each of these components in turn.

II. POLITICAL IDENTITY

The cosmopolitan idea of political identity has been well known since antiquity.[9] Citizenship has often been identified with human civility. Soc-

---

[6] John Beynon and David Dunkerley, eds., *Globalization: The Reader* (London: Athlone Press, 2000), 3.

[7] See, e.g., Darren J. O'Byrne, *The Dimensions of Global Citizenship: Political Identity beyond the Nation-State* (London: Frank Cass, 2003); Derek Heather, *World Citizenship and Government: Cosmopolitan Ideas in the History of Western Political Thought* (New York: St. Martin's Press, 1996); and April Carter, *The Political Theory of Global Citizenship* (New York: Routledge, 2001).

[8] Darren J. O'Byrne distinguishes "four essential components": membership, rights, duties, and participation; Stuart Hall and David Held identify "three leading notions": membership, rights and duties in reciprocity, and real participation in practice. I have synthesized their classifications into a more comprehensive set. See O'Byrne, *The Dimensions of Global Citizenship*, 5-10; Stuart Hall and David Held, "Citizens and Citizenship," in Stuart Hall and Martin Jacques, eds., *New Times: The Changing Face of Politics in the 1990s* (London: Lawrence and Wishart, 1989), 175-76.

[9] Cf. Heather, *World Citizenship and Government*, 1-59; and Carter, *The Political Theory of Global Citizenship*, 11-32.

rates called himself "a citizen of the world." According to Democritus, "the home of a great soul is the whole world"; hence, wise men belong to all countries. Zeno and other Stoics viewed all men as their "fellow-countrymen." In the Middle Ages, the Catholic Church claimed to be a united Christian community. Renaissance thinkers advanced similar ideas. In *The Education of a Christian Prince,* Erasmus referred to the *res publica Christiana.* Francis Bacon, Justus Lipsius, and Michel de Montaigne looked upon "all men as compatriots." As travel and trade increased, these philosophical ideas reflected a changing world that grew beyond borders. Merchants, bankers, priests, artists, musicians, teachers, philosophers, and mercenary soldiers journeyed all over Europe and did not identify themselves as the subjects of any French or Dutch or Italian ruler.

The classical republicans of the Renaissance were well acquainted with the cosmopolitan trend that had gained currency during the Middle Ages and was embraced by many of their contemporaries, but republicans explicitly rejected this trend. Machiavelli passionately declared that he loved Florence more than his own soul.[10] *The Prince* subverted the idea of a Christian state founded on universal moral values. Republicans identified themselves with their polity and its values. The cultivation of patriotic solidarity and loyalty created a strong collective bond—a sense of unity and integrity that made living together possible.

Contemporary republicans continue the classical legacy. Political theorist Michael Sandel emphatically rejects globalization: "Despite its merits . . . the cosmopolitan ideal [of democracy] is flawed, both as a moral ideal and as a public philosophy for self government in our time."[11] In particular, cosmopolitan values do not have the same motivating power as patriotism. In discussing patriotism, Philip Pettit remarks upon "the unchosen nature of [patriotic] identification": such "identification is not an intentional initiative but something that comes to people as naturally as breathing."[12] "Habitual" and "natural" civility are part of a republic's cultural heritage. Every member of the community should acknowledge and cherish that heritage since "this is where you are coming from: *this is what you are.*"[13] Political theorist Iseult Honohan compares the civic community to the family, with its distinctive emotional and moral ties.[14]

In both its classic and its contemporary versions, the republican notion of patriotic citizenship is quite exclusionary in character. The strong collective identity that republicans seek to cultivate does not accommodate other identities and values. Republican civic morality is in many respects hostile to nonrepublican values. For Machiavelli, the Roman republic's

---

[10] Niccolò Machiavelli, letter to Francesco Vettori, April 16, 1527, in *The Chief Works and Others,* ed. and trans. Allan Gilbert (Durham, NC, and London: Duke University Press, 1989), 1011.

[11] Sandel, *Democracy's Discontent,* 342.

[12] Pettit, *Republicanism,* 258.

[13] Ibid., 257.

[14] Honohan, *Civic Republicanism,* 268.

ability to impose its civil values on other peoples was even more glorious than its power to conquer them. Political philosopher Charles Taylor argues that modern states require their citizens to exhibit "much greater solidarity toward compatriots than toward humanity in general."[15] Maurizio Viroli puts it strongly: "[M]y patriotism is explicitly particularistic, because it describes love of country as the citizens' passionate love of their republic's institutions and way of life."[16]

Contemporary republicans realize that today the only form of passionate patriotism is nationalism, which is often incompatible with toleration and pluralism. Taylor accepts nationalism as a natural implication of patriotism: "Civic humanism requires a strong identity with a community and the nation is the community of modern times."[17] Honohan worries that "the nation is an inadequate substitute for participation; it does not generate the sense of responsibility in citizens in areas where it matters,"[18] but then she realistically admits that "it is hard to find examples of places where citizens do see themselves as bound together without some kind of national commonality."[19] Others try to establish a moderate line of "enlightened patriotism." Viroli tentatively argues that love of country "easily extends beyond the national borders and translates into solidarity."[20] He envisions a kind of "rooted republican patriotism" that is supposed to be "patriotism without nationalism."[21] Pettit claims that patriotism, properly understood, is an admiration of "my country for the values it realizes."[22] It seems to be Pettit's tacit assumption that a republican patriot would never face a dilemma when his country pursues values that he does not admire. For classical republicans, such a dilemma did not exist: the common interests of the *res publica* should always prevail. Machiavelli brutally declared that human lives could be sacrificed when the common interest was at stake. Preemptive strikes could be used to crush potential opponents; innocent citizens could be sacrificed to appease an angry mob. It is hard to imagine that Pettit would accept such conclusions.

Obviously, those who hope that global citizenship becomes a realistic objective would rather see the evolution of political identity go in a quite

[15] Charles Taylor, "Why Democracy Needs Patriotism," in Joshua Cohen, ed., *For Love of Country* (Boston: Beacon Press, 1996), 120.

[16] Viroli, *Republicanism*, 14.

[17] Charles Taylor, *Reconciling the Solitudes*, ed. Guy Laforest (Montreal: McGill-Queen's University Press, 1993), 42. Cf. David Miller, *On Nationality* (Oxford: Oxford University Press, 1995); David Miller, "Bounded Citizenship," in K. Hutchings and R. Dannreuther, eds., *Cosmopolitan Citizenship* (Basingstoke: Macmillan, 1995); and Ross Poole, *Nation and Identity* (London: Routledge, 1999).

[18] Honohan, *Civic Republicanism*, 279.

[19] Ibid., 280.

[20] Maurizio Viroli, *For Love of Country: An Essay on Patriotism and Nationalism* (Oxford: Oxford University Press, 1995), 12; Honohan, *Civic Republicanism*, 270.

[21] Viroli, *Republicanism*, 14; cf. Margaret Canovan, "Patriotism Is Not Enough," in Catriona McKinnon and Iain Hampsher-Monk, *The Demands of Citizenship* (Cambridge: Cambridge University Press, 2000).

[22] Pettit, *Republicanism*, 260.

different direction. After all, despite the continuous turmoil of national-istic and ethnic movements, there are some indications that national iden-tity has been losing its dominant status.[23] The relationship between one's citizenship and one's nationality is becoming less rigid, and in some cases the link between the two is merely symbolic. For many people, citizen-ship is no longer inherited for life but becomes a matter of choice. The citizens of one country live and work in other countries. Some have dual citizenship. Their overlapping identities are no longer strongly attached to a specific nation, language, and territory. Instead, many nonnational and nonterritorial identities have emerged. Individuals identify them-selves as environmentalists, pacifists, human rights activists, gays and lesbians, and so forth. As global issues attract more attention, people become more aware of international interests and more disposed toward international cooperation. The meaning of patriotism has evolved in a similar fashion. As national identity has become less intense, it has become more tolerant, less exclusionary, and less prone to fanaticism. The ele-ments of national and local identities have not disappeared but have become weaker. The ideas of "enlightened patriotism," "constitutional patriotism," and "civic cosmopolitanism" have emerged as hopeful alter-natives. Political activists appeal to "global consciousness" and seek "com-mon identity."

The conflict between republican and global identities is unavoidable and acute. Timid attempts to propose the concept of "republican plural-ism" or "patriotism without nationalism" merely paper-over the contra-diction. For republicans, universal moral values are too abstract to motivate citizens to engage in civic activity. Members of a global community would be less politically engaged than citizens of the *res publica.* They would lack healthy feelings of collective unity, solidarity, and civic *virtus.* Almost by definition, global citizenship flies in the face of the civic spirit.

III. Rights and Liberties

Contemporary politics is firmly grounded on the ideas of human and political rights. Most international organizations have defined their goals and policies in those terms. In 1948, the United Nations General Assem-bly adopted the Universal Declaration of Human Rights. The 1966 Cov-enant of Economic, Social, and Cultural Rights, the 1975 Helsinki Accords, and other international agreements have further developed the universal standards of rights and liberties. These documents reiterate the funda-mentals: freedom of speech, conscience, and religion; the free exchange of ideas; protection of the rights of minorities; the right to travel internation-

---

[23] Cf. Maryann Cusimano Love, ed., *Beyond Sovereignty* (Belmont, CA: Thomson-Wadsworth, 2003); Stephen D. Krasner, *Problematic Sovereignty: Contested Rules and Political Possibilities* (New York: Columbia University Press, 2001); and Gerard Delanty, *Inventing Europe: Idea, Identity, Reality* (London: Macmillan, 1995).

ally; and so on. Currently, a great number of international organizations—the International Court of Justice, the Red Cross, Amnesty International, the World Health Organization, and the UN Educational, Scientific, and Cultural Organization (UNESCO), to name just a few—are deemed, despite many problems, to protect these rights.

It would be hard to overestimate the enormous influence of international human rights agreements. They have systematically pressured nondemocratic states to respect the rights of their citizens. Governments who have violated international standards of human rights have compromised their own legitimacy. For anti-Communist activists in Eastern Europe and the Soviet Union, the Universal Declaration of Human Rights and the Helsinki Accords were powerful weapons against Communist ideology and propaganda. In a sense, the agreements contributed to the collapse of the Communist empire. Today, in Iran, Myanmar, Sudan, and China, the standards of universal human rights help to rein in autocratic regimes. It seems almost self-evident that political globalization will continue that historical process. The universality of individual rights transcends the confines of national, ethnic, religious, and civil identities. The ideals of global citizenship and global community bring with them aspirations toward the unification of all human beings independently of their identities as Spaniards, Tutsis, Sikhs, Jews, and so on. A citizen of the world has to respect the universal rights of others, and his rights have to be universally respected.

Just as civic republicans disregard the ideal of global identity, they also disregard the notion of universal rights. When they use the concept of rights, it is merely a legal concept, not a philosophical or moral one. It is a concept that follows the Roman legal tradition. "Rights are in fact only rights if custom or law recognizes them as such and are therefore always historical, not natural," writes Viroli.[24] "In the republican view," Honohan adds, rights "will not be formulated in terms of absolute boundaries.[25] Even the rights to privacy or property "are not absolute or primary."[26] The *res publica* grants rights and privileges to its citizens, and it has the authority to trump those rights when public interests make it necessary to do so. Clearly, as Pettit observes, "republicanism cannot be represented by any stretch of the imagination . . . as a tradition of rights akin to that which is sometimes associated with liberalism."[27]

This approach to rights is deeply rooted in the classical republican heritage. Republicanism has been strongly connected with the rhetorical

---

[24] Viroli, *Republicanism*, 60.

[25] Honohan, *Civic Republicanism*, 194.

[26] Ibid., 194, 209.

[27] Pettit, *Republicanism*, 303–4; cf. Honohan, *Civic Republicanism*, 206–11; Skinner, *Liberty before Liberalism*, 19–21; and Viroli, *Republicanism*, 60–63. Most republicans are very critical of political theorists, such as Richard Dagger or William Galston, who combine liberal rights and republican virtues. Cf. Richard Dagger, *Civic Virtues: Rights, Citizenship, and Republican Liberalism* (Oxford: Oxford University Press, 1997); and William Galston, "Liberal Virtues," *American Political Science Review* 82 (December 1988): 1277–90.

tradition of antiquity and the Renaissance.[28] Both Cicero and Machiavelli were champions of rhetorical eloquence, and modern-day republicans continue that tradition, arguing that the key tool of republican political reasoning is not rational analysis but effective rhetorical persuasion. According to Viroli, contemporary republicans need to rediscover a piece of "classical republican wisdom": "political theory is a department not of philosophy, or law, or science but of rhetoric."[29] For republicans, "[e]valuations of all political actions tend to be partisan, subjective, driven by passion; disputes in the real world are neither scientific nor philosophical." The goal of republicans is not "to ascertain or demonstrate the truth"[30]—because there are no universal moral values or truths for which to argue. The common good, justice, and freedom are just "regulative ideas that political deliberation should aim at, though what this implies in practice will be different in each case."[31] Thus, rhetorical discourse is the domain of moral relativism.[32] On this view, when political opponents appeal to rights, what they have in mind never goes beyond partial interests. Political actors use the language of rights only when it serves their interests. Viroli makes it clear that, in political debate, ideological bias and manipulative propaganda are both unavoidable and useful. From the republican point of view, the Sophists decisively won the ancient debate with Socrates.

The notion that eclipses rights-oriented thought in classical and contemporary republicanism is liberty. Both Quentin Skinner and Philip Pettit build their interpretations of classical republicanism on the basis of this central notion—and for good reason. The classical republican tradition refers to the Roman legacy of *libertas* and *civitas*, a community of free citizens. In the Renaissance, republicans revitalized that heritage. As Pocock demonstrates, Machiavelli, Francesco Guicciardini, and Donato Giannotti were the key figures in this revival. Contemporary republicanism's challenge to liberalism inevitably leads to a debate over the concept of freedom.

The idea of republican liberty has evolved into several versions, but two of them have emerged as the most cogent: liberty as *self-government* and liberty as *nondomination*.[33] Charles Taylor and Quentin Skinner have developed the self-government version. Skinner reminds us that the ancient republican paradigm of *libertas* and *civitas*, revived in the Renaissance as *vivere libero e civile*, establishes "an intimate connection between the defense

---

[28] Jerrold Seigel, *Rhetoric and Philosophy in Renaissance Humanism* (Princeton, NJ: Princeton University Press, 1968); Eugene Garver, *Machiavelli and the History of Prudence* (Madison: University of Wisconsin Press, 1987).

[29] Viroli, *Republicanism*, 18; cf. Pettit, *Republicanism*, 187–90.

[30] Viroli, *Republicanism*, 55, 92.

[31] Honohan, *Civic Republicanism*, 24.

[32] Peter Levine, *Living without Philosophy: On Narrative, Rhetoric, and Morality* (Albany: SUNY Press, 1998); Robert Hariman, ed., *Prudence: Classical Virtue, Postmodern Practice* (University Park: Pennsylvania State University Press, 2003).

[33] Iseult Honohan's concept of "republican political autonomy" is a combination and elaboration of both ideas. See Honohan, *Civic Republicanism*, 180.

of free communities and the capacity of individual citizens to secure and maximize their own liberty." The connection is very tight: "the one is a necessary condition of the other." Thus, within the classical tradition, "the discussion of political liberty is generally embedded in an analysis of what it means to live in a 'free state'." [34]

The state is free when its citizens are free to decide how to live, when they participate in their own system of self-rule. Charles Taylor interprets the connection this way: "[W]e cannot do what we really want, or follow our real will, outside a society of a certain canonical form, incorporating true self-government. It follows that we can only be free in such a society, and that being free *is* governing ourselves collectively according to this canonical form." In other words, "freedom involves at least partially collective self-rule." [35] As Skinner notes, "a self-governing republic is the only type of regime under which a community can hope to attain greatness at the same time as guaranteeing its citizens their individual liberty." [36] Individual freedom is not possible without collective freedom understood as self-government. Needless to say, the conception of liberty as "self-government" or "collective self-rule" is for Taylor and Skinner a key alternative to the liberal conception of the freedom of the individual to make choices.

The other concept of republican liberty, nondomination, has been developed by Philip Pettit. [37] Most recent republican theory revolves around this concept. [38] On Pettit's view, an agent is free when not under someone else's domination, that is, when not subject to someone else's capacity to interfere in an arbitrary manner in the choices the agent should make himself. Pettit adds that liberty as nondomination is not a mere lack of domination; it is itself a form of power to act: "It represents a control that a person enjoys in relation to their own destiny and such control constitutes one familiar type of power: the power of the agent who can prevent various ills happening to them." [39]

A defining feature of nondomination is its difference from the liberal "negative" conception of liberty as noninterference. The two concepts overlap but are not identical. An agent may interfere in another agent's actions yet not dominate him. Since only arbitrary interference qualifies as domination, the agent who legitimately interferes due to fair principles or democratic laws is not engaging in domination. In particular, when it

---

[34] Quentin Skinner, "On Justice, the Common Good, and the Priority of Liberty," in Chantal Mouffe, ed., *Dimensions of Radical Democracy: Pluralism, Citizenship, Community* (London: Verso, 1992), 221, 216.

[35] Charles Taylor, "What's Wrong with Negative Liberty," in Alan Ryan, ed., *The Idea of Freedom* (Oxford: Oxford University Press, 1979), 181, 178.

[36] Quentin Skinner, "The Paradoxes of Political Liberty," in David Miller, ed., *Liberty* (Oxford: Oxford University Press, 1991), 197.

[37] Pettit, *Republicanism*, 51–79; Philip Pettit, *A Theory of Freedom* (Oxford: Oxford University Press, 2001), 138–51.

[38] In his recent book *Liberty before Liberalism*, even Quentin Skinner presents a view on republican liberty that is very close to Pettit's.

[39] Pettit, *Republicanism*, 69.

is not an individual but a legal institution or a democratic political body that interferes, the intrusion is not considered domination. At the same time, it is possible to be wholly dependent on and subservient to another and yet free from interference. Pettit illustrates this point with an allegory of a master-slave relationship. It is possible to imagine a slave with a very permissive master. The slave may be allowed to do practically anything, but behind his activity there is always the master's capability to intrude without any respect for the slave's interests and wants. That potential power is arbitrary and dominating.

Both conceptions of republican liberty—self-government and non-domination—face serious difficulties. For Taylor, Skinner, Viroli, and Adrian Oldfield, the superiority of collective liberty over individual liberty is undeniable. No member of the republic can achieve the common good fully "without its being achieved for all members."[40] Collective self-government is "a necessary condition" of individual liberty, and a republican constitution is "the only type of regime" that ensures liberty. Republican thought contradicts the liberal philosophy of individual freedom: "republicans speak of societies as the primary subjects of freedom, individuals as the secondary, so that individuals count as free in virtue of the freedom of their society, and not vice versa."[41] In his most elaborate presentations of the ideal of nondomination, Pettit pays relatively more attention to the individual side of republican liberty, but that does not alter the fundamental thesis: "freedom as non-domination is a communitarian ideal."[42] For Oldfield, too, republicanism is a form of communitarianism.[43] Collective interests should prevail, and an individual can be forced, in his own best interest, to choose wisely; as Skinner writes, "the enjoyment of our personal liberty may often have to be a product of coercion and constraint."[44] Yes, declares Taylor, "men can, in short, be forced to be free."[45] In addition, as I have indicated, the republican emphasis on rhetoric transforms liberty, individual as well as collective, into a mere device of political persuasion. It is ultimately a matter of subjective judgment which institutions serve self-government and which political agents have the potential to be dangerously dominant. Those political actors who are rhetorically more skillful and persuasive are able to impose their own normative judgments. Finally, as we will see in the next section, for republicans, collective duties easily override individual liberties.

It seems hard to imagine how global citizenship could be based on principles steeped in moral relativism and collective partiality. One can-

---

[40] Ibid., 259.
[41] Pettit, "Negative Liberty, Liberal and Republican," 32.
[42] Pettit, *Republicanism*, 144.
[43] See Oldfield, *Citizenship and Community*, chap. 1 and passim.
[44] Skinner, "The Paradoxes of Political Liberty," 247.
[45] Taylor, "What's Wrong with Negative Liberty," 175; cf. Skinner, "The Paradoxes of Political Liberty," 229, 235; and Quentin Skinner, "Machiavelli's *Discorsi* and the Pre-Humanist Origins of Republican Ideas," in Gisela Bock et al., eds., *Machiavelli and Republicanism* (Cambridge: Cambridge University Press, 1990), 295.

not be a citizen of the world if one's individual goals and values are secondary to multiple group interests, local community values, and national policies. Moral and civic norms, even if they are not intended to be universal, lose their meaning when subject to ideologically biased interpretations and partisan rhetoric. The republican model of liberty (in either version) seems to remain at odds with the idea of global citizenship.

IV. GOALS AND RESPONSIBILITIES

Republican citizenship is not about rights but about the common good and the duties associated with achieving it. The common good is the ultimate goal of the republic and the essence of republican citizenship is commitment to this goal. Laws and civic institutions protect the common good; political activity is directed toward it. To depict the republican understanding of the ultimate goal of citizenship, modern-day republicans constantly return to their classical forerunners. Every study of republicanism begins with an extensive presentation of its historical context, and in particular, Machiavelli's thought.[46] For Machiavelli, "it is not the particular good but the common good (*bene comune*) that makes cities great. And without doubt the common good is not observed if not in republics." According to him, the ancient founders, such as Moses, Lycurgus, or Solon, established laws "for the purpose of the common good," and every prudent ruler should have the same intent. The Roman people, as "lover[s] of the glory and common good of [their] fatherland," were the perfect model of spirited citizenship.[47]

Contemporary republicans continue the tradition but struggle to define the common good. The notion includes a complex set of goals and values: the satisfaction of communal needs, liberty, the rule of law, security and strength, civic spirit and unity, dignity and honor. The rhetorical approach makes the complex notion even more difficult to untangle. After all, both the common good and its various components are just regulative ideas that, in political practice, "will be different in each case."[48] The republic's common good may have an entirely different meaning at different times and contexts. Iseult Honohan accepts such vagueness as inevitable and proposes a pluralistic model of this key notion: "if there is not a single common good, or goal of society, there are *common goods*."[49]

The common good requires high standards of responsibility. When there is a conflict between one's liberties and one's duties, the choice is

---

[46] See Honohan, *Civic Republicanism*, 13–144; Maynor, *Republicanism in the Modern World*, 20–32; Pettit, *Republicanism*, 17–50; Pocock, *The Machiavellian Moment*, 156–218; Viroli, *Republicanism*, 21–34; and Onuf, *The Republican Legacy*, 31–109.

[47] Machiavelli, *Discourses on Livy*, II 2, I 9, I 58. For a modern edition, see *Discourses on Livy*, trans. Harvey C. Mansfield and Nathan Tarcov (Chicago: University of Chicago Press, 1996).

[48] Honohan, *Civic Republicanism*, 24.

[49] Ibid., 150–58.

simple: "Republicanism does give a heavier weight to duties as they are better guides to action for citizens."[50] Both self-government and non-domination are unattainable without individual motivations that make civic actions effective. Skinner writes:

> A self-governing republic can only be kept in being . . . if its citizens cultivate that crucial quality which Cicero had described as *virtus*, which the Italian theorists later rendered as *virtù*, and which the English republicans translated as civic virtue or public-spiritedness. The term is thus used to denote the range of capacities that each one of us as a citizen most needs to possess: the capacities that enable us willingly to serve the common good, thereby to uphold the freedom of our community, and in consequence to ensure its rise to greatness as well as our individual liberty.[51]

This motivation to serve the common good is a theme that runs through the writings of contemporary republicans. Viroli appeals to "the passions that political liberty needs."[52] Sandel refers to "the moral energies of a vital democratic life."[53] Since only a free and strong republic can guarantee individual liberty, in order to be truly free we have to, in Skinner's words, "devote ourselves wholeheartedly to a life of public service."[54] Political institutions serve the common good and so should every citizen. Citizens should fulfill their duties with comprehension and commitment. It should go without saying that such service overrides individual freedoms. Skinner openly admits the enigmatic character of the relationship between service and freedom: "Public service, paradoxically enough, constitutes our only means of ensuring and maximizing our own personal liberty."[55]

The relationship between liberty and strong civic responsibility goes both ways. The republic's security, freedom, law, and order must rely on the principles of good citizenship. Good citizenship flourishes in a free and secure community. Civility needs freedom, freedom needs civility.[56] The republic is founded on citizens' emotional involvement, dedication, and public-spiritedness. It needs an intense sense of responsibility, self-

[50] Ibid., 206–7.
[51] Skinner, "The Paradoxes of Political Liberty," 242.
[52] Viroli, *Republicanism*, 12.
[53] Sandel, *Democracy's Discontent*, 24.
[54] Skinner, "On Justice, the Common Good, and the Priority of Liberty," 217, 222. Cf. Skinner, "The Paradoxes of Political Liberty," 197.
[55] Skinner, "On Justice, the Common Good, and the Priority of Liberty," 222. For Machiavelli and James Harrington, public service meant mainly military service and other demanding duties, so it could be necessary to coerce some citizens to participate. Again, it could be necessary "to force them to be free."
[56] Interesting comments on this subject can be found in Onuf, *The Republican Legacy*, 44–45.

constraint, patriotism, loyalty, courage, solidarity, and commitment. Liberal normative neutrality, as republicans see it, "is not a real option." [57]

A part of that spirited commitment is what republicans usually call "vigilance." "The price of liberty is eternal vigilance," writes Pettit.[58] In order to protect freedom and to prevent corruption, virtuous citizens should monitor public officers, authorities, and lawmakers. Citizens should stay alert and be ready to act in case they see that the *res publica* is in danger of corruption or abuse of power. Historically speaking, the ideas of civil militia and the right to bear arms are the republican instruments of political protection. Pettit argues that such vigilance may be very helpful today in order to make people aware of important issues (for instance, issues related to environmental protection). Vigilant citizens should be ready to act if such matters are neglected by authorities.

Modern-day republicans do not discuss the historical origins of the idea of vigilant citizenship because they are clearly uncomfortable with it, and rightly so. For Machiavelli and other classical republicans, public service meant, first of all, military service. Courage and discipline were key virtues because public service could require making the ultimate sacrifice. To die for the republic was to achieve eternal glory. Most importantly, public service was not only about defending the state's freedom. External conquest was a vital goal of a free republic: glorious victory was one of the greatest goals—if not *the* greatest goal—of the *res publica.* A free state was a regime superior to an autocratic princedom because freedom generated more power. As Machiavelli put it, republics had two major goals: remaining free from the domination of others and conquering them. Free states did not just enjoy their freedom; they either conquered or were conquered, since they were constantly pressed to compete with neighbors who were nothing but potential threats or victims. "The end of the republic is to enervate and to weaken all other bodies so as to increase its own body," Machiavelli wrote. Republican Rome, for instance, "became a great city through ruining the surrounding cities." [59] In the name of a free republic, on this view, virtuous citizens have to be not only alert and vigilant but also militant and powerful. Hence, such values as global peace or worldwide cooperation are left undiscussed by contemporary republicans, because such values do not express the republican civic spirit. Such values were significant to Erasmus and Kant, but not to Machiavelli and Harrington.

To be fair, it seems that the republican notion of civic virtue does have something to offer today. The challenges of global development are demanding and impose pressing responsibilities on the citizens of the global world. Engagement in international projects and institutions can no longer be founded on the traditional structures of authority and obe-

---

[57] Honohan, *Civic Republicanism,* 265.
[58] Pettit, *Republicanism,* 250.
[59] Machiavelli, *Discourses on Livy,* II 2, II 3.

dience. The global communications system makes cooperation between distant agents routine. Dispersed political and economic institutions generate networks of connections between people who never meet and often remain anonymous. The monitoring of the accountability and responsibility of various global actors can be difficult and costly. Under such circumstances, the need for social capital is growing. Global cooperation demands mutual trust between distant partners and commitment to follow the rules even when it is relatively easy to break them. In a global society, a work ethic based on accountability and trustworthiness is more needed than ever. The citizens of the world have to be well motivated, responsible, and knowledgeable.

Of course, the emphasis on civic virtue, participation, and accountability does not counterbalance all the drawbacks of republican morality. The list of drawbacks is long. The central notion of the common good remains vague and breaks into a variety of particular goods which, in a sense, are no longer truly common. Rhetorical relativism makes the principles of the common good and civic virtue easy to manipulate. It also seems contradictory to extend universally the scope of republican civic spirit. Such notions as "commitment to humanity" or "global civility" may sound appealing to some, but republicans themselves reject such slogans as not capable of stimulating civic engagement. Finally, the militant spirit of republican citizenship does not fit the common vision of a peaceful global world, free from terrorism, genocide, and ethnic cleansing.

V. Civic Participation

Modern history can be seen as a constant process of increasing political participation. The Glorious Revolution, the American Revolution, and the French Revolution were all about changing "subjects" into "citizens." Since then politics has become a sphere of civic engagement. Modern democratic regimes are founded on the universal rights to vote, to freely express political opinions, to organize political parties, and to participate in political decision making.

The republican ideas of civic virtue and liberty as self-government are firmly connected to civic engagement and participation. As I have already indicated, republicans view public service as a salient form of civic participation. But the republican citizen not only serves the *res publica*, his active involvement constitutes the *civitas*, the community of agents working for the common good. The pioneers of the republican renaissance, Pocock and Skinner, were inspired by Hannah Arendt's efforts to reanimate the participatory tradition of democracy. Arendt ranked the *vita activa* over the *vita contemplativa* as the unique expression of human nature. A person who wants to be in command of her life, and not subject to the will of others, should act in the public sphere. Freedom, the highest value, is impossible without action, since "to be free and to act are the same."

Although action is vital in all spheres of social life, Arendt argues that politics is the essential sphere. She virtually identifies freedom with political activity: "political freedom means the right to be a participator in government." [60] To maximize liberty, echoes Skinner, we must "take charge of the political arena ourselves." [61]

The reasons to participate in politics are numerous. First, citizens who want their interests to be represented and realized must get involved in order to manage the political process. Without citizens' active involvement, governments often lose track of citizens' interests and of the common good. Political participation shapes the republic. Second, citizens who participate in civic life strengthen their own motivation and admiration for common values. They express their independence and freedom from domination. By taking initiatives and fighting corruption, active citizens build mutual recognition among their peers. Third, participation is a form of civic education. It shapes and consolidates the habits of civic virtue. Without effective participation, citizens would be unable to consciously control their political bodies and their own destinies. Finally, political activity is not a mere means to achieve a goal. For Arendt, political engagement is a goal in itself, perhaps the most important goal.

Most modern-day republicans modify Arendt's project and follow the recent trends of democratic theory. They distinguish two major forms of political activity: political *deliberation* and *contestation*. Honohan puts stress on the former.[62] Deliberative democracy is based on the assumption that political legitimacy is to be found not in representation but in public deliberation. In a free republic, decision making should be a process of public debate:

> In a republican politics of deliberation, all individuals and groups are entitled to make proposals, advance views in their best light, and offer their reasons for these—there are no barriers to the claims and demands that they can make. Any voice may be heard and any claim expressed. . . . Every claim can be dismantled and subject to further scrutiny by others.[63]

On this view, public forums should be the main form of political institutions and the primary means for resolving civic disagreements. All citi-

---

[60] Hannah Arendt, "Freedom and Politics," in A. Hunold, ed., *Freedom and Serfdom* (Dordrecht: Reidel, 1961), 191–92; Hannah Arendt, *Between Past and Future* (New York: Penguin Books, 1991), 64; and Hannah Arendt, *On Revolution* (New York: Penguin Books, 1977), 218, 268.

[61] Skinner, "On Justice, the Common Good, and the Priority of Liberty," 217, 222.

[62] Honohan, *Civic Republicanism*, 221–38. Honohan refers to the numerous projects of deliberative democracy described in Sandel, *Democracy's Discontent*; Seyla Benhabib, ed., *Democracy and Difference* (Princeton, NJ: Princeton University Press, 1996); John S. Dryzek, *Deliberative Democracy and Beyond* (Oxford: Oxford University Press, 2000); and other works. See also David Ingram, *Rights, Democracy, and Fulfillment in the Era of Identity Politics: Principled Compromises in a Compromised World* (Lanham, MD: Rowman and Littlefield, 2004).

[63] Honohan, *Civic Republicanism*, 228.

zens would have an equal opportunity to debate their interests and bargain to achieve them.

Philip Pettit and John Maynor develop the idea of contestation as a form of political participation. While public deliberation is a form of direct participation in decision-making procedures, contestation is the ability to monitor and challenge governmental decisions. Pettit argues that the ability to contest political decisions and policies is more fundamental than the ability to vote and actively participate in decision making.[64] The political process is subject to public criticism by those whose interests are affected by its outcomes. Pettit directly opposes the principles of liberal democracy; according to him, nondominant, nonarbitrary political authority "requires not so much consent as contestability."[65] Such authority exercises democratic rule "without unduly forcing institutions." On this view, government is controlled by the people "to the extent that the people individually and collectively enjoy a permanent possibility of contesting what government decides."[66]

On the one hand, it is easy to understand why contemporary republicans have welcomed and joined recent discussions on new forms of political participation. Technological advancements in the field of communications have generated new possibilities and have made widespread participation in social debates practicable. As international communications networks develop, international political debates become standard procedure. Political theorists attach great expectations to these advancing technologies. Technological progress has made "globalization from below" an appealing project. Some theorists hope that global communications networks can enhance the prospects for participatory (as opposed to representative) democratic politics. Increasingly, social and civil associations are using the Internet to interact and to spread their ideas. People are better educated, and more information is available to them. They become aware of a variety of issues and can make knowledgeable decisions. Despite the fact that international communications networks are still far from being global—since many countries, comprising roughly three-fourths of the world's population, do not have the necessary resources to join the global community—the required technology is becoming more and more available.

On the other hand, however, it is rather surprising that republicans have embraced the trendy models of deliberative and contestatory democracy. In many respects, the new paradigm flies in the face of fundamental republican principles. Political deliberation is the kind of approach to politics that the republican tradition has emphatically opposed. Civic republicanism is not about rational analysis and seeking political consen-

---

[64] Pettit, *Republicanism,* 185; cf. ibid., 183–200; and Maynor, *Republicanism in the Modern World,* 155–73.

[65] Pettit, *Republicanism,* 185. He refers to Ian Shapiro's *Political Criticism* (Berkeley: University of California Press, 1990).

[66] Pettit, *Republicanism,* 184–85; Honohan, *Civic Republicanism,* 216.

sus. It is about devoted engagement and loyal service. Republican political discourse excels in rhetorical effectiveness rather than thoughtful philosophical deliberation. Classical republicans did not debate new civic values but demanded unconditional respect for old ones. They did not appeal to tolerance and fairness but to faith and duty. The paradigms of deliberative democracy and civic republicanism are not merely mismatched; they are fundamentally at odds.

Contestatory democracy is even more at odds with republicanism. For classical republicans, the concept of a "contestatory republic" would be a contradiction in terms. Civic activity means protecting and executing the laws of the *res publica,* not contesting them. Civic virtue means fulfilling duties and responsibilities, not questioning them. In addition, contestation is not a kind of political activity that produces mutual trust and solidarity. As republicans themselves put it, contestation is an expression of distrust toward political institutions.

Finally, there is a serious danger that deliberation and contestation would actually decrease civic participation. While contemporary political theorists and politicians alike complain about too few people participating in elections and other political activities,[67] one may predict that even fewer citizens might be actively involved in deliberation and contestation. One can easily imagine these new models of democracy leaving a great part of society uninvolved and inactive. Citizens who are not motivated strongly enough to learn about political affairs and devote energy to participating in politics would probably remain passive. Political deliberation demands standards that could be too high for many. Only educated citizens with a substantial knowledge of law, politics, the economy, and current events can effectively deliberate about political decisions and economic policies. There would be a grave danger of a deliberative republic turning into a highly elitist and discriminatory regime dominated by educated experts and talented propagandists.

Thus, attempts to combine the traditional principles of republicanism with the trendy inventions of recent democratic theory are bound to fail. Pettit, Honohan, and Maynor try to make old republican principles more practicable in the contemporary world, but the price they must pay is high. Leaving aside whether the models of deliberative and contestatory democracy are practicable in the first place, their basic assumptions are inconsistent with essential republican values: passionate patriotism, devotion to the *res publica,* and loyalty, not to mention determination to sacrifice in the name of the common good. As a matter of fact, the contradiction cannot possibly be more acute: contestation and deliberation are closely tied to republicanism's persistent nemesis, the liberal tradition of social contract and political consensus. In their efforts to embrace contestation and deliberation, contemporary republicans seem to be indirectly admit-

---

[67] Cf. Robert Putnam, *Bowling Alone: The Collapse and Revival of the American Community* (New York: Touchstone Books, 2000).

ting that some nonrepublican models of civic engagement may be more constructive in today's world.

VI. THE COMMUNITY

The idea that civic participation on the part of ordinary citizens is the essence of community has been a mainstay of the republican tradition. Civic activity creates the realm of civil society. Civic virtue and mutual trust make interpersonal bonds stronger and make civil society work more effectively. Adrian Oldfield presents Machiavelli, Rousseau, Hegel, and de Tocqueville as republicans who distinguished two levels of the republican community. While the *res publica* is a well-organized political body that secures liberty and executes law, the *civitas* is a moral community. The republic is a centralized body able to formulate and enforce policies and perform military tasks; civil society is a decentralized social order integrating individual and collective interests. Both elements of the republican community need each other, and neither can exist without civic virtue.

Surprisingly enough, the most recent republican literature pays very little attention to the two-sided character of the republican community. Pettit, Viroli, and Honohan express their distrust toward the decentralized nature of civil society. Pettit declares that "freedom as non-domination is not the sort of good that can be left to people to pursue for themselves in a decentralized way; all the signs are that it is best pursued for each under the centralized, political action of all: it is best pursued via the state."[68] For Honohan too, the state must be the catalyst, since "purely social groups do little to encourage political activism."[69] Since civil society tends to resemble the functioning of a market, it generates a variety of inequalities and unintentional side-effects. Moreover, the state must be strong. Pettit writes: "[W]e are going to be relatively well-disposed towards giving the state considerable power; we are going to look more fondly on state interference, provided that such interference can be bound by constraints that make it non-arbitrary."[70] "A strong and active state," Honohan believes, is "not a necessary evil but a real asset,"[71] and Maynor adds that it is "a positive force in the everyday lives of individuals."[72]

The strong republican state has numerous functions. Broadly speaking, its main goal is to foster the common good. Some elements of that task have already been indicated. The state brings external security and internal political stability. It defends justice and resolves the tensions between particular and common interests. It promotes the idea of liberty as nondomination and constitutes an institutional framework for self-

---

[68] Pettit, *Republicanism,* 274; cf. ibid., 241–46.
[69] Honohan, *Civic Republicanism,* 234–35.
[70] Pettit, *Republicanism,* 78.
[71] Honohan, *Civic Republicanism,* 184.
[72] Maynor, *Republicanism in the Modern World,* 5.

government. By preventing domination, it advances individual autonomy and independence. All forms of political participation, deliberation, and contestation are administered by the state. The economic market is so notoriously ineffective in providing public goods that the state must secure them.[73] In order to defend civic equality, the republican state administers taxation and other forms of redistribution, since this might be necessary to provide "the material preconditions for autonomy"[74] and "to restrict the wealth of the very rich and powerful in order to ensure equal freedom for all."[75] The state can intervene when people "are driven or manipulated to act in ways that undermine their autonomy." Central government is supposed to protect those who are under duress, dominated by others, misled, or disadvantaged in terms of education or access to information, and who therefore act in ways that jeopardize their interests.[76]

Such a radical model would be impossible without intense civic virtue. The moral legitimacy of powerful governmental institutions must be strong enough to make vast state intervention unobjectionable. Civic education is the heart of the matter.[77] Following the classical teaching of Cicero, Machiavelli, and Rousseau, contemporary republicans elaborately discuss the process of "shaping citizens" and "internalization" of civic norms in a democratic republic.[78] This is when citizens can be "forced to be free"; they can be encouraged through education to be accountable, dutiful, and loyal. Needless to say, the state manages the system of civic education.[79] Part of this management, on Pettit's view, would involve sound measures of governmental media regulation.[80] According to Pettit, the project of strong and virtuous governance may be difficult to accomplish, but it is far from impossible: "the contemporary state . . . is well up to the task of realizing such an ideal."[81]

Major questions arise concerning the applicability of the ideals of the *res publica* at the level of nation-states or even on a global scale. Classical republicans considered their ideal polity to be relatively small, similar to the Greek city-states or the early Roman republic. (The utopia of James Harrington's *Commonwealth of Oceana* [1656], described as a large territorial republic, seems to be the sole exception.) Hannah Arendt intended to rejuvenate the classical model of the republic as a small civic body. For centuries, only in such small communities has intense civic engagement

---

[73] Honohan, *Civic Republicanism*, 159.

[74] Ibid., 198–201.

[75] Pettit, *Republicanism*, 116–17.

[76] Ibid., 23; Honohan, *Civic Republicanism*, 201–3.

[77] Pettit, *Republicanism*, 241–70; Maynor, *Republicanism in the Modern World*, 174–202; Honohan, *Civic Republicanism*, 170–79; Dagger, *Civic Virtues*, 117–31.

[78] In classical republicanism, civic religion was a key educational tool. Viroli (*Republicanism*, 90–97) and Honohan (*Civic Republicanism*, 175–76) briefly discuss Machiavelli's and Tocqueville's views on religion in the republic but do not incorporate the classical idea of civic religion in their own theories of republicanism.

[79] Maynor, *Republicanism in the Modern World*, 180–92; Honohan, *Civic Republicanism*, 174–75.

[80] Pettit, *Republicanism*, 169.

[81] Ibid., 48.

been viable. Self-government is most effective when fellow-citizens are also neighbors and believe that their voices will be heard in the community. Citizens are most willing to get involved in civic discussions when they care about small-scale issues: clean and safe streets, good schools, reliable utility systems, and good local hospitals.

Today, global interdependence makes large-scale problems omnipresent and daunting. Environmental hazards, nuclear risks, terrorist threats, international crime, human rights violations, and genocide require well-organized, usually internationally coordinated, responses. The classical models of the *res publica* offer no realistic answers to such problems. Given the manifold functions of the state as the primary vehicle of republican politics, should modern-day republicans expand their ideal to encompass strong international, perhaps global, governance? Few people embrace the idea of such a world government as a viable option. For many, the prospect is a frightening one.

Likewise, if we are concerned with problems of governance on a global scale, the republican flirtation with deliberative or contestatory democracy seems to hold little promise. Leaving aside whether the vast structures of deliberative or contestatory democracy could be effectively organized in the first place, they would be extremely hard to manage on a global scale. They might be susceptible to malfunctions and lead to frequent gridlocks, which would be especially dangerous in situations of crisis. In that sense, these new models of the democratic state are essentially incompatible with the republican ideal of decisive and resolute executive power. The republic should be vigorous and dynamic, vehement and forceful. When contemporary republicans reshape the classical republic into a deliberative and contestatory democracy, they have to abandon those traditional ideals. One may expect that politics based mainly on deliberation and contestation would make executive power slower to act and less potent.

Finally, as I have noted, the strong moral and civic bonds among citizens that form the cement of the *res publica* are hardly imaginable on a very large scale. It is much too early to talk about a "global village" or a "global community," or about social bonds that extend beyond national and religious borders. It is unclear what such notions as international civic spirit or global solidarity would really mean. The ideas of "enlightened global citizenship" and "commitment to humanity" still sound utopian and resemble the goals of rationalistic liberalism rather than spirited republicanism. A global system of civic education also sounds both unrealistic and unattractive. It is rather disappointing that contemporary republicans do not even try to solve these daunting problems related to civic virtue—the very heart of republicanism.

Thus, on the one hand, the traditional republican conception of the strong state, applied on a global scale, would bring more serious dangers than it would potential advantages. A free and strong global republic, resolutely administering far-reaching economic redistribution or civic education, does not seem to be a real option. On the other hand, the new models of deliberative or contestatory democracy coopted by many contemporary republicans are inconsistent with important republican ideas. The strong republic cannot be based on contestation and deliberation. Devoted civic engagement repudiates rational political deliberation. Contestation does not build strong civic bonds.

VII. Conclusion

It remains an open question whether the concept of global citizenship can inspire billions of people, and not just a few political theorists and activists. I argue that the civic republican concept of citizenship fails as a fertile source of such inspiration. The list of reasons for this failure is long. The republican idea of identity is too narrow. Rhetorical relativism makes republican liberties and responsibilities dangerously partisan. Deliberative and contestatory political participation seems both ineffective and essentially nonrepublican. The strong republic could not be managed on a global scale. Some elements of the contemporary republican concept of citizenship are mutually inconsistent and often rather anachronistic. All in all, it is hard to conceive of the republican citizen as a "citizen of the world." Since we are still at the beginning of the globalization process, we should seek other models of citizenship that would enable us to deal with global problems in an effective way.

Philosophy, Politics, and Economics, University of Pennsylvania

INDEX